To the memory of my parents,
Norma Cubría de León and
Jorge Luis de Varona Ortiz,
to my brother Jorge and to my sister Norma
and to the two most important
women in my life,
my wife, Haydée, and my daughter, Irene,
to her husband Mark and to my grandson,
Daniel Francisco.
May God grant all of them the privilege
to live in a free, prosperous, and democratic
United States

Table of Contents

PART 1

THE 2016 PRESIDENTIAL CAMPAIGN

CHAPTER 1

CHAPTER 2

CHAPTER 3

CHAPTER 4

CHAPTER 5

CHAPTER 6

CHAPTER 7

Part 2

DONALD J. TRUMP IN THE WHITE HOUSE9

Acknowledgments

In this book, like the 24 others that I have written previously, my wife, Dr. Haydée Prado de Varona, has helped me immensely by writing and editing parts of the manuscript. Without her valuable cooperation, this book would not have been written. I am also deeply grateful for her patience and understanding during the many long hours and weekends that I have spent working and researching the topics included in this book. I am forever indebted to her as in 2011, she donated me, with immense love, one of her kidneys. Thanks to her, I did not have to receive dialysis. My health has improved immensely due to her most generous gift.

My thanks go to my friend, Rolando Perez, president and founder of Bear Witness Central, a patriot organization that defends freedom and liberty in the United States of America and in the world. Mr. Perez, a successful businessman, lives with his wife, children, and grandchildren in Jacksonville, Florida. He has created this great organization that has two websites: one in English, BWCentral.org, and one in Spanish, *www.LibertadUSA.com*. Rolando Perez has published all the articles that I have written in English and Spanish in both of these websites. Moreover, he has enhanced my articles by incorporating beautiful pictures and in some cases even videos.

Rolando Perez appointed me Director of Bear Witness Central and LibertadUSA in South Florida. Thanks to this website this book was written since Mr. Perez was able to publish there all my articles in English. BWCentral.org is one of the most important websites in the nation. It publishes the work of many well-known writers who describe and analyze the important events in our nation and the world. The website includes a multitude of videos and political cartoons. *BWCentral.org* has received up to 17,000 hits in one day. *www.LibertadUSA.com* is one of the most popular websites in Spanish in the United States and Latin America. It has a radio component of interviews by the directors of Bear Witness Central. I am also very grateful to Dr. Juan Torres, a successful physician, who lives with his wife and two children in Orlando, Florida. He is the Director of Bear Witness Central and LibertadUSA in central Florida and works closely with Rolando Perez and with me. Dr. Torres has introduced me to many patriots and leaders of various conservative, religious, and Tea Party organizations in the nation, who are extremely concerned with what is happening in our beloved country since 2008.

I have participated with Dr. Torres and Mr. Perez in numerous and important national conferences. I called Dr. Torres "Mr. Network" for his active participation in many organizations throughout the nation and for his effectiveness in working with a multitude of leaders of conservative and religious organizations. He is frequently invited to speak all over the nation. Dr. Torres founded one of the earliest Hispanic Tea Parties in the nation, the Latin American Tea Party. When Dr. Torres met Rolando Perez, he decided to join forces with him in Bear Witness Central.

I am proud of Alex Newman, also Director of Bear Witness Central, who is an author of books and the foreign correspondent of the excellent magazine *New American*. I am also proud Armando Escalante, who is the Director of Bear Witness Central in the greater Daytona, Florida area and Nevin Gussack, Director of Bear Witness Central in Palm Beach County. Mr. Gussack has helped me with computer issues and exchanged ideas with me frequently. Mr. Newman and Mr. Escalante have presented with me at numerous Bear Witness conferences in many cities.

I am grateful to Aldo Tuero Rosales of *El Nuevo Acción* and Lorenzo del Toro of *Ideal* magazine who have published some of my articles. I am appreciative to the late Dr. Horacio Aguirre, former owner of the Spanish newspaper *Diario Las Américas*, and his daughter, Helen Aguirre de Ferrer, for publishing many of my articles since 1973. Likewise, I am very appreciative to Antonio Purriños, the owner of the Spanish newspaper *La Voz de Miami Beach*, which was published once a month, for allowing me to be one of his columnists.

My appreciation goes to Jorge Rodriguez, president and owner of two Spanish radio stations in Miami, La Poderosa 670 AM and Cadena Azul 1550, who gave me the opportunity to have a weekly 90-minute program from 2008 to 2009. In 2013 and 2016 I was invited to participate in a series of programs regarding the Hispanic heritage of America.

While I had the radio program, I was able to cover the 2008 presidential campaign which led me to write a book in Spanish entitled ¿Obama o McCain? (2008). Since that time until today, my research on Barack Obama and his destructive administration has never stopped.

Numerous employees of those two radio stations, including the late Ruby Feria, Roger Vivas, and Enrique Encinosa have interviewed me countless times regarding domestic and international issues. My thanks go to Mariano González Solis who interviews me once a week in La Estación del Pueblo Radio Station in Orlando, Florida. Lastly, my thanks go to Kiko Arocha from Alexandria Library Press for publishing this book and for his efforts in that endeavor. I am the only one responsible for any errors that may appear on this book.

About the Author

Frank de Varona is an educator, historian, journalist, and internationally known expert on politics, economics, foreign affairs, and national security issues. He was an Associate Professor in the Curriculum and Instruction Department, College of Education, at Florida International University (FIU) from 1997 to 2004. During his seven years at FIU, he taught many graduate and undergraduate courses and supervised social studies student teachers in secondary schools.

Frank de Varona was born in Camagüey, Cuba in 1943 but his ties to the United States are very strong. One of his ancestors, Vasco Porcallo de Figueroa, came as Lieutenant Governor of La Florida and Lieutenant General of the expedition of Hernando De Soto in 1539. Later, his ancestor Spanish conquistador, returned to Cuba. His son went on with De Soto's army and explored ten Southern states. Unlike Hernando De Soto, he survived the expedition and returned to his father in Cuba.

Professor de Varona's great aunt, Mercedes Cubria, came to live in the United States at the age of six. She joined the Women Army Corps (WACs) during World War II as a second lieutenant. Mercedes Cubria served in the Army with distinction during the Second World War, the Korean War, and the Cold War as an intelligence officer. She retired from the Army as a highly-decorated Lieutenant Colonel.

At the age of 17, Frank de Varona participated in the Bay of Pigs invasion in an effort to eradicate communism in Cuba. After the defeat, he was sentenced to 30 years in prison and served two years. When Frank de Varona returned to the United States, he continued his education and received a Bachelor's degree in political science and economics and a certificate in Latin American Studies from the University of Florida in 1966. He earned a Master's degree in social studies at the University of Miami in 1969 and a Specialist in Education degree in educational administration and supervision at the University of Florida in 1976. He completed additional graduate work at the University of Florida, Florida International University, and Boston University.

From April to August 1966 and during the summer of 1968, Mr. de Varona worked as an escort interpreter for the U.S. State Department. In this position, he traveled with Latin American professionals from many fields throughout the United States. One of the visitor participants, Jorge Sánchez Méndez, became Minister of Industry and Vice President of Costa Rica.

Republican presidential candidate Senator Bob Dole talked with Frank de Varona in Orlando, Florida.

Professor de Varona had a 37-year distinguished career in the Miami-Dade County Public Schools (M-DCPS) as a social studies teacher; intergroup relations specialist; assistant principal; coordinator of adult education; principal of an adult education center, middle school, and senior high school; region director for personnel and labor relations; region superintendent; associate superintendent responsible for the pre-kindergarten through 12th grade, adult, and vocational curriculum; and the direct supervision of alternative, magnet, community, and adult and vocational schools, public radio and television, and student services; and interim deputy superintendent of schools for federal programs, equal education opportunity, food service, and transportation.

Secretary of Education Shirley Hufsteader and Commissioner of Education Ralph Turlington visited Miami Edison Senior High School and Principal Frank de Varona showed them around.

President Jimmy Carter and Congressman Pepper visited Miami Edison High School in 1980.

Professor de Varona retired from M-DCPS, the fourth largest school district in the United States, in February 2012. On February 2013, Mr. de Varona returned to work as a part-time adult education coordinator with M-DCPS and retired in February 2014. Upon his retirement, he continued his career as a journalist and writer in Miami, Florida, where he lives with his family.

Professor de Varona has written 25 books and published many articles in magazines and books in the United States and Spain. His book *Latino Literacy: A Complete Guide to Our Hispanic History and Culture* (Henry Holt & Company, 1996) received outstanding national reviews. Congresswoman Ileana Ros-Lehtinen wrote the preface of the book.

Frank de Varona's other books are *Hispanics in U.S. History, Volume I* (1989), *Hispanics in U.S. History, Volume II* (1989), *Bernardo de Gálvez* (1990), *Simón Bolívar* (1992), *Benito Juárez* (1992), *Miguel Hidalgo y Costilla* (1993), *Hispanic Presence in the United States* (1993), *Perspectives: Authentic Voices of Latinos* (1995), *Florida Government Lessons* (1996), *World History: The Human Odyssey* (Bilingual Supplement) (1997), *Florida Resource Book* (1997), *Multicultural Guide to Dade County* (1997), *Florida Government and Economics Resource Book* (1998), *Simón Bolívar: The Liberator* (2003), *Florida: History, Geography, Government, and Economics* (2005), and *Presencia Hispana en los Estados Unidos Quinto Centenario* (2013).

Professor de Varona is the only individual in the nation who has written seven books on the Obama administration. Three of those books are in Spanish: ¿Obama o McCain? (2008), *El Ver-*

dadero Obama: Sus conexiones marxistas, socialistas y radicales (2010), y *¿Obama o Romney?* (2012). The other four books are *America in Decline* (2014), *Obama, Hillary Clinton and Radical Islam* (2016) *Russia, China, and their Allies Threaten America* (2016). He is also wrote the book *The New World Order Threatens America and the World* (2017) and the current one.

Professor de Varona has worked as a contributing writer and/or editorial consultant for over 18 different publishers. In this capacity, he has reviewed over 70 world history, world geography, U.S. history, civics, government, economics, Spanish, language arts, and elementary textbooks as well as biographies.

Professor Frank de Varona was awarded on November 15, 2015 the Grand Cross of the Knight of the National Brotherhood of the Monarchy of Spain in Seville, Spain. In the picture he appears with his wife Dr. Haydée Prado de Varona, a clinical psychologist.

King Juan Carlos I of Spain awarded Professor de Varona the Cross of the Royal Order of Isabel La Católica with the rank of Encomienda in 1994. He was awarded the Grand Cross of the Knight of the National Brotherhood of the Monarchy of Spain in 2015. Professor de Varona received the Byzantine Imperial Order of Constantine the Great with the rank of Commander in 1991. These awards were given to him for his many books and articles regarding the Hispanic contributions to the United States and his work to include these contributions in U.S. textbooks.

Frank de Varona wrote several articles and biographies as well as summarized documents for the CD-ROM *The Hispanic American Experience* produced by Primary Source Media. He was also a consultant for the Spanish language arts program of Jostens Corporation and for the software program of U.S. history of Davidson and Associates.

Professor de Varona has written curriculum programs for school districts and conducted workshops for teachers and school administrators in Miami-Dade, Broward, and Palm Beach Counties in Florida. He has also conducted workshops in the Alexandria, Virginia, and New York City Public Schools. He has been a consultant in Spain, Dominican Republic, and Honduras. The Agency for International Development asked Professor de Varona to assist Honduras in the establishment of middle schools.

As a journalist, Professor de Varona has written many articles on political, economics, national security, foreign affairs, Hispanic presence and contributions to the United States, and historical and educational issues for the following newspapers: *Diario Las Américas, La Voz de Miami Beach,* El *Nuevo Herald,* and *El 20 de Mayo* (from Los Angeles). He has written over 300 political and historical articles for the following electronic magazines or websites: *Gaspar Lugareño, Emilio Ichikawa, Neoliberalismo, La Nueva Nación El Nuevo Acción, Baracutey Cubano, Bear Witness Central, and LibertadUSA.* He also writes articles for the following magazines: *El Camagüeyano Libre, Girón (Bay of Pigs Veteran Association), Hispania, and Ideal.*

Frank de Varona has produced four television documentaries for Channel 17 in Miami, Florida. He was producer, director, and interviewer for a one-hour weekly program in Channel 14 in Miami from 1990 to 1992.

Professor de Varona had a radio program in La Poderosa and Cadena Azul radio stations from 2007 to 2008 and for several months in 2013 and 2016. For the last five years Professor de Varona is interviewed once or twice a week by journalist Mariano González Solis at the Estación del Pueblo radio station in Orlando, Florida on current political, economic, and social events in the United States and the world.

Professor de Varona appears frequently on numerous local, national, and international television and radio programs, including *C Span,* the *Voice of Americas, radio and TV Marti,* and

FoxNews in Spanish. He is a frequent contributor to *NTN 24 Television* with headquarters in Bogotá, Colombia which is seen in Latin America and the United States.

He has conducted workshops at various colleges and universities and at national conferences such as National Association of Bilingual Educators (NABE), Teachers of English for Speakers of Other Languages (TESOL), National Council for the Social Studies (NCSS), Florida Council for the Social Studies (FCSS) and Dade County Council for the Social Studies (DCCSS).

Professor de Varona has been invited as a speaker during the Hispanic Heritage Month celebrations at the Department of Labor, Nuclear Regulatory Commission, Internal Revenue Service, Drug Enforcement Administration, and Naval Observatory as well many school districts and universities across America.

Frank de Varona served as vice president, secretary, and treasurer of the Governor's Hispanic Affairs Commission. He is in the middle on the first row and behind him Governor Bob Graham. The Governor's Hispanic Affairs Commission help meetings in many cities in Florida to listen and try to resolve the problems encountered by Hispanics in the state.

To Frank De Varona
With best wishes,

Vice President George H.W. Bush met with Frank de Varona (second from left) and the members of the Florida Hispanic Affairs Commission in the White House.

Active in state, regional and national organizations, he has been appointed to various state commissions by governors. He served as vice president, secretary, and treasurer of the Governor's Hispanic Affairs Commission, Governor's Commission on a Free Cuba, Florida Humanities Council, Florida Historical Markers Commission, Florida Cuban Heritage Trail, Florida Historical Preservation Board Commission, Board of Dentistry (consumer member), and the International Education Commission.

Secretary of Education Lamar Alexander appointed Professor de Varona to the U.S. Department of Education National Council on Educational Statistics Advisory Committee under the administration of George H.W. Bush. He served on the Advisory Board of the U.S. Department of Educational Southeastern Educational Improvement Laboratory.

Presidential candidate Ronald Reagan and Nancy Reagan are placing a wreath at the Bay of Pig Monument in Miami in 1980. Four veterans of the Brigade 2506, including the author, were selected to greet the president.

To Frank de Varona
With best wishes,
Ronald Reagan

Reagan and Secretary of Education Bell are meeting with Hispanic educators, including the author, in the West Wing of the White House next to the Oval Office in 1983.

Professor de Varona was invited to the White House on three occasions during the presidency of Ronald Reagan. Professor de Varona also met with Vice President George H.W. Bush in the White House when, as an officer of the Florida Hispanic Affairs Commission, he visited Washington, D.C. to lobby Congress on behalf of Contra military aid. Professor de Varona is the South Florida Director of Bear Witness Central and LibertadUSA director. He is an advisor and a member of the International Assembly of the Cuban Patriotic Council, Press Secretary of the Partido Auténtico, Chairman of the Keep Government Accountable Coalition, Vice Chairman of the Miami-Dade Conservative Republican Coalition and Vice President of the Partido Ortodoxo del Pueblo. Professor de Varona is a member of the Republican Party Executive Committee of Miami-Dade County.

Republican 2016 Presidential Candidate, Senator Marco Rubio, with Frank de Varona and wife Dr. Haydée Prado de Varona at a breakfast in West Miami in December 2015.

After dropping from the presidential race Senator Rubio was reelected to the Senate. Senator Rubio meets with President Donald Trump frequently and has recommended strong economic sanctions on the oppressive Cuban and Venezuelan regimes.

The author met with Republican Senator Ted Cruz from Texas
and former 2016 Presidential Candidate in Miami.

Secretary of the Treasury Catalina Vasquez Villalpando dedicated a dollar bill to the author

The author presented candidate Donald Trump the insignia of the Assault Brigade 2506 along with two other brigade members at the Bay of Pigs Veterans Brigade 2506 museum in Little Havana in Miami.

The author did the pledge of allegiance to the flag and spoke at the noon Trump Rally held at Bayfront Park in downtown Miami a few days before the presidential election. Next to the author is former Hialeah Mayor Julio Martinez who was the chairman of the Donald J. Trump campaign in Miami-Dade County. Several thousand Trump supporters endured the intense heat to hear presidential candidate Donald Trump speak as well as others.

Secretary General of the Organization of American States (OAS) Luis Almagro and the author at a meeting held at Miami-Dade College dealing with democracy and political parties in Latin America. The author praised Almagro for denouncing the Venezuelan communist regime but asked him to do the same with the mass-murdering Cuban regime.

Former Bolivian President Jorge Quiroga with the author and the president of the Cuban Patriotic Council Antonio D. Esquivel at the meeting dealing with democracy and political parties in Latin America held at Miami-Dade College in Miami.

Jorge Quiroga served as president from Bolivia from 2001 to 2002. He is a strong anti-communist who is an opponent of the Communist President of Bolivia Evo Morales. Former Bolivian President Quiroga spoke eloquently at the forum and said that when he goes to Bolivia Cuban intelligence services agents follow him everywhere.

He denounced both the Cuban and Venezuelan brutal and merciless regimes. The author praised former Bolivian President Jorge Quiroga for his defense of democracy and market economy.

Presidential Assistant Dr. Carlos Díaz-Rosillo appears in the picture with the author and the President of the Cuban Patriotic Council Antonio Esquivel. He met with Americans of Cuban descent in Miami and spoke on President Donald Trump's Cuban policy. The author and others at the meeting held at the Cuban Diaspora Museum praised the first steps taken by the president but stated the sanctions against the mass-murdering regime in the island needed to be strengthen considerably. Dr. Carlos Díaz-Rosillo receives intelligence briefings at the White House and provides the president and others with recommendations on foreign policy. Dr. Díaz-Rosillo and the author spoke at the Trump Bayfront Park Rally in downtown Miami a few days before the presidential election

On December 3, 2017, the author met and talked with the brilliant writer and film producer Dinesh D' Souza and his Venezuelan wife at the American at Crossroads Conference in Jacksonville Dinesh D' Souza dedicated one of his books to the author.

Excellent writer and former CIA official and a member of the Citizens' Commission on Benghazi Clare Lopez met with the author in Jacksonville, Florida. Clare Lopez spoke on Obama's secret Presidential Directive 11 which was Obama's plan to turn the Middle East to Iran and North Africa to al-Qaida and the Muslim Brotherhood.

Investigative journalist Roger Aronoff, who set up the Citizens' Commission on Benghazi with retired CIA officials, generals, admirals, former members of Congress, and Pentagon officials, with the author in Jacksonville. The Commission published a report titled *Dereliction of Duty* pointing out how President Barack Obama and Secretary of State Hillary Clinton entered in an unnecessary war in Libya against the national interest.

The author has met previously with Roger Aronoff in Washington, D.C. and communicated with him frequently. Based upon this report and the articles written by the patriots who served on the Benghazi Commission, the author wrote a book titled, *Obama, Hillary Clinton, and Radical Islam* which has several chapters on Libya. The author denounced Obama and Hillary Clinton for committing high treason, criminal negligence, and dereliction of duty.

This writer had lunch with political consultant and writer Roger Stone at the Europa Café Restaurant and Alex Newman in Ft Lauderdale. Later, Alex interviewed Roger in his studio for the New American magazine. This writer helped with the video camera and gave Roger Stone his book on The New World Order Threatens America and the World (October 2017) where he included part of an article written by Stone. This writer also gave Roger Stone a copy of his article on Obama's Presidential Directive 11 since Stone was going to see his friend President Donald Trump at Mar-a-Lago in a couple days, This writer asked Stone to share the article with the president and request him to declassify the Directive 11 document.

Introduction

Republican presidential candidates from right to left: New Jersey Governor Chris Christie, Senator Marco Rubio (R-FL), Ben Carson, Wisconsin Governor Scott Walker, Donald Trump, Jeb Bush, Mike Huckabee, Senator Ted Cruz (R-TX), Senator Rand Paul (R-KY), and John Kasich take the stage for the first prime time presidential debate hosted by *Fox News* and *Facebook* at the Quicken Loans Arena on August 6, 2015 in Cleveland, Ohio.

There were in addition to Donald Trump, 16 other Republican presidential candidates. Very few pundits believed Donald Trump could defeat these well-known and powerful politicians in the Republican Party. As opposed to Trump, some of them were great debaters. Even less in the media believed that if Donald Trump became the nominee of the Republican Party, he could defeat the likely Democratic Party candidate Hillary Clinton.

On August 6, 2015, the first debate of Republican presidential candidates was hosted by *Fox News* and *Facebook* at the Quicken Loans Arena in Cleveland, Ohio – the same location as the future 2016 Republican National Convention. The two-hour debate invited the 10 highest-polling candidates, as measured by the average of the top five national polls selected by *Fox News*.

In addition, all other seven candidates were invited to a one-hour debate earlier that same day.

The candidates in the main debate were Donald Trump, Jeb Bush, Scott Walker, Mike Huckabee, Ben Carson, Ted Cruz, Marco Rubio, Rand Paul, Chris Christie, and John Kasich. The moderators of this debate were Bret Baier, Megyn Kelly, and Chris Wallace. Seven candidates, who did not qualify for the debate, were invited to participate in the 5 p.m. forum. These seven candidates were Rick Perry, Bobby Jindal, Rick Santorum, Lindsey Graham, Carly Fiorina, Jim Gilmore, and George Pataki.

In the prime-time debate, frontrunner Donald Trump's overall performance was criticized as he was described as rude and erratic by many pundits, while others said his comments were popular and his criticisms were overdue, including his criticism of Bush's description of illegal immigration as an "act of love." Cruz, Rubio, Christie, and Huckabee received praise.

Donald Trump won the nomination of the Republican Party. Only two newspapers in the nation endorsed Trump. Two former Republican President, George H.W. Bush and his son George W. Bush, announced that they were not going to vote for Trump. Many Never Trump Republicans, including Mitt Romney, constantly criticized Republican presidential candidate Donald Trump. In fact, Donald Trump ran against the Republican and Democratic Parties establishment and the biased corrupt mainstream media.

Why so much hatred towards Donald Trump? On reason was that Trump frequently insulted his Republican opponents and ridiculed them, such as Marco Rubio as "Little Marco" and Ted Cruz as "Lying Ted." However, the most important reason was that Donald Trump attacked the members of the globalist elite of the New World Order who had selected Hillary Clinton to quickly move to a one-world government under the United Nations but controlled by the billionaires' globalists.

Donald Trump ran an anti-globalist, nationalistic, and America First campaign that resonated with millions of Americans who believed that both political parties had abandoned them. They had watched how well-paying jobs had evaporated as multinational corporations moved their factories and research centers from the United States to countries like China and Mexico as well as Third World nations to maximize profits. Candidate Trump criticized the free trade agreements and globalization that were responsible for the loss on tens of thousands of well-paying jobs. He gave American workers hope for a better future.

Obama has been constantly criticizing President Trump of colluding with Russia, but it was Obama who approved the sale of 20% of the uranium mines in America to Russia and who shared with that nation America's technology. It was Obama who made the unconstitutional and terrible Iranian Deal and gave the mass murdering Cuban regime a series of unilateral concessions in return for nothing.

Donald Trump's election as president was a political earthquake and a major political upset. It ended eight years of a Marxist and pro-Muslim Brotherhood presidency that divided the American people, turned the nation into a surveillance state by spying on journalists and citizens, weakened the military, created civil wars in the Middle East and North Africa, violated the Constitution, engaged in many crimes and scandals, eroded American sovereignty, reduced freedom and liberty, weaponized the IRS, EPA and other federal agencies to attack conservatives and religious organizations, made enemy lists in the White House, increased the size of the federal government, and continued on the road to a planetary government.

Books that describe the Obama administration, the Trump campaign, and the president

David Horowitz in his best seller book *Big Agenda: President Trump's Plan to Save America* (2017) said that Donald Trump's election win was "The beginning of a major political, economic, and social revolution that would change America and the world."

David Horowitz wrote the book *Big Agenda: President Trump's Plan to Save America* (2017).

Amazon describes the book as follows:

"One of the nation's foremost conservative commentators, *New York Times* bestselling author, and a mentor to many of Donald Trump's key advisers, David Horowitz presents a White House battle plan to halt the Democrats' march to extinguish the values America holds dear.

Big Agenda details President Trump's likely moves, including his

• First wave of executive orders — restoring Guantanamo, Keystone XL, nixing amnesty

• Surprising judicial appointments — Supreme Court and the federal judiciary

• Radical changes to federal rules & regulations — ObamaCare, EPA overreach, and a New Deal for black America."

"With the White House and Senate in GOP hands and a Supreme Court soon to follow, President Trump will have a greater opportunity than even Ronald Reagan had to reshape the American political landscape while securing the nation's vital security interests abroad.

No president since FDR and his famed '100 Days' has the chance Donald Trump has, Horowitz argues."

"But he writes that the GOP and Trump must recognize they are not fighting policy ideas, but an ideology — a progressive one with a radical agenda to stop Trump to reduce America's power and greatness. *Big Agenda* is a rallying cry and indispensable guide for how to claim ultimate victory for the conservative cause. Horowitz writes, "One battle is over, but there are many more to come. This book is a guide to fighting the opponents of the conservative restoration. It identifies who the adversaries are — their methods and their motivations. It describes their agenda — not merely the issues with which they advance their goal, but the destructive goal itself. And it lays out a strategy that can defeat them.""

David Horowitz wrote the following: "Half the country had voted for a candidate who vowed in favor to continue the Obama administration policies that brought the nation to the brink. Half of the nation voted for a candidate in favor of open borders, a candidate who willingly prosecuted the genders and racial wars of the political left. Half of the nation voted for a candidate who viewed the Constitution as a changeable document, a candidate ready to appoint Supreme Court Justices who believe its decisions should be based not on the law but whether they achieved a progressive result."

Horowitz explained that the nation is "facing daunting threats to its security, prosperity, and freedom." He pointed out that Obama gave America a massive government debt with an anemic economic recovery. Ninety-four million Americans dropped from the work force and 47 million receive food stamps. Obama reduced our sovereignty by creating porous national borders. Because of Obama's failed policies, there was an influx of thousands of criminals and unknown number of terrorists. This author wrote a book expressing similar concerns in terms of national security as *Big Agenda: President Trump's Plan to Save America.*

This author wrote the book *The Gathering Threat of Russia, China, and Their Allies Against America* that described the damage done to the national security by the presidency of Barack Obama. The progressive agenda of former President Obama intentionally reduced the power of America around the world.

This author wrote the book *The Gathering Threat of Russia, China, and their Allies Against America* in 2017 where he criticized Obama's foreign policy of weakness and appeasement toward America's enemies.

President Barack Obama made the United States a superpower in complete retreat in the world. The enemies of America, including Russia, China, Iran, North Korea, Venezuela, Cuba, and radical Islam, did not fear President Obama. The allies of America did not trust or respect Obama to defend them from their enemies. Obama and Congress severely cut the Pentagon's budget for many years while the enemies of America significantly improved their Armed Forces and nuclear arsenals with new weapons.

Russia annexed part of Georgia, Ukraine's Crimean Peninsula, and occupied parts of eastern Ukraine. China has built military bases on islands in the South China Sea that belong to U.S. allies. China claims illegally as its territory 90% of the South China Sea and islands that belong to Japan in the East China Sea.

Both China and Russia are harassing U.S. aircrafts and Navy ships around the world. These nations and their allies represent an existential threat to America. President Trump understands why America needs to drastically increase the budget of the Pentagon and improve our nuclear arsenal and missiles to match or exceed the better-equipped Russian and Chinese missiles and other weapons. Anti-ballistic missile defense must be improved. Failure to do so will severely endanger the national security of the United States.

President Trump needs to improve the military quickly to prevent a possibly devastating Russian-Chinese surprise nuclear attack upon America as weakness invites aggression from the dictators who rule those two nations. This writer revealed how Russia and China are developing hypersonic glide vehicles to defeat the increasingly sophisticated anti-ballistic missile (ABM) defense of the United States and its allies. These two enemy nations are more advanced in the development of hypersonic weapons.

The nation that achieves mastery of hypersonic weapons first will overturn the principles of how wars are waged. The development of hypersonic weapons is like the development of nuclear arms. America is in great danger as the balance of military power has shifted against it. The only area in which America has superior weapons is in space. Russia and China are working diligently to develop weapons superior to America's weapons in space, such as the hypersonic glide vehicles.

The Gathering Threat explained how Vladimir Putin has frequently threatened nuclear war against America and its allies. It is very important for Americans to understand that Russia is the number one geopolitical enemy of America. Equally important is to know that Russia is using jihadists throughout the world as a weapon against the United States and the West. China, Russia, North Korea, Iran, and other nations are waging successful cyber warfare against America and stealing its industrial and military secrets.

Unfortunately, the Obama-Clinton administration did very little to stop the cyber warfare waged by our enemies. Another serious threat to America is an electromagnetic pulse (EMP) event provoked either from an atomic bomb exploded high in space in the middle of America or from solar flares that would destroy all electronics and the electrical grid of America and result in the death of 80% to 90% of Americans in a few months due to starvation.

Obama failed to protect the nation. As result America, at all levels, is unprepared for an EMP nuclear attack or an EMP provoked by solar flares despite their catastrophic consequences. President Trump needs to quickly spend whatever is necessary to protect the electronics and the electrical grid of America.

Now President Trump needs to clean the mess left by the Obama administration. While Obama created the Islamic State, President Trump eliminated all the rules of engagement that tied the hands of the military in fighting the Islamic State. In less than a year, the Trump administration dropped over 30,000 bombs killing over 70,000 jihadists and capturing 98% of the territory of the Islamic State in both Iraq and Syria.

Amazon describes the book as follows:

"From Roger Stone, a *New York Times* bestselling author, longtime political adviser and friend to Donald Trump, and consummate Republican strategist, comes the first in-depth examination of how Trump's campaign tapped into the national mood to deliver a stunning victory that almost no one saw coming."

"In the early hours of November 9, 2016, one of the most contentious, polarizing, and vicious presidential races came to an abrupt and unexpected end when heavily favored presidential hopeful Hillary Clinton called Donald J. Trump to concede, shocking a nation that had, only hours before, given little credence to his chances. Donald Trump pulled the greatest upset in American political history despite a torrent of invective and dismissal of the mainstream media. Here is the first definitive explanation about how the "silent majority" shifted the election to Donald Trump in reliable Democratic Pennsylvania, Wisconsin, and Michigan, thus handing him the presidency."

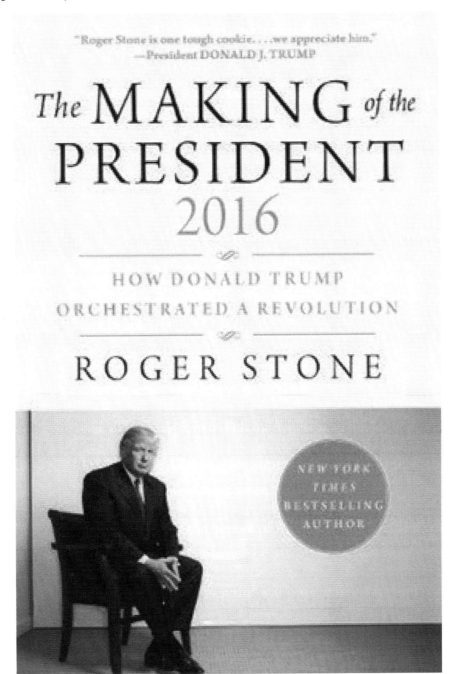

Roger Stone wrote *The Making of the President 2016: How Donald Trump Orchestrated a Revolution* in 2016.

"Stone, a long time Trump retainer and confidant, gives us the inside story of how Donald Trump almost single-handedly harnessed discontent among Forgotten Americans despite running a guerrilla-style grass roots campaign to compete with the smooth running and free-spending Clinton political machine. From the start, Trump's campaign was unlike any seen on the national stage—combative, maverick, and fearless. Trump's nomination was the hostile takeover of the Republican party and a resounding repudiation of the failed leadership of in the tradition of Theodore White's landmark books, the definitive look at how Donald J. Trump shocked the world to become president both parties whose policies have brought America to the brink of financial collapse as well as endangering our national security."

"Here Stone outlines how Donald Trump skillfully ran as the anti-Open Borders candidate as well as a supporter of American sovereignty, and how he used the Globalist trade deals like NAFTA to win over three of ten Bernie Sanders supporters. The veteran adviser to Nixon, Reagan, and Trump charts the rise of the alt-conservative media and the end of the mainstream media monopoly on voter impacting information dissemination. This is an insider's view that includes studying opposition research into Bill, Hillary, and Chelsea Clinton's crimes, and the struggle by the Republican establishment to stop Trump and how they underestimated him. Stone chronicles Trump's triumph in three debates where he skillfully lowered expectation levels but skewered Mrs. Clinton for the corruption of the Clinton Foundation, her mishandling of government e-mail, and her incompetence as Secretary of State."

"Stone gives us the inside word on Julian Assange, *WikiLeaks*, Clinton campaign chief John Podesta, Huma Abedin, Anthony Weiner (Carlos Danger), Doug Band, Jeffery Epstein, and the efforts to hide the former first lady's infirmities and health problems. Stone dissects the phony narrative that Trump was in cahoots with Russian strongman Vladimir Putin or that the e-mails released by *WikiLeaks* came from the Russians."

"The grizzled political veteran of ten Republican presidential campaigns from Richard Nixon to Ronald Reagan to Donald Trump explains how Trump's election has averted near certain war with Russia over Syria and the rejection of the neocon policies of the Obama/Clinton Administration. *The Making of the President 2016* reveals how Trump brilliantly picked at Hillary Clinton's weaknesses, particularly her reputation as a crooked insider, and ignited the passions of out-of-work white men and women from the rust belt and beyond, at a time when millions of Americans desperately wanted change. Stone also reveals how and why the mainstream media got it wrong, including how the polls were loaded and completely misunderstood who would vote. Stone's analysis is akin to Theodore H. White's seminal book *The Making of the*

President 1960. It is both a sweeping analysis of the trends that elected Trump as well as the war stories of a hard-bitten political survivor who Donald Trump called one tough cookie."

The author presented his book *The New World Order Threatens America and the World* (October 2017) to Roger Stone during lunch at the Europa Café in Fort Lauderdale. Alex Newman and James F. Fitzgerald are also in the picture.

This author has met with Roger Stone twice. The second time was on December 28, 2017 when he had lunch with Stone, with investigative reporter and writer Alex Newman, and the president of the Law Enforcement Charitable Foundation James Fitzgerald at the Europa Cafe restaurant in Fort Lauderdale. Later the author and the other two went to the studio of Roger Stone where he participates in interviews with Alex Jones of *Infowars*. Alex Newman conducted an interview with Stone for the magazine *New American* and this writer taped the interview.

Among the things that Roger Stone told us was the plan that Trump haters have for ending the presidency of Donald Trump. First, is the Fake Russian Collusion investigation of Special Counsel Robert Mueller hoping for an impeachment. Second, is the use of the 25th Amendment of the Constitution to declare President Trump unfit for office due to insanity, if most of the cabinet and the vice president vote in favor of taking this action. Third, is to assassinate the president. This writer is convinced that the members of the globalist elite of the New World Order are behind some of these efforts to terminate the presidency of the duly elected leader of America. This author prays to God every day for the safety and protection of President Donald Trump, his family and the members of his administration.

A third book that gives you an insight on the president is Newt Gingrich's book *Understanding Trump* that was published in June 2017.

Amazon describes the book as follows:

"Donald Trump is unlike any president we've ever had. He is the only person ever elected to be commander in chief who has not first held public office or served as a general in the military.

His principles grow out of five decades of business and celebrity success-not politics-so he behaves differently than do traditional politicians. In *Understanding Trump*, Newt Gingrich shares what he learned from more than two years helping Trump and his team throughout the campaign, the election, and during the first months of the presidency."

"Mr. Gingrich provides unique insight into how the new president's past experiences have shaped his life and style of governing. This book also includes Mr. Gingrich's thorough analysis of how President Trump thinks and makes decisions, as well as the president's philosophy, doctrine, and political agenda going forward."

"Further, these pages hold a detailed discussion of Trump-style solutions for national security, education, health care, economic growth, government reform, and other important topics. Mr. Gingrich also identifies the forces in the Washington establishment, media, and bureaucracy that will oppose the president at every turn. Finally, book *Understanding Trump* explains the president's actions so far and lays out a vision for what Americans can do to help make President Trump's agenda a success."

"The president owes his position to the people who believed in him as a candidate, not to the elites in government and media who have expressed contempt for him since he began his campaign to become president. The very essence of Trump's mission is a willingness to enact policies and set goals that send our country in a bold new direction - one that may be unreasonable to Washington but is sensible to millions of Americans outside the Beltway. Only with the country's help will President Trump be able to overcome the entrenched interests in Washington and fulfill his promise to make America great again for all Americans."

The election of Donald Trump

The presidency of Donald Trump marks a profound change in the trajectory of American government, politics, and culture. Like his administration, the movement that put him in office represents a phenomenon that is worth studying.

Tweeter-in-Chief

No American president has sent so many tweeters in history as Donald Trump. In 2017, the president sent over 2,200 tweets using more than 40 hours. Since 80% to 90% of the articles and editorials published by the Destroy Trump corrupt mainstream media are negative, the president has fought back with tweeters. His most frequent tweet has been "Fake News."

Donald Trump was elected as the 45th president of the United States on November 8, 2016 after a very dirty and polarizing campaign ran by the Democratic Party and Hillary Clinton.

No president in history has called dictators who threaten the nation "Rocket man" and "Short and Fat" as Donald Trump has when referring to the bloody tyrant of North Korea Kim Jong Un. In another tweet by the president, he said the Pakistan had accepted billions of dollars in aid from the United States while failing to act against the terrorist networks. President Trump was correct in pointing out that America has given Pakistan $33 billion since 2002 and yet that nation gives sanctuary to the Afghan Taliban and terror group, the Haqqani network. The president is withholding $255 million in aid to Pakistan. President Trump is also threatening to end aid to the Palestinian Authority. The United States has given billions to the Palestinian Authority that refuses to enter peace negotiations with America's ally Israel and pays $20,000 to the family of any Palestinian who kills Israelis.

President Trump uses tweeter frequently to explain Americans and the world his intentions and to praise and criticize people and nations. Here are some recent examples:

"Such respect for the people of Iran as they try to take back their corrupt government. You will see great support from the United States at the appropriate time"!

"I will be announcing THE MOST DISHONEST & CORRUPT MEDIA AWARDS OF THE YEAR on Monday (January 7, 2016) at 5:00 o'clock. Subjects will cover Dishonesty & Bad Reporting in various categories from the Fake News Media. Stay tuned"!

"North Korean Leader Kim Jong Un just stated that the "Nuclear Button is on his desk at all times." Will someone from his depleted and food starved regime please inform him that I too have a Nuclear Button, but it is a much bigger & more powerful one than his, and my Button works"!

"Peace treaty with Israel. We have taken Jerusalem, the toughest part of the negotiation, off the table, but Israel, for that, would have had to pay more. But with the Palestinians no longer willing to talk peace, why should we make any of these massive future payments to them"?

"It's not only Pakistan that we pay billions of dollars to for nothing, but also many other countries, and others. As an example, we pay the Palestinians HUNDRED OF MILLIONS OF DOLLARS a year and get no appreciation or respect. They don't even want to negotiate a long overdue."

President Trump congratulated Senator Orrin Hatch on his retirement.

"Congratulations to Senator Orrin Hatch on an absolutely incredible career. He has been a tremendous supporter, and I will never forget the (beyond kind) statements he has made about me as President. He is my friend and he will be greatly missed in the U.S. Senate"!

Huma Abedin mishandled e-mails that had classified information. This is a crime.

These e-mails were found in the computer of her former husband Anthony Weiner. Weiner went to jail for improper sexual behavior with a minor. President Trump used a tweet to request that she would be prosecuted.

"Crooked Hillary Clinton's top aid, Huma Abedin, has been accused of disregarding basic security protocols. She put Classified Passwords into the hands of foreign agents. Remember sailor's pictures on submarine? Jail! Deep State Justice Department must finally act? Also on Comey & others."

"We will not rest until all of America's GREAT VETERANS can receive the care they so richly deserve. Tremendous progress has been made in a short period of time. Keep up the great work".

"Democrats are doing nothing for DACA - just interested in politics. DACA activists and Hispanics will go hard against Dems, will start "falling in love" with Republicans and their President! We are about RESULTS."

".... impartial journalists of a much higher standard, lose all of your phony and non-existent "sources," and treat the President of the United States FAIRLY, so that the next time I (and the people) win, you won't have to write an apology to your readers for a job poorly done"!

"The Failing New York Times has a new publisher, A.G. Sulzberger. Congratulations! Here is a last chance for the Times to fulfill the vision of its Founder, Adolph Ochs, "to give the news impartially, without fear or FAVOR, regardless of party, sect, or interests involved."

Most presidential tweets are helpful to Donald Trump in responding to the frequent and mostly unfair attacks by the mainstream media. However, other tweets are not necessary as when the president attacks a Hollywood liberal actress who despises him. All tweets should be reviewed by White House lawyers and by political and national security advisers. The president needs also to be careful on the remarks he uses for it can damage him politically and used against him by the Destroy Trump media.

President Trump was accused of insulting people from Haiti, El Salvador, and countries from Africa

On January 11, 2018, President Trump held a meeting in the Oval Office with a bipartisan group of members of Congress to discuss immigration policy. After the meeting Democratic Senator Dick Durbin from Illinois said the the president denigrated nations from Africa, Haiti, and El Salvador by calling them "shithole countries" while expressing a preference to admit immigrants from Norway. The Destroy Trump liberal mainstream media, Democrats and some Republicans denounced the president alleged remarks. Republican Congresswoman Mia Love from Utah, whose family comes from Haiti, stated that "The remarks by the president were unkind, divisive, and fly on the face of our national values. This behavior is unacceptable from the leader of our nation."

Presidential spokesman Raj Shah said, "Certain Washington politicians choose to fight for foreign countries, but President Trump will always fight for the American people." "Like other nations that have merit-based immigration, President Trump is fighting for permanent solutions that make our country stronger by welcoming those who can contribute to our society, grow our economy, and assimilate into our great nation," he added. Later, the president denied making those comments.

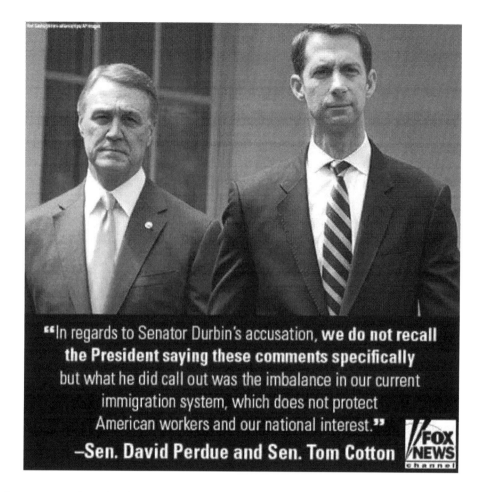

Republican Senators David Purdue from Georgia and Tom Cotton from Arkansas, who were present at the meeting, said that they did not recall the president saying those comments specifically but heard the president discuss the imbalance in our current immigration system. The Destroy Trump media has continued to attack the president on a daily calling him a racist and a White Supremacist. The anti-Trump media has barely reported the strong denial of the two Republican senators. The mainstream media has repeated the version of the radical Democratic Senator Durbin from Illinois hoping to hurt him politically in the midterm elections.

Regardless of what the president's comments were, those alleged remarks damaged him poliT-Illy as well as his image in the nation and internationally. There are thousands of Haitian and Central American voters in Florida and other states that may not support the president, if he runs for reelection in 2020 and may not support Republicans running in the 2018 midterm elections. Therefore, it is so important for the president to be careful in what he says to avoid misunderstandings and damage his image as president. In the future the president should record every future meeting with Democrats and reporters. This incident in the Oval Office came after a very successful televised 55-minutes White House bipartisan meeting where Democrats and Republicans praised President Trump for the way he ran the meeting.

The attempt to declare President Trump unfit for office

Michael Wolff wrote the book *Fire and Fury: Inside the Trump White House* in January 2018. This book written by a liberal author, who writes for left-wing publications, such as *Vanity Fair* and the *Guardian* newspaper, portrays the president as erratic, uninformed, and lacking focus. This writer believes this is a Fake book written by a Fake author whose intention Wolff says is to end the presidency of Donald Trump. Obviously, it would take much more than a false book full of lies to do that!

Michael Wolff, in an interview by *NBC*, said on January 5, 2018, that the people around the president in the White House said the following: "Trump is like a child. What they mean by that is he has a need for immediate gratification. It's all about him. This man does not read, does not listen. He's like a pinball, just shooting off the sides. They say he's a moron, an idiot."

Basically, Wolff is saying that Trump's associates question his fitness for office and 100% of those around him in the White House question his intelligence. Wolff is making the rounds in the Destroy Trump television channels. This is part of a concerted plan by Democrats, communists, and globalists, including two retiring Republican senators, Bob Corker of Tennessee and Jeff Flake of Arizona, who have stated that the president is insane. These individuals are hoping to invoke the 25th Amendment of the Constitution that states that if over half of President Trump's cabinet declare the president unfit or crazy to continue in office, he would be replaced by the vice president.

Michael Wolff wrote the book *Fire and Fury: Inside the Trump White House* in January 2018.

Steve Bannon is quoted in the book as describing a June 2016 meeting involving Donald Trump, Jr., Jared Kushner, and Paul Manafort with a Russian lawyer during the campaign as "treasonous" and unpatriotic." Bannon is also quoted calling Ivanka Trump as being "dumb as a brick." Later Bannon denied that he made those comments to the author as well as many others.

These quotes by Bannon led to a break with President Donald Trump. This is unfortunate since both are anti-globalist nationalists. However, if it is true that Bannon said these negative comments, it is understandable the statement released by the president against Bannon. The White House 266-word statement from President Donald Trump severely criticized the former Chief Strategist Steve Bannon.

Michael Wolff, as the Republican National Committee said, "Has a long history of making stuff up." Several individuals quoted in the book have denied that they ever told the author those comments. The president's lawyer is seeking to block the distribution of this book.

President Trump has stated that the book is "full of lies, misrepresentations, and sources that don't exist." Later, on Twitter, he said he is "a stable genius." White House Press Secretary Sarah Huckabee Sanders said on *Fox News* on January 5, 2018, "It's absolutely outrageous to make this type of allegations about Trump's mental fitness." "They're desperate attempts to attack Trump, what's I think is really mentally unstable is people not seeing the progress Trump is making," she said.

The *Conservative Tribune* website reported on January 6, 2018 that the book makes wild claims, some of which Wolff has said he is not even sure are true. One of the most outrageous claims concerns the mental health of the president.

Press Secretary Sarah Sanders stated at a recent news briefing "I am not going to waste my time or the country's time going page by page talking about a book that is a complete fantasy and just full of tabloid gossip because it is bad, pathetic, and our focus is going to be on moving the country forward." A reporter asked Sanders about the claim concerning Trump's mental health, "It's disgraceful and laughable, if he was unfit, he probably wouldn't be sitting there and wouldn't have defeated the most qualified group of candidates the Republican Party has ever seen." "This is an incredibly strong and good leader. That's why we've had such as successful in 2017 and why we're going to continue to do great things as we move forward in this administration," Sanders said.

On January 9, 2018, Steve Bannon resigned from his position as executive chairman at *Breitbart News.*

Because of Steve Bannon's quotes in the book, the president released a statement larger than a tweet on January 3, 2018. President Trump said the following:

"Steve Bannon has nothing to do with me or my Presidency. When he was fired, he not only lost his job, he lost his mind. Steve was a staffer who worked for me after I had already won the nomination by defeating seventeen candidates, often described as the most talented field ever assembled in the Republican Party."

"Now that he is on his own, Steve is learning that winning isn't as easy as I make it look. Steve had very little to do with our historic victory, which was delivered by the forgotten men and women of this country. Yet Steve had everything to do with the loss of a Senate seat in Alabama held for more than thirty years by Republicans. Steve doesn't represent my base — he's only in it for himself."

"Steve pretends to be at war with the media, which he calls the opposition party, yet he spent his time at the White House leaking false information to the media to make himself seem far more important than he was. It is the only thing he does well. Steve was rarely in a one-on-one meeting with me and only pretends to have had influence to fool a few people with no access and no clue, whom he helped write phony books."

"We have many great Republican members of Congress and candidates who are very supportive of the Make America Great Again agenda. Like me, they love the United States of America and are helping to finally take our country back and build it up, rather than simply seeking to burn it all down."

Because of the quotes attributed to Steve Bannon in the shameful and Fake book, which several days later he said he was misquoted, the president broke completely with Bannon. The former chief strategist also lost the support of Rebekah Mercer, multimillionaire conservative donor and who holds a minority stake in *Breitbart News*.

On January 9, 2018, *Breitbart News* announced that Bannon had resigned as executive chairman of the conservative news organization. This writer is sad to see Steve Bannon, a nationalist and anti-globalist, break with the president and quit *Breitbart News*, but he understands that those comments and allowing the Fake and dishonest writer Michael Wolff to enter the White House was a mistake.

Donald Trump is a politically incorrect and unconventional president. And this is precisely what the Trump base that elected him wants. America and the world need to get use to the style of this president.

The Deep State is trying to destroy the presidency of Donald Trump

Cartoon showing the president trying to drain the D.C. Swamp, but will he succeed?

Frank de Varona

The rank-and-file officials in the CIA, NSA, FBI, and other intelligence agencies are patriotic individuals. But some of the high-ranking officials of the 17 intelligence agencies as well as the members of the globalist elite serving in the Council of Foreign Relations, the Bilderberg Group, and the Trilateral Commission are part of the Deep State. President Trump needs to fire as many as possible Deep State officials who are working in the federal government!

As is described in this book, since his election, the Deep State is trying to destroy the presidency of Donald Trump in whatever way possible. Many Democrats in Congress are calling for his impeachment and are describing him as unbalanced and crazy. Two Trump haters Republican senators, Senator Bob Corker from Tennessee and Jeff Flake from Arizona, who are not running for reelection, have joined the chorus and are also calling the president crazy. They are hoping that half of the cabinet would declare President Trump "insane" so that he can be removed under the 25th Amendment of the Constitution.

Crimes and scandals of Clinton campaign and why Hillary and Obama need to be indicted

Donna Brazile and Hillary Clinton

After being fired by *CNN* for providing Hillary Clinton questions in advance of the presidential debates, Donna Brazile was appointed Interim Chair of the Democratic National Committee (DNC) to replace the scandal-ridden Congresswoman Debbie Wasserman-Schultz. The

Democratic Congresswoman Wasserman-Schultz from South Florida was forced to resign after *WikiLeaks* published almost 20,000 DNC e-mails.

Some of the e-mails indicated that DNC top employees were discussing how to manipulate events to favor Hillary Clinton in obtaining the nomination of the Democratic Party in 2016. This was done in direct violation of the DNC charter which mandates this committee to remain neutral during the Democratic Party primaries.

The leaked DNC e-mails showed the DNC efforts to destroy the campaign of the Marxist Senator Bernie Sanders from Vermont. After Americans found out how the DNC rigged the primaries to help Clinton, the DNC went into an unsuccessful damage control mode.

Presidential candidate Hillary Clinton was once again exposed as a very corrupt woman who would do anything to be elected president. When Hillary Clinton received her party nomination on July 26, 2016, she was a tainted candidate.

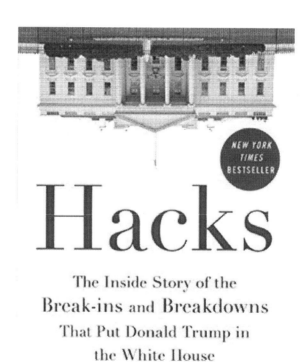

Donna Brazile wrote *Hacks: The Inside Story of the Break-ins and Breakdowns That Put Donald Trump in the White House* in November 2017.

In her 288-page book Hacks, the former Democratic National Committee Interim Chairwoman Donna Brazile accused the Democratic Party and the DNC of favoring Hillary Clinton over Bernie Sanders. Brazile criticized the Clinton campaign and accused it of being dismissive of her after she took over as DNC chair following the resignation of Debbie Wasserman Schultz. Brazile published an article in *Politico* on November 2, 2017. Her book and the article claimed that Clinton stole the nomination and then blew the election.

Brazile stated that she promised Senator Sanders that she would find out if the DNC rigged the system to give Clinton the presidential nomination of the party. Brazile wrote that she found out a signed August 2015 agreement between the Clinton campaign and the DNC that assured the party would be bailed out of debt by Clinton's fundraising efforts. In turn, the Clinton campaign would assume control of the DNC, make staffing decisions at the DNC, and have input over its finances.

Former Bernie Sanders campaign officials complained about the actions taken by the DNC after the first excerpt of Brazile's book was released. Senator Sanders' supporters had long accused the DNC of favoring Clinton, who won 34 primaries and nearly four million more votes than Sanders. Jeff Weaver, former Sanders campaign manager, said he was worried about the future of the Democratic Party. Weaver stated the following: "The electoral history of the last seven or eight years is pretty abysmal, America's oldest political party may go the way of the Federalist. It needs to reconnect with grass roots supporters."

Brazile contemplated switching out Clinton for Vice President Joe Biden after the former Secretary of State fainted in September 2016. The Clinton campaign said it was just pneumonia.

Brazile's book was criticized by Hillary Clinton's supporters. During her press tour for the book, Brazile told *ABC News* that critics of her book could "go to hell."

C. Mitchell Shaw wrote an article titled "Clinton Campaign Scandals" which was published in the December 4, 2017 *New American* issue. Shaw said that the "past few weeks have shed much new light on political corruption, illegal practices, and unethical activities in both the Clinton campaign and the DNC, to such a degree that it is difficult to imagine either of them bouncing back unscathed."

Shaw explained that when it was clear that the DNC e-mail scandal was not going to disappear, the DNC and Clinton campaign began blaming the leaked e-mails on Russia. *WikiLeaks* denied the accusation. Hillary Clinton and the DNC continued to claim that the e-mails were not leaked but that they had been *hacked*.

When the scandal did not go away, Hillary Clinton took it to the next level and said that Russia rigged the election to favor Donald Trump. During the third and final presidential debate, Hillary Clinton — while avoiding questions about the content of the e-mails — went so far as to call Donald Trump "Putin's puppet," Shaw said.

The Clinton campaign, the DNC, and the complicit Destroy Trump corrupt mainstream media repeated the Trump-"Putin's puppet" accusation again and again during the rest of the campaign. It is very difficult for Democrats to continue making this false accusation now that President Trump has authorized the sale of anti-tank missiles and other weapons to Ukraine over the strong objection of Putin. In contrast, Obama never sold a bullet to Ukraine.

Who killed Seth Rich?

Seth Rich, a 27-year-old computer-voting specialist at the DNC, was murdered on July 10, 2016 in Washington, D.C

Some people believe that Seth Rich leaked the e-mails of the DNC to WikiLeaks. Julian Assange, founder of WikiLeaks, hinted that Rich was the source of the hacked e-mails. He offered a $20,000 reward for the apprehension of his killer(s). While many have called his murder a botched robbery, the police found Rich's wallet, credit cards, and cellphone on his body.

Some people think Rich was assassinated by a hired killer as punishment for his alleged leaking of the DNC's e-mails. Others blame Russia, a charge rejected by that nation. The D.C. police department is still investigating. No one has been arrested in the assassination of this young man.

The 35-page dossier prepared by Christopher Steele commissioned by the opposion research firm Fusion GPS with the purpose of destroying candidate Donald J. Trump

C. Mitchell Shaw wrote that just before President-elect Donald J. Trump was inaugurated, the liberal media published "an intelligence dossier containing unsubstantiated, salacious accusations that Trump was being controlled by the Kremlin as a form of blackmail and supported by the Kremlin to help in his race against Clinton."

Bruce Ohr and his wife Nellie Ohr

Nellie Ohr, the wife of a Justice Department (DOJ) official Bruce Ohr, was hired by Fusion GPS, the company that together with Christopher Steele, the former British spy, wrote the anti-Trump dossier that contains salacious and unsubstantiated accusations against Donald Trump. Later, Bruce Ohr was demoted for concealing the work of his wife on the fake dossier.

FoxNews reported that the Fusion GPS connections with Nellie and Bruce Ohr have raised Republican concerns about the objectivity of the Justice Department and even prompted a call from President Donald Trump's outside counsel for a separate special prosecutor. Mrs. Ohr was indeed involved in the Trump research. Bank records reveal that Fusion GPS contracted with her "to help our company with its research and analysis of Mr. Trump."

Christopher Steele wrote, together with Fusion GPS, the unverified anti-Trump dossier.

FoxNews reported that Bruce Ohr met during the 2016 campaign with Christopher Steele, the former British spy who authored the dossier. The FBI used the dossier, which is an unproven 35-page document, to investigate and possibly obtain surveillance warrants. Now Christopher Steele is faced with a libel lawsuit filed by a Russian and is changing his accusation of Donald Trump's links with Russia to "possible" collusion.

FoxNews said that Fusion GPS "attracted scrutiny because Republican lawmakers have spent the better part of this year investigating whether the dossier, which was funded by the Hillary Clinton campaign and the Democratic National Committee, served as the basis for the Justice Department and the FBI to obtain FISA surveillance last year on a Trump campaign adviser named Carter Page."

FoxNews stated that Trump's lawyer, Jay Sekulow, has asked for the appointment of a separate special prosecutor to look into potential conflicts of interest involving the Justice Department and FBI officials. A group of House of Representatives Republicans have called for months for the appointment of a second special counsel to investigate certain Barack Obama and Hillary Clinton-related controversies. Attorney General Jeff Sessions is reviewing the request for a special counsel.

Attorney General Jeff Sessions stated the following: "I've put a senior attorney, with the resources he may need, to review cases in our office and make a recommendation to me ... if things aren't being pursued that need to be pursued, if cases may need more resources to complete in a proper manner, and to recommend to me if the standards for a special counsel are met."

The dossier was fake and rapidly discredited. Moreover, it was later discovered that the dossier was paid by the Clinton campaign and the DNC and then shared with James Comey's FBI. As previously stated, Nellie Ohr, the wife of a Justice Department official, Bruce Ohr, was hired by Fusion GPS, the company that wrote the unsubstantiated accusations against Donald Trump. The Clinton campaign broke campaign finance laws by failing to disclose the payment of the anti-Trump dossier. This would be one of the many election laws broken by the corrupt Hillary Clinton and her campaign workers.

C. Mitchell Shaw wrote the following: "Clinton and the DNC were so dedicated to keeping their involvement in the creation of the dossier a secret that they described the payments to Fusion GPS as legal services paid to Marc Elias. This is a clear violation of campaign finance laws requiring campaigns and parties to show an accounting of what monies come in (and from whom) and what monies go out (and to whom and for what). The non-profit Campaign Legal Center filed a complaint with the Federal Election Commission (FEC) on October 25, 2017 claiming that the Clinton campaign and the DNC violated federal law when they undermined the vital public information role of campaign disclosures by filing misleading reports. If the FEC decides to investigate, this could be added to the list of new investigations on the Clinton campaign."

C. Mitchell Shaw pointed out that Brazile wrote that she had made a promise to Bernie Sanders to "get to the bottom of whether Hillary Clinton's team had rigged the nomination process, as a cache of e-mails stolen by Russian hackers and posted online had suggested." Brazile was a willing participant in the corruption she is now exposing. It is also important to note that the most damning of her claims are well documented, said Shaw.

Lastly, Shaw explained that Brazile wrote in her *Politico* article that by the time she took over as Interim Chair of the DNC, the party was in deep financial trouble because of the poor leadership of Congresswoman Wasserman Schultz and the "neglect" of President Obama. On September 7, 2017, Brazile called Senator Sanders and told him that Hillary Clinton had stolen the Democratic Party nomination from him and that she was a "cancer" in the body of the DNC. President Donald Trump later pounced on Brazile's account and stated on Twitter that he always thought he would square off against Sanders.

FBI Deputy Director Andrew McCabe recently testified in a close hearing of the House of Representatives Permanent Select Committee on Intelligence.

McCabe announced that he will retire from the FBI early in 2018. McCabe, whose wife received over $700,000 from Democrats when she ran unsuccessfully for a state senate seat in the Legislature of Virginia in 2005, said the FBI could not verify the accusation of the collusion of Trump campaign with Russia. Yet the fake dossier was used to receive court-approval for the wiretapping of members of the Trump campaign as well as Donald Trump.

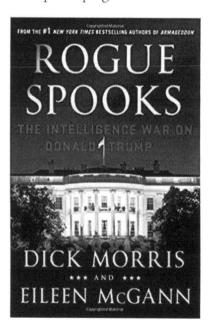

Dick Morris and Eileen McGann wrote *Rogue Spooks: The Intelligence War on Donald Trump* in August 2017.

During the campaign and after the election of Donald Trump, Deep State rogue intelligence agents began an attempted coup d'état—now in progress— with the goal of overthrowing the presidency of Donald Trump and subvert the will of the electorate.

Amazon describes *Rogue Spooks* as follows:

"Donald Trump's first 100 days in office were roiled by allegations of treasonous contacts between his campaign team and the Kremlin to rig the election. These outrageous charges first surfaced in the notorious Trump Dossier, an unverified document of suspect provenance, full of wild and salacious accusations."

"This dossier—filled with little more than gossip, rumor, and innuendo—was compiled by Christopher Steele, a former British intelligence operative who teamed up with the FBI and anti-Trump partisans. Hillary Clinton supporters paid for Steele's work."

"When no news media would publish the unverified dossier, the ex-spook enlisted the help of a former UK ambassador to Russia, who arranged in turn for a former U.S. assistant secretary of state to get the document to Senator John McCain, in the hope that he would then bring it to FBI Director James Comey's attention. McCain did just that."

"Comey himself played a critical role in the dossier ultimately going public, giving a confidential summary to President Obama and congressional leaders. It was immediately leaked by rogue spooks in order to demean, destabilize, and destroy Donald Trump's nascent presidency."

"The dossier and this mythical intelligence are the basis for the phony claims about a Russia-Trump collusion to steal the election. No proof was found. No substantiation uncovered. Even Comey told Trump he was not under investigation for the Russian meddling charges. But that didn't end the leaks or the allegations. Working in concert with liberal news outlets, these rogue spooks have formed a new Intel/Media complex that threatens our democracy. *Rogue Spooks* will reveal how it works."

"Readers of *Rogue Spooks,* from bestselling authors Dick Morris and Eileen McGann, will be shocked to learn the truth about the false accusations against President Trump in the flawed dossier. They'll be interested to know how leaks to the media fueled the phony scandal, and how intelligence agencies will try to use the newly appointed special prosecutor to oust President Trump. They will also learn what we can do—specifically—to stop them."

On January 4, 2018, Senate Judiciary Chairman Charles Grassley and Senator Lindsey Graham have asked the Justice Department to investigate Christopher Steele for a possible criminal investigation for lying to federal authorities regarding his fake dossier. The two senators sent a letter to Deputy Attorney General Rod Rosenstein and FBI director Christopher Wray.

On January 6, 2018, Byron York wrote an article called "What the Trump Dossier Criminal Referral Means" which was published in the *Washington Examiner*. York explained that the letter by two Republican senators related "to certain communications between Christopher Steele and multiple U.S. news outlets regarding the so-called 'Trump dossier' that Mr. Steele compiled on behalf of Fusion GPS for the Clinton campaign and the Democratic National Committee and also provided to the FBI."

York wrote that "Grassley and Graham said that, on the basis of the classified information laid out in the memo, we are respectfully referring Mr. Steele to you for investigation of 18 U.S.C. 1001, for statements the committee has reason to believe Mr. Steele made regarding his distribution of information contained in the dossier." (18 U.S.C. 1001 is the same federal false statements law that special counsel Robert Mueller has used to charge Michael Flynn and George Papadopoulos in the Trump-Russia investigation.)

York said that Steele communicated frequently with the FBI. "It is a crime to make false statements to the FBI – does not have to be under oath, does not have to be in a formal interview or interrogation setting, it's simply a criminal act to knowingly make a false statement to the FBI. As a result of their talks, Steele and the FBI reached a tentative agreement whereby the FBI would pay Steele to continue the anti-Trump work," explained York.

While Steele was also working for the opposition research firm Fusion GPS – his dossier was the result of a Fusion GPS anti-Trump project funded by the Clinton campaign and the Democratic National Committee. York said that "As part of that, Steele briefed reporters on what he had found. In a London court case, Steele's lawyers said that in September 2016, Fusion GPS directed Steele to brief reporters individually from the *New York Times*, the *Washington Post*, *CNN*, the *New Yorker*, *Yahoo News*, and, later, *Mother Jones*."

York stated the following: "One serious question is whether Steele told the FBI that he was telling reporters the same information – those explosive allegations about Trump and Trump associates – that he was bringing to bureau investigators. If the FBI knew that, would they have agreed to an arrangement to make Steele a paid FBI operative investigating the Trump-Russia affair? That would have been a most unorthodox arrangement, with Steele disseminating his allegations to the FBI and the press simultaneously."

The Deep State is the D.C. Swamp

On December 1, 2017, Monica Crowley wrote an article titled "Why the Swamp Hates Donald Trump?" which was published by the website *Frontpage magazine*. Crowley asks does the swamp always win?. She answers, "Yes, of course, the swamp always won, but the way we answer that question now, because it's an open question for the first time in a long time, is going to determine the future of this exceptional nation."

Crowley described the swamp as follows: "The swamp is the ruling class and it's comprised of the elites on all sides of the political spectrum. Why has it always dominated? We sort of take it for granted. Why has it always dominated despite repeated attempts by noble patriots over many years to try to chip away at its monstrous power? The short answer is that the swamp controls all the levers of power in this country, and they have the capability and the will to destroy anyone and anything that threatens its grip. The swamp is the perfect embodiment of Lord Acton's warning that power tends to corrupt and absolute power corrupts absolutely."

"It's elected officials on both sides. It's the establishment on both sides. Their staffs, the media, federal bureaucracies, special interests, lobbyists, even some in the deep state who are supposed to only be focused on America's external threats, and even some in law and law enforcement who are only supposed to be interested in applying equal justice under the law. They've all become corrupted, and this ruling class has dined out on this rotten status quo for a hell of a long time until now," she wrote.

Crowley explained that finally this nation has elected a person who is not part of the swamp and who does not fear the creatures of the swamp. The swamp hates Donald Trump and is trying to destroy his presidency. Donald J. Trump came in and he promised to smash their corrupt existing order, to overturn the money changers' tables. The president wants to restore respect for the Constitution, to restore government back to its proper place, and to restore economic growth, and to make America great again.

"Of course, most of these things, if not all of them, scare the living hell out of the ruling class. Having failed to destroy their nemesis during the campaign, they have now redoubled their efforts to kill his presidency" wrote Crowley.

Crowley pointed out that "It is true that this President is an imperfect warrior, but he is the kind of disrupter that we have been waiting for, the kind of disrupter that we have been longing for, but while disrupters in the private sector are celebrated, right? Government is supposed to serve the people but instead, it serves only itself and that's why anyone who comes along like Donald Trump promising to restore the country to the vision the Founders intended has got to be crushed. The swamp will not be threatened."

These individuals, such as Barack Obama, Hillary Clinton, James Comey, Robert Mueller, George Soros, John Brennan, Eric Clapper, Democrats in Congress, and many others, are engaged in an ongoing coup against elected President Donald Trump. President Donald Trump has been trying to drain the Washington, D.C. Swamp with great difficulty. The globalists never expected Donald Trump to win and defeat their chosen candidate Hillary Clinton. Even though the globalists Insiders in Wall Street gave tens of millions to Hillary Clinton and only two newspapers endorsed Donald Trump, he won.

President Trump ran an anti-globalist, nationalistic, America First campaign. However, he has named 40 globalists to his administration since they are too powerful to be completely ignored. Nevertheless, the president is a patriot and has named the least amount of globalists to his administration when compared to any other president.

The Clinton campaign and Obama paid thugs to beat up Trump supporters and used agent provocateurs to damage candidate Trump

On October 19, 2016, Moderator Chris Wallace asked questions to Hillary Clinton and Donald Trump during the third and last presidential debate in Las Vegas, Nevada.

On October 20, 2016, Steve Contorno wrote an article titled "Trump says Clinton and Obama paid people to cause violence at his rallies" that was published by the website *Politifact*. Contorno said that during the third and final presidential debate, Republican presidential candidate Donald Trump accused Hillary Clinton and Barack Obama of paying people to incite violence at his rallies.

Trump stated the following: "If you look at what came out today on the clips. I was wondering what happened with my rally in Chicago and other rallies where we had such violence. She's the one, and Obama, that caused the violence. They hired people, they paid them $1,500, and they're on tape saying, be violent, cause fights, do bad things. When I saw what they did, which is a criminal act by the way, where they're telling people to go out and start fist-fights and start violence. In particular in Chicago people were hurt, and people could've been killed in that riot. And that was now all on tape started by her."

Contorno said that Donald Trump was talking about the video released that week by Project Veritas Action, a conservative group that went undercover to secretly record Democratic operatives discussing plans to cause trouble at Trump rallies and then blamed Trump's supporters. Project Veritas is an organization founded by James O'Keefe, a 32-year-old conservative activist.

In 2009, O'Keefe posted undercover videos that showed illegal activities by employees of ACORN, the Marxist organization led by Barack Obama. These videos destroyed ACORN. Its communist leaders and employees then joined other radical organizations. Previous operations from Project Veritas have led to resignations of Democratic operatives and NPR executives.

Contorno wrote that a 16-minute video posted by James O'Keefe's Project Veritas called "Rigging the Election," dramatically begins with O'Keefe promising to expose "the dark background dealings of the Hillary Clinton presidential campaign." O'Keefe said the following: "What you're about to see will make you uncomfortable and angry. It's graphic, uncensored and disturbing. Our attorneys say there is strong evidence of criminality."

The video showed Scott Foval, who is the national field director at Americans United for Change. He was a subcontractor working for Democracy Partners, a consulting firm founded by Robert Creamer, who is also featured in the video. Democracy Partners worked for the Democratic National Committee.

Contorno wrote that the video showed Foval saying the following: "If you're there and you're protesting and you do these actions, you will be attacked at Trump rallies. That's what we want. The whole point of it is, we know Trump's people will freak the (expletive) out, the security team will freak out, and his supporters will lose their (expletive). There's a script. There's a script of engagement. Sometimes the crazies bite, and the crazies don't bite. The key is initiating the conflict by having leading conversations with people who are naturally psychotic."

"I mean honestly, it is not hard to get some of these (expletive) to pop off. It's a matter of showing up, to want to get in the rally in a Planned Parenthood T-shirt. Or Trump is a Nazi. You can message to draw them out and message them to punch you."

The outrageous comments were rejected by DNC Interim Chair Donna Brazile, who said they "do not in any way comport with our long-standing policies on organizing events, and those statements and sentiments do not represent the values that the Committee holds dear." The scandal forced the dismissal of Foval by Americans for Change and the departure of Creamer from his work with the DNC and the Clinton campaign.

Another individual mentioned in the video, Contorno pointed out, was Zulema Rodriguez. She bragged that she "did the Chicago event where they shut down" during the Republican Convention.

Rodriguez was referring to the Trump March 11, 2016 Chicago rally that was cancelled due to a massive anti-Trump protest, whose participants clashed with Trump supporters, causing several injuries. Campaign finance reports showed that the Clinton campaign paid Rodriguez $1,610 in Arizona on February 29, 2016 -- less than two weeks before the Chicago rally.

Contorno stated the following: "Other people and groups have been given credit for shutting down the Chicago rally. Multiple news reports suggest that University of Illinois Chicago students, MoveOn.org and Bernie Sanders supporters mobilized online to shut down the rally. Hundreds of anti-Trump protesters planted themselves inside the event with the goal of preventing it from even taking place. They succeeded, and clashed with Trump supporters after it was announced the Republican businessman wouldn't be attending. FEC reports show Rodriguez also worked for *MoveOn.org*."

Robert Creamer, a convicted felon, is a radical leftist political consultant
and a great friend of Barack Obama.

Robert Creamer is the husband of socialist Democratic congresswoman Jan Schakowsky from the Illinois's 9th congressional district. Creamer's firm, Democracy Partners, works with Democratic campaigns. He also leads the radical nonprofit group Americans United for Change.

In 2005, Creamer pleaded guilty to tax violations and $2.3 million in bank fraud in relation to payments with checks with insufficient funds to fund his public interest group in the 1990s. He repaid the funds and was convicted and sentenced to five months in prison and eleven months of house arrest.

On October 19, 2016, Jen Lawrence wrote an article titled "Robert Creamer Visited Obama's White House 340 Times" that was published by *Breitbart*. Lawrence said that the Obama's White House logs show Creamer making 340 visits to the White House, with 45 of those meetings including President Obama. Creamer's political consulting firm Democracy Partners is at the center of the investigation of Project Veritas that exposes Democrat operatives instigating violence at Trump rallies and plotting potential voter fraud.

Jen Lawrence pointed out that in addition to the regular visits of Creamer to the White House, "Creamer's own statements contradict Brazile's claim that Democracy Partners was just a bit player in the Clinton campaign and the DNC." Lawrence explained the following: "In hidden camera video filmed at Creamer's Washington, D.C. office, Creamer explains that Hillary Clinton is aware of all of his activities, directly or indirectly, and that Democracy Partners has a daily conference call with the Clinton campaign, as well as frequent calls with the White House. Creamer's meetings at the White House include two meetings with President Obama in March 2011 and June 2013 where the total number of people is listed as just two."

In the second O'Keefe video, Lawrence stated the following: "Scott Foval said that Bob Creamer is diabolical and I love him for it. While discussing the potential voter fraud plot, Foval credits Creamer for coming up with most of these ideas, and describes Democracy Partners as a dark hat. Creamer boasts having more than four decades as a political organizer and strategist on his Democracy Partners page. Creamer's biography also details a long history working with the DNC at the presidential campaign level. During the 2008 and 2012 presidential elections he worked with the Democratic National Committee as a consultant to the Obama Presidential Campaign coordinating field based rapid response to Republican Presidential candidates. During his career, Creamer has worked on hundreds of electoral campaigns at the local, state and national level."

On November 7, 2017, William Jasper wrote an article titled "Alt-Right and Agents Provocateurs" that was published in *New American*. Jasper wrote that due to the undercover camera work of James O'Keefe's Project Veritas, the nation learned that top Democratic Party operatives were boasting about infiltrating Trump campaign rallies and events, staging conflicts, and "creating anarchy." Jasper explained that "Scott Foval, Bob Creamer, and other dirty tricks agents for Hillary Clinton's campaign and the Democratic National Committee were caught *in flagrante* admitting to staging and instigating conflicts for maximum media effect."

Jasper stated the following: "Foval made it clear that he knew that many of his tactics are illegal and that he didn't care that some of the DNC's legal experts were worried about possible prosecution, if discovered. It doesn't matter what the frigging legal and ethics people say, we need to win this mother foc***," he said, adding, We're starting anarchy here. Did the same media go back and clobber Clinton and the DNC for the deception after the Foval revelations? Of course not; instead they went after O'Keefe and Project Veritas."

Hillary Clinton wrote her dissertation in college on the communist Saul Alinsky. She was a friend and a disciple of Alinsky. Obama considered Alinsky his spiritual guide.

Jasper pointed out that Bob Creamer, who was a mentor of Scott Foval, appeared on the video describing the anarchy he was orchestrating. Creamer and Foval were following the program advocated by the Marxist and Chicago-based community organizer Saul Alinsky, the author of Rules for Radicals and a close friend of Hillary Clinton.

Jasper explained that Sanford D. Horwitt wrote a biography of this Marxist agitator from Chicago and founder of the community organizers movement. Horwitt wrote in his book about a revealing incident dealing with Alinsky's advice to students at Tulane University in 1972. The radical students were planning to protest a speech by George H. W. Bush, who was then the U.S. ambassador to the United Nations.

Horwitt wrote the following: "The students told Alinsky they were thinking about picketing or disrupting Bush's address. That's the wrong approach, he rejoined, not very creative — and besides causing a disruption might get them thrown out of school. He told them, instead, to go to hear the speech dressed as members of the Ku Klux Klan, and whenever Bush said something in defense of the Vietnam War, they should cheer and wave placards reading, The KKK supports Bush. And that is what they did, with very successful, attention-getting results." Those students acted as agent provocateurs, a tactic used by communists and others throughout the world.

Shirley Teeter was a paid agent provocateur by the Clinton campaign.

Teeter was used cynically and illegally to validate Hillary Clinton's charge that Trump supporters were "a basket of deplorables." Jasper discussed the role of agent provocateurs in the Clinton campaign as well as how these individuals are currently employed in the Anti-Trump Deep State and resistance movement. He cited as prime example Shirley Teeter, a woman agent provocateur used by the Clinton campaign to discredit Trump and his supporters.

Shirley Teeter, a 69-year-old woman who was wearing an oxygen mask and carrying an oxygen tank, claimed she was hit by a supporter of candidate Trump at a Trump rally in North Carolina. The corrupt Destroy Trump mainstream media featured photos of the handicapped woman on the ground with her wheelchair as a victim of despicable and inhumane Trump's supporters. However, it turned out that Teeter was a paid agent provocateur. She "was one of our activists," Scott Foval bragged on the video. He also said that she "had been trained up to birddog" and perform her stunt exactly as it was planned.

Agent provocateurs were present at the August 12, 2017 deadly confrontation in Charlottesville, Virginia, said Jasper. He explained that the violent confrontation between neo-Nazis/white nationalists on one side with masked Antifa thugs and Black Lives Matter radicals on the other side culminated with the death of demonstrator Heather Heyer. The Deep State and the leaders of the resistance who are virulent Trump haters could not have asked for a better-staged event to reinforce their false narrative of President Trump as a reincarnated Hitler and a supporter of the Ku Klux Klan, said Jasper.

Jasper wrote the following: "The alt-Right, at least as represented in Charlottesville, provided the precise optics needed by the Fake News media not only to boost its relentless anti-Trump campaign, but also to associate legitimate concerns about illegal immigration with xenophobia, and efforts to retain Confederate symbols and Southern heritage with racism. They also served to boost the image of the communist-directed Antifa mobs as heroic opponents of fascism and bigotry… While some of the alt-Right celebrities are merely losers seeking fame by attaching themselves to Donald Trump's coattails, others more closely fit the profile of agent provocateurs — that is, saboteurs whose purpose is to discredit from within."

Jason Kessler is an agent provocateur who wants to discredit conservatives and President Trump and his supporters by portraying them as racist pro-Nazi white nationalists.

Jasper mentioned another agent provocateur, Marxist Jason Kessler, who was a pro-abortion, pro-gun control, pro-radical environmentalist, pro-Obama, and atheist and who participated in the radical Occupy Wall Street movement and suddenly "converted" to a white nationalist and alt-right activist. He is known for being the main organizer of the white nationalist Unite the Right rally in Charlottesville, Virginia, which resulted in the death of Heather Heyer after a car was driven into the crowd.

Kessler celebrated her death by saying that the victim was "a fat, disgusting Communist" in a tweet that was linked to an article on the *Daily Stormer,* a neo-Nazi website. Kessler is a plant to advance the Marxist-globalist agenda and identify anti-communists as fascists.

Richard Spencer is a neo-Nazi 39-year-old agent provocateur who pretends to like Trump while saying he likes socialism and socialized medicine and government expending. He says "Heil Trump" with the intension to identify Trump with Hitler. Marxists are experts in using agent provocateurs to demonize and destroy their enemies.

Investigating the investigators

Hillary Clinton and Special Counsel Robert Mueller are both part of the Swamp.

On October 23, 2017, Victor Davis Hanson wrote an article titled "Investigating the investigators" which was published in the website *America Greatest.* Hanson explained that as the

President Donald Trump investigators—in Congress, in the Justice Department, and the legions in the media— are unable to charge the president with collusion with Russia, he raises the following two questions: "Was the zeal of the original accusers of felony behavior with the Russian collusion merely an attempt at deflection? Was it designed to protect themselves from being accused of serious crimes"?

Hanson raises the question: What did the FBI do?

Hanson stated the following:

"It was bad enough that the original narrative had the authors of the so-called Fusion GPS/Steele dossier leaking their smears to the media. Worse, the FBI, in the earlier fashion of the Clinton campaign, may have paid to obtain the Fusion concoction."

"Now it appears that some of the leakers who had the file in their possession also may have belonged to the American intelligence community. Did the FBI pass around its purchased smears to other intelligence agencies and the Obama administration in the unspoken hope that, in seeing the file had been so sanctioned and widely read, some intelligence operative or one of the Obama people would wink and nod as they leaked it to the press?"

"And why did the progenitors of the Steele dossier fraud—the Fusion GPS consortium and former *Wall Street Journal* reporters (a firm that had a prior history of smearing political enemies with "opposition research") and working indirectly on behalf of Russian interests—reportedly behind closed doors invoke the Fifth Amendment to avoid testifying about the dossier, its origins, and its funding before the House Intelligence Committee?"

"Increasingly, James Comey seems to be caught in contradictions of his own making. The former FBI director may well have misled the U.S. Congress in deliberate fashion, both about the timeline of events that led him to recommend not charging Hillary Clinton and about his denials that the FBI had communications about the bizarre "accidental" meeting on an Arizona tarmac between the U.S. Attorney General and Bill Clinton."

"How does an FBI Director get away with leaking his own notes, ostensibly FBI property, to the media with the expressed intent of leveraging the selection of a special prosecutor, only to succeed in having his friend, former FBI Director Robert Mueller, appointed to that very post—an official who presumably and earlier had been investigating possible Clinton collusion with Russian uranium interests?"

This writer believes there is sufficient evidence of wrong doing by some officials and individuals in the FBI, the Justice Department, other intelligence agencies, the Obama White House, and the Clinton campaign that a special counsel should be appointed to conduct a full investigation. The investigation should also include the Clinton Foundation, the mishandling of classified information by Hillary Clinton and Huma Abedin, the war in Libya, and Obama's secret Presidential Directive 11.

Imran Awan is a Pakistani-American information technology worker. He is currently awaiting trial on charges of bank fraud.

Imran Awan worked as a shared employee for Democrats in the House of Representatives. At the time of his arrest in July 2017, he had been working as an information technologist in Congress for 13 years. He has been involved in multiple investigations in 2017. He is currently awaiting trial on charges of bank fraud. Awan's relationship with the corrupt former Democratic National Chairman Congresswoman Debbie Wasserman Schultz is a mystery.

So Many Questions, So Few Answers

Hansen raises several questions regarding the strange relationship between former Democratic National Chairman Debbie Wasserman Schultz and her IT "expert," the now-indicted Imran Awan. Hansen asked the following:

"Why would Wasserman-Schultz go out of her way to protect him and by extension his network from government investigations—even as Awan's criminal familial enterprises, as well as his unauthorized and perhaps illegal conduct concerning government communications, were being exposed? Why is Awan apparently eager to talk to prosecutors about his relationships with Wasserman-Schultz and other congressional representatives? Why did an "in-the-know" Wasserman-Schultz apparently allow Awan to act so illegally for so long? In other words, the behavior of the former head of the DNC seems inexplicable."

Susan Rice served as Obama's White House National Security Advisor from 2013 to 2017.

Susan Rice was formerly U.S. Ambassador to the United Nations. Rice's was mentioned as a possible replacement for retiring Secretary of State Hillary Clinton after President Barack Obama's re-election in 2012. However, since Rice lied on five national television channels on December 13, 2012 on the Benghazi attack, Republicans in the Senate would have opposed her nomination.

Hansen wrote that after lying again, "Susan Rice now admits that she unmasked the names of private U.S. citizens swept up in Obama administration intelligence surveillance and seems to have no regrets about it." "Samantha Power, the Obama administration's former U.N. ambassador, does not deny that she, too, unmasked names—but strangely is reported to have argued that she was not responsible for all the unmaskings that appear under her authorizations on the transcripts," said Hanson.

Samantha Power served as Special Assistant to the President on the National Security Council.

Power worked in the White House from January 2009 to February 2013. She was then appointed ambassador to the United Nations. Power was responsible for implementing Obama's secret classified Presidential Directive 11 which stated that the Middle East was to be given to Iran and the North of Africa to al-Qaida and the Muslim Brotherhood.

Hansen stated the following: "If true, does that astonishing statement mean that Samantha Power has amnesia or that her own staff or others improperly used her name to access classified documents? Has anyone ever admitted to unmasking American citizens under surveillance, and then claimed that her authorizations were not as numerous as they appear in documents? And what were the connections between those who unmasked and those who illegally leaked information to the press?"

President Trump was ridiculed by the corrupt mainstream media when he tweeted that "Obama" (members of the Obama administration) had Trump "wires tapped" (electronically surveilled) at Trump Tower. He was correct. Donald Trump was spied upon by the NSA before he even ran for president, then during his campaign and the transition, and now as president as well. Sadly, we live in a surveillance society and this writer has also been a victim of being illegally spied upon and harassed by intelligence agencies due to his writings and publications.

Hansen pointed out that *The Hill*, not known as a conservative organ, "now is reporting that as early as 2009 some within Robert Mueller's FBI knew of possible blackmail, bribery, and money-laundering by Russian interests in seeking, through various means, control of sizable uranium sources inside the United States—an agenda Putin's surrogates apparently knew to be impossible without a waiver from Hillary Clinton's State Department."

Where did the real collusion lurk?

Hansen explained that it was Hillary and Bill Clinton and Barack Obama the ones who colluded with Russia and not Donald Trump. He stated the following:

"Even as Mueller presses ahead and even as anti-Trump journalists have sought for a year to find any proof that Trump was a Russian patsy, the charge of collusion may be proved accurate after all—but it seems to have had little to do with Trump *per se*. Instead, Bill and Hillary Clinton, the former directly, the latter via the family foundation, may well have been empowering and profiting from Russian insiders who were eager to obtain control of 20 percent of North America's uranium holdings. Indeed, Russian agents caught spying in connection with the deal were swapped out—in a not very favorable trade for the United States—without much audit. Stranger still, so far the denials have not contested the facts, but only the efficacy of the Russian-Clinton deal: there was supposedly not any wrongdoing given that so far the Russians have not shipped out any uranium as if a habitually drunk driver is not culpable until he kills someone on the road."

"Barack Obama was strangely in no hurry to move on the opportunistic Russian collusion charges against Donald Trump during the campaign or between his election and inauguration—and perhaps not just because he knew there was no there there. Instead, Obama wisely may have concluded that if *quid pro quo* election-timed concessions to Russian interests constitute a criminal or treasonous offense, then his own hot-mic offer to the Putin government was a similar transgression. But more important, it seems likely now that Obama knew that any such reopening of the Russian question would not only expose a compromised Clinton in an election cycle but also his own administration—as knowledge of politically motivated decisions to ignore what might well have indictable offenses came to light."

"At this point, it would be silly to ask why there will be no more $145 million gifts from Russian interests to the Clinton Foundation (or from anyone, for that matter), or no more $500,000 fees for a single Bill Clinton speech. Whereas the Clintons are always willing to sell something that properly belongs to the government, they are no longer in any position to negotiate anything and thus by their own financial standards have zero monetary value to the sorts who in the past were eager to buy them."

"Are we finally nearing the end of our own Jacobin cycle of revolutionary fervor—as wild charges of criminality are exposed to be little more than the bitter feelings over a blown election or, worse, efforts either to nullify that election or an attempt to cloak the accusers' own felonious behavior? But the inquisitions will likely stop only when the inquisitors, under intense pressures, learn that they have far more exposure to the very charges that they have leveled—and thus finally beg to call the whole sordid matter off."

On January 6, 2018, the Destroy Trump newspaper the *Washington Post* reported that the FBI had been investigating the Clinton Foundation for months. The investigation is being conducted out of the FBI's field office in Little Rock, Arkansas, where the Clinton Foundation has its office in the Bill Clinton Presidential Library. FBI agents are trying to determine whether any donations made to the Clinton Foundation were linked to official acts when Hillary Clinton was Secretary of State from 2009 to 2013. The Clinton Foundation investigation dates back to 2015 when the FBI offices in Washington, D.C., Los Angeles, New York, and Little Rock began investigating the donations. The *Washington Post* also reported that officials from the Justice Department have said that they are reviewing investigative records on the Clinton e-mail case to determine if any of the concerns raised by Republican members of congress merit the appointment of a special council for federal investigation.

The lie about Russian collusion has sired truths beyond our wildest nightmares

Hansen concluded his illuminating article by saying the following:

"In a fair world, Robert Mueller would find that his original agenda had proved irrelevant, other than incidentally colliding with far more serious culpability on the part of many of those who had energized him. He then would either drop the investigation, recuse himself, or expand it to include far more likely charges of collusion that affected our national security."

"In a fair world, those in the House Ethics Committee long ago would have dropped politically motivated and empty complaints against Rep. Devin Nunes (R-Calif.), chairman of the House Intelligence Committee, and would have agreed that he was simply a political target. He was preemptively targeted not for leaking classified government information (which he did not do), but for presciently long ago announcing to intelligence agencies and to the president that Obama Administration officials had likely improperly unmasked information about private

U.S. citizens that was subsequently unlawfully leaked to the press—a tawdry process that ultimately may well be connected to many of the scandals mentioned above."

"And in a fair world, those who were determined to indict all who profited from Russian largesse would conclude that the Clinton machine always should have been their most likely target. America is in a radical state of flux, or rather in a great accounting and recalibration, ranging from government to popular culture."

President Donald Trump thinks that the Mueller probe in bad for the nation

It was reported that Special Counsel Robert Mueller may be looking to accuse the president and his family of money laundering which would be outside the scope of his investigation. If true, this may provoke a constitutional crisis. During his years as FBI director under Obama, Mueller never investigated the many crimes and scandals of the Obama administration. There is no doubt in this writer's mind that Mueller was named as special counsel to bring down the presidency of Trump.

On December 29, 2017, President Trump told the Destroy Trump *New York Times* that Special Counsel Robert Mueller's investigation is "bad for the country." The president stated that the only collusion with Russia during the presidential campaign was the one by Democrats.

President Trump said the following: "It makes the country look very bad, and it puts the country in a very bad position. So the sooner it's worked out, the better it is for the country. I actually think it's turning to the Democrats because there was collusion on behalf of the Democrats. There was collusion with the Russians and the Democrats. A lot of collusion. Starting with the dossier. But going into so many other elements. And Podesta's firm." The president said that a Russia investigation led by House Republicans is getting closer to the heart of the real Russia story — that Moscow was working with Democrats during the 2016 campaign.

FBI agents biased against Donald Trump

The *Daily Mail* reported on January 20, 2017, that Peter Strzok is the FBI's top counter-intelligence investigator. He worked on the Hillary Clinton email probe then went to work for Special Counsel Robert Mueller investigation of a possible Russian connection with the Trump campaign. Strzok watered down key findings of Clinton removing language which could have had her charged. The disclosure has led to hearings in Congress, with the deputy FBI director for eight hours on apparent anti-Trump bias in his agency.

FBI agents Peter Strzok, 47, and his mistress Lisa Page, 38, exchanged 10,000 texts of email insulting President Donald Trump.

FBI agent Peter Strzok whose anti-Trump texts to his lover have plunged the Robert Mueller investigation into crisis - leaving home with the wife he cheated on. Strzok was dismissed from the Mueller probe, but the reason why only emerged months later. President Donald Trump said the FBI's conduct was "really disgraceful" after the texts were revealed and said the "system is rigged."

It has been revealed by the FBI that about 50,000 text messages from the FBI lovers over a period of several months have not been preserved. Additionally, in one text message a "secret society" at the FBI was discussed. These revelations have created a political storm in Congress regarding how top officials at the FBI and the Department of Justice had anti-Trump bias

Conclusion

Hillary Clinton violated multiple federal election laws. She committed serious crimes when she paid thugs to beat up Trump's supporters at his rallies. The Clinton campaign paid for the anti-Trump unverified fake dossier and concealed the payment. The fake dossier was rapidly discredited after it was published. She also used agent provocateurs to demonize Donald Trump and his supporters. Clinton's supporters appeared in the concealed video discussing voter fraud. The dossier was then shared with James Comey's FBI and the Obama administration used it to illegally investigate members of the Trump campaign.

However, Congress is currently investigating the role of Obama and Hillary Clinton in meddling with the Trump campaign. It is also investigating the bribes paid by Russia to members of the Obama administration and especially to the Clinton Foundation with the approval of the sale of 20% of the uranium mines to Russia, a geopolitical enemy of America. Hillary Clinton was also involved in having an unsecure server at home where she illegally received classified documents. Clinton and Obama engaged in treason, dereliction of duty, and criminal negligence in the Libyan civil war and later in the gunrunning of weapons from Libya to Turkey to Syria that ended in the hands of the Islamic State and the al Nusra Front in Syria.

James Comey, Robert Muller, Susan Rice, Samantha Power, Eric Clapper, John Brennan, Eric Holder, Loretta Lynch, and others in the Obama administration as well as Debbie Wasserman Schultz need to be investigated. The Clintons need to be investigated and indicted for all the many crimes and scandals. Former President Barack Obama also needs to be investigated and indicted as well.

In spite of the relentless attacks by the Deep State, President Trump had many accomplishments during his first year in office. The president destroyed the Islamic State capturing 98% of territory in Iraq and Syria. He began rebuilding the military and is dealing forcefully with North Korea. The president by eliminating costly regulations to businesses and passing the Tax Cuts and Jobs Act has improve the economy which is now growing at more than 3% of the GNP with a 4.1% unemployment rate the lowest in 17 years and a 6.8 % African American unemployment rate, the lowest in 45 years. The stock market has surpassed the Dow Jones 25,000 mark. Two million less people are receiving food stamps. Two millions jobs were created. However, draining the D.C. Swamp will be very difficult for the president. If President Trump fails to drain the Swamp, the creatures living the swamp may eat him alive!

PART 1

THE 2016 PRESIDENTIAL CAMPAIGN

CHAPTER 1

The 2016 Bilderberg conference

The Taschenbergpalais Hotel is located just south of the river in Dresden's historic city center, the "Innere Altstadt."

The 2016 Bilderberg conference took place from June 9-12, 2016 in Dresden, Germany. The conference venue was the five-star Taschenbergpalais Hotel. The 64th Bilderberg meeting included around 130 participants from 20 countries. According to the official website the participants were a diverse group of political leaders and experts from industry, finance, academia, and the media. During the 2015 B.G. meeting in Austria, six individuals from Turkey were invited, probably due to Middle East concerns, and one from Russia.

The key topics for discussion included:

- Current events (Even though not announced, the U.S. presidential elections was in the agenda).

- China

- Europe: migration, growth, reform, vision, unity

- Middle East

- Russia

- US political landscape, economy: growth, debt, reform

- Cyber security

- Geo-politics of energy and commodity prices

- Precariat and middle class

- Technological innovation

The Bilderberg Group (B.G.) official website explains the following: "Founded in 1954, the Bilderberg conference is an annual meeting designed to foster dialogue between Europe and North America. Every year, between 120-150 political leaders and experts from industry, finance, academia and the media are invited to take part in the conference. About two thirds of the participants come from Europe and the rest from North America; approximately one third from politics and government and the rest from other fields."

"The conference is a forum for informal discussions about major issues facing the world. The meetings are held under the Chatham House Rule, which states that participants are free to use the information received, but neither the identity nor the affiliation of the speaker(s) nor any other participant may be revealed. Thanks to the private nature of the conference, the participants are not bound by the conventions of their office or by pre-agreed positions. As such, they can take time to listen, reflect and gather insights. There is no desired outcome, no minutes are taken and no report is written. Furthermore, no resolutions are proposed, no votes are taken, and no policy statements are issued."

But is this an accurate description of the B.G. and its objectives? Not at all. Of course, there is a desired outcome which upon return all individuals were to implement!

What is the Bilderberg Group?

The Bilderberg Group (BG) was founded in 1954 by Polish-born Joseph Retinger to promote a greater understanding between Europe and the United States. The organizers met at the Hotel Bilderberg for a three-day meeting in Oosterbeek, Netherlands and that is why it received that name.

During the first meeting, very powerful individuals from the United States and Europe decided that the group would decide all issues regarding the politics and economic policies that their nations would follow and the strategies that they would follow to rule the world and eventually create a planetary government.

Since 1954, the Bilderbergers meet once a year in different cities in Europe, Canada, and the United States. The members of the B.G. have represented the wealthy elite of the Western World bankers, industrialists, CEO of multinational corporations, financiers, prime ministers, presidents, monarchs, key politicians, owners of the media, powerful university professors, presidents of the European Union, European Central Bank, World Bank, the International Monetary Fund, chair of the Federal Reserve Bank and other presidents and governors of central banks in Europe and other parts of the world, secretary generals of NATO, and important cabinet and military leaders.

Similar to the Council of Foreign Relations (CFR), the B.G. meetings are secret. All U.S. presidents since Dwight D. Eisenhower have belonged to the B.G. global ruling class or sent representatives to the meetings.

A founding member was German-born ex-Nazi Prince Bernhard, husband of Queen Juliana of Holland.

David Rockefeller, the billionaire banker and former president of the Council on Foreign Relations, was one of the founders of the Bilderberg Group. He later founded the Trilateral Commission (T.C.) in 1972. He always advocated for a global government.

In his book, *Memoirs* (2003), he stated the following: "Some even believe we are a part of the secret cabal working against the best interests of the United States, characterizing my family and me as internationalists and of conspiring with others around the world to build a more integrated global political and economic structure-one world, is you will. If that's the charge, I stand guilty, I am proud of it."

From the very beginning of the B.G., various members of the Rockefeller families and its ally, the Rothschild dynasty in Europe, have been the most powerful force of the organization. Baron Edmond de Rothschild, the French-born financier who was said to be the wealthiest of the surviving descendants of the legendary banking family, has been a most active member of the B.G. Baron Edmond de Rothschild died in Geneva in 1997 at the age of 71.

Many years ago, in an interview, Baron Edmond de Rothschild said that of all the countries in the world where he did business, the United States appealed to him most. "For me it symbolizes free enterprise, where a man is responsible only to himself, a place of endless opportunity and limitless space," he said. Then he added, "I am fundamentally a citizen of the world, devoted to France, where I was born, to Switzerland, where I was made welcome, and to Israel because I am a Jew." These two families, the Rockefellers and Rothschilds, as well as European monarchs and a small group of very wealthy individuals determine who will be invited to participate at the B.G. meetings.

George Soros is known as "The Man Who Broke the Bank of England" because of his short sale of U.S. $10 billion worth of pounds, resulting in a profit for him of $1 billion during the 1992 Black Wednesday United Kingdom currency crisis. Soros is one of the 30 richest people in the world. Soros is a well-known supporter of progressive and extreme radical political causes. He is also known as Obama's godfather.

There are between 120 and 150 participants at these meetings of which about 80 are regulars, such as Henry Kissinger. Many Obama's advisors, cabinet members, and important White House officials are Bilderbergers, such as Obama's Godfather George Soros, Zbigniew Brzezinski, Hillary Clinton, Robert Gates, Timothy Geithner, Janet Napolitano, Susan Rice, Paul

Volcker, and James Jones. Approximately 2/3 of the participants come from Europe and the rest from the United States and Canada.

George Soros was born on August 12, 1930 as Schwartz György in Hungary. He is a billionaire business magnate who is chairman of Soros Fund Management.

David Rockefeller has always been close to the bloody assassin Fidel Castro

David Rockefeller is shaking the bloody hands of the oppressive Cuban dictator Fidel Castro. They met frequently in New York City and Havana.

The most powerful individuals in the planet, such as David Rockefeller, are members of these three organizations. The Americans who participate in the B.G., C.F.R., and T.C. meetings with head of nations and high government officials are in violation of the U.S.'s Logan Act that prohibits elected officials to meet in private with influential business and banking executives to debate and design public policy.

Promising politicians are invited and interviewed by B.G., such as the governor of the small state of Georgia, Jimmy Carter, and Arkansas, Bill Clinton. If these politicians support the one-world government objective of the B.G., then the B.G. will give them enormous financial support. With the established media owned by them, the globalist elite provide massive positive coverage to make them presidents. Of course, after Carter and Clinton were elected, they staffed their administrations with C.F.R., T.C., and B.G. members and consulted with B.G. constantly on domestic and international affairs issues.

The meetings are held under the Chatham House Rule, which states that participants are free to use the information received, but the identity or the affiliation of the speaker(s) and of any other participant may not be revealed. Due to the private nature of the conferences, the participants are not bound by the conventions of their office or by pre-agreed positions. As such, they can take time to listen, reflect, and gather insights. There is no detailed agenda, no resolutions are proposed, no votes are taken, and no policy statements are issued.

Final list of participants of the 2016 Bilderberg conference was announced in the Bilderberg Group official website

The invited individuals were as follows:

CHAIRMAN

Castries, Henri de (FRA), *Chairman and CEO, AXA Group*

Aboutaleb, Ahmed (NLD), *Mayor, City of Rotterdam*

Achleitner, Paul M. (DEU), *Chairman of the Supervisory Board, Deutsche Bank AG*

Agius, Marcus (GBR), *Chairman, PA Consulting Group*

Ahrenkiel, Thomas (DNK), *Permanent Secretary, Ministry of Defence*

Albuquerque, Maria Luís (PRT), *Former Minister of Finance; MP, Social Democratic Party*

Alierta, César (ESP), *Executive Chairman and CEO, Telefónica*

Altman, Roger C. (USA), *Executive Chairman, Evercore*

Altman, Sam (USA), *President, Y Combinator*

Andersson, Magdalena (SWE), *Minister of Finance*

Applebaum, Anne (USA), *Columnist Washington Post; Director of the Transitions Forum, Legatum Institute*

Apunen, Matti (FIN), *Director, Finnish Business and Policy Forum EVA*

Aydin-Düzgit, Senem (TUR), *Associate Professor and Jean Monnet Chair, Istanbul Bilgi University*

Barbizet, Patricia (FRA), *CEO, Artemis*

Barroso, José M. Durão (PRT), *Former President of the European Commission*

Baverez, Nicolas (FRA), *Partner, Gibson, Dunn & Crutcher*

Bengio, Yoshua (CAN), *Professor in Computer Science and Operations Research, University of Montreal*

Benko, René (AUT), *Founder and Chairman of the Advisory Board, SIGNA Holding GmbH*

Bernabè, Franco (ITA), *Chairman, CartaSi S.p.A.*

Beurden, Ben van (NLD), *CEO, Royal Dutch Shell plc*

Blanchard, Olivier (FRA), *Fred Bergsten Senior Fellow, Peterson Institute*

Botín, Ana P. (ESP), *Executive Chairman, Banco Santander*

Brandtzæg, Svein Richard (NOR), *President and CEO, Norsk Hydro ASA*

Breedlove, Philip M. (INT), *Former Supreme Allied Commander Europe*

Brende, Børge (NOR), *Minister of Foreign Affairs*

Burns, William J. (USA), *President, Carnegie Endowment for International Peace*

Cebrián, Juan Luis (ESP), *Executive Chairman, PRISA and El País*

Charpentier, Emmanuelle (FRA), *Director, Max Planck Institute for Infection Biology*

Coeuré, Benoît (INT), *Member of the Executive Board, European Central Bank*

Costamagna, Claudio (ITA), *Chairman, Cassa Depositi e Prestiti S.p.A.*

Cote, David M. (USA), *Chairman and CEO, Honeywell*

Cryan, John (DEU), *CEO, Deutsche Bank AG*

Dassù, Marta (ITA), *Senior Director, European Affairs, Aspen Institute*

Dijksma, Sharon A.M. (NLD), *Minister for the Environment*

Döpfner, Mathias (DEU), *CEO, Axel Springer SE*

Dyvig, Christian (DNK), *Chairman, Kompan*

Ebeling, Thomas (DEU), *CEO, ProSiebenSat.1*

Elkann, John (ITA), *Chairman and CEO, EXOR; Chairman, Fiat Chrysler Automobiles*

Enders, Thomas (DEU), *CEO, Airbus Group*

Engel, Richard (USA), *Chief Foreign Correspondent, NBC News*

Fabius, Laurent (FRA), *President, Constitutional Council*

Federspiel, Ulrik (DNK), *Group Executive, Haldor Topsøe A/S*

Ferguson, Jr., Roger W. (USA), *President and CEO, TIAA*

Ferguson, Niall (USA), *Professor of History, Harvard University*

Flint, Douglas J. (GBR), *Group Chairman, HSBC Holdings plc*

Garicano, Luis (ESP), *Professor of Economics, LSE; Senior Advisor to Ciudadanos*

Georgieva, Kristalina (INT), *Vice President, European Commission*

Gernelle, Etienne (FRA), *Editorial Director, Le Point*

Gomes da Silva, Carlos (PRT), *Vice Chairman and CEO, Galp Energia*

Goodman, Helen (GBR), *MP, Labour Party*

Goulard, Sylvie (INT), *Member of the European Parliament*

Graham, Lindsey (USA), *Senator*

Grillo, Ulrich (DEU), *Chairman, Grillo-Werke AG; President, Bundesverband der Deutschen Industrie*

Gruber, Lilli (ITA), *Editor-in-Chief and Anchor "Otto e mezzo", La7 TV*

Hadfield, Chris (CAN), *Colonel, Astronaut*

Halberstadt, Victor (NLD), *Professor of Economics, Leiden University*

Harding, Dido (GBR), *CEO, TalkTalk Telecom Group plc*

Hassabis, Demis (GBR), *Co-Founder and CEO, DeepMind*

Hobson, Mellody (USA), *President, Ariel Investment, LLC*

Hoffman, Reid (USA), *Co-Founder and Executive Chairman, LinkedIn*

Höttges, Timotheus (DEU), *CEO, Deutsche Telekom AG*

Jacobs, Kenneth M. (USA), *Chairman and CEO, Lazard*

Jäkel, Julia (DEU), *CEO, Gruner + Jahr*

Johnson, James A. (USA), *Chairman, Johnson Capital Partners*

Jonsson, Conni (SWE), *Founder and Chairman, EQT*

Jordan, Jr., Vernon E. (USA), *Senior Managing Director, Lazard Frères & Co. LLC*

Kaeser, Joe (DEU), *President and CEO, Siemens AG*

Karp, Alex (USA), *CEO, Palantir Technologies*

Kengeter, Carsten (DEU), *CEO, Deutsche Börse AG*

Kerr, John (GBR), *Deputy Chairman, Scottish Power*

Kherbache, Yasmine (BEL), *MP, Flemish Parliament*

Kissinger, Henry A. (USA), *Chairman, Kissinger Associates, Inc.*

Kleinfeld, Klaus (USA), *Chairman and CEO, Alcoa*

Kravis, Henry R. (USA), *Co-Chairman and Co-CEO, Kohlberg Kravis Roberts & Co.*

Kravis, Marie-Josée (USA), *Senior Fellow, Hudson Institute*

Kudelski, André (CHE), *Chairman and CEO, Kudelski Group*

Lagarde, Christine (INT), *Managing Director, International Monetary Fund*

Levin, Richard (USA), *CEO, Coursera*

Leyen, Ursula von der (DEU), *Minister of Defence*

Leysen, Thomas (BEL), *Chairman, KBC Group*

Logothetis, George (GRC), *Chairman and CEO, Libra Group*

Maizière, Thomas de (DEU), *Minister of the Interior, Federal Ministry of the Interior*

Makan, Divesh (USA), *CEO, ICONIQ Capital*

Malcomson, Scott (USA), *Author; President, Monere Ltd.*

Markwalder, Christa (CHE), *President of the National Council and the Federal Assembly*

McArdle, Megan (USA), *Columnist, Bloomberg View*

Michel, Charles (BEL), *Prime Minister*

Micklethwait, John (USA), *Editor-in-Chief, Bloomberg LP*

Minton Beddoes, Zanny (GBR), *Editor-in-Chief, The Economist*

Mitsotakis, Kyriakos (GRC), *President, New Democracy Party*

Morneau, Bill (CAN), *Minister of Finance*

Mundie, Craig J. (USA), *Principal, Mundie & Associates*

Murray, Charles A. (USA), *W.H. Brady Scholar, American Enterprise Institute*

Netherlands, H.M. the King of the (NLD)

Noonan, Michael (IRL), *Minister for Finance*

Noonan, Peggy (USA), *Author, Columnist, The Wall Street Journal*

O'Leary, Michael (IRL), *CEO, Ryanair Plc*

Ollongren, Kajsa (NLD), *Deputy Mayor of Amsterdam*

Özel, Soli (TUR), *Professor, Kadir Has University*

Papalexopoulos, Dimitri (GRC), *CEO, Titan Cement Co.*

Petraeus, David H. (USA), *Chairman, KKR Global Institute*

Philippe, Edouard (FRA), *Mayor of Le Havre*

Pind, Søren (DNK), *Minister of Justice*

Ratti, Carlo (ITA), *Director, MIT Senseable City Lab*

Reisman, Heather M. (CAN), *Chair and CEO, Indigo Books & Music Inc.*

Rutte, Mark (NLD), *Prime Minister*

Sawers, John (GBR), *Chairman and Partner, Macro Advisory Partners*

Schäuble, Wolfgang (DEU), *Minister of Finance*

Schieder, Andreas (AUT), *Chairman, Social Democratic Group*

Schmidt, Eric E. (USA), *Executive Chairman, Alphabet Inc.*

Scholten, Rudolf (AUT), *CEO, Oesterreichische Kontrollbank AG*

Schwab, Klaus (INT), *Executive Chairman, World Economic Forum*

Sikorski, Radoslaw (POL), *Senior Fellow, Harvard University; Former Minister of Foreign Affairs*

Simsek, Mehmet (TUR), *Deputy Prime Minister*

Sinn, Hans-Werner (DEU), *Professor for Economics and Public Finance, Ludwig Maximilian University of Munich*

Skogen Lund, Kristin (NOR), *Director General, The Confederation of Norwegian Enterprise*

Standing, Guy (GBR), *Co-President, BIEN; Research Professor, University of London*

Svanberg, Carl-Henric (SWE), *Chairman, BP plc and AB Volvo*

Thiel, Peter A. (USA), *President, Thiel Capital*

Tillich, Stanislaw (DEU), *Minister-President of Saxony*

Vetterli, Martin (CHE), *President, NSF*

Wahlroos, Björn (FIN), *Chairman, Sampo Group, Nordea Bank, UPM-Kymmene Corporation*

Wallenberg, Jacob (SWE), *Chairman, Investor AB*

Weder di Mauro, Beatrice (CHE), *Professor of Economics, University of Mainz*

Wolf, Martin H. (GBR), *Chief Economics Commentator, Financial Times*

The Bilderberg Group chose Hillary Clinton as the next United States president

Republican Senator Lindsey Graham from South Carolina
endorsed Donald Trump but later withdrew his endorsement.

It is strongly suspected that the secretive Bilderberg Group discussed how to prevent Donald Trump from becoming president, the possibility of mass riots as a result of wealth inequality, and the migrant crisis as well as the United Kingdom's vote on leaving the European Union. The attendance of anti-Trump Senator Lindsey Graham was an obvious sign that Bilderbergs were planning on how to prevent Donald Trump from defeating Bilderberg's chosen candidate, Hillary Clinton.

Donald Trump's self-funded campaign and his public opposition to globalism and internationalist trade deals like NAFTA shocked the Bilderberg globalist elitists. Three other interesting names on the list included Richard Engel, NBC News' chief foreign correspondent, Vernon E. Jordan, Jr., Senior Managing Director, Lazard Frères & Co., and Roger Charles Altman.

Richard Engel, NBC News' chief foreign correspondent, also worked for ABC News. Both television organizations are part of the mainstream pro-Democratic Party news media.

Roger Charles Altman is an American investment banker, the founder and executive chairman of Evercore, and a former Democratic politician. He served as Assistant Secretary of the Treasury in the Carter administration and as Deputy Secretary of the Treasury in the Clinton administration from January 1993 until he resigned in August 1994, amid the Whitewater controversy. He supported Hillary Clinton for president

Vernon E. Jordan, Jr., is Senior Managing Director, Lazard Frères & Co. LLC.

Jordan is a civil rights activist in the United States who was chosen by President Bill Clinton as a close adviser. Jordan, a member of the Democratic Party, has become an influential figure in American politics.

Thomas E. "Tom" Donilon is an attorney and former high government official
who served as White House National Security Advisor in the Obama administration.

Donilon served as Agency Review Team Lead for the State Department in the Obama transition team. Obama appointed Donilon as Deputy to National Security Advisor James Jones. Donilon replaced Jones as National Security Advisor on October 8, 2010. Donilon tendered his resignation as National Security Adviser on June 5, 2013. He was followed by Susan Rice. Donilon is a former member of the Steering Committee of the Bilderberg Group.

This writer pointed out that Hillary Clinton was the chosen presidential candidate of the B.G. Two very powerful Democrats were invited to attend the 2015 Bilderberg Group meeting held in Austria. One was Tom Donilon, a Democrat operative who served in the Obama White House as National Security Director. The other one was Jim Messina, a Democratic Party operative and chief advisor to Hillary Clinton. Many suspect that the B.G. decided to try to place the very corrupt former Secretary of State in the White House to continue to advance the agenda of the B.G. for a planetary government.

Who is Jim Messina and why was he invited to the Bilderberg Group meeting in Austria?

Jim Messina was the White House Deputy Chief of Staff for Operations
under President Barack Obama from 2009 to 2011.

Jim Messina was the White House Deputy Chief of Staff for Operations under President Barack Obama from 2009 to 2011. He became campaign manager of Obama's 2012 re-election campaign. Messina was hired as National Chief of Staff of the Obama campaign in the 2008 general election. After Obama was elected, Messina was named Director of Personnel of the Obama-Biden Transition team, helping Obama pick his cabinet.

Messina became President Obama's White House Deputy Chief of Staff and earned the nickname "the fixer." Dan Pfeiffer called Messina "the most powerful person in Washington that you haven't heard of." He also said that Messina and Chief of Staff Rahm Emanuel (present mayor of Chicago) had a "crazy relationship" and explained that "You'd be in a meeting, and Rahm would bark out that something needed to be done; Jim would disappear from Rahm's office, pop through the door a few minutes later and say, 'Got it!' or 'Got him!'" Messina had a crucial role in the passage of the disastrous Affordable Care Act or ObamaCare and was widely credited with the effort to repeal Don't Ask Don't Tell regarding gays in the Armed Forces.

Jim Messina celebrated Obama's reelection in November 2012

Messina was Obama's campaign manager during the 2012 Presidential Election. In January 2013, Messina became head of Organizing for Action (OFA) and used the Obama for America database and other resources to support President Obama's dangerous legislative agenda in his second term. While OFA was formed in 2009 by Obama, it was reformed as a political-action non-profit group in January 2013. Obama is the only president in history to have created such an organization.

Obviously, Obama intends to continue pushing his destructive anti-American, pro-Muslim, Marxist, and New World Order agenda when he leaves the White House. Obama's former White House and campaign official also founded The Messina Group, a full-service consulting firm with offices in Washington, D.C., New York, San Francisco, and London.

Steve Watson wrote an article entitled "Bilderberg Backs Hillary for 2016 Presidency" which was published in *InfoWars* on June 8, 2015. He explained that Jim Messina of The Messina Group was the chief advisor to Hillary Clinton. Messina also headed the super PAC Priorities USA, which supported Barack Obama and is now firmly involved in the Hillary Clinton camp.

Messina conducted Barack Obama's reelection campaign in 2012 and returned to the United States after leading the unpopular United Kingdom Prime Minister David Cameron to a surprise majority victory in British elections. Messina said on MSNBC's "Morning Joe" program a month ago, "I'm coming home tomorrow and it's whatever it will take to get Hillary [elected]," Watson wrote that "Messina's presence at Bilderberg will be focused around ensuring none of Hillary's potential challengers get the big bucks from the innumerable transnational banks and corporations that will also be represented at Bilderberg."

As it has been reported by many, including this writer, in June 2008 the Bilderberg Group met in secret with both Hillary Clinton and Barack Obama while the globalists were meeting in Chantilly in Northern Virginia. As always, the nation's press was shunted. Watson pointed out that it is believed that the group endorsed Barack Obama over Hillary Clinton, as a more immediate candidate, with the plan being that Hillary Clinton would essentially be picked up as president for a third Obama term. A powerful Bilderberg member and top corporate elitist, James A. Johnson, also had a direct hand in selecting Obama's running mate for the 2008 election, acting as kingmaker for America's then future president.

Hillary Clinton has a deep-rooted connection to the Bilderberg New World Order globalist elitist. Bill Clinton attended the 1991 meeting in Germany. Shortly before becoming president, he attended again in 1999 when the B.G. annual meeting was held in Sintra, Portugal (even though Clinton that he had not attended a B.G. meeting in 15 years). Hillary Clinton was rumored to have attended the 2006 meeting in Ottawa, Canada. It is important to note that some individuals attend the meetings and their names are not published in the official list of attendees.

Conclusion

Some of the individuals who attended the 2015 and 2016 Bilderberg Group meetings were strong supporters of the very corrupt Hillary Clinton. It is obvious that she was the one chosen by the members of the globalist elite to be president of the United States.

This writer believes that the Bilderberg Group, the Council of Foreign Relations, and the Trilateral Commission are part of the New World Order's objective of a one-world government to enslave humanity. If Hillary Clinton would have been elected president, the road to a world government would have continued full speed ahead. Unfortunately, the United States is similar to the nation described in George Orwell's book *1984*, a Big Brother surveillance society and police state!

The world could be on the verge of an economic collapse in the near future as a result of the central bankers of the United States and Europe, which are controlled by private banking cartels which are the owners of these financial institutions and have printed over $11 trillion out of thin air. The economic crisis in Greece, Spain, Portugal, Italy, and other European countries could also contribute to this impending economic catastrophe. Fortunately, President Trump's policies have improved the economy, which is now growing at a rate of more than 3% per quarter. The stock market is soaring and unemployment is at its lowest in 17 years

Americans need to fight the global government that is being planned under the United Nations, but controlled by the members of Bilderberg Group, the Council of Foreign Affairs, and the Trilateral Commission. If this diabolical plan is ever successful, the United States will lose its sovereignty, wealth, Constitution, and laws.

The Bilderberg Group selected the very corrupt Hillary Clinton as the next president of the United States. Both Hillary and former president Bill Clinton have always believed that they are above the law and that rules and regulations that apply to others do not apply to them. It is clear why Hillary Clinton's destruction of 30,000 e-mails was a risk she was willing to take. Bill and Hillary are devious, unprincipled, and dishonest liars and both have committed many crimes. The Clinton Foundation is a criminal enterprise as Hillary Clinton, when she served as Secretary of State, traded favors in exchange for millions for the corrupt foundation. Both of them should be indicted.

Similar to Barack Obama, Hillary Clinton frequently lies. Similar to Barack Obama, Hillary Clinton has been involved in numerous scandals and has committed crimes. Similar to Barack Obama, Hillary Clinton believes that she is above the law. Similar to Obama, she has ties to the Muslim Brotherhood.

Hillary Clinton, unlike her husband, is not a charming and charismatic politician. She had a poor rollout of her presidential campaign. No matter how hard she has tried to connect with ordinary people, many feel that she lacks authenticity. Together with her campaign staffers, Hillary Clinton tried very hard to distance herself from the many scandals involving Bill Clinton and her. Hillary Clinton has a very serious problem and that is that her many scandals will not go away.

The fact that the Clinton Foundation has accepted millions from foreign countries and shady individuals over the years, which constitutes a major scandal, hurt Hillary Clinton's presidential campaign. How could Hillary Clinton pretend to be a defender of the rights of women in the United States when she accepted millions of dollars from Middle Eastern countries where women are severely oppressed and stoned to death for infidelity? How could she pretend to be a defender of women when she covered up and attacked the many women that her husband raped and sexually harassed? Hillary became an enabler of Bill Clinton.

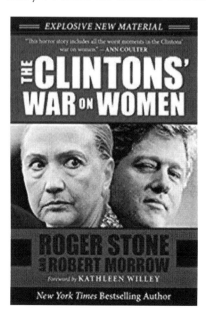

Roger Stone and Robert Morrow wrote *The Clintons' War on Women* in 2015.

Stone and Morrow said that Hillary Clinton pretends to be an "advocate of women and girls." However, there is a shocking side to her story that has been carefully covered up—until now. *The Clintons' War on Women* "reveals for the first time how Bill and Hillary Clinton systematically abused women and others—sexually, physically, and psychologically—in their scramble for power and wealth."

Hillary Clinton is a tremendous hypocrite! The former first lady is a corrupt and dishonest politician. Never before in our history has a leading presidential candidate been campaigning while 147 FBI agents were investigating that candidate for misusing classified top secret information in an illegal private server at her home and for corruption while serving as Secretary of State. More than likely, China, Russia, Iran, North Korea, and others are enemy nations that have cyber capabilities and probably have all the Clinton's e-mails. Some of the top secrets e-mails had the names of many of the CIA spies in foreign enemy countries. Most likely, these CIA spies have been killed or imprisoned due to Hillary's criminal negligence as in Benghazi and Libya.

The FBI agents are also investigating Mrs. Clinton's trading favors for cash donations to the Clinton Foundation or for tens of thousands of dollars received by the couple for speeches. Recently, it was reported that Russia paid many bribes to the Clintons and others in the Obama administration.

If Hillary Clinton had won the presidential election in 2016, this would have been the final death knell for America! Her whole public life has been one scandal after another with cover-ups and lies. It would have also meant that the globalist elite had won one more time.

CHAPTER 2

Hillary Clinton connections with communists and radicals

Barbara Olson wrote the book *Hell to Pay: The Unfolding Story of Hillary Rodham Clinton* in 1999.

The author, Barbara Olson, was a conservative commentator and a lawyer who died when al-Qaida terrorists hijacked American Airlines Flight 77 and crashed it into the Pentagon on September 11, 2001.

Barbara Olson also wrote another book on the Clintons,
The Final Days: The Last Desperate Abuses of Power, in 2001.

Cliff Kincaid wrote an article titled "Hillary Clinton's Biggest Cover-Ups: A Look Back" which was published in *Accuracy in Media* (AIM) on August 17, 2016. Kincaid explained that the 1999 book, *Hell to Pay: The Unfolding Story of Hillary Rodham Clinton,* asked "Will there be another President Clinton?"

Cliff Kincaid stated the following: "These two books are absolute must-reads in order to understand the power-driven Bill and Hillary Clinton relationship. Olson provides the best account of Hillary's emergence as a budding Leninist who studied Saul Alinsky and understood the Leninist concept of acquiring, accumulating and maintaining political power at any cost. Her work went into our own August 2003 *AIM Report*. The *AIM Report* was titled "Hillary Clinton's Biggest Cover-Ups."

Below is the devastating *AIM Report* which explained the many connections of Hillary Clinton with members of the Communist Party USA, radicals, and globalists who want a planetary government under the United Nations (U.N.) but controlled by them:

Of all the scandals of Hillary Clinton and cover-ups, none is more significant than her attempt to whitewash her own personal transformation from Goldwater girl to Marxist. No mainstream media organization has examined how she is determined in her new book to keep people in the dark about what Hillary's biographer, the late Barbara Olson, described as her "roots in Marxism."

"In her formative years," Barbara Olson explained, "Marxism was a very important part of her ideology…" Olson's important 1999 book, *Hell to Pay: The Unfolding Story of Hillary Rodham Clinton* (Regnery Publishing, Inc., 1999) remains as the best account of Hillary Clinton's communist connections and emergence as a "budding Leninist" who "understood the Leninist concept of acquiring, accumulating and maintaining political power at any cost."

As an example, Hillary's book gripes that the end to her illegal closed-door health-care task-force meetings, where a socialized medicine scheme was hatched, was the result of her opponents citing an "obscure federal law" in court. Hillary, a lawyer, never wanted the law to get in her way.

Hillary Clinton, similar to Obama, admired the extreme radical Saul Alinsky, author of *Rules for Radicals*. Hillary Clinton wrote her college dissertation on Alinsky and was his friend until his death.

Leaving the GOP

Hillary Clinton's book, *Living History* (Simon & Schuster), does attempt to explain her move from the political right to the left. But it stops far short of explaining her involvement with extreme left-wing groups and individuals in league with America's enemies.

Hillary Clinton wrote the book *Living History* in 2004.

The book says that Hillary was the daughter of a staunch Republican and that, in high school, she read Senator Barry Goldwater's book, *The Conscience of a Conservative*, and wrote a term paper on the American conservative movement. She dedicated the book to her parents, "who have always taught me to be an individual."

Hillary Clinton was a Goldwater supporter in 1964 and had "strong anti-Communist views," she says. She also got deeply involved in the United Methodist Church, which "opened my eyes and heart to the needs of others?" However, her conservative views persisted until she entered Wellesley College in 1965, where she served as president of the Young Republicans during her freshman year. However, she says that she began having more doubts about the war against communism in Vietnam -doubts fed by a Methodist magazine she was receiving while in college as well as reports from the *New York Times*.

Defending the Black Panthers

Hillary Clinton moved on to Yale Law School in 1969, which was a hotbed of activity on behalf of the violent and racist Black Panther organization. She stated the following: "The world and its realities came crashing down on Yale in April 1970, when eight Black Panthers, including party leader Bobby Seale, were put on trial for murder in New Haven. Thousands of angry protesters, convinced the Panthers had been set up by the FBI and government prosecutors, swarmed into the city. Demonstrations broke out in and around campus. "

Hillary Clinton also wrote the following: "The campus was bracing for a huge May Day rally to support the Panthers when I learned, late on the night of April 27, that the International Law Library, which was in the basement of the law school, was on fire. Horrified, I rushed to join a bucket brigade of faculty, staff and students to put out the fire and to rescue books damaged by flames and water." So *Living History* portrays Hillary as someone who did not participate in the pro-Panther demonstrations but just tried to save some books from a fire.

Panther justice

A former radical David Horowitz from the 1960s said that both Hillary Rodham and Bill Lann Lee, who later became President Clinton's head of the U.S. Justice Department's Civil Rights Division, helped organize the pro-Panther demonstrations at Yale. Others sympathetic to Hillary contend that she was merely among a group of law students who monitored the trial on behalf of the ACLU, which was concerned that law enforcement officers were violating the civil liberties of members of the party. However, Hillary says nothing in her book about this role.

What is not in dispute is that she served on the Board of Editors of the Yale Review of Law and Social Action, a "progressive" alternative to the school's traditional review. Its fall 1970 issue was devoted to the trial and glorification of the Panthers.

The red lawyer

During the summer of 1971, Mrs. Clinton writes in her book, she was a law clerk at the Oakland firm of Treuhaft, Walker and Burnstein. "I spent most of my time working for Mal Burnstein researching, writing legal motions and briefs for a child custody case," she said. The public record shows that Clinton worked for Robert Treuhaft, a member of the Communist Party USA (CPUSA) and Harvard-trained lawyer for the party.

Citing public sources, Peter Flaherty's book, *The First Lady* (Vital Issues Press, 1996), says that "Hillary was recommended to Treuhaft by some of her professors at Yale. She was looking for a 'movement' law firm to work at for the summer. As it turns out, Hillary would continue her association and support of the Black Panther cause while working as a law clerk for Treuhaft." Flaherty notes that Treuhaft told Herb Caen of the *San Francisco Examiner*, "That was the time we were representing the Black Panthers, and she worked on that case."

Robert Treuhaft, a member of the Communist Party USA (CPUSA)
and Harvard-trained lawyer for the party.

Don't ask, don't tell

Mrs. Clinton's involvement with Treuhaft is no secret, although Hillary clearly does not want to talk about it. A *New York Times* obituary of Treuhaft, who died in 2001, said that he had "accepted a young Yale lawyer named Hillary Rodham (now Senator Hillary Rodham Clinton) as an intern." A British newspaper, the *London Times*, said that "generations of liberal lawyers were groomed under his [Treuhaft's] tutelage, including a young Yale law student named Hillary Rodham."

These two obituaries are posted at a website in honor of Treuhaft's famous wife, British author Jessica Mitford, herself a member of the Communist Party USA (CPUSA), whose lobbying of Bill Clinton on the death penalty issue was reportedly facilitated by Hillary.

The *Harvard Law Bulletin* said the following about Treuhaft: "He belonged to and served as attorney to the Communist Party of the United States for many years and defended the civil rights of groups such as the Black Panther Party, Vietnam War draft resisters, and members of Berkeley's free speech movement."

The *London Times* said Treuhaft and Mitford left the CPUSA in 1958 and that "Khrushchev's denunciation of the crimes of Stalin had been influential in driving away lots of believers." But Khrushchev had denounced Stalin's crime in February 1956.

The *Times* said that "the Mitford/Treuhaft idea that the American Communist ideal should be an indigenous affair never took root," suggesting they left the party not because of what Stalin did but because working through the CPUSA had proven to be ineffective in establishing a communist America. The British newspaper *The Independent* said that Treuhaft and Mitford continued to sing the "Internationale," once the Soviet national anthem, after they left the party.

Barbara Olson reported, "Hillary has never repudiated her connection with the Communist movement in America or explained her relationship with two of its leading adherents. Of course, no one has pursued these questions with Hillary. She has shown she will not answer hard questions about her past, and she has learned that she does not need to-remarkable in an age when political figures are allowed such little privacy."

David Mixner is a gay activist who was investigated for his involvement
with communists and backing from North Vietnam.

In her book, however, Hillary does write about some of her radical associates. She notes a meeting in 1969 with David Mixner of the Vietnam Moratorium Committee, an anti-Vietnam war protest group that came under investigation by the House Internal Security Subcommittee for its involvement with communists and backing from Hanoi. Mixner would go on to become a leading homosexual activist, adviser to and friend of President Clinton. He was credited for the delivery of some six million votes to Clinton in 1992.

Robert Borosage is a radical leftist who is director of the Institute for Policy Studies (IPS), a Marxist think tank.

Former conservative David Brock's book, *The Seduction of Hillary Rodham*, links Hillary with Robert Borosage, a Yale Law School graduate and one of the founders of the Yale Review. Borosage later became director of the Institute for Policy Studies (IPS), a Marxist think tank.

Borosage is now co-director of the Campaign for America's Future, a group that is trying to move the Democratic Party further to the political left.

Hillary writes about her involvement with the Children's Defense Fund, headed by Marian Wright Edelman, but omits any mention of the New World Foundation (NWF). Hillary followed Edelman's husband, Peter, as chairman of the NWF. Mrs. Clinton chaired the group during a time (1982-1988) when it gave grants to the Committee in Solidarity with the People of El Salvador, a front group for the communist terrorists; the National Lawyers Guild, a one-time-identified communist front; and the Christic Institute, an extreme left-wing group of lawyers which practiced "legal terrorism" against citizens, retired military, intelligence officials, and others who were perceived to be supporting the cause of freedom from communism in Central America.

The cover-up continues

Peter Flaherty writes, "Hillary's official biography prepared by the '92 Clinton campaign makes no mention of her stint as NWF chairman, despite the fact that she oversaw some $23 million in foundation assets. A few journalists, like Dan Wattenberg of *The American Spectator*, did report on the NWF grants during the summer of 1992, but the major media paid almost no attention. There was no need for Hillary to defend herself."

Hillary also took advantage of Bill Clinton's radical connections, many developed during his trips abroad. Strobe Talbott and Bill Clinton had been Rhodes Scholars in England together, for example, and Talbott and his wife, Brooke Shearer, "became friends of mine," she writes. Brooke's brother, Derek Shearer, another Yale graduate, became a friend of Bill and pro-Marxist economic adviser to Clinton.

Talbott, who also graduated from Yale and is now president of the Brookings Institution, a branch of the New World Order Council of Foreign Relations, became Deputy Secretary of State in the Clinton administration. Before that, he had been a columnist for *Time* magazine. He write a July 20, 1992, column, "The Birth of the Global Nation," stating that in the next century "nationhood as we know it will be obsolete," that we would all someday become world citizens, and that wars and human rights violations in the 20th century had clinched "the case for world government."

To help accomplish this, Talbott pressed for the use of the U.S. military to restore an extreme leftist defrocked Catholic priest, Jean Bertrand Aristide, to power in Haiti in 1994. Confidential documents from the U.N., publicized by AIM at the time, said that Talbott and other officials viewed an invasion as "politically desirable." Aristide, a Marxist-oriented advocate of the Liberation Theology, had been booted from the presidency by the military because. Aristide was inciting mobs to threaten to burn to death judges and legislators if they did not support his bidding.

Hillary's book describes this as a case of "the elected President" of Haiti being returned to power "after a harrowing year of diplomacy and the landing of American troops." However, the book *Voodoo Politics* by Lynn Garrison tells a far different story, exposing Aristide as an anti-American figure, not only allegedly involved in murder but involved in drug trafficking. Garrison was an adviser to one of the generals involved in the anti-Aristide coup.

The political reasons for the invasion can be seen in the make-up of the "Aristide Foundation for Democracy." The foundation board included left-wing Democrats such as Reps. Maxine Waters, John Conyers, and Joseph Kennedy, and former Rep. Michael Barnes.

Talbott's global left-wing vision was endorsed by President Clinton, who had sent a letter on June 22, 1993 to the World Federalist Association (WFA) when it gave Talbott its Norman Cousins Global Governance Award. In the letter, Clinton noted that Norman Cousins, the WFA founder, had "worked for world peace and world government" and that Talbott was a "worthy recipient" of the award.

Congresswoman Bella Abzug was a member of the Communist Party USA.

Hillary and China

Hillary does not discuss the financial contributions of communist Chinese to her husband's campaign for re-election. She does admit that the communist dictatorship wanted to use her appearance at a 1995 U.N. women's conference in Beijing as "a public relations tool to improve its image around the world." Hillary went anyway. She does not mention that radical feminist and Marxist Bella Abzug played a role in getting her to go. Hillary was a big fan of Abzug, having hailed her work and career in a major speech at the U.N.

FBI files obtained by *AIM* identify Abzug as a member of the Communist Party USA. She ran for Congress but was opposed by the Socialist Party for having shown "a general unwillingness to be outspokenly critical of Communist actions threatening the peace and freedom of the world." Not too far from the five-star hotel where Hillary and the feminists were meeting in Beijing, baby girls and boys were being starved to death at Chinese orphanages.

Pictures of this brutality were smuggled out of the country by Human Rights Watch. One showed an emaciated 11-year-old girl tied down to a bed, withering away. A British film about the problem, The Dying Rooms, showed children tied to wooden toilets, sleeping in their own excrement.

The brutality reflects the Chinese policy of one child per family, enforced through mandatory abortions, sterilization, and outright killings. Hillary calls such a policy "barbaric" in her book but admits that in her speech at the conference she did not criticize China by name. Ironically, all of this is recounted in a chapter entitled "Women's Rights Are Human Rights."

For Hillary, the villains are not the communists and fellow travelers but the "extreme conservatives" who oppose them. She rails against conservative talk radio, suggesting that it played a role in provoking the 1994 Oklahoma bombing. This is a ridiculous charge that Bill Clinton used in a brazen political attempt to discredit his political opponents on talk radio. Hillary takes it further, claiming that executed bomber Timothy McVeigh was a member of the "extreme right-wing" and had ties to "militant anti-government groups."

This is an exaggeration that borders on fantasy. McVeigh may have attended a meeting of a militia group at some point and had some anti-government views stemming from the violent federal assault on the Branch Davidian religious compound in Waco, Texas, in 1993. But the evidence developed by McVeigh's attorney, Stephen Jones, and other experts suggests that foreign terrorists may have ultimately been behind the Murrah Building bombing. However, the Clinton administration stopped the investigation and prosecution of McVeigh and his alleged partner, Terry Nichols, both of whom had served in the Army. Jones' book, *Others Unknown* (Public Affairs, 1998), explores this. Terrorism analyst Laurie Mylroie, author of *The War Against America* (Regan Books, 2001), has also cited evidence of a foreign or even Iraqi role in the Oklahoma City bombing.

Foreign policy expert

Mrs. Clinton, who abandoned her pro-Palestinian stance and became pro-Israel when she ran for the Senate, speaks out on foreign policy, confirming the role of co-president she assumed in domestic and foreign affairs. Her book defends the Clinton administration's military campaigns on behalf of the Muslims in Bosnia and Kosovo. She says the Bosnian Serbs were attacked because they "were besieging the Muslim town of Srebrenica in a frenzy of 'ethnic cleansing.'" In fact, Srebrenica, a so-called U.N. "safe haven," was being used to train and refurbish Muslim troops and may have been serving as a base for foreign terrorists in the region. Hillary conveniently ignores the Clinton-approved "ethnic cleansing" by Croatian forces against the Serbs.

"I had spoken out strongly in favor of Bill's leadership of NATO in the bombing campaign to force Slobodan Milosevic's troops out of Kosovo," a province of Yugoslavia, she says. But the House refused to authorize the bombing, making the intervention illegal. The bombing campaign, which resulted in the deaths of thousands of innocent civilians, amounted to interference in a sovereign state that posed no threat to the U.S. Indeed, the bombing benefited the Kosovo Liberation Army, a group linked to al-Qaeda. In Hillary's book, though, President Clinton "sounded the alarm on global terrorism" and tried to get the "diabolical" Osama bin Laden.

In Rwanda, she writes, "rape and sexual assault were committed on a mass scale, tactical weapons in the genocidal violence that raged there in 1994." Yet she also notes that Bill later "publicly expressed regret that our country and the international community had not done more to stop the horror" of perhaps one million dead. The program Triumph of Evil noted that the Clinton administration even hesitated to label it genocide.

More lies by Hillary Clinton

Hillary Clinton told about her close friend, Webb Hubbell, who went to prison for stealing from his partners and clients at the Rose Law Firm. Hillary says in her book that she did not know that Webb was in serious trouble until November 24, 1994. That is a lie. She and Bill had been told in March that Hubbell faced prosecution and that he should be ousted from the Justice Department. They promptly sought and got his resignation. Fearing he would reveal their darkest secrets, they and their aides set out to raise money to buy his silence. The final OIC report says he was paid $541,750 for his services, but he performed little or no work.

The claim that the Clintons did not know Hubbell was in deep trouble until November 1994 enabled them to say they had nothing to do with the solicitation of hush money because they did not know that Hubbell faced prosecution. The more that lie is publicized, the more difficult it will be for the Clintons to return to the White House as President and First Mate. They should have been evicted when the hush-money scandal broke.

Conclusion

Hillary Clinton has a deep-rooted connection to the Council of Foreign Relations, the Trilateral Commission and the Bilderberg Group, which are part of the New World Order's objective of a one-world government to enslave humanity. Bill Clinton attended the 1991 B.G. meeting in Germany. Shortly before becoming president, he attended again the meeting in 1999 when the B.G. annual meeting was held in Sintra, Portugal (Clinton had said that he had not attended in 15 years). Hillary Clinton was rumored to have attended the 2006 meeting in Ottawa, Canada. It is important to note that some individuals attend the meetings and their names are not published in the official list of attendees.

If Hillary Clinton would have been elected president, the road to a world government would have continued full speed ahead. Unfortunately, the United States is similar to the nation described in George Orwell's book *1984*, a Big Brother surveillance society and police state!

The world may be on the verge of an economic collapse as a result of the central banks of United States and European (controlled by the private banking cartels who are the owners of these financial institutions) and have printed over $11 trillion out of thin air. The economic crisis in Greece, Spain, Portugal, Italy, and other European countries could also contribute to this impending economic catastrophe.

Americans need to fight the global government being planned under the United Nations, but controlled by the members of Bilderberg Group, the Council of Foreign Affairs, and the Trilateral Commission. If this diabolical plan is ever successful, the United States will lose its sovereignty, wealth, Constitution, and laws.

The Bilderberg Group selected the very corrupt Hillary Clinton as the next president of the United States. Both Hillary and former president Bill Clinton have always believed that they are above the law and that rules and regulations that apply to others do not apply to them. It is clear why Hillary Clinton's destruction of 30,000 e-mails was a risk she was willing to take. Bill and Hillary are devious, unprincipled, and dishonest liars and both have committed many crimes. Both should be indicted.

Similar to Barack Obama, Hillary Clinton frequently lies. Similar to Barack Obama, Hillary Clinton has been involved in numerous scandals and committed crimes. Similar to Barack Obama, Hillary Clinton believes that she is above the law. Similar to Obama, she has ties to the Muslim Brotherhood.

CHAPTER 3

The Clinton Foundation is a criminal enterprise

More than 6,000 donors have given to the Clinton Foundation more than $2 billion in funding since its creation in 2000.

Former President Bill Clinton and former Secretary of State Hillary Clinton have been involved in a great number of scandals over the years. One of the worst scandals is how the Clinton Foundation has accepted tens of millions from governments of foreign countries and individuals from the United States and foreign nations seeking favors from the State Department or from the Obama administration over a number of years.

Hillary Clinton speaks at a fundraising of the corrupt Clinton Foundation.

Incredibly, more than 6,000 donors have given the Clinton Foundation more than $2 billion in funding since its creation in 2000. No other president or secretary of state has ever created such a foundation to raise money in such a corrupt and criminal manner. There is no question that the Clinton Foundation is a criminal enterprise created to enrich Bill and Hillary Clinton.

Donald J. Trump has demanded that a special prosecutor be appointed to investigate the evidence of a "pay-to-play scheme" of trading favors for millions in donations to the corrupt Clinton Foundation. The Republican Party presidential candidate said on August 22, 2016 in Akron, Ohio that the Clinton Foundation is "the most corrupt enterprise in the history of politics" and that it should be shut down. On August 22, almost 15,000 additional e-mails that Hillary Clinton failed to give were published. The trading favors for cold cash by the very corrupt Hillary Clinton was a very important issue during the 2016 presidential campaign.

It is quite clear that there was a pattern of trading favors for millions of dollars in donations to the Clinton Foundation or paying significant amounts to Bill Clinton for his speeches. Judge Andrew Napolitano and Rudy Giuliani have stated several times that in their opinion the trading of favors and access to Secretary of State Hillary Clinton could be grounds for a criminal indictment.

Peter Schweizer wrote a 186-page book entitled *Clinton Cash: The Untold Story of How and Why Foreign Governments and Businesses Helped Make Bill and Hillary Rich.*"

Peter Schweizer analyzed large donations made to the Clinton Foundation by foreign governments and individuals. He explained that the leaders of foreign nations who made large donations to the Clinton Foundation and to former President Bill Clinton through very high speaking fees received favors from the State Department under Hillary Clinton in return. Schweizer wrote that "We will see a pattern of financial transactions involving the Clintons that occurred contemporaneous with favorable U.S. policy decisions benefiting those providing the funds."

Peter Schweizer revealed in his book that the Hillary Clinton State Department traded favors for big donations to the Clinton Foundation and speaking fees for Bill Clinton. The author wrote that he has evidence of a "pay-to-play scheme." Schweizer raised questions about donors and conflicts of interest.

An Associate Press (AP) Report published on August 23, 2016 indicated that more than half of the individuals outside the government who met with Hillary Clinton while she was Secretary of State gave money — either personally or through companies or groups — to the Clinton Foundation. At least 85 of 154 people from private interests who met or had phone conversations scheduled with Hillary Clinton while she served at the State Department donated to the Clinton Foundation or pledged commitments to its international programs, according to a review of State Department calendars released to the Associated Press. The 85 donors combined contributed as much as $156 million. At least 40 donated more than $100,000 each and 20 gave more than $1 million.

These e-mails are among many from Secretary Clinton and her assistants that showed visitors and phone contacts in her official calendar that was turned over by the State Department to AP. The AP sought Clinton's calendar and schedules three years ago, but delays led the AP to sue the State Department last year in federal court for those materials and other records. The AP's findings represent the first systematic effort to calculate the scope of the intersecting interests of Clinton Foundation donors and people who met personally with Clinton or spoke to her by phone about their needs.

Clearly, Hillary Clinton has stonewalled the release of this damaging information about her "pay-to-play scheme" of trading favors for cold cash. AP reviewed calendar information and detailed schedules that cover half of Mrs. Clinton's State Department tenure.

Below are the alarming findings of the Associate Press Report:

Donors who were granted time with Clinton included an internationally known economist who asked for her help as the Bangladesh government pressured him to resign from a nonprofit bank he ran; a Wall Street executive who sought Clinton's help with a visa problem; and Estee Lauder executives who were listed as meeting with Clinton while her department worked with the firm's corporate charity to counter gender-based violence in South Africa.

The meetings between the Democratic presidential nominee and foundation donors do not appear to violate legal agreements Hilary Clinton and former president Bill Clinton signed before she joined the State Department in 2009. But the frequency of the overlaps shows the intermingling of access and donations and fuels perceptions that giving the foundation money was the admission price for face time with Clinton. Her calendars and e-mails released describe scores of contacts she and her top aides had with foundation donors.

The 154 from private interests did not include U.S. federal employees or foreign government representatives. Clinton met with representatives of at least 16 foreign governments that donated as much as $170 million to the Clinton foundation. However, these meetings were not included in AP's calculations because such meetings were considered part of her diplomatic duties.

S. Daniel Abraham

S. Daniel Abraham, whose name was included in e-mails released by the State Department as part of another lawsuit, is a Clinton fundraising bundler who was listed in Clinton's planners for eight meetings with her at various times. A billionaire behind the Slim-Fast diet and founder of the Center for Middle East Peace, Abraham told the AP last year that his talks with

Clinton concerned Mideast issues. Big Clinton Foundation donors with no history of political donations to the Clintons also met or talked by phone with Hillary Clinton and top aides, AP's review showed.

Muhammad Yunus

Muhammad Yunus, a Bangladeshi economist who won the 2006 Nobel Peace Prize for pioneering low-interest "microcredit" for poor business owners, met with Clinton three times and talked with her by phone during a period when Bangladeshi government authorities investigated his oversight of a nonprofit bank and ultimately pressured him to resign from the bank's board. Throughout the process, he pleaded for help in messages routed to Clinton and she ordered aides to find ways to assist him.

American affiliates of his nonprofit Grameen Bank had been working with the Clinton Foundation's Clinton Global Initiative programs as early as 2005, pledging millions of dollars in microloans for the poor. Grameen America, the bank's nonprofit U.S. flagship, which Yunus chairs, has given between $100,000 and $250,000 to the foundation — a figure that bank spokeswoman Becky Asch said reflects the institution's annual fees to attend CGI meetings. Another Grameen arm chaired by Yunus, Grameen Research, has donated between $25,000 and $50,000.

As a U.S. senator from New York, Clinton, as well as then-Massachusetts Sen. John Kerry and two other senators, sponsored in 2007 a bill to award a congressional gold medal to Yunus. He got one but not until 2010, a year after Obama awarded him a Presidential Medal of Freedom.

Yunus first met with Clinton in Washington in April 2009. Six months later, an announcement was made by USAID, the State Department's foreign aid arm that it was partnering with the

Grameen Foundation, a nonprofit charity run by Yunus, in a $162 million commitment to extend its microfinance concept abroad. USAID also began providing loans and grants to the Grameen Foundation, totaling $2.2 million over Clinton's tenure.

By September 2009, Yunus began complaining to Clinton's top aides about what he perceived as poor treatment by Bangladesh's government. His bank was accused of financial misman-agement of Norwegian government aid money — a charge that Norway later dismissed as baseless. But Yunus told Melanne Verveer, a long-time Clinton aide who was an ambassa-dor-at-large for global women's issues, that Bangladesh officials refused to meet with him and asked the State Department for help in pressing his case.

"Please see if the issues of Grameen Bank can be raised in a friendly way," he asked Verveer. Yunus sent "regards to H" and cited an upcoming Clinton Global Initiative event he planned to attend. Clinton ordered an aide to "Give to EAP rep," referring the problem to the agency's top East Asia expert. Yunus continued writing to Verveer as pressure mounted on his bank. In December 2010, responding to a news report that Bangladesh's prime minister was urging an investigation of Grameen Bank, Clinton told Verveer that she wanted to discuss the matter with her East Asia expert "ASAP."

Clinton called Yunus in March 2011 after the Bangladesh government opened an inquiry into his oversight of Grameen Bank. Yunus had told Verveer by e-mail that "the situation does not allow me to leave the country." By mid-May, the Bangladesh government had forced Yunus to step down from the bank's board. Yunus sent Clinton a copy of his resignation letter. In a sep-arate note to Verveer, Clinton wrote, "Sad indeed."

Clinton met with Yunus again in Washington in August 2011 and in the Bangladesh capital of Dhaka in May 2012. Clinton's arrival in Bangladesh came after Bangladesh authorities moved to seize control of Grameen Bank's effort to find new leaders. Speaking to a town hall audience, Clinton warned the Bangladesh government that "we do not want to see any action taken that would in any way undermine or interfere in the operations of the Grameen Bank."

Blackstone Group chairman Stephen Schwarzman is an American business magnate and fi-nancier. He is the chairman and CEO of the Blackstone Group, a global private equity and fi-nancial advisory firm he established in 1985. His personal fortune is estimated at $12.9 billion, according to *Forbes*. As of 2015, *Forbes* ranked Schwarzman at 100th on its World's Billionaires List. Blackstone donated between $250,000 and $500,000 to the Clinton Foundation.

In another case, Clinton was host at a September 2009 breakfast meeting at the New York Stock Exchange that listed Blackstone Group chairman Stephen Schwarzman as one of the attendees. Schwarzman's firm is a major Clinton Foundation donor, but he personally donates heavily to GOP candidates and causes. One day after the breakfast, according to Clinton e-mails, the State Department was working on a visa issue at Schwarzman's request. In December that same year, Schwarzman's wife, Christine, sat at Clinton's table during the Kennedy Center Honors. Clinton also introduced Schwarzman, then chairman of the Kennedy Center, before he spoke.

Blackstone Group chairman Stephen Schwarzman is a business magnate and financier.

Blackstone donated between $250,000 and $500,000 to the Clinton Foundation. Eight Blackstone executives also gave between $375,000 and $800,000 to the foundation. Blackstone's charitable arm has pledged millions of dollars in commitments to three Clinton Global aid projects ranging from the U.S. to the Mideast. Blackstone officials did not make Schwarzman available for comment.

Clinton met in June 2011 with Nancy Mahon of the MAC AIDS, the charitable arm of MAC Cosmetics, which is owned by Estee Lauder. The meeting occurred before an announcement about a State Department partnership to raise money to finance AIDS education and prevention. The public-private partnership was formed to fight gender-based violence in South Africa, the State Department said at the time.

The MAC AIDS fund donated between $5 million and $10 million to the Clinton Foundation. In 2008, Mahon and the MAC AIDS fund made a three-year unspecified commitment to the Clinton Global Initiative. That same year, the fund partnered with two other organizations to beef up a USAID program in Malawi and Ghana. In 2011, the fund was one of eight organizations to pledge a total of $2 million over a three-year period to help girls in southern Africa. The fund has not made a commitment to CGI since 2011.

Estee Lauder executive, Fabrizio Freda, also met with Clinton at the same Wall Street event attended by Schwarzman. Later that month, Freda appeared on a list of attendees to a meeting between Clinton and a U.S.-China trade group. Estee Lauder has given between $100,000 and $250,000 to the Clinton Foundation. The company made a commitment to CGI in 2013 with four other organizations to help survivors of sexual slavery in Cambodia. MAC AIDs officials did not make Mahon available to AP for comment.

Kate, the Duchess of Cambridge, shakes hands with Hillary Rodham Clinton.

Kate and her husband Prince William were attending a reception that was co-hosted by the Royal Foundation and the Clinton Foundation at British Consul General's Residence in New York on December 8, 2014.

When Clinton appeared before the U.S. Senate in early 2009 for her confirmation hearing as secretary of state, then- Senator Richard Lugar, a Republican from Indiana, questioned her at length about the foundation and potential conflicts of interest. His concerns were focused on foreign government donations, mostly to CGI.

Senator Lugar wanted more transparency than was ultimately agreed upon between the foundation and Obama's transition team. Now, Lugar hopes Hillary and Bill Clinton make a clean break from the foundation.

"The Clintons, as they approach the presidency, if they are successful, will have to work with their attorneys to make certain that rules of the road are drawn up to give confidence to them and the American public that there will not be favoritism," Lugar said.

"There's a lot of potential conflicts and a lot of potential problems," said Douglas White, an expert on nonprofits who previously directed Columbia University's graduate fundraising management program. "The point is, she can't just walk away from these 6,000 donors."

Clinton campaign official criticized the AP report

"It is outrageous to misrepresent Secretary Clinton's basis for meeting with these individuals," spokesman Brian Fallon said. He called it "a distorted portrayal of how often she crossed paths with individuals connected to charitable donations to the Clinton Foundation." Clinton campaign spokesman Brian Fallon did not respond to the AP's questions about Clinton transition plans regarding ethics, but said in a statement Tuesday the standard set by the Clinton Foundation's ethics restrictions was "unprecedented, even if it may never satisfy some critics."

The Clinton Foundation acknowledges that mistakes were made

In 2015, the Clinton Foundation's acting CEO, Maura Pally, admitted to some mistakes in the organization's listing of donations from foreign governments on its tax forms. Maura Pally, the acting CEO wrote in a statement the following: "Our total revenue was accurately reported on each year's form—our error was that government grants were mistakenly combined with other donations. Those same grants have always been properly listed and broken out and available for anyone to see on our audited financial statements, posted on our website. So yes, we made mistakes, as many organizations of our size do, but we are acting quickly to remedy them and have taken steps to ensure they don't happen in the future. We are committed to operating the Foundation responsibly and effectively to continue the life-changing work that this philanthropy is doing every day."

A spokeswoman for Chelsea Clinton said the former first daughter planned to remain on the board because she "is committed to ensuring that those benefiting from the foundation's work will be able to continue receiving that often-life-changing help." It said Chelsea Clinton was remaining on the board to "steward the implementation of changes," including "new fundraising policies."

Chelsea Clinton planned to remain on the board of the Clinton Foundation if Hillary Clinton was elected president in November 2016.

Bill Clinton told supporters in a letter sent on August 22, 2016 that he would resign from the board and stop raising money for the foundation and that he and Chelsea had decided the foundation would "raise money only from U.S. citizens, permanent residents, and U.S.-based independent foundations." Foreign government and corporate gifts, which have raised ethical questions in the past, would not be accepted. The purpose of these changes, Bill Clinton said, was to eliminate "legitimate concerns about potential conflicts of interest." Clinton also said that while leaving the board, "I will continue to support the work of the foundation."

Bill Clinton also said the foundation was going to change its name from the Bill, Hillary & Chelsea Clinton Foundation back to the Clinton Foundation. The name changed when Mrs. Clinton left the State Department and began raising money for the foundation in the period before she launched her presidential bid.

Ray Madoff, a Boston College Law School professor and director of the Forum on Philanthropy and the Public Good, said that it would make sense for Chelsea to remain on the board. However, in this case, it is complicated by its history. "The Clinton Foundation has been way too inattentive to the appearance of impropriety," Ms. Madoff said. "Chelsea clearly has access to her parents so the appearance of impropriety continues." She added, "If the Clintons didn't have this ongoing problem, then it is a more difficult case. After all, Chelsea is a working adult and it makes sense that she would work on the Clinton Foundation."

As Secretary of State Hillary Clinton hosted at a dinner an Ukrainian billionaire donor to Clinton Foundation

Ukrainian billionaire Victor Pinchuk

Ukrainian billionaire Victor Pinchuk was hosted at a dinner at Hillary Clinton's home while she was Secretary of State in 2012. He donated at least $8.6 million to the Clinton Foundation when Mrs. Clinton was secretary of state.

Peter Nicholas wrote an article titled "Clinton Hosted Ukrainian at 2012 Dinner" which was published in the *Wall Street Journal* on August 24, 2016. He explained that while she was secretary of state, Hillary Clinton hosted a dinner involving Clinton Foundation donors, including an Ukrainian businessman who had given money to the foundation and retained a lobbyist to arrange State Department meetings. The dinner attended by Victor Pinchuk four years ago was mentioned in a new batch of State Department e-mails obtained by the conservative group Citizens United through public records requests and released on August 23, 2016.

Peter Nicholas stated the following: "A note about the dinner from a foundation official to Huma Abedin, one of Mrs. Clinton's top deputies at the State Department, described the event as a Clinton Foundation dinner in June 2012 at the home of the Democratic presidential nominee and included a list of guests attending. The dinner guest list is an elite corps of Obama administration officials, Democratic donors, political consultants and foundation donors."

Mr. Pinchuk is described in a short background briefing on all the guests as a "successful businessman, whose role in civic, international affairs and charitable organizations has made him a leader in Ukraine's growing interaction with Europe and the world." Republican critics said that the dinner is an illustration of what they describe as the overlapping interests between Clinton Foundation donors and the Clinton-led State Department. Republican presidential candidate Donald Trump called for a special prosecutor to examine dealings during Mrs. Clinton's tenure as the nation's top diplomat.

Victor Pinchuk's Ukraine-based foundation donated at least $8.6 million to the Clinton Foundation when Mrs. Clinton was secretary of state. He is a former member of the Ukrainian Parliament whose wealth comes from a pipe-making business. The 85 donors, including Victor Pinchuk, contributed $156 million to the Clinton Foundation.

Pinchuk also hired Doug Schoen as a lobbyist to help set up meetings with the State Department and White House officials in part to promote the goal of democratization in the Ukraine. Schoen is a former adviser to former President Bill Clinton. Thus, it is clear that in order to meet with Secretary Clinton foreigners had to donate millions to the corrupt foundation and sometimes hire a former adviser to the Clintons. Afterwards favors were traded for cold cash!

Hillary Clinton and Obama approved the purchase by Russia of 20% of the uranium mines of America

Hillary Clinton and Obama approved the purchase by Russia of 20% of the uranium mines of America which seriously endangered our national security. This deal suggests that Bill and Hillary Clinton have put "America for sale" to a potential enemy of the nation solely to enrich themselves. Russia has as a client state and an ally, Iran. Currently, Congress has reopened the Uranium One sale as there is evidence that Russia gave bribes to members of the Obama administration.

Uranium One sign points to a 35,000-acre ranch owned by John Christensen, near the town of Gillette, Wyoming. Uranium One had the mining rights to John Christensen's property and it was sold to Russia.

Uranium One began to buy companies with assets in the United States. In April 2007, the corporation announced the purchase of a uranium mill in Utah and more than 38,000 acres of uranium exploration properties in four Western states, followed quickly by the acquisition of the Energy Metals Corporation and its uranium holdings in Wyoming, Texas, and Utah. That deal made clear that Uranium One was intent on becoming a powerhouse in the United States uranium sector with the potential to become the domestic supplier of choice for U.S. utilities, the company declared.

Frank Giustra made a contribution of $31.3 million to the Clinton Foundation.

Five months later, Frank Giustra held a fund-raiser for the Clinton Giustra Sustainable Growth Initiative, a project aimed at fostering progressive environmental and labor practices in the natural resources industry, to which he had pledged $100 million. Frank Giustra, a multimillionaire mining financier, donated $31.3 million to the foundation run by Bill Clinton. He sold his Uranium One Company to Russia and earned an immense profit.

Political campaigns in the United States are prohibited from accepting foreign donations. However, foreigners may give to foundations in the United States. When Hillary Clinton declared that that she was running for president, the Clinton Foundation announced changes to lessen concerns about potential conflicts of interest with such donations. The foundation stated that it would only accept donations from Western countries.

Russia's annexation of Crimea and military invasion of Eastern Ukraine have created a new Cold War between Russia and the United States and its European allies. Allowing the dictator Vladimir Putin to acquire such a large portion of America's uranium has seriously endangered our national security.

The Russian dictator has used the oil and gas resources of his country to threaten Ukraine and our European allies and project power around the world. Former U.S. Ambassador to Russia Michael McFaul, who served under Secretary of State Hillary Clinton, stated the following: "Should we be concerned? Absolutely. Do we want Putin to have a monopoly on this? Of course we don't. We don't want to be dependent on Putin for anything in this climate." The ambassador stated that he was unaware of the Uranium One deal until asked about it.

Bill Clinton met with Vladimir V. Putin in Moscow in 2010.

President Bill Clinton, shortly after the Russians announced their intention to acquire a majority stake in Uranium One, was paid $500,000 for a Moscow speech by a Russian investment bank with links to the Kremlin. The records indicate that at the time, both Rosatom and the

United States government made promises intended to eliminate concerns about giving control of the company's assets to the Russians. Those promises were broken.

Conclusion

A Rasmussen poll published on April 29, 2015 revealed that 63% likely voters that Hillary Clinton may have helped foreign donors as Secretary of State and 30% that this was unlikely. Many polls in 2016 revealed that the majority of Likely Voters did not trust Hillary Clinton, while only a minority trusted her.

Attorney General Loretta Lynch failed to appoint a special prosecutor, as recommended by Donald J. Trump, to investigate Bill Clinton and Hillary Clinton for their worldwide influence peddling and trading multimillion donations to their foundation for favors. Like any American citizen, the Clintons should be given the presumption of innocence.

Lynch met with Bill Clinton in the tarmac of an airport while the FBI investigation was going on. To many this was improper and raised the questions of collusion.

The American people, as well as Republican members of Congress, are tired of cover-ups and failure to prosecute the many crimes committed by President Obama and members of his administration. Loretta Lynch needs to remember that her job is not to protect the Obama administration officials but to serve the American people. If crimes were committed, federal prosecutors need to indict Bill and Hillary Clinton and, if convicted, they must go to jail. The Clintons have been involved in numerous scandals and crimes during their lives. Both seem to believe that that they are above the law. The Clintons believe that rules and regulations must be followed by other people, but not by them.

Attorney General Lynch did not investigate Bill and Hillary Clinton's involvement in a "pay-to-play scheme," which is nothing more than bribes. Lynch is as corrupt as the previous Attorney General Eric Holder.

There is definitely a pattern of financial transactions involving the Clintons that occurred at the same time that favorable decisions were made by Secretary Clinton. These transactions benefitted those providing the contributions, but endangered our national security as in the case of Uranium One.

Secretary Clinton approved a multinational from Canada to sell to Russia 20% of the uranium mines of America which seriously endangered our national security. The Canadian multinationals donated tens of millions to the Clinton Foundation.

The Clintons have always believed that they are above the law and that rules and regulations that apply to others do not apply to them. Hillary Clinton also lies frequently. Astoundingly, Hillary Clinton stated when she was presenting her new book that at one time she was flat broke. She also lied when she stated that all of her grandparents were immigrants.

Similar to Barack Obama, Hillary Clinton frequently lies. Similar to Barack Obama, Hillary Clinton has been involved in numerous scandals and committed crimes. Similar to Barack Obama, Hillary Clinton believes that she is above the law. Similar to Obama she has ties to the Muslim Brotherhood.

Together with her campaign staffers, Hillary Clinton tried very hard to put out the fire brought by the AP report and the findings documented in the *Clinton Cash* book and movie. Hillary Clinton has a very serious problem and that is that she needs to start putting out fires from the many other scandals that will simply not go away.

How could Hillary Clinton pretend to be a defender of the rights of women in the United States when she has accepted millions of dollars from Middle Eastern countries where women are severely oppressed and are stoned to death for infidelity?

Hillary Clinton is a tremendous hypocrite! The former first lady is a corrupt and dishonest politician who has been involved in many crimes and high treason, dereliction of duty, and criminal negligence in Libya. Hillary Clinton has placed America for sale.

Hopefully, in light of the new revelations that indicate that Russia gave bribes to members of the Obama administration, the Clintons and others should be indicted and prosecuted.

CHAPTER 4

Huma Abedin and her entire family work with terror groups and the global jihad movement

Anthony Weiner announced his withdrawal from the race for mayor of New York City next to his terror-link wife Huma Abedin in 2013. Later, Huma separated from her pervert husband who ended in prison.

Weiner spent 12 years in the House of Representatives before resigning in June 2011 after posting an explicit image of him on his twitter account. At the time, he admitted that he had "exchanged messages and photos of an explicit nature with about six woman" over the previous three years. After leaving office, the pervert and disgraced politician went into rehabilitation for sexual addition. Now the pervert is involved in another sexting scandal.

Huma Abedin, the Democratic presidential nominee Hillary Clinton's longtime top adviser and assistant, announced on August 29, 2016 that she and husband Anthony Weiner are separating after news of the former congressman's latest sexting scandal emerged. Abedin stated the following: "After long and painful consideration and work on my marriage, I have made the decision to separate from my husband. Anthony and I remain devoted to doing what is best for our son, who is the light of our life. During this difficult time, I ask for respect for our privacy."

On September 25, 2017, Weiner was sentenced to 21 months in prison and ordered to pay a $10,000 fine. He was also required to register as a convicted sex offender at this place of residence and work for the rest of his life. Abedin filed for divorce.

Huma Abedin, who is connected to the global jihad movement and the Muslim Brotherhood, had a very strange marriage. Perhaps being married to the Jewish pervert Anthony Weiner was to cover up her activities on behalf of the Muslim Brotherhood and other Islamic terror groups. Huma Abedin, who served as Secretary of State Hillary Clinton's Deputy Chief of Staff, has ties, as well as her late father, mother, and brother with Muslim Brotherhood operatives and terror organizations. Abedin was Vice Chair to the Hillary Clinton presidential campaign.

The announcement came on August 29 after the *New York Post* reported that Weiner, once again, had exchanged sexual messages with a woman starting in 2015. One of the exchanges reported by the *New York Post* included a risqué photo of Weiner with his infant son on the bed beside him.

The sexual message/picture showed "a bulge in his white, jokey-brand boxer briefs and his son cuddle up to his left." Weiner, age 51, sent the image via twitter direct message to a divorcee with whom he had been sex texting for over a year and a half. According to the *New York Post*, the former congressman wrote in other messages of masturbating as he thought about her, describing the woman as "literary a fantasy chick."

Donald Trump was quick to issue a statement, stating the following: "Huma is making a very wise decision. I know Anthony Weiner well, and she will be far better off without him. I only worry for the country in that Hillary Clinton was careless and negligent in allowing Weiner to have such close proximity to highly classified information. Who knows what he learned and who he told? It's just another example of Hillary Clinton's bad judgment. It is possible that our country and its security have been greatly compromised by this."

Weiner, the former Democratic Congressman, resigned from Congress in 2011 after the first sex scandal came to light. Weiner had been sending lewd messages and photos online to random women. Weiner then ran for New York City mayor until it was revealed he had again been exchanging messages with women on line, using the pseudonym Carlos Danger.

Paul Sperry, the author of the book, **wrote** an article titled "Huma Abedin's Mom Linked to Shocking anti- Women Book" which was published in the *New York Post* on August 28, 2016.

Sperry wrote that as secretary of state, women's-rights champion Hillary Clinton not only made a presentation at a Saudi university run by her top aide Huma Abedin's anti-feminist and terror link mother, but invited Dr. Saleha M. Abedin to participate in a State Department event for "leading thinkers" on women's issues.

This occurred despite evidence at the time that Saleha M. Abedin had explored the religious merits of sexual submissiveness, child marriage, the lashing and stoning of adulterous women, and even the circumcision of girls. Saleha M. Abedin, whose daughter Huma Abedin was Vice Chair of Hillary Clinton's presidential campaign, did take a pro-gender-equality stance on at least one issue, Muslim women's right to participate in violent jihad alongside men.

As the *New York Post* first reported, Huma's mother edits the *Journal of Muslim Minority Affairs*, which has suggested that America had 9/11 coming to it because of "sanctions" and "injustices" the United States allegedly imposed on the Muslim world. The *Journal of Muslim Minority Affairs* also opposed women's rights as un-Islamic, arguing that "empowerment' of women does more harm than benefit."

In 1999, Dr. Saleha Abedin translated and edited a book titled *Women in Islam: A Discourse in Rights and Obligations*, which was published by the *Institute of Muslim Minority Affairs*. This book was written by her Saudi colleague, Fatima Naseef, who explained that the stoning and lashing of adulterers, the killing of apostates, sexual submissiveness, and even female genital mutilation are all permissible practices under Shariah law. On Page 202 of the book, the author stated the following: "The wife should satisfy her husband's desire for sexual intercourse (even if she is not in the mood). She has no right to abstain except for a reasonable cause or legal prohibition." However, as Paul Sperry said, getting in the mood may be difficult since millions of Islamic women have been sexually mutilated.

Fatima Umar Naseef wrote in her book that female genital mutilation is permissible and said that "circumcision for women is allowed." Naseef explained that laws promoting feminist equality, moreover, are ineffectual, since "man-made laws have in fact enslaved women, submitting them to the cupidity and caprice of human beings. Islam is the only solution and the only escape."

Naseef described the job of Islamic woman as follows: "The women cannot mix and social interact with the opposite sex, which is forbidden in Islam. Moreover, women's biological constitution is different from that of men. Women are fragile, emotional and sometimes unable to handle difficult and strenuous situations. Men are less emotional and show more perseverance." There is one exception to the sexual division of roles--"Women can also participate in fighting when jihad becomes an individual duty."

Huma Abedin was the closest adviser and body woman of Hillary Clinton. This picture shows Abedin on the campaign trail with Hillary Clinton.

Sperry pointed out that on the back cover of the book, Dr. Saleha Abedin says she is "pleased to launch" the book as part of a series on the study of women's rights in Islam sponsored by the International Islamic Committee for Woman and Child (IICWC), for which she is listed as chairperson. This organization, founded by Huma's mother, the Cairo-based IICWC, has advocated for the repeal of Egypt's Mubarak-era laws in favor of of the implementation of Shariah law, which could allow female genital mutilation, child marriage, and marital rape.

Dr. Saleha Abedin is paid by the Saudi government to advocate and spread Shariah law in non-Muslim countries like America and to also spread Saudi Arabia's diabolical Wahhabi Islamic religion.

Sperry wrote that in 1995, less than three weeks before Clinton gave her famous women's rights speech in Beijing, Saleha Abedin headlined an unusual Washington conference organized by the Council on American-Islamic Relations (CAIR), a Muslim Brotherhood front organization, to lobby against the United Nation platform drafted by Hillary Clinton and other feminists. Visibly angry, Saleha Abedin argued that it ran counter to Islam and was a "conspiracy" against Muslims. Specifically, she called into question provisions in the platform that condemned domestic battery of women, apparently expressing sympathy for men who commit abuse. Pakistan-born Saleha Abedin claimed that men who serially beat women tend to be unemployed, making their abuse somehow more understandable. "They are victims of a different kind," she claimed. "And they are simply taking their frustrations out on women."

Despite all this, in 2010, Huma Abedin arranged for Hillary Clinton, then the secretary of state, to travel to Jeddah, Saudi Arabia, to meet with her mother and talk at the university that she helped found and where she worked as a professor of sociology and Vice Dean. Speaking to a room full of women, Clinton said Americans have to stop stereotyping Saudi women as oppressed, before assuring the audience that not all American women go "around in a bikini bathing suit." While Hillary Clinton was there, she formed a partnership with Saleha Abedin's Dar al-Hekma College called the U.S.-Saudi Women's Forum on Social Entrepreneurship and promised to reverse post-9/11 curbs on Saudi student visas to America.

Saleha Abedin appears in the picture to the right of Secretary of State during her shameful trip to Jeddah, Saudi Arabia, arranged by her top assistant Huma Abedin to meet with her mother and talk at her university.

Similar to President Barack Obama, Hillary Clinton has no difficulty working with operatives of the Muslim Brotherhood such Huma Abedin and her mother. The so-called defender and champion of women's right, Hillary Clinton, accepted millions in donations to the very corrupt and criminal Clinton Foundation from Middle Eastern countries. Hillary Clinton is very aware that these nations oppress women, mutilate them sexually, and even stone them to death for infidelity. Hillary Clinton's pretends to be a defender of the gay community yet she accepts millions in donations to the Clinton Foundation from Middle Eastern nations even though 10 of those countries have death penalty for gays, lesbians, and transgender individuals.

The strong collaboration of Dr. Saleha Abedin with the global jihad movement and multiple terrorist organizations did not stop Secretary of State Hillary Clinton from visiting her in Jeddah, Saudi Arabia at Dar Al-Hehma College where she works. In February 2010, Secretary of State Hillary Clinton accompanied by her loyal Deputy Chief of Staff Huma Abedin, visited Huma's mother at the Saudi college.

In her speech at the college, Hillary Clinton praised the terror-linked professor Saleha Abedin for her "pioneering work" and told her how much she appreciated the work of her daughter at the State Department. Secretary Clinton's stated the following: "I have to say a special word about Dr. Saleha Abedin, you heard her present the very exciting partnerships that have been pioneered between colleges and universities in the United States and this college. And it is pioneering work to create these kinds of relationships."

"But I have to confess something that Dr. Abedin did not, and that is that I have almost a familial bond with this college, Dr. Abedin's daughter, one of her three daughters, is my Deputy Chief of Staff, Huma Abedin, who started to work for me when she was a student at George Washington University in Washington, D.C., she added."

Instead of praising Huma's mother "pioneering" work with our nation's colleges and universities as well as other in the Western nations, Secretary Clinton should have asked the FBI to investigate her contacts with Islamic institutes and programs in our colleges and universities. Sadly, there is no difference between Hillary Clinton and Barack Obama in their connections with members of the Muslim Brotherhood.

Author Frank Gaffney wrote that Huma's brother, Dr. Hassan Abedin, is also closely connected to the Muslim Brotherhood. Dr. Abedin is a fellow of the Islamic Trust's Oxford University Center for Islamic Studies in Great Britain. The Oxford Center presented an award for great scholarly achievement to Shaykh Abd Al-Fattah Abu Gudda, who was involved with the Muslim Brotherhood since his meeting with Hassan al-Banna, the founder of the Brotherhood during the 1940s.

As revealed by internal e-mails released in response to a lawsuit filed by Judicial Watch, the following year, Hillary Clinton invited Dr. Saleha Abedin and the president of the Saudi university to Washington to participate in a State Department colloquium on women. Incredibly, the Hillary Clinton campaign spokesman Nick Merrill told the *New York Post* that while Huma Abedin was in fact listed as an editorial staffer of her mother's radical Islamic journal from 1996 to 2008, she did not do anything for the publication in her long tenure there. When asked if Clinton regrets honoring the Islamist mother and bestowing legitimacy on her extreme views, Merrill had no comment.

Huma Abedin is the body woman and former Vice Chair of the Hillary Clinton presidential campaign. Both are very close friends.

Huma Mahmood Abedin was born in Kalamazoo, Michigan in 1976. When she was two years old, her family moved to Jeddah, Saudi Arabia. Her father, Syed Zaimul Abedin, was born in the British India in 1928 and died in 1993. Her mother, Saleha Mahmood Abedin, was born in Pakistan. Both of her parents came to study to the United States and received Ph.D.'s from the University of Pennsylvania. They later moved to Saudi Arabia, a country with many radical Islamist groups, including the Muslim Brotherhood.

The Ikhwan, the name of the Muslim Brotherhood, has been supported by Saudi Arabia and other Sunni Middle Eastern nations. It has engaged in assassinations, terrorism, and violence for almost a century. It is anti-Western and anti-Semitic.

The Brotherhood is the world's oldest and most influential of all the radical Islamist organizations. It is also the most anti-American and represents a direct threat to our national security.

Unfortunately, former President Obama, with the support of former Secretary of State Hillary Clinton, has allowed the Muslim Brotherhood to infiltrate his administration. Both Hillary Clinton and Barack Obama supported the Muslim Brotherhood government of Egypt and tried unsuccessfully to prevent the coup d'état that overthrew President Mohamed Morsi.

Obama and Hillary Clinton also supported the Libyan Muslim Brotherhood, Ansar al Sharia, and al-Qaeda in the Maghreb to overthrow Muammar Qaddafi in Libya, who at the time was America's ally in the war of terror. Obama and Hillary Clinton committed treason, dereliction of duty, and criminal negligence in Libya.

This writer wrote the book *Obama, Hillary Clinton, and Radical Islam* in 2016.

This writer documented in his book how the royal family of Saudi Arabia has been spending billions of dollars spreading the country's perverse and extremist Wahhabist religion throughout the world. This religion from Saudi Arabia preaches hatred and mistrust of infidels (nonbelievers), calls rival religious sects apostates, and promotes violent jihad.

Osama bin Laden and almost all of the terrorists who attacked the United States on 9/11 came from Saudi Arabia. It is now known that the Saudi royal family was directly involved in the

9/11 terrorist attacks. Saudi Arabia pretends to be an ally of the United States, but it is and has always been our enemy.

As stated earlier, Huma Abedin, who served as Secretary of State Hillary Clinton's Deputy Chief of Staff, was connected as well as her late father, mother, and brother to the Muslim Brotherhood operatives and organizations. She is very close to Hillary Clinton. Huma Abedin's mother, Dr. Saleha Abedin, has lived in Saudi Arabia for many years. Dr. Saleha Abedin currently is a professor of sociology and Vice Dean at Dar Al-Hehma College in Jeddah, Saudi Arabia.

Frank Gaffney, in his book *The Muslim Brotherhood in the Obama Administration* (2012) described Huma Abedin's and her family´s connections to the Muslim Brotherhood while living in Saudi Arabia.

Gaffney explained that together with Abdullah Omar Naseef, a financier of al-Qaeda, Huma's parents founded and managed the Institute of Muslim Minority Affairs (IMMA) at the King Abdulaziz University in Saudi Arabia. This organization became a family business that continues to exist to this day.

Syed Abedin was recruited by the influential Muslim Brotherhood operative, Abdullah Omar Naseef, who was at the time the Secretary-General of the Muslim World League (MWL) and a financial supporter of al-Qaida. Thus, it began the long lasting association of Syed and Saleha Abedin, as well as their daughter Huma, with the Muslim Brotherhood and other terrorist organizations involved in the global jihad movement.

Dr. Naseef is currently an officer of the international Islamic Council for Dawa and Relief, (IICDR), which is composed of more than one hundred Islamic organizations from around the world and is headquartered in Cairo, Egypt. The IICDR website includes a large number of affiliated organizations, many of which are associated with the global Muslim Brotherhood, Hamas fundraising, or support for al-Qaeda. Dr. Naseef is also the President of the Muslim World Congress and the chairman of the Oxford Center of Islamic Studies.

Dr. Abdullah Omar Naseef is supporter of many world-wide terrorist organizations. He is also a financial supporter of al-Qaeda. He has worked closely with Huma Abedin's parents.

Dr. Naseef has held many important positions in Saudi Arabia including serving as Vice-President of the Kingdom's Shura Council, President of King Abdul Aziz University, and, most importantly, as Secretary-General of the Muslim World League (MWL) from 1983 to 1993.

Gaffney explained in his book that the former Justice Department attorney Andrew C. McCarthy, the lead prosecutor of Omar Abdel Rahman, the so-called "Blind Sheikh" who organized the first attack to the Twin Towers in New York City in 1993, had stated the following regarding the MWL: "Perhaps the most significant Muslim Brotherhood organization in the world... It was launched by Muslim Brotherhood activists with the financial backing of the Saudi royal family. It is often referred to as a charity, but it is really a global propagation enterprise-exporting the Muslim Brotherhood's virulently anti-Western brand of Islamist ideology throughout the world, very much including in the United States... According to Osama bin Laden himself, the Muslim World League was one of al-Qaeda's three top funding sources."

World Net Daily (*WND*), the electronic publication, was the first to report that Dr. Saleha Abedin reportedly represented the Muslim World League (MWL), a Saudi-financed charity that has spawned Islamic groups accused of terror ties, in a meeting in Beijing, China. The MWL was one of the groups declared by the United States government to be an official al-Qaeda front. The MWL was founded in Mecca, Saudi Arabia in 1962 and presents itself as one of the largest Islamic nongovernmental charity organizations. However, according to documents and testimony from the United States government, this charity is heavily financed by the Saudi Arabia, which pretends to be our strong ally.

The Anti-Defamation League's profile of the Muslim World League accuses the organization of promulgating the following: "A fundamentalist interpretation of Islam around the world through a large network of charities and affiliated organizations. Its ideological backbone is based on an extremist interpretation of Islam and several of its affiliated groups and individuals have been linked to terror-related activities."

Gaffney pointed out that Dr. Naseef not only founded and chaired the Institute of Muslim Minority Affairs (IMMA) but also founded in 1988 the Rabita Trust, an organization that was designated a terrorist funding entity by the United States government in October 2001. In 1989, when Dr. Naseef was Secretary-General of the Muslim World League, he wrote the following: "The secular world view is the total negation of Islamic faith... Therefore, the struggle of Islamic thought with modern secularism is part of the terrible warfare of Islam against... the powers of atheism, lies and evil..."

Gaffney wrote that the Institute for Muslim Minority Affairs and its publication, *The Journal of Muslim Minority Affairs*, both established by Huma Abedin's father, "has been vehicles for promoting Abdullah Omar Naseef's Islamist program in Western societies and the indoctrination of young Muslims in Islamic supremacist ideology." The purpose of the institute and its journal is the recruitment of Muslims who live in non-Muslim countries into a social and religious unit that would resist Western assimilation.

Saudi Arabia has spent billions of dollars in the Western world and in our country establishing educational centers, mosques, and organizations, such as the Islamic Society of North America

(ISNA) and the Muslim Student Association (the organization in which Huma Abedin was active while at the university). The ultimate diabolic objective of the IMMA is the spread of Islam until it dominates the non-Muslim nations of the world. Creating a worldwide Muslim caliphate, where the nonbelievers or the infidels will be killed or enslaved, is the long-term dream of the IMMA as well as the Muslim Brotherhood and Muslim Brotherhood front organizations.

These organizations are helping fundamentalist Muslims to organize and gain government influence committed to the spread of Shariah law and the transformation of governments from within. Gaffney pointed out that this was the vision of the Institute of Muslim Minority Affairs that Abdullah Omar Naseef and Huma's parents had. They wanted to build peaceably over time an Islamist infrastructure in the United States and other countries in the West and "create enclaves, in colleges and universities, in social organizations in the larger community and in the government itself, where Shariah is honored as the basic law and Muslims are pressured not to assimilate into the culture and laws of the United States and other Western countries where they lived."

Upon the death of Huma Abedin's father, Syed, in 1993, her mother, Saleha, took over the IMMA and its journal. Huma's brother Hassan is associate editor of the journal. Gaffney explained that Saleha Abedin is a prominent figure in another group, the Muslim Brotherhood's secret International Women's Organization, also known as the Muslim Sisterhood. The Sisterhood's goal is to establish Shariah as the guiding legal code, ensuring the subjugation of women worldwide.

Andrew C. McCarthy reported that Dr. Saleha Abedin translated and edited a book entitled *Women in Islam: A Discourse in Rights and Obligations (1999)* that stated that man-made laws enslave women. The book justifies the support of Shariah law of practices such as the legal subordination of women, the death penalty for apostates or blasphemers of Islam, and the participation of women in violent jihad. It is absolutely incredible that some individuals in the Obama mainstream progressive media have called Dr. Saleha Abedin a leading voice of women's rights in the Muslim world. Have these misinformed journalists failed to read about the oppression of women under Shariah law?

Author Walid Shoebat wrote that Dr. Saleha Abedin was one of 63 leaders of the Muslim Sisterhood, the de-facto female version of the Muslim Brotherhood. Shoebat also reported that Saleha Abedin served with Najla Ali Mahmoud, the wife of the Muslim Brotherhood ousted

President Mohammed Morsi of Egypt. Both women were members of the Sisterhood´s Guidance Bureau.

Dr. Saleha Abedin reportedly represented the Muslim World League (MWL), a Saudi-financed charity that has spawned Islamic groups accused of terror ties in a meeting in Beijing, China. One of the groups was declared by the United States government to be an official al-Qaeda front. The MWL was founded in Mecca, Saudi Arabia in 1962 and presents itself as one of the largest Islamic nongovernmental charity organizations. Andrew C. McCarthy wrote an article entitled "The Huma Unmentionables" in the *National Review Online* on July 24, 2013. He explained that among her activities, Dr. Saleha Abedin directs the International Islamic Committee for Woman and Child. This organization is a component of the Union for Good, a formerly designated terrorist organization.

Yusuf al Qaradawi, who is the spiritual leader of the Muslim Brotherhood, has issued fatwas (orders) calling for the killing of U.S. military in Iraq as well as suicide bombings in Israel.

The Union for Good is led by Sheikh Yusuf al Qaradawi, the spiritual leader of the Muslim Brotherhood who has issued fatwas (orders) calling for the killing of American military and support personnel in Iraq as well as suicide bombings in Israel. Shamefully and outrageously,

Obama's White House hosted Qaradawi's chief deputy, Sheikh Abdulla bin Bayyah, who also endorsed the fatwa calling for the killing of American troops and personnel in Iraq.

What an insult to our brave soldiers, marines, and other armed forces personnel who fought and died in the Iraqi war! Sheikh al Qaradawi helped write the charter for the International Islamic Committee for Woman and Child, the organization that is run by Dr. Saleha Abedin.

The Muslim Students Association and Huma Abedin's involvement in one of its chapters

Huma Abedin returned or was sent to the United States and graduated from George Washington University. While attending this university, she was on the executive board and the social committee of the university's chapter of the Muslim Students Association (MSA), an organization that is a front of the Muslim Brotherhood, according to documents captured by the FBI.

In her book *Stop the Islamization of America* (2011), Pamela Geller describes the MSA as a Muslim student organization that "creates an atmosphere of intimidation for Jewish students on campuses nationwide and brings speakers who preach jihad and hatred." Geller explained that following the disruption of a conference presented by Israeli ambassador Michael Oren in February 2010 by members of MSA chapter at the University of California-Irvine, the MSA was suspended and several leading members were arrested. Geller pointed out that the "MSA still operates on campuses all over the country, trafficking freely on intimidation, thuggery, disinformation, and hate."

Andrew C. McCarthy pointed out that the Muslim Students Association has a large network of chapters at colleges and universities across North America and "it is the foundation of the Muslim Brotherhood's infrastructure in the United States." He explained that not all Muslim students who join the MSA become a member of the Muslim Brotherhood. The MSA has an extensive indoctrination program which leads to Muslim Brotherhood membership for those who qualify. MSA leaders founded the Islamic Society of North America (ISNA), the largest Islamist organization in the United States.

McCarthy wrote that the MSA and ISNA consider themselves the same organization. Due to the support of the ISNA to the terrorist organization Hamas, which is the Palestinian branch of the Egyptian Muslim Brotherhood, the organization was named an unindicted co-conspirator in the Holy Land Foundation case. Several members were sent to prison for many years.

Wael Jalaidan ran the MSA chapter at the University of Arizona. Later, Jalaidan went on to help Osama bin Laden found al-Qaeda. This terrorist also worked closely with the parents of Huma Abedin's friend and patron, Abdullah Omar Naseef, in establishing the Rabita Trust, another organization that was labeled a terrorist organization under the United States law due to its funding of al-Qaeda.

Huma Abedin, as reported by Gaffney and McCarthy, was listed from 1996 to 2008 as an assistant editor of the *Journal of Muslim Minority Affairs* with a worldwide circulation that is published by her mother's Institute of Muslim Minority Affairs. Her name appeared during seven of those years alongside that of Abdullah Omar Naseef, the Muslim Brotherhood's and al-Qaeda´s financial supporter. When the United States government designated Naseef as a sponsor of terrorism in 2003, her name was removed from the IMMA Journal. Abedin speaks English, Arabic, and Urdo.

Anwar al-Awlaki, the al-Qaeda operative who was killed by a U.S. drone in Yemen, was the leader of the MSA chapter at Colorado State University during the 1990s.

During the years that Huma Abedin was active in the Muslim Brotherhood front organization, the MSA, at the chapter in George Washington University, she was working as an assistant editor of the journal of the Institute of Muslim Minority Affairs. First Lady Hillary Clinton hired Huma Abedin. She was initially hired as an unpaid intern and later as a member of the White House staff. Hillary Clinton kept Huma Abedin as a member of her staff when she became a United States senator from New York.

The alarming close relationship of Huma Abedin with Hillary and Bill Clinton and Barack Obama

Later, Abedin worked from 2007 to 2008 in the presidential campaign of Senator Hillary Clinton. Michelle Cottle wrote in the August 13, 2007 issue of the *New York Magazine* that "Huma Abedin, Hillary's beautiful enigmatic body person spends nearly every waking minute with Hillary and so she has the best sense of her daily routine." Others have stated that when someone called Hillary Clinton, the telephone was usually answered by Huma Abedin. Both were and still are very close.

When Hillary Clinton became Secretary of State, she appointed Huma Abedin, her longtime assistant, to the position of Deputy Chief of Staff. In that position, Abedin continued to work closely with Secretary Clinton and became her advisor on Muslim affairs. Former President Bill Clinton, Secretary of State Hillary Clinton, or President Barack Obama was bothered by the long standing association with the Muslim Brotherhood and Muslim Brotherhood's front organizations of Huma Abedin and her family. Abedin, as well as other Muslim Brotherhood connected individuals, were instrumental in changing the United States foreign-policy with respect to the Middle East and the Muslim Brotherhood government in Egypt, Libya, and Tunisia.

These Islamists have also been instrumental in making major changes in the manuals that describe Islam and are used to train personnel by the Pentagon, the FBI, and the Department of Homeland Security. Instructors who taught our personnel about Islam were fired or transferred if they did not comply with the information given in the rewritten manuals.

Any information critical of Islam or the oppressive Shariah law was purged from the manuals. Information and freedom of speech suppression is the first step to dominate and conquer Western countries pushed by Islamic supremacists. Regrettably, they were quite successful in our nation under the leadership of pro-Muslim or hidden Muslim president Barack Obama.

Barack Obama even allowed radical Islamists to write his own speeches at the White House. Several high-ranking retired two-star and three-star generals and four-star admirals as well as high-ranking government officials of the George W. Bush administration were appalled and denounced the rewriting of these manuals and the ever increasing infiltration in the Obama regime of the Muslim Brotherhood and other radical Islamists.

The then-President Obama celebrated during each of his eight years in office in the White House the end of Ramadan with an Iftar dinner. This is the dinner that breaks the day of fasting of Ramadan. During the Iftar dinner celebrated at the White House on August 10, 2012, Obama said the following: "Huma is an American patriot, and an example of what we need in this country, more public servants with her sense of decency, her grace and her generosity of spirit. So, on behalf of all Americans, we thank you so much."

Conclusion

It is appalling and shameful that the mainstream media continues to cover up the work of Hillary Clinton with operatives of the Muslim Brotherhood and that of her closest assistant Huma Abedin. The failure to tell the truth about Hillary Clinton and her body woman and closest adviser Huma Abedin seriously endangers our national security. The media needs to tell the truth regarding Hillary Clinton's connections to the terror group of the Muslim Brotherhood.

It is quite concerning and appalling that both Obama and Hillary Clinton have completely ignored the well-documented ties of Huma Abedin and her entire family to the Muslim Brotherhood and its supremacist agenda for conquering our nation and establishing Shariah law in the land of the free and home of the brave. Dr. Saleha Abedin, the mother of Huma Abedin, is paid by the Saudi government to advocate and spread Shariah law in non-Muslim countries like America as well as its diabolical Wahhabi Islamic religion. This writer finds it incomprehensible that the alarming professional and family associations of Huma Abedin were not investigated by the State Department. How in the world did she ever receive the security clearance needed to work closely with then-Secretary of State Hillary Clinton?

Obviously, the hiring of this terror-linked woman, as well as the criminal negligence, lies, and cover-up at Benghazi by Hillary Clinton made the former first lady and secretary of state unfit to be elected president of the United States. Hillary Clinton stole the nomination for president from Marxist Senator Bernie Sanders as Donna Brazile indicated in her book *Hacked*. As far as the Muslim Brotherhood is concerned, this writer believes that there is no difference between

Hillary Clinton and Barack Obama since it is obvious that both allowed radical Islamists to infiltrate our government.

The news media must break the conspiracy of silence and expose the damage done to our national security by Huma Abedin and her mentor and patron, Hillary Clinton, by changing our foreign policy in favor of the Muslim Brotherhood and allowing many Islamic supremacists to come to our country. Obama wrote a secret and classified Presidential Directive 11 where he said that the Middle East should be given to Iran and the North of Africa to al-Qaida and the Muslim Brotherhood. Clinton and others implemented this policy in violation of multiple U.S and international laws.

It is was very sad that the FBI's criminal investigation regarding Hillary Clinton misused of her e-mail and server, revealing national security and classified information to unauthorized individuals and her allowing Huma Abedin and other staffers to use her e-mail server continues to be covered up. More than likely there was a great deal of the Obama White House and Department of Justice interference.

Hillary and Bill Clinton have been involved in numerous scandals over the years and that is why both of them have employed a top Washington lawyer, David Kendall, on a full-time basis. It is time for justice to be done regarding the corrupt Hillary Clinton. It is also time for the media to expose her top aide, the Muslim Brotherhood princess Huma Abedin, and her entire ties to the global jihad movement. Barack Obama should have been impeached and Bill and Hillary Clinton indicted for corruption a long ago.

President Donald Trump asked the Justice Department to prosecute Huma Abedin for mishandling classified documents in her private computers and some in her divorced husband's computer. Time will tell if the Justice Department prosecutes Huma Abedin and others for this criminal conduct.

CHAPTER 5

Tim Kaine's connections to communists and radicals and the Theology of Liberation

Senator Timothy "Tim" Kaine, Democrat from Virginia, was the unsuccessful candidate for Vice President of his party in 2016. After the 2016 election, Kaine said that he would run for re-election to the Senate in 2018.

Timothy Kaine was born in Kansas on February 26, 1958. He graduated from Harvard Law School. He is currently serving as Senator from Virginia. He was elected to the Senate in 2012 and was the nominee of his party for Vice President in the 2016 election.

Previously, Kaine served as governor of Virginia from 2006 to 2010. He was also chairman of the Democratic National Committee from 2009 to 2011. On July 22, 2016, Hillary Clinton announced that she had selected Tim Kaine to be her vice-presidential running mate.

Sadly, this writer discovered Tim Kaine's very radical and dangerous past associations. This explains why Obama considered him as his Vice President pick and why Clinton chose him for the same spot.

On September 12, 2016, Mark Tapson wrote an article titled "Hillary VP Pick Kaine's Radical Roots" which was published in the website *Truth Revolt*. Tapson explained that with the uncertainties regarding Hillary Clinton's health, her Vice President pick attracted more attention than usual in the 2016 presidential election.

Ken Blackwell

Ken Blackwell, ambassador to the United Nations Commission on Human Rights and a former Secretary of State of Ohio and Cincinnati Mayor, wrote an article titled "Tim Kaine's Radical Roots" which was published on the website *Hill* on September 9, 2016. Blackwell's article focuses on Kaine's "radical roots" and "Soviet sympathizing mentors."

Blackwell pointed out that Tim Kaine speaks proudly of his life-changing "mission" trip to Latin America in 1980. Conveniently left out of these stories are Tim Kaine's Soviet sympathizing mentors. In fact, "whatever Kaine's intentions, he more likely met Karl Marx than Jesus Christ while there." A very alarming picture emerges of Kaine's adventures with radicals and communist revolutionaries in the 1980s in Latin America.

Reports indicate that in Honduras Kaine adopted an interpretation of the gospel known as Marxist Catholic Liberation Theology. This is not and was not mainstream "Catholic thought." It is and was a radical Marxist-based ideology at odds with the Church, the United States, and the West but supportive of (and supported by) the Soviet Union. Sadly, since the selection of Pope Francis as leader of the Church, this Marxist-based Catholic Liberation Theology has gained new strength.

What is the Marxist Liberation Theology and why Pope Francis supports it?

Thomas D. Williams wrote an article entitled "Highest ranking core war defector: the KGB invented liberation theology" which was published by the website BWCentral.org on May 14, 2015.

Ion Mihai Pacepa was born October 28, 1928 in Bucharest, Romania.

Pacepa is a former three-star general in the Securitate, the secret police of Communist Romania, who defected to the United States in July 1978 following President Jimmy Carter's approval of his request for political asylum. He is the highest-ranking defector from the former Eastern Bloc and has written several books and news articles on the inner workings of the communist intelligence services. At the time of his defection, General Pacepa was advisor to the bloody dictator Nicolae Ceaușescu, acting chief of his foreign intelligence service, and state secretary of Romania's Ministry of Interior.

Williams explained that Ion Mihai Pacepa stated that the Theology of Liberation was the creation of the Soviet KGB as a way of bringing communism to Latin America and around the world. Williams stated that General Pacepa has been called "the Cold War's most important defector." After his defection, the Romanian totalitarian regime, under the bloody communist dictator Nicolae Ceausescu, placed "two death sentences and a $2 million bounty on his head." He pointed out that Pacepa worked more than ten years with the CIA.

General Pacepa made, what the agency described as, "an important and unique contribution to the United States." In fact, he is reported to have given the CIA "the best intelligence ever obtained on communist intelligence networks and internal security services."

Williams pointed out that the Liberation Theology has been generally understood to be a marriage of Marxism and Christianity. Pacepa wrote in his recent article that "what has not been understood is that it was not the product of Christians who pursued Communism, but of Communists who pursued Christians." Cardinal Joseph Ratzinger, future Pope's Benedict XVI, in his role as doctrinal watchdog, called Liberation Theology a "singular heresy" and a "fundamental threat" to the Church.

General Pacepa further explained that he learned details of the involvement of the KGB with the Liberation Theology from Soviet General Aleksandr Sakharovsky, the chief foreign intelligence adviser of Romania, who later became head of the Soviet espionage service, the PGU. In 1959, General Sakharovsky went to Romania, together with Soviet Premier Nikita Khrushchev, for what would become known as "Khrushchev's six-day vacation." According to General Ion Mihai Pacepa, Soviet leader Nikita Khrushchev "wanted to go down in history as the Soviet leader who had exported communism to Central and South America." Khrushchev selected Romania since it was the only Latin country in the Soviet bloc and provided an ideal vehicle to Latin America because of some similarity of language and culture. Cuba was selected first.

Fidel Castro and Nikita Khrushchev supported Liberation Theology as a way to infiltrate communists in the Catholic Church.

General Pacepa pointed out that the theology of liberation was not merely infiltrated by the KGB. This theology was actually invented by Soviet intelligence services. Pacepa said that "The movement was born in the KGB, and it had a KGB-invented name: liberation theology." According to General Aleksandr Sakharovsky, during those years, the KGB liked to use the name liberation for the communist insurgencies throughout the world. Thus, the name theology of liberation was coined.

Mihai Pacepa wrote that the National Liberation Army of Colombia (FARC), created by the KGB with help from Fidel Castro; the National Liberation Army of Bolivia, created by the KGB with help from Ernesto "Che" Guevara; and the Palestine Liberation Organization (PLO), created by the KGB with help from Yasser Arafat, were "liberation" movements born at the Lubyanka — the headquarters of the KGB in Moscow, Soviet Union.

Pacepa explained that the liberation theology was born of a 1960s top-secret "Party-State Dezinformatsiya Program." It was approved by Aleksandr Shelepin, the chairman of the KGB, and by Politburo member Aleksey Kirichenko, who coordinated the Communist Party's international policies. The program ordered that "the KGB take secret control of the World Council of Churches (WCC) based in Geneva, Switzerland, and use it as cover for converting liberation theology into a South American revolutionary tool." The KGB knew that the WCC was the largest international ecumenical organization after the Vatican, representing some 550 million Christians of various denominations throughout 120 countries.

According to Pacepa, the KGB established an intermediate international religious organization called the Christian Peace Conference (CPC), headquartered in Prague. Its main objective "was to bring the KGB-created Liberation Theology into the real world." He explained that "The new Christian Peace Conference was managed by the KGB and was subordinated to the venerable World Peace Council, another KGB creation, founded in 1949 and by then also headquartered in Prague." In his work with the Soviet bloc intelligence community, Pacepa managed the Romanian operations of the World Peace Council (WPC).

Pacepa wrote the following: "In 1968 the KGB-created Christian Peace Conference, supported by the world-wide World Peace Council, was able to maneuver a group of leftist South American bishops into holding a Conference of Latin American Bishops at Medellín, Colombia. In spite of the fact that the Conference's objective was to seek solutions to poverty, its undeclared goal was to recognize a new religious movement encouraging the poor to rebel against the 'institutionalized violence of poverty,' and to recommend the new movement to the World Council of Churches for official approval. The Medellin Conference achieved both goals. It also bought the KGB-born name Liberation Theology." Pacepa stated the following: "I recently glanced through priest Gustavo Gutiérrez's book, *A Theology of Liberation: History, Politics, Salvation* (1971), and I had the feeling that it was written at the Lubyanka. No wonder he is now credited with being the founder of Liberation Theology."

Six years after Pacepa's defection to the United States, the Vatican issued the first of two very strong critiques of liberation theology under the guidance of Cardinal Joseph Ratzinger and His Holiness Pope John Paul II. The Vatican also warned that the theologies of liberation generate "a disastrous confusion between the 'poor' of the Scripture and the 'proletariat' of Marx." In so doing, it said, "they pervert the Christian meaning of the poor, and they transform the fight for the rights of the poor into a class fight within the ideological perspective of the class struggle." Pacepa concluded his article by saying the following: "Liberation theology was deliberately designed to undermine the Church and destabilize the West by subordinating religion to an atheist political ideology for its geopolitical gain."

Even though Pope Francis has said that he is not a Marxist and that he is opposed to the Marxist Liberation Theology followed by radical communist priests, nuns, bishops, and cardinals, his actions betray his statements. Historian Roberto Bosca at the Austral University in Buenos Aires said that Pope Francis supported Liberation Theology's preferential option for the poor, although "in a non-ideological fashion." Before becoming Pope, Cardinal Jorge Mario Bergoglio of Buenos Aires described Liberation Theology's preferential option for the poor as part of a long Christian tradition rooted in the Gospels.

Priest Miguel D'Escoto Brockmann, age 83, was minister of Foreign Relations during the communist Sandinista regime in Nicaragua and also president of the General Assembly of the United Nations.

Pope Francis ended the punishment of this communist priest, which had been imposed by his Holiness Pope John Paul II for refusing to abandon communist politics. His Holiness John Paul II, who after his death was canonized, was a great anti-communist and an enemy of the Marxist Liberation Theology of the Catholic Church. In 1984, his Holiness Pope John Paul II punished Miguel D'Escoto for refusing to get out of politics and did not allow him to celebrate masses or offer sacraments.

It was most unfortunate that in August 2014 Pope Francis lifted the almost 30-year ban imposed by the Church on Maryknoll priest Miguel d'Escoto Brockmann that forbade him to celebrate Mass and offer sacraments. By taking this unwise action, Pope Francis sent the wrong message of tolerance and acceptance to all the communists within the Catholic Church. Unfortunately, many now believe that Pope Francis sympathizes with the Marxist Liberation Theology of the Church.

After the punishment was lifted by Pope Francis, the communist priest Miguel d'Escoto immediately attacked the late Pope John Paul II, now a saint of the Church, for "an abuse of authority." He also said that Fidel Castro is a messenger of the Holy Spirit in "the necessity of struggle" to establish "the reign of God on this earth that is the alternative to the empire."

The totalitarian Castro dictators, the late Fidel Castro and his brother Raúl Castro, were and continue to be responsible for the assassination of more than 17,000 men, women, and boys, the incarceration of over 500,000, and the dangerous journeys of tens of thousands who have escaped from Cuba in rafts and small boats, with an estimated 100,000 having perished at sea trying to reach America.

The Castro brothers are responsible for the over two million Cubans who were forced to leave the land of their birth. The serial Cuban assassin, the late Fidel Castro, was the messenger of the devil, not God!

D'Escoto belongs to the Maryknoll Missionary Congregation, which supports the Liberation Theology. Some Maryknoll nuns and priests have supported and fought with communist guerrillas in Central America.

Miguel d'Escoto was born in the United States and was ordained in New York in 1961. He became one of the strongest proponents of the Marxist Liberation Theology. He collaborated with the National Sandinista Liberation Front (Frente Sandinista de Liberación Nacional).

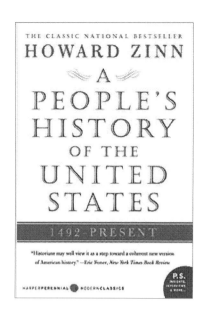

Howard Zinn is the author of a communist textbook, *A People's History of the United States*, used in many schools and universities across the United States by liberal, socialist, and Marxist teachers and professors.

When this writer was an associate professor of social studies at Florida International University, another professor recommended him to use this Marxist book in his classes. Being an anticommunist his entire life, this writer was appalled at the suggestion.

After the coming to power of the Sandinista dictator Daniel Ortega, the communist priest d'Escoto was named Minister of Foreign Relations. When Miguel d'Escoto became President of the United Nations General Assembly, he chose a communist, Howard Zinn, as his personal assistant. Zinn is the author of a communist textbook, *A People's History of the United States*, which is used in many schools and universities across the United States by liberal, socialist and Marxist teachers and professors. Pope Francis welcomed with open arms the communist Miguel d'Escoto to the Vatican.

Pope Francis also invited to the Vatican the Marxist Peruvian priest Gustavo Gutiérrez, who is usually regarded as the "Father" of Liberation Theology. Gutiérrez co-authored a book with Cardinal Gerhard Ludwig Miller, the Prefect of the Congregation for the Doctrine of the Faith. The Vatican's semiofficial newspaper, *L'Obsservatore Romano*, said at the time that the Marxist Liberation Theology should not continue to be ignored.

Rather than continuing to be not ignored, this writer believes that liberation theology needs to be completely eradicated since communism and the Catholic religion are incompatible. Our Lord Jesus Christ preached liberty from oppression and communism does the opposite.

Who are Marxist Cardinal Gerhard Ludwig Müller and Marxist priest Gustavo Gutiérrez?

Marxist Cardinal Gerhard Ludwig Müller

Gerhard Ludwig Müller was born on December 31, 1947. He is currently Cardinal and Prefect of the Congregation for the Doctrine of the Faith. On February 22, 2014, Pope Francis made him a cardinal since Müller, like him, supports the Theology of Liberation. In an interview by the German newspaper *Frankfurter Allgemeine Zeitung*, Cardinal Müller said Pope Francis "is not so much a liberation theologian in the academic sense, but as far as pastoral work is concerned, he has close ties with liberation theology's concerns."

In the 1980s Cardinal and Prefect of the Congregation for the Doctrine of the Faith and future Pope, Joseph Ratzinger, attacked liberation theology as borrowing "from various currents of Marxist thought" and said that it was a "heresy". Other Popes have stated the same thing. In 1988, priest Gerhard Ludwig Müller visited Peru and met the communist priest Gustavo Gutiérrez, regarded as the father of the movement. It was Gustavo Gutiérrez who convinced Müller of the value of Liberation Theology.

Priest Gustavo Gutiérrez, a Peruvian, is regarded as the father of the Marxist Liberation Theology.

The Marxist Müller stated the following: "Liberation Theology wants to make God's liberating actions visible in the Church's religious and social practice... It would stop being genuine theology if it were to confuse the Christian message with Marxist or other social analysis." When the German newspaper asked Müller if Liberation Theology was recognized as a form of thought on an equal footing with the other traditional forms of theology, Cardinal Müller explained that Liberation Theology's basic concern was congruent with the Gospel for the Poor – "for those on the periphery," as Pope Francis never tired of emphasizing, he said.

Cardinal Müller has been a pupil and friend of communist priest Gustavo Gutiérrez, the father of the Latin American liberation theology. Commenting on Gutiérrez, Archbishop Müller stated the following: "The theology of Gustavo Gutiérrez, independently of how you look at it, is orthodox because it teaches us the correct way of acting in a Christian fashion since it comes from true faith."

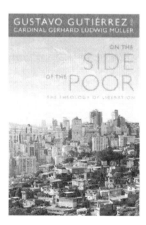

Marxist Father Gustavo Gutiérrez co-authored the book *On the Side of the Poor* with Marxist Cardinal Gerhard Ludwig Müller in 2015.

Cardinal Müller stated the following: "In my judgment, the ecclesial and theological movement that began after the Second Vatican Council in Latin America under the name 'liberation theology, is one of the most significant currents of Catholic theology in the 20th century."

The book points out that for many years the Theology of Liberation, which emerged from Latin America in the 1970's, was viewed with suspicion by the Vatican in Rome. It was the subject of a critical notification from the Vatican Congregation for the Doctrine of the Faith and many of its leading proponents were disciplined or silenced. Now, this is no longer the case thanks to Pope Francis. Cardinal Muller, a former student of communist Gutiérrez who spent many summers working in Peru, writes with deep feeling and conviction about the contributions of Liberation Theology to Church teaching--particularly in articulating the preferential option for the poor. The book explains the essential Marxist ideas of Liberation Theology.

It is extremely sad that the Vatican has been infiltrated by communists over the years. Since the cardinals selected the first pro-Muslim Marxist Pope, Pope Francis has brought to Rome several Liberation Theology advocates. This writer is convinced that Pope Francis will create a serious breach between Marxists in the Church and anticommunist priests, bishops, cardinals, and parishioners.

Gustavo Gutiérrez was born on June 8, 1928 in the Montserrat barrio of Lima, Peru. He is of Indian (Quechua) and Spanish heritage. Gutiérrez studied medicine and literature in Peru. From 1951 to 1955, he studied Psychology and Philosophy at the University of Louvain in Belgium. From 1955 to1959, Gutiérrez studied at the University of Lyons where he received his Doctor of Philosophy in Theology. At both European universities, Gutiérrez continued his studies of Karl Marx. He had studied Marxism earlier in Lima. His experiences and learning in Europe were important for the development of liberation theology.

Gustavo Gutiérrez, age 88, is a Peruvian theologian and Dominican communist priest who is considered as the father of liberation theology.

Gutiérrez wrote a book in Spanish, *La Teología de la Liberación* (*Liberation Theology History, Politics, and Salvation*), in 1972. As previously stated, Gutiérrez also co-authored the book *On the Side of the Poor* in 2015 with his Marxist friend Gerhard Ludwig Müller, Prefect of the Congregation for the Doctrine of the Faith on Liberation Theology. Pope Francis invited Gustavo Gutiérrez to the Vatican to honor him and let him write.

In 1959, at the age of 31, Gutiérrez returned to Lima and decided to infiltrate the Catholic Church as Nikita Khrushchev and Fidel Castro wanted. He was ordained as a priest that year.

The Soviet KGB had already made plans to use the Church to bring communism to Latin America and the world. As a parish priest, Gutiérrez began working as a tutor in the Department of Theology and Social Science at the Catholic University of Lima. He holds the John Cardinal O'Hara Professorship of Theology at the University of Notre Dame. This American Jesuit university gave Obama an honorary degree even though he voted in favor of abortion and infanticide and persecutes Christians. Gutiérrez has been professor at the Pontifical Catholic University of Peru and is a visiting professor at many major universities in North America and Europe.

On May 15, 2015, Mary Anastasia O'Grady wrote in the *Wall Street Journal* an article entitled "Behind the Pope's Embrace of Castro Speculation Runs from a Trojan Horse Plan to Latin American Antipathy of the U.S." She explained that priest Gustavo Gutiérrez, the Peruvian who launched liberation theology and wrote a book on this topic, was back at the Vatican. He told journalists that the Church never condemned his Marxist theology and praised Pope Francis' views on poverty. This writer knows that this Peruvian Marxist priest is lying and ignoring the fact that the two previous popes denounced and suspended many Marxist priests who were adherents of liberation theology.

O'Grady pointed out that the warmth and hospitality that Pope Francis Pope showed to Cuban dictator Raúl Castro at the Vatican baffled many Catholics. The dictator went to "Rome for a public-relations boost and Pope Francis obliged him." During their encounter, dictator Castro mocked the Catholic faith by saying "that he would return to the Church if the pope behaved." He also insulted every Cuban refugee by giving the Pope, of all things, an art piece, which depicted a migrant at prayer, done by a Cuban artist.

O'Grady wrote that Pope Francis gave the Cuban dictator a copy of his 2013 apostolic exhortation titled "The Joy of the Gospel" in which he sharply criticizes economic freedom. The Pope is preaching to the converted. As Raúl Castro puts it, "The pontiff is a Jesuit, and I, in some way, am too. I studied at Jesuit schools."

Some Catholics have tried to excuse Pope Francis's hostility toward economic freedom and market economics conveyed in his article "The Joy of the Gospel" by saying that he grew up in a corrupt state-run economy. However, O'Grady wrote an article on the *Wall Street Journal* pointing out the following: "This is nonsense. Argentine statism explicitly denounces market economics. I can only speculate about the Holy Father's Cuba views. But he is earning a dubious political reputation."

Upon becoming Pope, Francis was praised by all Marxist Catholic religious officials who practice the Marxist Liberation Theology throughout the world. They now think that they have an ally in the Vatican.

Pope Francis has implemented a complete reversal of the policy practiced by His Holiness John Paul II and Cardinal Joseph Ratzinger, now Pope emeritus Benedict XVI, who expelled thousands of priests who practiced Liberation Theology throughout the world. This is very sad and alarming!

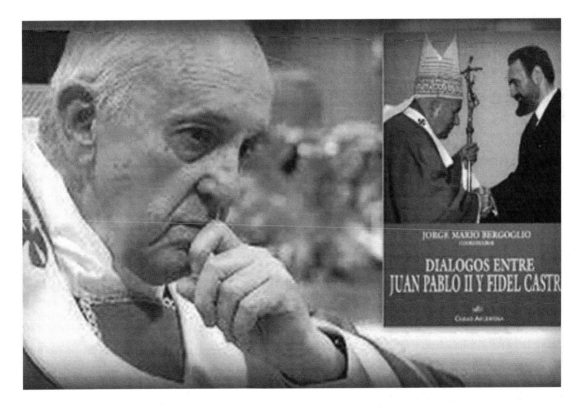

Pope Francis, who was known as Cardinal Jorge Mario Bergoglio in Argentina, is a supporter of the Marxist Liberation Theology of the Church.

Cardinal Bergoglio wrote a book, *Dialogues Between Pope John Paul II and Fidel Castro* (1998) (*Diálogos entre Juan Pablo II y Fidel Castro*), which was published in Buenos Aires, Argentina. He has always demonstrated a rare interest in the affairs of communist Cuba, even saying that the U.S. naval base at Guantánamo should be returned to Cuba. Is that in the Bible?

César Vidal, a well-known Spanish writer and journalist, wrote an article on May 18, 2015. He explained in this article that the prologue of over 50 pages of this book written by the then Cardinal Jorge Mario Bergoglio Archbishop of Buenos Aires is very revealing of the ideology of the current pope.

Cardinal Bergoglio attributed the poverty of Cuba solely to the blockade (Cuban communist term for the U.S. commercial embargo) by the United States and not to the enormous mismanagement by the bloody tyranny of the Castro brothers and its failed command communist economy. The Argentinean cardinal quoted Fidel Castro in his book, who said that the social and political system that was the closest to the social doctrine of the Catholic Church was the Cuban socialism, if only God was added to its regime! Vidal explained that anyone who read the prologue of the now Pope Francis would have no doubt that he was sympathetic to the Cuban regime.

Tim Kaine is also supportive as a Catholic of the Marxist Theology of Liberation. Ken Blackwell wrote the following: "Published documents from the Soviet and East German archives show active measures were undertaken to undermine the Vatican and the pope — key barriers to a Soviet influence in Latin America. The documents are detailed in books by former Associated Press Berlin bureau chief, John Koehler and the Mitrokhin Archive data published by Cambridge University Professor Christopher Andrew."

"Journalistic and academic research has now shown that Liberation Theology itself was quite possibly a product of a Kremlin disinformation campaign designed to undermine the Church and bring Catholic countries into the Soviet sphere. The top-ranking Soviet Bloc defector of the Cold War, Rumanian General Ion Pacepa admits that he was personally involved in the operation."

Ken Blackwell explained that Tim Kaine's political formation was not pro-American or pro-Catholic, it was pro-Soviet. Kaine adopted a Marxist ideology contrary to the institutional Catholic Church and to the United States.

Tim Kaine in Honduras and Father Jim Carney

Blackwell wrote the following: "Just how hardcore were his Jesuit teachers? Well, around the time Kaine was there, Jesuits were arrested for gunrunning, and, the next year, the Honduran government banned any more American Jesuits from coming to that country because of their left-wing activism."

"They also expelled one American-born Jesuit, who also had to leave that religious community because he was too radical even for them. That priest was Father Jim Carney, and he was the one the *New York Times* tells us that Kaine sought out across the border in Soviet-supported Nicaragua, taking a bus and then walking several miles to meet him, Blackwell added."

Father Jim Francis Carney was born in 1924.

Carney was a Jesuit priest who worked with communist rebels in Honduras and was killed in that country's armed insurgency in 1983. Father Carney was part of a 96-man unit that invaded Honduras to bring the Nicaraguan Communist revolution to that country.

"Carney was a full-blown revolutionary. A recent *New York Times* report says his death was "murky" and hardened Kaine's distrust of American involvement in the region. What isn't murky is what led to his death. In 1983, Carney was part of a 96-man unit that invaded Honduras to bring the Nicaraguan Communist revolution there too. The insurgents were Cuban and Nicaraguan trained and led by Jose Reyes Mata, Cuban-educated, and Honduras' top Marxist. Reyes Mata had previously served with Che Guevara in Bolivia."

José María Reyes Mata (1943-1983) was a Honduran revolutionary communist and a sympathizer of the bloody dictator Fidel Castro. He became both a doctor and an internationalist revolutionary in Cuba. He participated in Che Guevara's ill-fated Bolivian revolution and, after surviving prison, moved to Chile. After the 1973 Chilean coup d'état, Reyes Mata returned to Honduras and fought with Nicaraguan Sandinistas, hoping to gain their support for a Revolutionary United Front to be established in Honduras.

In 1983, he led a group of Honduran rebels from Nicaragua into Honduras. Honduran troops fought the communist rebels and Reyes Mata was captured and killed. Father Carney was captured and killed too. Tim Kaine worried about a possible participation of the United States in an extrajudicial killing of his Marxist Jesuit priest friend, but he did not seem bothered by Father Carney's participation in a Communist-sponsored insurgency and invasion of Honduras, according to Blackwell.

Blackwell pointed out that the Nicaraguan Sandinistas had been founded by KGB operative Carlos Fonseca. Eastern Bloc archives also show they were supported massively by the Cubans, Soviets, and East Germans — with guns, ammunition, money, prison building, and so forth. The Sandinistas were brutal too, with more political prisoners than any other country in the region except for Cuba.

Blackwell stated the following: "Some prisoners were executed by being hacked to death, or by being flayed alive. Others had family members sexually assaulted in front of them. By every measure, the atrocities the Sandinistas committed were far worse than the dictatorship they had replaced…Why Kaine felt the need to go Nicaragua, and meet a friend of violent revolutionaries is murky. But his relationship with Carney's successor, Father Melo, continues in the open. Melo, incidentally, wants to redistribute land throughout Latin America by 2021. Did Kaine's mentors teach him the art of Soviet disinformation — call yourself the very thing you seek to undermine and try to destroy it from within?"

Tim Kaine today

In Virginia, Tim Kaine ran as a moderate and governed as a liberal. As governor of Virginia, Kaine appointed operatives of the Muslim Brotherhood to important positions in his state, as Obama did in the White House and elsewhere in the federal government and as Hillary Clinton did in the Department of State. Today, Kaine defines himself as a "Pope Francis" Catholic but, with respect to abortion and marriage, he opposes Pope Francis.

On the conscience rights of groups like the Little Sisters of the Poor, Kaine sided with Obama. Pope Francis sided with the Little Sisters, whom he visited in Washington a year ago to publicly show his support.

Blackwell concluded his article by asserting that Kaine's questionable Catholicism "serves neither his Church nor his country, but a Leftist political agenda" that runs "against the interests of freedom and the United States."

Conclusion

Tim Kaine, like Hillary Clinton and Barack Obama, has connections with communists and radicals. It was very fortunate that Donald Trump was elected president. Otherwise, the United States would have had a third term of Obama in the White House. Senator Kaine said he would run for reelection in 2018. Hopefully, Republicans in Virginia will nominate a strong candidate to defeat Kaine and in that way, eliminate another Marxist from the Senate.

CHAPTER 6

America Resurgent:
The Republican Party platform of 2016

"To be prepared for war is one of the most effectual means of preserving peace." President George Washington

The Republican Platform is a statement of who Republicans are and what Republicans believe as a Party. Every four years, at the Republican National Convention, delegates gather to update the Platform to address the current challenges we face as a country.

After almost eight years, the Obama administration made America a superpower in complete retreat. The allies of America did not trust the Obama administration. America's enemies were emboldened. In all of America's history, there is no parallel to what President Barack Obama and his former Secretary of State Hillary Clinton did to weaken the nation and seriously endanger its security.

Donald J. Trump was elected to the White House and he is now restoring greatness to America and improving the national security. The Republican Party Platform of 2016 is outstanding and, if implemented completely by President Trump, will make America Great and Safe again.

The Republican Party Platform of 2016 rejects the New World Order promoted by members of the globalist elite who wants to take America and other nations to a planetary government under the United Nations (U.N.), which would have disastrous consequences for the United States and the world.

The Republican Party Platform wants the Congress – the Senate through its ratifying power and the House of Representative through its power of the purse – to reject all the U.N. agreements and treaties whose long-range impact will take away the sovereignty, armed forces, currency, wealth, laws, courts, and Constitution of America. Americans will lose their freedom and liberty under a world government which is Barack Obama and Hillary Clinton wanted.

The Platform of the Republican Party strongly rejects the U.N. Agenda 21 as damaging to American sovereignty and opposes any form of U.N. global tax. It opposes any diplomatic efforts that could result in giving the United Nations unprecedented control over the internet.

The Republican Party does not accept the jurisdiction of the International Criminal Court. It supports statutory protection for U.S. personnel and officials as they act abroad to meet our global security requirements.

With regards to Cuba, the Republican Party is opposed to the series of shameful and unilateral concessions made by President Obama without a "Quid Pro Quo" or nothing in return. It supports the Helms Burton law, which sets the conditions for the lifting of trade embargo, travel, and financial sanctions.

Under the Helms Burton Law, the bloody Cuban regime is required to legalize all political parties, free all political prisoners, restore all human and civil rights, allow an independent media, and conduct free and fair internationally-supervised elections before lifting the embargo. The Republican Party renews its commitment to Cuba's courageous pro-democracy movement as the protagonists of Cuba's inevitable liberation and democratic future.

The Platform of the Republican Party addressed the situation of Venezuela. The Republican Party recognizes that Venezuela represents a gathering threat to U.S. security, a threat intensified much more under Barack Obama's watch.

Venezuela has become a narco-terrorist nation, turning into an Iranian outpost in the Western Hemisphere. The oppressive regime of Nicolás Maduro issues Venezuelan passports or visas to thousands of Middle Eastern terrorists and offers safe haven to Hezbollah trainers, operatives, recruiters, and fundraisers.

Below is part of the Republican Party Platform of 2016 dealing with foreign policy and national security issues:

"We are the party of peace through strength. Professing American exceptionalism – the conviction that our country holds a unique place and role in human history – we proudly associate ourselves with those Americans of all political stripes who, more than three decades ago in a world as dangerous as today's, came together to advance the cause of freedom...

We pledge to our servicemen and women the authority and resources they need to protect the nation and defend America's freedom. Continued vigilance, especially in travel and commerce, is necessary to prevent bioterrorism, cyber terrorism, and other asymmetric or non-traditional warfare attacks and to ensure that the horror of September 11, 2001 is never repeated on our soil.

History proves that the best way to promote peace and prevent costly wars is to ensure that we constantly renew America's economic strength. A healthy American economy is what underwrites and sustains American power. The current administration is weakening America at home through anemic growth, high unemployment, and record-setting debt. We must therefore rebuild our economy and solve our fiscal crisis. In an American century, America will have the strongest economy and the strongest military in the world...

In 1981, President Ronald Reagan came to office with an agenda of strong American leadership, beginning with a restoration of our country's military strength. The rest is history, written in the rubble of the Berlin Wall and the Iron Curtain.

We face a similar challenge today. The current Administration has responded with weakness to some of the gravest threats to our national security this country has faced, including the proliferation of transnational terrorism, continued belligerence by a nuclear-armed North Korea, an Iran in pursuit of nuclear weapons, rising Chinese hegemony in the Asia Pacific region, Russian activism, and threats from cyber espionage and terrorism. In response to these growing threats, President Obama has reduced the defense budget by over $487 billion over the next decade and fought Republican efforts to avoid another $500 billion in automatic budget cuts through a sequestration in early 2013 that will take a meat ax to all major defense programs...

Nuclear forces and missile defense imperiled

We recognize that the gravest terror threat we face today – a nuclear attack made possible by nuclear proliferation – requires a comprehensive strategy to reduce the world's nuclear stockpiles and prevent the spread of those armaments. But the United States can lead that effort only if it maintains an effective strategic arsenal at a level sufficient to fulfill its deterrent purposes, a notable failure of the Obama administration.

The United States is the only nuclear power which was not modernizing its nuclear stockpile. It took the Obama administration just one year to renege on the president's commitment to modernize the neglected infrastructure of the nuclear weapons complex – a commitment made in exchange for approval of the New START treaty. In tandem with this, the Obama administration systematically undermined America's missile defense, abandoning the missile defense bases in Poland and the Czech Republic, reducing the number of planned interceptors in Alaska, and cutting the budget for missile defense. In an embarrassing open microphone discussion with former Russian President Medvedev, Obama made clear that, if he won a second term, he intended to exercise "more flexibility" to appease Russia, which meant further undermining our missile defense capabilities. A Republican president will be honest and forthright with the American people about his policies and plans and not whisper promises to authoritarian leaders.

A twenty-first century threat: The cyber security danger

The frequency, sophistication, and intensity of cyber-related incidents within the United States increased steadily over the past decade and will continue to do so until it is made clear that a cyber-attack against the United States will not be tolerated. The Obama administration's cyber security policies failed to curb malicious actions by our adversaries, and, no wonder, for there was no active deterrence protocol. The deterrence framework was overly reliant on the development of defensive capabilities and was unsuccessful in dissuading cyber-related aggression. The United States cannot afford to risk the cyber-equivalent of Pearl Harbor.

An America that leads: The Republican national security strategy for the future

We will honor President Reagan's legacy of peace through strength by advancing the most cost-effective programs and policies crucial to our national security, including our economic security and fiscal solvency. To do that, we must honestly assess the threats facing this country, and we must be able to articulate candidly to the American people our priorities for the use of taxpayer dollars to address those threats…In order to deter aggression from nation-states, we must maintain military and technical superiority through innovation while upgrading legacy systems including aircraft and armored vehicles. We must deter the threat posed by rogue aggressors with the assurance that justice will be served through state-of-the-art surveillance, enhanced special operations capabilities, and unmanned aerial systems…

Honoring and supporting our veterans: A sacred obligation

America has a sacred trust with our veterans, and we are committed to providing them and their families with care and dignity. This is particularly true because our nation's warriors are volunteers, who served from a sense of duty. The work of the department of veteran's affairs – with a staff of 300,000 – is essential to meet our obligations to them: providing health, education, disability, survivor, and home loan benefit services and arranging memorial services upon death.

Sovereign American leadership in international organizations

Since the end of World War II, the United States, through the founding of the United Nations and NATO, has participated in a wide range of international organizations which can, but sometimes do not, serve the cause of peace and prosperity. While acting through them, our country must always reserve the right to go its own way. There can be no substitute for principled American leadership.

The United Nations remains in dire need of reform, starting with full transparency in the financial operations of its overpaid bureaucrats. As long as its scandal-ridden management continues, as long as some of the world's worst tyrants hold seats on its Human Rights Council, and as long as Israel is treated as a pariah state, the U.N. cannot expect the full support of the American people.

The United Nations Population Fund has a shameful record of collaboration with China's program of compulsory abortion. We affirm the Republican Party's long-held position known as the Mexico City Policy, first announced by President Reagan in 1984, which prohibits the granting of federal monies to non-governmental organization that provide or promote abortion.

Under our Constitution, treaties become the law of the land. So, it is all the more important that the Congress – the Senate through its ratifying power and the House through its appropriating power – shall reject agreements whose long-range impact on the American family is ominous or unclear…To shield members of our Armed Forces and others in service to America from ideological prosecutions overseas, the Republican Party does not accept the jurisdiction of the International Criminal Court. We support statutory protection for U.S. personnel and officials as they act abroad to meet our global security requirements.

Protecting human rights

To those who stand in the darkness of tyranny, America has always been a beacon of hope, and so it must remain. That is why we strongly support the work of the U.S. Commission on International Religious Freedom, established by Congressional Republicans to advance the rights of persecuted peoples everywhere. It has been shunted aside by the current Administration at a time when its voice more than ever needs to be heard… A Republican administration will return the advocacy of religious liberty to a central place in our diplomacy.

America's generosity: International assistance that makes a difference

Americans are the most generous people in the world. Apart from the taxpayer dollars our government donates abroad, our foundations, educational institutions, faith-based groups, and committed men and women of charity devote billions of dollars and volunteer hours every year to help the poor and needy around the world. This effort, along with commercial investment from the private sector, dwarfs the results from official development assistance, most of which is based on an outdated, statist, government-to-government model, the proven breeding ground for corruption and mismanagement by foreign kleptocrats. Limiting foreign aid spending helps keep taxes lower, this frees more resources in the private and charitable sectors, whose giving tends to be more effective and efficient.

Foreign aid should serve our national interest, an essential part of which is the peaceful development of less advanced and vulnerable societies in critical parts of the world. Assistance should be seen as an alternative means of keeping the peace, far less costly in both dollars and human lives than military engagement.

Combating human trafficking

As we approach the 150th anniversary of the Emancipation Proclamation, issued by the first Republican President Abraham Lincoln, we are reminded to be vigilant against human bondage in whatever form it appears. We will use the full force of the law against those who engage in modern-day forms of slavery, including the commercial sexual exploitation of children and the forced labor of men, women, and children…

Promoting a free marketplace of ideas: Public diplomacy

International broadcasting of free and impartial information during the Cold War kept truth and hope alive in the captive nations. Today, Radio Free Europe/Radio Liberty and Radio/TV Marti do the same in other lands where freedom is unknown or endangered. We support these essential extensions of American values and culture and urge their expansion in the Middle East. Recognizing the vital role of social media in recent efforts to promote democracy, we support unrestricted access to the Internet throughout the world to advance the free marketplace of ideas.

Strengthening ties in the Americas

We will resist foreign influence in our hemisphere. We thereby seek not only to provide for our own security, but also to create a climate for democracy and self-determination throughout the Americas.

The current administration has turned its back on Latin America, with predictable results. Rather than supporting our democratic allies in the region, the president has prioritized engagement with our enemies in the region. Venezuela represents an increasing threat to U.S. security, a threat which has grown much worse on the current president's watch. In the last three years, Venezuela has become a narco-terrorist state, turning it into an Iranian outpost in the Western hemisphere. The current regime issues Venezuelan passports or visas to thousands of Middle Eastern terrorists offering safe haven to Hezbollah trainers, operatives, recruiters and fundraisers.

Alternatively, we will stand with the true democracies of the region against both Marxist subversion and the drug lords, helping them to become prosperous alternatives to the collapsing model of Venezuela and Cuba.

We affirm our friendship with the people of Cuba and look toward their reunion with the rest of our hemispheric family. The anachronistic regime in Havana which rules them is a mummified relic of the age of totalitarianism, a state-sponsor of terrorism. We reject any dynastic succession of power within the Castro family and affirm the principles codified in U.S. law as conditions for the lifting of trade, travel, and financial sanctions: the legalization of political parties, an independent media, and free and fair internationally-supervised elections. We renew our commitment to Cuba's courageous pro-democracy movement as the protagonists of Cuba's inevitable liberation and democratic future. We call for a dedicated platform for the transmission of Radio and TV Marti and for the promotion of Internet access and circumvention technology as tools to strengthen the pro-democracy movement. We support the work of the Commission for Assistance to a Free Cuba and affirm the principles of the Cuban Adjustment Act of 1966, recognizing the rights of Cubans fleeing Communism.

The war on drugs and the war on terror have become a single enterprise. We salute our allies in this fight, especially the people of Mexico and Colombia. We propose a unified effort on crime and terrorism to coordinate intelligence and enforcement among our regional allies, as well as military-to-military training and intelligence sharing with Mexico, whose people are bearing the brunt of the drug cartels' savage assault.

Our Canadian neighbors can count on our close cooperation and respect. As soon as possible, we will reverse the current Administration's blocking of the Keystone XL Pipeline so that both our countries can profit from this vital venture and there will no need for hemispheric oil to be shipped to China.

Advancing hope and prosperity in Africa

PEPFAR, President George W. Bush's Plan for AIDS Relief, is one of the most successful global health programs in history. It has saved literally millions of lives. Along with the Global Fund to fight AIDS, tuberculosis and malaria, another initiative of President Bush, it represents America's humanitarian commitment to the peoples of Africa, though these are only one aspect of our assistance to the nations of that continent. From Peace Corps volunteers teaching in one-room schools to U.S. Seabees building village projects, we will continue to strengthen the personal and commercial ties between our country and African nations...

U.S. leadership in the Asian-Pacific community

We are a Pacific nation with economic, military, and cultural ties to all the countries of the oceanic rim, from Australia, the Philippines, and our Freely Associated States in the Pacific Islands to Japan and the Republic of Korea. With them, we look toward the restoration of human rights to the suffering people of North Korea and the fulfillment of their wish to be one in peace and freedom. The United States will continue to demand the complete, verifiable, and irreversible dismantlement of North Korea's nuclear weapons programs with a full accounting of its proliferation activities...

South Asia

We welcome a stronger relationship with the world's largest democracy, India, both economic and cultural, as well as in terms of national security. We hereby affirm and declare that India is our geopolitical ally and a strategic trading partner. We encourage India to permit greater foreign investment and trade. We urge protection for adherents of all India's religions...The working relationship between our two countries is a necessary, though sometimes difficult, benefit to both, and we look toward the renewal of historic ties that have frayed under the weight of international conflict...

Taiwan and China

We salute the people of Taiwan, a sound democracy and economic model for mainland China. Our relations must continue to be based upon the provisions of the Taiwan Relations Act. America and Taiwan are united in our shared belief in fair elections, personal liberty, and free enterprise...If China were to violate those principles, the United States, in accord with the Taiwan Relations Act, will help Taiwan defend itself. We praise steps taken by both sides of the Taiwan Strait to reduce tension and strengthen economic ties. As a loyal friend of America, Taiwan has merited our strong support, including free trade agreements status, as well as the timely sale of defensive arms and full participation in the World Health Organization, International Civil Aviation Organization, and other multilateral institutions.

We will welcome the emergence of a peaceful and prosperous China, and we will welcome even more the development of a democratic China. Its rulers have discovered that economic freedom leads to national wealth. The next lesson is that political and religious freedom leads to national greatness. The exposure of the Chinese people to our way of life can be the greatest force for change in their country. We should make it easier for the people of China to experience our vibrant democracy and to see for themselves how freedom works. We welcome the increase in trade and education alliances with the United States and the opening of Chinese markets to American companies.

The Chinese government has engaged in a number of activities that we condemn: China's pursuit of advanced military capabilities without any apparent need; suppression of human rights in Tibet, Xinjiang, and other areas; religious persecution; a barbaric one-child policy involving forced abortion; the erosion of democracy in Hong Kong; and its destabilizing claims in the South China Sea. Our serious trade disputes, especially China's failure to enforce international standards for the protection of intellectual property and copyrights, as well as its manipulation of its currency, call for a firm response from a new Republican administration.

Europe

The West has been the bulwark of democracy and freedom, providing hope and faith to the oppressed around the globe. Our historic ties to the peoples of Europe have been based on shared culture and values, common interests and goals. Their endurance cannot be taken for granted, especially in light of the continent's economic upheaval and demographic changes. Ensuring the continued vitality of our political alliance with Europe through NATO will require effort and understanding on both sides of the Atlantic. We honor our special relationship with the United Kingdom and appreciate its staunch support for our fight against terrorism worldwide...

Russia

The heroism – and the suffering – of the people of Russia over the last century demand the world's respect. As our allies in their Great Patriotic War, they lost 28 million fighting Nazism. As our allies in spirit, they ended the Soviet terror that had consumed so many millions more. We do have common imperatives: ending terrorism, combating nuclear proliferation, promoting trade, and more. To advance those causes, we urge the leaders of their government to reconsider the path they have been following: suppression of opposition parties, the press, and institutions of civil society; unprovoked invasion of the Republic of Georgia, alignment with tyrants in the Middle East; and bullying their neighbors while protecting the last Stalinist regime in Belarus. The Russian people deserve better, as we look to their full participation in the ranks of modern democracies…

Our unequivocal support of Israel

Israel and the United States are part of the great fellowship of democracies who speak the same language of freedom and justice, and the right of every person to live in peace. The security of Israel is in the vital national security interest of the United States; our alliance is based not only on shared interests, but also shared values… The United States seeks a comprehensive and lasting peace in the Middle East, negotiated between the parties themselves with the assistance of the U.S., without the imposition of an artificial timetable.

The challenges of a changing Middle East

We recognize the historic nature of the events of the past two years – the Arab Spring – that have unleashed democratic movements leading to the overthrow of dictators who have been menaces to global security for decades. In a season of upheaval, it is necessary to be prepared for anything…On the other hand, radical elements like Hamas and Hezbollah must be isolated because they do not meet the standards of peace and diplomacy of the international community. Iran's pursuit of nuclear weapons capability threatens America, Israel, and the world. A continuation of its failed engagement policy with Iran will lead to nuclear cascade. In solidarity with the international community, America must lead the effort to prevent Iran from building and possessing nuclear weapons capability.

Conclusion

President Trump was elected president. Everyone must work hard to help Donald Trump implement the Republican Party platform. Republicans must unite to preserve America as the shining light and the beacon of freedom of the world.

CHAPTER 7

Donald J. Trump, the law and order candidate

Donald Trump spoke at a rally in West Bend, Wisconsin on August 16, 2016 on how to restore law and order, improve the economy, and keep America safe from Islamic terrorists.

As a result of the constant agitation and demonstrations in cities throughout America where many radical members of Black Lives Matter ask their followers to attack police, a significant number of police officers have been assassinated or seriously wounded. Its leaders have meet with the radical and former community agitator President Barack Obama and Valery Jarrett in the White House. Hillary Clinton and Gary Johnson, who ran for president on the Libertarian Party ticket, also endorse and support this domestic terror group.

In his August 16, 2016 speech from West Bend, Wisconsin, then Republican presidential nominee Donald Trump discussed ways to deal with lawlessness, improve the economy, and keep

America safe from Islamic terrorists. Trump started by praising law enforcement officers as he always does in his rallies. He condemned the riots that were happening in Wisconsin and stated that law and order must be restored. He said that what America needs is more police officers, especially in the poorest communities.

Black Lives Matter is a domestic terrorist organization led by Marxists and anarchists who have been promoting violence and assassinations of police officers throughout the nation for the past two years.

The Republican candidate said that the war against police must end and accused Hillary Clinton of being against law enforcement. He also said that the Democratic Party has failed the African American community and called upon black voters to support him.

Below is the transcript of Donald Trump's speech:

"We are at a decisive moment in this election. Last week, I laid out my plan to bring jobs back to our country. Yesterday, I laid out my plan to defeat Radical Islamic Terrorism. Tonight, I am going to talk about how to make our communities safe again from crime and lawlessness.

Let me begin by thanking the law enforcement officers here in this city, and across this country, for their service and sacrifice in difficult times. The violence, riots and destruction that have taken place in Milwaukee is an assault on the right of all citizens to live in security and peace.

Law and order must be restored. It must be restored for the sake of all, but most especially the sake of those living in the affected communities. The main victims of these riots are law-abiding African-American citizens living in these neighborhoods. It is their jobs, their homes, their schools and communities which will suffer as a result. There is no compassion in tolerating lawless conduct. Crime and violence is an attack on the poor, and will never be accepted in a Trump Administration…

The war on our police must end. It must end now. The war on our police is a war on all peaceful citizens who want to be able to work and live and send their kids to school in safety. Our job is not to make life more comfortable for the rioter, the looter, the violent disruptor. Our job is to make life more comfortable for the African-American parent who wants their kids to be able to safely walk the streets…

Hillary Clinton-backed policies are responsible for the problems in the inner cities today, and a vote for her is a vote for another generation of poverty, high crime, and lost opportunities. I care too much about my country to let that happen. We all care too much about our country to let that happen…

It's easy for Hillary Clinton to turn a blind eye to crime when she has her own private security force. I believe all Americans, not just the powerful, are entitled to security. Hillary Clinton has had her chance. She failed. Now it's time for new leadership. The Hillary Clinton agenda hurts poor people the most.

There is no compassion in allowing drug dealers, gang members, and felons to prey on innocent people. It is the first duty of government to keep the innocent safe, and when I am President I will fight for the safety of every American – and especially those Americans who have not known safety for a very, very long time…

The Democratic Party has taken the votes of African-Americans for granted. They've just assumed they'll get your support and done nothing in return for it. It's time to give the Democrats some competition for these votes, and it's time to rebuild the inner cities of America – and to reject the failed leadership of a rigged political system…

Jobs, Safety, Opportunity, and Fair and Equal Representation

We reject the bigotry of Hillary Clinton which panders to and talks down to communities of color and sees them only as votes, not as individual human beings worthy of a better future.

She doesn't care at all about the hurting people of this country, or the suffering she has caused them. The African-American community has been taken for granted for decades by the Democratic Party. It's time to break with the failures of the past – I want to offer Americans a new future. It is time for rule by the people, not rule by special interests.

Every insider, getting rich off of our broken system, is throwing money at Hillary Clinton. The hedge fund managers, the Wall Street investors, the professional political class. It's the powerful protecting the powerful. Insiders fighting for insiders. I am fighting for you.

When we talk about the insider, who are we talking about? It's the comfortable politicians looking out for their own interests. It's the lobbyists who know how to insert that perfect loophole into every bill. It's the financial industry that knows how to regulate their competition out of existence. The insiders also include the media executives, anchors and journalists in Washington, Los Angeles, and New York City, who are part of the same failed status quo and want nothing to change…

The leadership class in Washington D.C., of which Hillary Clinton has been a member for thirty years, has abandoned the people of this country. I am going to give the people their voice back. Think about it.

The people opposing our campaign are the same people who have left our border open and let innocent people suffer as a result. The people opposing our campaign are the same people who have led us into one disastrous foreign war after another. The people opposing our campaign are the same people who lied to us about one trade deal after another. Aren't you tired of a system that gets rich at your expense? Aren't you tired of big media, big businesses, and big donors rigging the system to keep your voice from being heard? Are you ready for change? Are you ready for leadership that puts you, the American people, first? That puts your country first? That puts your family first…

The Democratic Party has run nearly every inner city in this country for 50 years, and run them into financial ruin. They've ruined the schools. They've driven out the jobs. They've tolerated a level of crime no American should consider acceptable. Violent crime has risen 17% in America's 50 largest cities last year. Killings of police officers this year is up nearly 50 percent. Homicides are up more than 60% in Baltimore. They are up more than 50% in Washington, D.C.

This is the future offered by Hillary Clinton. More poverty, more crime, and more of the same. The future she offers is the most pessimistic thing I can possibly imagine. It is time for a different future. Here is what I am proposing.

First, on immigration. No community in this country has been hurt worse by Hillary Clinton's immigration policies than the African-American community. Now she is proposing to print instant work permits for millions of illegal immigrants, taking jobs directly from low-income Americans. I will secure our border, protect our workers, and improve jobs and wages in your community. We will only invite people to join our country who share our tolerant values, who support our Constitution, and who love all of our people.

On trade, I am going to renegotiate NAFTA, stand up to China, withdraw from the TPP, and protect every last American job.

On taxes, I am going to give a massive tax cut to every worker and small business in this country, bring thousands of new companies and millions of new jobs onto our shores – and make it very difficult for our businesses to leave.

I am going to reform our regulations, so jobs stay in America, and new businesses come to America to hire workers right here in Milwaukee. Every policy my opponent has sends jobs overseas. I am going to bring trillions in new wealth back to the United States. On education, it is time to have school choice, merit pay for teachers, and to end the tenure policies that hurt good teachers and reward bad teachers. We are going to put students and parents first.

Hillary Clinton would rather deny opportunities to millions of young African-American children, just so she can curry favor with the education bureaucracy. I am going to allow charter schools to thrive, and help young kids get on the American ladder of success: a good education, and a good-paying job.

On crime, I am going to support more police in our communities, appoint the best prosecutors and judges in the country, pursue strong enforcement of federal laws, and I am going to break up the gangs, the cartels and criminal syndicates terrorizing our neighborhoods. To every lawbreaker hurting innocent people in this country, I say: your free reign will soon come crashing to an end.

On healthcare, we are going to get rid of Obamacare – which has caused soaring double-digit premium increases – and give choice to patients and consumers. Aetna, just today, announced they are dropping out – as are many of the major insurance companies.

On government corruption, I am going to restore honor to our government. We've seen the corruption of Hillary Clinton, the mass e-mail deletions, the pay-for-play at the State Department, the profiteering, the favors given to foreign corporations and governments at your expense. We've seen a former Secretary of State lie to Congress about her illegal e-mail scheme, risk innocent American lives, and bring dishonor onto our government.

In my Administration, I am going to enforce all laws concerning the protection of classified information. No one will be above the law. I am going to forbid senior officials from trading favors for cash by preventing them from collecting lavish speaking fees through their spouses when they serve.

We are going to make this a government of the people once again. This is our chance to take back power from all the people who've taken it from you. The reason you see the establishment media lining up behind my opponent is because they are scared that you, with your vote, can take away their power and return it to your family and community.

These are tough times. But I know we can make American Greater Than Ever Before. To do this, we are going to need a fighter in the White House. I will be your fighter.

To defeat crime and Radical Islamic Terrorism in our country, to win trade in our country, you need tremendous physical and mental strength and stamina. Hillary Clinton doesn't have that strength and stamina. She cannot win for you.

Most importantly, she has bad judgment. Bad judgment on terrorism, bad judgement on foreign policy, bad judgment on trade. The only individuals she's ever delivered for is her donors – not the people.

I've said it before, and I'll say it again. My opponent asks her supporters to repeat a three-word pledge. Her pledge reads: "I'm With Her." I choose to recite a different pledge. My pledge reads: "I'm With You – the American people."

I will fight to ensure that every American is treated equally, protected equally, and honored equally. We will reject bigotry and hatred and oppression in all of its forms, and seek a new future of security, prosperity and opportunity – a future built on our common culture and values as one American people.

I am asking for your vote, so I can be your champion in the White House. We will once again be a country of law and order, and a country of great success. To every parent who dreams for their children, and to every child who dreams for their future, I say these words to you tonight: I'm with you, I will fight for you, and I will win for you.

Conclusion

This was a brilliant speech by Donald J. Trump. He explained how he was going to improve the economy creating new jobs everywhere and, in the inner cities, discarding free trade agreements that create unemployment, fighting Islamic terrorism, stopping illegal immigration, and restoring law and order. Trump criticized Hillary Clinton's massive corruption, catering to special interests and donors as well as trading favors for lots of cash.

CHAPTER 8

Trump held a rally at the Bayfront Park in Miami

The author led the pledge of allegiance to the flag and spoke at the Trump Rally held at Bayfront Park in downtown Miami a few days before the presidential election.

On November 2, 2016, Donald J. Trump held a rally at Bayfront Park in Miami, which was attended by approximately 3,000 people, before heading off to campaign events in Orlando and Pensacola. Former Hialeah Mayor and Chairman of the Trump campaign in Miami-Dade County Julio Martinez served as Master of Ceremony. He introduced a pastor for a prayer and then this writer, who had been invited by the Trump campaign to say a few words and do the Pledge of Allegiance to the Flag.

Remarks by Frank de Varona at the Trump Rally at Bayfront Park

"I am a veteran of the Bay of Pigs Invasion. I also serve as Office Manager to the Donald J. Trump for President Campaign Republican National Committee Office in West Dade.

Since we lost our birthplace to a Marxist totalitarian regime, the Cuban exile community in every election has looked for the most conservative candidate available with the best chance of winning. In this election, Donald Trump represents that candidate. The country cannot continue to go in the direction that it was been going for the last eight years.

The Democratic Party has injured, at every opportunity, the cause of Cuba's freedom and the return to self-government. We remember the Mariel exodus that took place under the Carter administration, a Democrat. Elián González, the son of a Cuban immigrant who drowned bringing her son to freedom, was returned to Castro's Cuba under a Clinton White House.

And now, Obama legitimizes the totalitarian government in Cuba to the eyes of the world and provides economic assistance, investment, and tourism in exchange for nothing. President Obama is working to undermine or eliminate the embargo.

For these reasons, the Cuban exile community feels naturally betrayed by the Democratic Party. It is a no-brainer that Mr. Trump is far more conservative than Mrs. Clinton.

Since we have arrived in the United States, in the last 20 years especially, the Democratic Party has been inimical to our values and to the cause of Cuban freedom. We still dream of achieving freedom and self-determination in a free Cuba."

This writer asked those in the audience who are members of the Brigade 2506, veterans of the Bay of Pigs Invasion, and the Cuban resistance to rise and be recognized. Lastly, he gave the pledge of allegiance to the flag.

Metro Dade Commissioner Bruno Barreiro, Republican National Committee Co-Chairwoman Sharon Day, Florida Attorney General Pam Bondi, and President of the National Republican Party Reince Priebus spoke to the audience under Miami's very hot sun.

Donald J. Trump's speech at the rally

Trump supporters from Miami-Dade and Broward counties began lining up at sunrise at the entrance of Bayfront Park in Miami as voters were anxious to see the Republican Party nominee. Donald J. Trump entered the stage just after noon and stated the following:

"Thank you women for Trump, Hispanics for Trump, Cubans for Trump, and Blacks for Trump. With your votes we can beat the system. The rigged system. So show up early and vote. The polls are saying we are going to win Florida. Don't believe it! Get out there and vote.

Pretend we're slightly behind. We don't want to blow this!" He said that the nation is down to just six days before the general election day and he urged all Republicans to go out and vote, if they have not already voted.

The Republican Party candidate said one of his top priorities would be get rid of the Affordable Care Act. "Real change begins with immediately replacing ObamaCare," Trump told the crowd. He said more than 90% of Florida's counties will lose ObamaCare insurers next year. He said companies are leaving, doctors are quitting and deductibles are going through the roof, "it wasn't supposed to be like this."

Trump repeatedly denounced Hillary Clinton over the scandal involving the e-mails she received in an illegal private unsecured server and the renewed investigation by the FBI. "Real change also means restoring honesty to our government. The FBI is reopening an investigation into crooked Hillary Clinton," said the Republican nominee. Trump called the FBI's investigation the biggest thing since Watergate.

Trump said it has been reported that the FBI is now looking into Clinton's entire inner circle and many of the things she has done over the years. "It's about time. Remember, it's a rigged system. She wants to blame everyone else for her mounting legal troubles but she really has no one to blame but herself," he said.

Barack Obama lied again when he said he did not know of the existence of Clinton secret and unsecured server since he sent e-mails to Clinton in her secret server. Both have violated the law. It has now been learned that several foreign intelligence services hacked Clinton's e-mails that had confidential and Special Access Program (SAP) e-mails. The SAP e-mails are the most secret and are sent to less than 10 individuals in the executive branch and none in Congress. Clinton received the list of spies the CIA has in foreign nations. Due to her incredibly irresponsible behavior, these spies have been probably captured and executed.

Trump again called out the media for biased reporting, saying they wanted "crooked Hillary." "This is not about me. It's about all of you and our magnificent movement to make America Great Again," said Trump. The GOP candidate said that as president he would go into the poorest communities and work on a national plan for revitalization. Trump said that if he were elected, he was going to create jobs unlike his predecessor.

Trump stated the following:" "America has lost 70,000 factories since China entered the World Trade Organization. Another Bill and Hillary backed disaster. We are living through the greatest jobs theft in the history of the world. Our jobs are going to Mexico, our jobs are going to other countries. China and others are making our products. A Trump administration will stop the jobs from leaving America." Trump criticized Obama and said that "President Obama should be working on jobs instead of campaigning for crooked Hillary."

Trump also promised to build a wall between the U.S. and Mexico to control immigration. "As Secretary of State, Hillary Clinton allowed dangerous aliens to go free because their countries would not take them back. Countless innocent Americans have been killed by illegal aliens," he said. Trump promised that he would take measures to take care of veterans, provide school choices, and end to Common Core.

This writer appears with Ivan Sanchez, Vice President of the Cuban Patriotic Council, and Antonio D. Esquivel, President of the Cuban Patriotic Council, at the Trump rally in Miami.

"We are asking for the vote of every American who believes in truth and justice, not money and power," said the Republican nominee. Trump said he was proud to receive the endorsement of the Bay of Pigs Brigade 2506 Veteran Association. He said, "I see all these signs Cubans for Trump. Love Cubans," Trump said.

The Republican candidate said he would help the African Americans and stated the following: "The inner cities are very sad. The crime is horrible. The education is terrible. And you can't get a job. Unbelievable numbers. We are doing great with the African-American community. We are doing great with the Hispanic community and the lines are 4, 5, and 6 blocks long. They've never seen anything like it."

Conclusion

Candidate Donald J. Trump was right, and he won Florida with 60% support from Cuban Americans.

CHAPTER 9

Cuban Americans Won Florida for Trump

Miguel Saavedra, leader of Vigilia Mambisa, an anti-communist organization, and a group of Cuban Americans showed their support for Donald Trump in front of the popular Versailles Restaurant in the Little Havana neighborhood of Miami.

The shameful Cuban policy of Barack Obama and its support by Hillary Clinton helped deliver Florida to Donald J. Trump

Mary Anastasia O'Grady wrote an article titled "Will Obama's Cuba Policy Lose Florida for Clinton?" which was published in the *Wall Street Journal* on November 8, 2016 before the election results came in. Barack Obama and Hillary Clinton did not understand the real sentiment of Cuban American voters in Florida and other states in the nation. They relied on false polls saying that the majority of Cuban Americans hated the embargo and wanted to restore diplomatic relations with the oppressive regime in Havana. Both of them forgot that Cuban Americans from both political parties have been elected and reelected to the Senate and the House of Representatives because they opposed Obama's unilateral concessions to the Cuban bloody regime with nothing in return as well as diplomatic recognition.

Democratic candidates should stop taking advice from a handful of very wealthy businessmen who are clueless with respect to the real pulse of the Cuban-American community. These very rich individuals and their globalist friends want to make Cuba the China of the Caribbean to enrich the U.S. multinationals that do not care about human and civil rights in Cuba.

O'Grady concluded her article by stating, "No matter who wins on Tuesday, the next president will have to clean up this Cuba mess. Decent Cuban-Americans on both sides of the aisle want answers." Hopefully, Trump would do just that as he said in various rallies.

Ileana Ros-Lehtinen, Marco Rubio, Carlos Curbelo, and Mario Diaz-Balart were reelected in Florida and all opposed the shameful Cuba policy of Obama and Clinton.

Obama's decisions on Cuba and his series of outrageous, illegal, and unilateral concessions, which have almost destroyed the commercial embargo against Cuba, did not help Hillary Clinton. These concessions made by Obama were in violation of the Helms Burton Law. Hillary Clinton said at a rally held at Florida International University that, if elected president, she was going to end completely the embargo with an (illegal) executive order. These actions made patriotic Cuban Americans angry and that is why most of them voted for Donald J. Trump. The vast majority of Cuban Americans in Florida and other states have opposed the series of unilateral concessions that Obama has given the bloody regime in Havana with no "Quid Pro

Quo" or nothing in return, except for more oppression against the suffering Cuban people of the island.

Oppenheimer, who wrote a series of columns severely criticizing Mr. Trump, was correct in pointing out how the policy on Cuba by Obama and its support by Clinton hurt the Democratic Party nominee. This writer, a veteran of the Bay of Pigs invasion, was asked by the Trump campaign at its headquarters in Trump Tower to do a short video on what Mr. Trump should do regarding the Cuban bloody regime if elected president. The short video of about nine minutes was sent to New York along with two even shorter videos done by Bay of Pigs veteran Eli César and Army veteran Jorge Rodriguez. Juan Fiol filmed the videos and sent them to New York.

Shortly after the videos were sent, Mr. Trump spoke in Texas. On August 6, 2016, Donald J. Trump said that, if elected president, he was going to impose severe economic sanctions on the Cuban regime unless the Castro brothers conduct a democratic election in the island. Similar statements were said by the Republican candidate at the James Knight Center in Miami and other places.

Donald Trump spoke at the Museum and Library of the Bay of Pigs Veteran Association Brigade 2506 in Miami.

Donald J. Trump spoke on his desire for a free democratic Cuba at the Museum and Library of the Bay of Pigs Veteran Association Brigade 2506 in Miami.

On October 25, 2016, Donald J. Trump met with a group of veterans of the Bay of Pigs who invaded Cuba in 1961 soon after their Association endorsed him for president. It was the first time that the Brigade 2506 had endorsed a candidate for president in 55 years. Mr. Trump thanked the veterans for their endorsement and praised them for their fight over many years for the freedom of Cuba calling them heroes. He said the Assault Brigade 2506 members were "true fighters for freedom and were committed in defense of human rights and justice." Mr. Trump also praised the Ladies in White who are frequently beaten and arrested in Cuba each time they walk to churches. The Republican nominee denounced Hillary Clinton as well as President Obama for shutting their eyes to the human rights violations in Cuba. He said that Obama has done a terrible deal with Cuba and if Hillary Clinton were to be elected she would do one even worse.

This writer had the great honor of being selected to present Donald J. Trump with the Brigade coat of arms together with Brigade President Humberto Díaz-Argüelles and another Brigade member.

Obama's diplomatic recognition and unilateral concessions to Cuba resulted in Hillary Clinton's loss of Florida

Mike Gonzalez, who is a senior fellow at the Heritage Foundation, wrote an article titled "Obama's Legacy Drive Lost Florida for Clinton" which was published in the *New York Post* on November 12, 2016. Gonzalez wrote the following: "The evidence is mounting that President Obama's overzealous defense of his opening Cuba gambit cost Hillary Clinton the state of Florida. That misstep could end up wiping out most of the president's carefully curated legacy achievements…Obama lifted limits on the import of cigars and rum, and then ordered our ambassador to the United Nations to abstain from a vote condemning the U.S. economic embargo on Cuba. That U.N. directive was especially galling. President Obama was, in fact, venting his frustration with Congress for not lifting the embargo upon his command — which Congress has the right to refuse to do — by letting the world body mock U.S. law unopposed."

The Cuban-American community in Miami and throughout the entire state was furious and decided to support Donald Trump, who promised that he would end relations unless Raúl Castro began democratic reforms. A New York Times-Siena poll, headlined "Cubans Come Home to Trump," confirmed that all this was enough to add almost 20 percentage points to Trump's support among Cuban-Americans.

An analysis of Cuban-American precincts put the support for Trump at 60% or higher. Hillary Clinton ended up losing the election to Trump by the razor-thin margin of 125,000 votes out of more than 9 million casted in a state where Cuban-Americans number more than a million. Florida with its 29 votes was decisive in winning the White House for Mr. Trump.

The West Dade Trump Victory Office

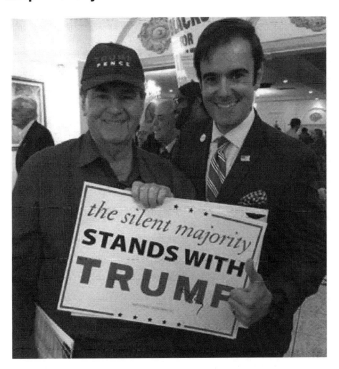

This author and John Pugh, Deputy State Political Director and South Florida Strategist of the Trump campaign in Florida, at the rally of Governor Mike Pence in Miami.

This author was appointed Office Manager of the West Dade Trump Victory Office by John Pugh, who was in charge of several counties in South East Florida. This office was one of 29 offices in Florida and one of four in Miami-Dade County.

This writer recruited over 200 volunteers. They worked very hard knocking several thousand doors, making several thousand phone calls, covering over 30 Early Voting precincts, and waiving Trump signs and passing flyers at precincts on Election Day.

Other volunteers stood in front of Sedano and Publix supermarkets and pharmacies seeking citizens who had not registered to vote and filling out voter registration forms and absentee ballot request forms. Over 7,000 were registered to vote by the three Miami-Dade County Trump offices. Many sign waiving events were held all over Miami-Dade where bumper stickers and yard signs were given away by Trump supporters. The West Dade Office gave thousands of wall and yard signs and bumper stickers to individuals who came to the office.

The author and a group of his volunteers at the West Dade Trump Victory Office

These offices in Miami-Dade County were assisted by Cuban Americans Jaime Figueras and Alex Garcia, who were full-time employees of the Florida Republican Party. These individuals worked extremely hard.

Juan Fiol and West Dade Office volunteers were participating in a sign waiving event in front of Versailles Restaurant in Miami.

One of our volunteers, Cuban American Juan Fiol, was frequently interviewed in radio and television as were Cuban-American lawyer Lorenzo Palomares and former Hialeah Mayor Julio Martinez, who served as Chairman of the Miami-Dade Trump campaign. Jaime Fiol organized four events at Las Vegas Restaurant, one for each presidential debate and a very special one on Election Day.

This writer appears with his daughter, Irene de Varona; grandson, Danny Linares de Varona; and West Dade Office volunteers George Garces, Ana Maria Lamar, and Lucy de Varona.

West Dade Office volunteers Barbara Grant and others at one of our events at Las Vegas Restaurant.

This writer and his wife Haydée are celebrating Donald J. Trump's victory with about 300 West Dade Office volunteers and volunteers from other offices at Las Vegas Restaurant in Miami on Election Day.

Conclusion

Cuban-Americans in Florida and Cuban-American volunteers in the Trump campaign were crucial in helping Donald J. Trump win the White House. Florida with its 29 electoral votes was decisive in winning the White House for Donald J. Trump.

CHAPTER 10

Trump supports a strong military

Donald Trump and Hillary Clinton answered questions from Matt Lauer at the NBC Commander-in-Chief Forum.

The NBC Commander-in-Chief Forum

On September 7, 2016, Donald Trump and Hillary Clinton participated in the NBC Commander-in-Chief Forum dealing with America's role in the world. The two presidential candidates argued that their experience better prepared them to make the life-or-death decisions required of the Commander-in-Chief.

Michael C. Bender and Colleen McCain Nelson wrote an article titled "Trump, Clinton Clash on Security" which was published on the *Wall Street Journal* on September 8, 2016. Bender and Nelson said that Trump stated that building a "great" company and traveling the world prepared him to make the difficult decisions required of a Commander-in-Chief, such as sending U.S. soldiers into harm's way. The Republican candidate for president said that "The main thing is I have great judgment I know what's going on, I've called so many of the shots." The forum came at a time when Americans ranked national security as a higher priority than in any other presidential election in the past. Bender and Nelson explained that moderator Matt Lauer questioned both candidates on issues that have dogged their campaigns: Clinton's use of a private e-mail server and her handling of classified information and Trump's apparent admiration of Russian President Vladimir Putin.

Hillary Clinton defended her handling of classified material by saying she took that responsibility seriously and acknowledging that using her own server was "a mistake" that she would not repeat. "I make no excuses for it," she said. "It was something that should not have been done."

A navy veteran asked a critical question to Clinton and, as usual, she lied by saying that none of the e-mails she received in her illegal private server was marked classified. The FBI said that several e-mails were clearly identified as classified. In addition, she received many SAP, Special Access Program, e-mails that only a few receive in the executive branch and none in Congress since these are the most sensitive of all the top secrets. Hillary Clinton's mishandling of top secrets and SAP e-mails have seriously endangered our national security. More than likely all enemy countries now have that information, including the list of our spies and the activities of drones.

Bender and Nelson said that Donald J. Trump stood by his controversial comments, saying that it was an honor to be praised by Putin. The GOP nominee has called Russia's president a strong leader and Trump noted that Vladimir Putin has an 82% approval rating in his own country. "I think when he calls me brilliant, I'll take the compliment. The GOP candidate said that he disagrees with the political system of Russia. Trump explained the following: "I think under the leadership of Barack Obama and Hillary Clinton, the generals have been reduced to rubble. They have been reduced to a point where it's embarrassing for our country."

Former New York City Mayor and U.S. Attorney Rudy Giuliani said that he believes Hillary Clinton violated 13 federal laws

Former New York City Mayor and U.S. Attorney Rudy Giuliani said on January 20, 2016 that he does not think there is any way Hillary Clinton should be able to avoid facing an indictment for the "secretive and highly classified" government information found on the private e-mail server she used while secretary of state. Giuliani told the *Fox and Friends* program the following: "There are 13 violations of federal law that she arguably committed, this is about as clear as it gets. It is a crime to negligently handle top secret material. Now, how can she put all this out there and not get proceeded against by the government."

Giuliani told *FoxNews* that Clinton "destroyed 34,000 e-mails" and that he would have argued, as a prosecutor, "that's evidence of a guilty knowledge . . . the destruction is evidence of guilty knowledge, evidential principle that you can use against someone when they're in a situation where who knows what's on those 34,000 e-mails." Later, it was discovered that her staff destroyed with a hammer or threw away many of the cell phones and tablets which were not given to the FBI.

Trump speech at the Union League of Philadelphia

The Republican presidential candidate wants a strong military to protect America from its enemies and vowed to rebuild the armed forces of America after the neglect and massive budget cuts of the Obama administration. Trump wants to increase the Army to 540,000 soldiers from its current level of 480,000 and expand the Marine Corps from 23 to 36 battalions, the Navy from 276 to 350 ships, and the Air Force from 1,100 to 1,200 fighter aircraft. All of these recommendations are supported by the report of the bipartisan defense panel. Trump advocates an improved ballistic missile defense system. If elected, he said he was going to request Congress to repeal the "sequester" provision of the 2011 Budget Control Act. "As soon as I take office, I will ask Congress to fully eliminate the defense sequester and will submit a new budget to rebuild our military," Trump said.

Donald J. Trump delivered an important speech on national security and national defense at the Union League of Philadelphia on September 6, 2016.

Donald J. Trump declared that he would implement a realistic foreign policy. He delivered a powerful critique of Obama-Clinton foreign policy. Trump stated the following: "Let's look back at the Middle East at the very beginning of 2009. Libya was stable. Syria was under control. Egypt was ruled by a secular president who was an ally of the United States. Iraq was experiencing a reduction in violence…. Iran was being choked off by economic sanctions… Unlike my opponent, my foreign policy will emphasize diplomacy, not destruction. Hillary Clinton's legacy in Iraq, Libya, and Syria has produced only turmoil and suffering and death."

Trump portrayed Hillary Clinton as "reckless" and "totally unfit to be our Commander-In-Chief." He questioned her fitness for the Oval Office and said the following: "Sometimes it seemed like there wasn't a country in the Middle East that Hillary Clinton didn't want to invade, intervene in, or topple. She's trigger-happy and very unstable when it comes to war… Hillary Clinton has taught us really how vulnerable we are in cyber hacking. It's probably the only thing that we've learned from Hillary Clinton."

Ashley Parker and Alan Rappeport wrote an article titled "Donald Trump Vows to Bolster Nation's Military Capacities" which was published in the *New York Times* on September 7, 2016.

They said that Trump pointed out that America's adversaries were preparing to capitalize on perceptions of American weakness around the world and vowed to improve the nation's military capabilities and defense spending. "Our adversaries are chomping at the bit," Trump said. "We want to deter, avoid and prevent conflict through our unquestioned military strength," he added.

Parker and Rappeport said that Trump called on allies to pay more for American military protection. "Early in my term, I will also be requesting that all NATO nations promptly pay their bills," he said. "Only five NATO countries, including the United States, are currently meeting their minimum requirements to spend 2 % of GDP on defense," he added.

Donald Trump said he would "make government leaner and more responsive to the public." He suggested reducing the size of the federal government through "responsible workforce attrition." He also accused the Obama administration of agreeing to bad deals with Iran. "Our president lied to us," Donald Trump said of President Obama, saying the nuclear deal with Iran put the country "on a path to nuclear weapons."

Parker and Rappeport pointed out that Trump's fiercest criticism was directed at Hillary Clinton. The reporters stated the following: "Trump accused her of being complicit in an array of foreign policy stumbles, and of deleting her e-mails as secretary of state to hide her participation in a pay for play scandal of granting access to Clinton Foundation donors."

Trump released a letter signed by 88 high-ranking retired military officials endorsing his campaign

Donald Trump's campaign released a letter on September 6, 2016 signed by 88 retired military leaders endorsing his presidential candidacy, including four four-star generals and 14 three-star flag officers. Two of the leaders of the group were retired military Major General Sidney Shachnow and Rear Admiral Charles Williams. Both praised Donald J. Trump and declared that "the 2016 election affords the American people an urgently needed opportunity to make a long-overdue course correction in our national security posture and policy."

The 88 retired military leaders who endorsed Trump's presidential campaign stated in their letter the following: "For the past eight years, America's armed forces have been subjected to a series of ill-considered and debilitating budget cuts, policy choices and combat operations that have left the superb men and women in uniform less capable of performing their vital missions in the future than we require them to be. America's military, we believe that such a change can only be made by someone who has not been deeply involved with, and substantially responsible for, the hollowing out of our military and the burgeoning threats facing our country around the world. For this reason, we support Donald Trump's candidacy to be our next Commander-in-Chief. For this reason, we support Donald Trump and his commitment to rebuild our military, secure our borders, to defeat our Islamic supremacist adversaries, and restore law and order domestically. We urge our fellow Americans to do the same."

The former U.S. military leaders were sharply critical of the Obama administration's national security and foreign policy. They warned that "enemies have become emboldened, sensing weakness and irresolution in Washington" and that "in our professional judgment, the combined effort is potentially extremely perilous."

Donald Trump called the endorsements a "great honor". He stated the following: "I thank each of them for their service and their confidence in me to serve as Commander-In-Chief. Keeping our nation safe and leading our armed forces is the most important responsibility of the presidency. Under my administration, we will end the weak foreign policy of the last eight years, rebuild our military, give our troops clear rules of engagement and take care of our veterans when they come home. We can only Make America Great Again if we ensure our military remains the finest fighting force in the world, and that's exactly what I will do as president."

Conclusion

Once elected president, Donald J. Trump proved that he is an outstanding Commander-in-Chief. Hillary Clinton demonstrated that she was unfit to be president in multiple ways, such as by committing treason, dereliction of duty, and criminal negligence in Benghazi and the war in Libya; mishandling classified e-mails in an illegal private server; destroying incriminating evidence by erasing thousands of e-mails and destroying multiple devices; doing favors to donors who gave tens of millions to the corrupt Clinton Foundation while serving as secretary of state, and committing perjury in her many testimonies in Congress. She should be indicted for all her crimes.

CHAPTER 11

Putin took advantage of Obama's weakness and the military balance of power has shifted in Russia's favor

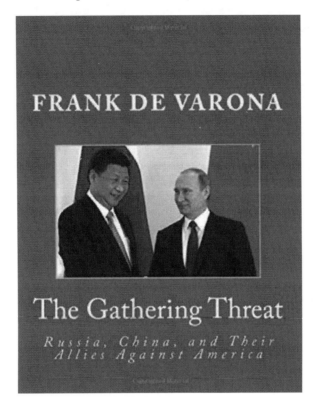

This writer wrote the book *The Gathering Threat of Russia, China, and Their Allies Against America* in 2016.

President Donald Trump has begun to reverse the military weakness left by Barack Obama's disastrous eight-year presidency. President Trump has increased the budget of the Pentagon and turbo charge the economy which has grown more than 3% in the last two quarters. Without a strong economy the United States will cease to remain a superpower.

President Barack Obama made the United States a superpower in complete retreat in the world. The enemies of America, including Russia, China, Iran, North Korea, Venezuela, Cuba, and radical Islam, did not fear President Obama. The allies of America did not trust or respect Obama to defend them from their enemies. Obama and Congress severely cut the Pentagon's budget for a number of years while the enemies of America significantly improved their Armed Forces and nuclear arsenals with new weapons.

Russia annexed part of Georgia, Ukraine's Crimean Peninsula, and occupied parts of eastern Ukraine. China has built military bases on islands in the South China Sea that belong to U.S. allies. China claims illegally as its territory 90% of the South China Sea and claims islands that belong to Japan in the East China Sea.

Both China and Russia are harassing U.S. aircrafts and Navy ships around the world. These nations and their allies represent an existential threat to America. President Trump understands why America needs to drastically increase the budget of the Pentagon and improve the nuclear arsenal and missiles to match or exceed the better-equipped missiles and other weapons of Russian and Chinese. Anti-ballistic missile defense must be improved. Failure to do so will severely endanger the national security of the United States.

President Trump needs to improve the military quickly to prevent a possibly devastating Russian-Chinese surprise nuclear attack upon America as weakness invites aggression from those who rule these two nations. This writer revealed how Russia and China are developing hypersonic glide vehicles to defeat the increasingly sophisticated anti-ballistic missile (ABM) defense of the United States and its allies. These two enemy nations are ahead in the development of hypersonic weapons.

The nation that achieves mastery of hypersonic weapons first will overturn the principles of how wars are waged. The development of hypersonic weapons is similar to the development of nuclear arms. America is in great danger as the balance of military power has shifted against it. The only area in which America has superior weapons is space. Russia and China are working diligently to develop weapons superior to America in space, such as the hypersonic glide vehicles.

The book *The Gathering Threat of Russia, China, and Their Allies Against America* (2016) explains how Vladimir Putin has frequently threatened nuclear war against America and its allies. It is very important for Americans to understand that Russia is the number one geopolitical enemy of America. Equally important is to know that Russia is using jihadists throughout the world as a weapon against the United States and the West. China, Russia, North Korea, Iran, and other nations are waging successful cyber warfare against America and stealing its industrial and military secrets.

Unfortunately, the Obama-Clinton administration did very little to stop the cyber warfare from our enemies. Another serious threat to America is an electromagnetic pulse (EMP) event provoked either from an atomic bomb exploded high in space in the middle of America or from solar flares that would destroy all electronics and the electrical grid of America. This catastrophe would result in the death 80% to 90% of Americans in a few months due to starvation. Obama failed to protect the nation and as result America, at all levels, is unprepared for an EMP nuclear attack or an EMP provoked by solar flares despite their catastrophic consequences. President Trump needs to quickly spend whatever is necessary to protect the electronics and the electrical grid of America.

Russia has violated with impunity the New START nuclear agreement

The Department of State has reported that, while Obama ordered America nuclear warhead stocks to be reduced sharply, Russia increased its deployed nuclear warheads over the past six months under a strategic arms reduction treaty. Since April 2016 Russia has added 61 new nuclear warheads. Incredibly, Obama ordered the Pentagon during the same period to reduce our deployed nuclear warheads by 114. Obviously, this ill-advised action has increased the disparity between America and Russia and has seriously endangered our national security.

Bill Gertz wrote an article titled "Russia Adds Hundreds of Warheads under Nuclear Treaty" which was published in the *Washington Free Beacon* website on October 4, 2016. The reporter explained that Russia's nuclear warhead increases since 2011 suggest that Putin does not intend to cut its nuclear forces and will abandon the New START arms treaty as part of a major nuclear buildup.

Vladimir Putin did not respect Barack Obama and now Russia has more nuclear warheads than America.

Gertz pointed out that Mark Schneider, a former Pentagon nuclear weapons specialist now with the National Institute for Policy, said that, in his opinion, it is highly unlikely that Russia intends to comply with New START. Schneider said the following: "Moscow appears to be on a path to doubling its warheads. With or without New START, Russian deployed strategic nuclear warheads are likely to increase to 3,000 by 2030. I think it is also clear that the Obama administration has an unannounced program to implement Obama's proposed one-third reduction in strategic nuclear forces from the New START level unilaterally. A strategic military balance that existed in 2011 when the treaty was approved has now been reversed by Russian increases and U.S. cuts. In 2011, the United States had a lead of 263 deployed warheads, we are now 429 deployed warheads below Russia. The Russians will think this is quite important. It could impact Putin's willingness to take risks."

Shamefully, the Obama administration continued a program of unilateral nuclear disarmament despite promises by President Obama to modernize and maintain U.S. nuclear forces as long as strategic dangers were present. This is happening as Russia and America have increased tensions over Syria. The Russian action followed the State Department's decision to cut off talks with Russia on Syria.

Gertz wrote that the nuclear buildup is raising new fears that Putin is planning to break out of New START treaty limits rather than comply with the accord. Russian forces have deployed 249 warheads above the warhead limit set by the treaty to be reached by February 2018. Since the treaty went into effect in 2011, Russia increased its total warhead stockpile from 1,537 to 1,796 warheads, an increase of 259 warheads. At the same time, the Obama administration cut U.S. nuclear forces by 433 warheads during the same period.

It is obvious that Obama willfully and deliberately downgraded America military superiority making America a lesser superpower. I think this is treason and dereliction of duty! Why do we not hear Republicans in Congress denouncing this unilateral disarmament while our enemies are getting stronger militarily? Why is the media not writing editorials criticizing Obama's endangering of our national security? After all, if Russia and China were to attack America and defeat it in a World War III, all Democrats, Republicans, and independents would suffer alike. This is not a matter of politics but of survival.

Gertz wrote that Air Force General John E. Hyten, nominee to be the next commander of the U.S. Strategic Command, warned the Senate during a hearing in September 2016 that Russia is modernizing both its strategic and tactical nuclear weapons. General Hyten stated the following to the Senate Armed Services Committee: "It seems clear that Russia has been making large investments in its nuclear weapon programs as well as modernizing both its strategic and non-strategic nuclear weapons. In addition to advancing nuclear capabilities, Russia is emphasizing new regional and strategic approaches, and declaring and demonstrating its ability to escalate if required. Collectively, Russian development of advancing weapons capabilities and its evolving war fighting doctrine is concerning."

Gertz explained the following: "Under New START, the United States and Russia agreed to reduce deployed nuclear warheads to 1,550 warheads. Deployed land-based and submarine-launched missiles and bombers will be cut to 700. Missile launchers and non-deployed heavy bombers will be reduced to 800. While U.S. nuclear forces are very old and in need of modernization, Russian nuclear forces are being modernized. By 2020, nuclear missile submarines, land-based missiles, and bombers will be modernized, with 70 percent of the nuclear forces replaced with advanced systems, according to U.S. officials."

Russia abandoned the 2000 agreement on plutonium reduction

Russia announced on October 4, 2016 that it abandoned a 2000 agreement to reduce stockpiles of plutonium originally intended for nuclear weapons. Gertz stated that Pentagon spokesman Peter Cook said the following of the Russian rejection of the plutonium agreement, "We're disappointed with their decision."

Gertz wrote that other alarming signs of the advances of Russian nuclear weapons include intelligence reports that Moscow is expanding underground nuclear command. This is a violation of the New START treaty. Putin is also planning to double its nuclear warhead stockpiles for new multiple-warhead missiles.

Obama, who is the architect of the destruction of the United States, ignored Russia's rapid reaming and modernizing of its nuclear arsenal and forward movement of its unilateral disarmament scheme. This is dereliction of duty and treason!

Putin and Obama shared a tense handshake at the G20 meeting in China.

Current tensions between Russia and the United States

Roger Aronoff wrote an article titled "Media Judgment Corrupted by Desire to Defeat Trump" which was published in the *Accuracy in Media* website on October 5, 2016. Aronoff said that under Secretary of State Hillary Clinton there was supposed to be a reset of relations between the United States and Russia. However, the reset failed miserably. The Obama administration suspended direct contacts with Russia on halting the war in Syria after Putin violated the cease fire.

Aronoff wrote that Caroline Glick of the *Jerusalem Post* stated the following: "In exchange for saving Bashar Assad's neck and enabling Iran and Hezbollah to control Syria, Russia has received the capacity to successfully challenge U.S. power. A recent agreement between the Syrian government and Russia permits—indeed invites—Russia to set up a permanent air base in Khmeimim [Syria], outside the civilian airport in Latakia. Russian politicians, media and security experts have boasted this base will be able to challenge both the U.S. Navy and NATO. The Syrian government is currently bombarding Aleppo to get rid of rebel forces. Bashar Assad's goal is to defeat the rebel forces by destroying the sheltering civilian populations."

Aronoff said the following: "The media should be asking whether Mrs. Clinton would as president be able to improve relations with Russia given her former failures… The media should be asking key questions of Mrs. Clinton, including about her support for the disastrous, unsigned Iran deal. Not only did the Obama administration pay Iran $1.7 billion in cash as a ransom payment for four American prisoners that Iran was holding, but recent reporting has revealed that the Obama administration supported the UN lifting sanctions on the regime's Bank Sepah and Bank Sepah International on January 17."

Conclusion

It is obvious that Obama with the help of Hillary Clinton willfully and deliberately downgraded America's military superiority and made America a lesser superpower. Both weakened American power abroad. Both allowed the Muslim Brotherhood to infiltrate our government and society. This is treason and dereliction of duty! The disastrous Obama and Clinton legacies foster danger and insecurity abroad. Both have seriously endangered our national security.

President of Donald J. Trump started to reverse the immense damage done by Obama and Clinton. Donald J. Trump has begun to rebuild our military. America's survival is at stake! Americans need America to be resurgent and not America in decline!

CHAPTER 12

Trump needs to upgrade the nuclear triad to defend America from China and Russia

The United States is the only nuclear power that has not modernized its nuclear stockpile. Barack Obama, several others previous presidents, and Congress have failed to protect the national security. America's nuclear arsenal and ICBMs are obsolete. This is why China and Russia do not fear America and this is very dangerous.

China captured a U.S. Navy drone in the South China Sea

A bright yellow unmanned underwater vehicle (UUV) drone is 10 feet long. It often moves slowly and autonomously around the sea to collect data about the ocean floor and environment for weeks or months before being retrieved by U.S. Navy ships.

The website *Stratfor* published an article on December 16, 2016 titled "China captures a U.S. Navy Drone in the South China Sea." It explained that a Chinese warship seized a U.S. Navy unmanned underwater vehicle (UUV) in the South China Sea. According to several reports,

China deployed a Navy ship on December 15, 2016 to steal the U.S drone about 57 nautical miles northwest of the Philippines' Subic Bay port. This occurred just before the *USNS Bowditch* was preparing to retrieve the underwater drone. Department of Defense officials have said that the United States has requested that Beijing return the drone. The incident occurred as then President-elect Donald Trump criticized China for unfair trade, currency manipulation, and imperialism on the South China Sea.

On December 17, 2016, China stated that it had seized the drone to ensure the "safe navigation of passing ships and personnel." China said it would give it back. This was an unacceptable excuse for what was a clear violation of international law and another affront to America. On that same day, then President-elect Donald J. Trump blasted the theft of U.S. equipment and tweeted to following: "China steals United States Navy research drone in international waters-rips it out of water and takes it out of water to China in unprecedented act."

On December 15, 2016, a U.S. Navy underwater drone deployed by the *USNS Bowditch* was captured and stolen by the Navy of China resulting in a formal diplomatic protest. This incident is one of many involving China, a nation that has harassed U.S. Navy ships and aircrafts for several years during the Obama administration.

Stratfor pointed out that *USNS Bowditch* is an oceanographic survey ship. This ship is part of a 29-ship Special Mission Ship program and operates in the South China Sea. *Stratfor* pointed out the following: "The *USNS Bowditch*, a Pathfinder-class survey ship under the Naval Oceanographic Office's Maritime Sealift Command, is routinely deployed to survey and map the ocean floor. Though this mission is ostensibly civilian in nature, the data the ship collects also has useful military applications that are particularly relevant for submarine navigation. In its demand for the UUV's safe return, the United States asserted that the vehicle had been captured in international waters. The latest episode appears to be a fairly bold move on China's part."

More than likely Chinese leaders are trying to assert that 90% of the South China Seas and its reefs and islands belong to China. The Permanent Court of Arbitration recently denied that claim.

The theft occurred more than 50 nautical miles from the Scarborough Shoal, China's nearest territorial claim. The underwater mapping that the *Bowditch* drone would have been engaged in can be used to support U.S. anti-submarine operations by identifying most likely paths of submarines.

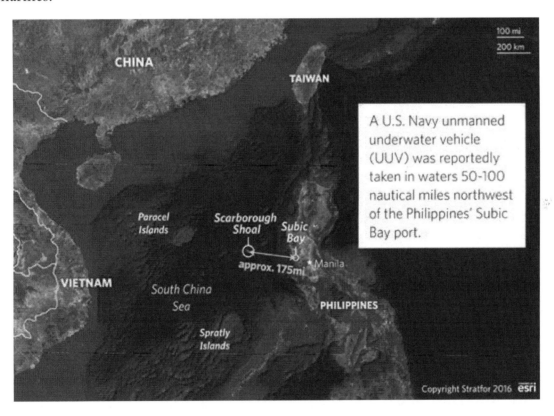

This map of the South China Sea shows where the Navy unmanned underwater vehicle (UUV) drone was captured about 800 miles from China. It was a final insult to Obama.

A serious incident between China and America occurred in April 2001. An EP-3 Navy surveillance aircraft was operating about 70 miles from Hainan Island when it was intercepted by two Chinese J-8 fighters. The collision between the EP-3 and one of the J-8s caused the death of the Chinese pilot. The EP-3 surveillance aircraft was forced to make an emergency landing on Hainan. The 24 crew members were detained and interrogated by the Chinese authorities. The Americans were eventually released.

The damaged EP-3 Navy surveillance aircraft is shown on the ground on Hainan Island.

Paul Sonne and Gordon Lubold wrote an article titled "U.S. Demands Return of Survey Drone Taken by China in South China Sea" which was published in the *Wall Street Journal* on December 16, 2016. Sonne and Lubold wrote that it was the first time Beijing has captured a U.S. drone since the Chinese took a Navy surveillance plane on Hainan Island following a midair collision on April 20, 2001. The drone is valued at approximately $150,000. It is one of many that the U.S. Navy uses around the world to collect "bathymetric data from the sea, along with data on the water's salinity, temperature and current flow."

The reporters explained the following: "The seizure of the drone marks the latest and perhaps sharpest point of tension between U.S. and Chinese military forces in and around the South China Sea, a critical trade waterway where China has built artificial islands and laid claim to a vast swath of maritime territory, to the dismay of neighbors and U.S. officials…The Chinese have installed antiaircraft weapons and other small arms on all seven of its reclaimed islands in the South China Sea. China's reclamation and militarization of the islands have raised concerns in Washington that Beijing is planning to enforce broad and disputed Chinese claims to the sea, a critical maritime hub that sees more than $5 trillion in trade transit its waters annually."

In violation of international law China has installed antiaircraft weapons and other arms on all seven islands it has built in the South China Sea. This was done despite President Xi Jinping's promise not to militarize the islands in the Spratly archipelago, where Beijing's territorial claims overlap with those of several other nations. President Donald J. Trump has said that he is ready to confront Beijing on territorial issues.

Senator John McCain, Republican from Arizona and Chairman of the Senate Armed Services Committee, denounced the Chinese government and demanded the U.S. to take action against the weaponry. He stated the following: "It appears China is intent on transforming these features into operational bases that will allow its military to project power and assert control of one of the most vital international waterways. This is unacceptable."

As usual, Obama did nothing except to ask that the drone be returned. He could have sent several Navy ships to the area to show strength. U.S. Pacific allies witnessed the weakness shown by America in dealing with the Chinese hybrid naval war. China is becoming emboldened. More serious incidents are likely be contemplated against the U.S. Navy ships and aircrafts.

Admiral Harry Harris is the commander of the U.S. Pacific Command.

Admiral Harry Harris, the head of the U.S. Pacific Command, said in a speech at an Australian think tank, the following: "The United States will not allow the shared domains to be closed down unilaterally no matter how many bases are built on artificial features in the South China Sea. We will cooperate where we can and be ready to confront where we must."

President Trump has indicated that he will take a harder line than Barack Obama toward China. He said recently that he would review U.S. commitments to Taiwan and **the one China**

policy. He also accused Beijing of building a "massive military complex" in the South China Sea.

USNS Impeccable

On March 8, 2009, the *USNS Impeccable* was 75 miles south of the island of Hainan, China, when it was followed by five Chinese ships. Two Chinese naval trawlers maneuvered close to the *USNS Impeccable* approaching it as close as 50 feet while waving Chinese flags and ordering the *Impeccable* to leave the area.

Two Chinese trawlers stopped directly in front of the *Impeccable*, forcing the ship to conduct an emergency halt in order to avoid collision.

The *Impeccable* sprayed water at one of the nearest Chinese ships and radioed the Chinese crews informing them of its intentions to leave the area and requesting a safe pass to travel.

When it was trying to leave the area, the two Chinese trawlers dropped pieces of wood in the *Impeccable's* path and stopped directly in front of it, forcing it to do an emergency stop to avoid a collision. Once the *Impeccable* got under way, the crew aboard one of the trawlers used a grappling hook to try to snag the *Impeccable's* towed sonar array.

One Chinese crewman waves a Chinese flag while another one uses a grappling hook to try to snag the *USNS Impeccable's* towed sonar array.

The United States filed a formal complaint following the incident stating that, under international law, the U.S. military can conduct activities "in waters beyond the territorial sea of another state without prior notification or consent" including in an exclusive economic zone of another country. The U.S. diplomatic note stated that "The unprofessional maneuvers by Chinese vessels violated the requirement under international law to operate with due regard for the rights and safety of other lawful users of the ocean."

China's Foreign Ministry responded stating that the Pentagon's complaint that five Chinese vessels had harassed the *Impeccable* was "totally inaccurate." This claim was disputed by several reports that have been released, all stating that the *Impeccable* was interfered numerous times, both while operating in the area and when attempting to leave.

On December 19, 2016, the *Wall Street Journal* wrote an excellent editorial titled "China Tests U.S. Resolve" regarding the efforts of China to illegally challenge the freedom of navigation in the South China Sea. Below is the editorial:

"China's theft of a U.S. Navy underwater drone in full view of the *USNS Bowditch* on Thursday is a telling episode. While Beijing agreed to return the drone over the weekend, along with bluster that the U.S. had hyped the heist, the Chinese navy's actions were a deliberate provocation. China is testing U.S. resolve to maintain freedom of navigation in international waters that Beijing illegally claims as its own.

Some think the theft is a response to Donald Trump's decision to take a congratulatory call from Taiwan's President. But the People's Liberation Army has pulled these stunts before. In April 2001, a PLA pilot tried a dangerous intercept with a U.S. spy plane in international airspace. He misjudged the distance, losing his own life and causing the U.S. plane to make an emergency landing in China. Beijing released the crew and plane after a 10-day standoff.

In March 2009, the PLA began a harassment campaign against the *USNS Impeccable* in international waters. After several days of dangerous maneuvers by five Chinese ships and one plane, the Chinese maritime militia tried to steal a towed sonar array from the ship. Whether China today is responding to Mr. Trump or offering a final insult to President Obama is beside the point because the drone theft is part of a larger Chinese pattern.

China's behavior shows its intention to intimidate its neighbors and establish hegemony in East Asia. In recent weeks the PLA air force has flown practice bombing missions, with fighter escorts, near the Japanese island of Okinawa and around Taiwan. The Japanese air force scrambled to intercept Chinese planes 571 times last year, up from 96 in 2010. Recently China has deployed military forces on disputed shoals in the South China Sea, contradicting President Xi Jinping's promise to Mr. Obama.

China objects to U.S. Navy and Air Force transits near these shoals. The Obama Administration promised to carry out such missions regularly but then restricted the Pentagon to a handful. That sent a message that the U.S. can be intimidated from exercising its rights.

The drone theft may be a Chinese warning that the U.S. Navy will face harassment if a Trump Administration steps up such patrols. China is also rapidly expanding its submarine fleet, as an asymmetric response to U.S. surface dominance, and undersea drones map the ocean floor and test currents and sonar for submarine passage and detection.

The Chinese interception occurred about 50 nautical miles from the U.S. base at Subic Bay in the Philippines. The recent anti-American rants by Philippine President Rodrigo Duterte may also have encouraged China to hope that an episode at sea could drive a larger rift between Manila and Washington. The Navy will have to expect more such interference.

All of this is occurring as Mr. Trump is signaling his intention to take a tougher line with China, at least initially, as he renegotiates the bilateral economic and strategic relationship. Mr. Trump's precise goals aren't clear, but one promise he's likely to fulfill is rebuilding the U.S. Navy to reinforce America's Pacific presence.

Chinese leaders may think these shows of force will intimidate the Trump Administration the way they did Mr. Obama. But they are likely to have the opposite effect. Mr. Trump doesn't separate economic from security issues, and the Chinese are playing with fire."

Russia is America's number one geopolitical enemy

Both China and Russia are harassing U.S. aircrafts and Navy ships around the world. These two nations and their allies represent an existential threat to America.

The nation needs to drastically increase the budget of the Pentagon and improve the nuclear arsenal and missiles to match or exceed the better-equipped Russian and Chinese missiles and other weapons. Anti-ballistic missile defense must be improved. Failure to do so will severely endanger the national security of the United States.

Vladimir Putin did not respect Barack Obama and now Russia has more nuclear warheads than America.

It might provoke a devastating combined Russian-Chinese surprise nuclear attack upon America as weakness invites aggression from the dictators who rule those two nations. This writer revealed how Russia and China are developing hypersonic glide vehicles to defeat the increasingly sophisticated anti-ballistic missile (ABM) defense of the United States and its allies. These two enemy nations are ahead in the development of hypersonic weapons.

The nation that achieves mastery of hypersonic weapons first will overturn the principles of how wars are waged. The development of hypersonic weapons is similar to the development of nuclear arms. America is in great danger as the balance of military power has shifted against it. The only area in which America has superior weapons is in space. Russia and China are working diligently to develop weapons superior to America in space, such as the hypersonic glide vehicles.

Vladimir Putin has frequently threatened nuclear war against America and its allies. It is very important for Americans to understand that Russia is the number one geopolitical enemy of America. Equally important is to know that Russia is using jihadists throughout the world as a weapon against the United States and the West. China, Russia, North Korea, Iran, and other nations are waging successful cyber warfare against America and stealing its industrial and military secrets. Unfortunately, the Obama-Clinton administration did very little to stop the cyber warfare from our enemies.

Russia has violated with impunity the New START nuclear agreement

The Department of State reported that Russia increased its deployed nuclear warheads over the past year under a strategic arms reduction treaty as Obama ordered America nuclear warhead stocks to be reduced sharply. Since April 2016, Russia has added 61 new nuclear warheads. Incredibly, Obama ordered the Pentagon during the same period to reduce its deployed nuclear warheads by 114. Obviously, this ill-advised action simply increased the disparity between America and Russia and seriously endangered our national security.

Bill Gertz wrote an article titled "Russia Adds Hundreds of Warheads under Nuclear Treaty" which was published in the *Washington Free Beacon* website on October 4, 2016. The reporter explained that Russia's nuclear warhead increases since 2011 suggest that Putin does not intend to cut its nuclear forces and will abandon the New START arms treaty as part of a major nuclear buildup.

Gertz pointed out that Mark Schneider, a former Pentagon nuclear weapons specialist who is now with the National Institute for Policy, said that, in his opinion, it is highly unlikely that

Russia intends to comply with the New START. Schneider said the following: "Moscow appears to be on a path to doubling its warheads. With or without the New START, Russian deployed strategic nuclear warheads are likely to increase to 3,000 by 2030. I think it is also clear that the Obama administration has an unannounced program to implement Obama's proposed one-third reduction in strategic nuclear forces from the New START level unilaterally."

"A strategic military balance that existed in 2011 when the treaty was approved has now been reversed by Russian increases and U.S. cuts. In 2011, the United States had a lead of 263 deployed warheads; we are now 429 deployed warheads below Russia. The Russians will think this is quite important. It could impact Putin's willingness to take risks."

Shamefully, the Obama administration continued a program of unilateral nuclear disarmament despite his promises to modernize and maintain U.S. nuclear forces as long as strategic dangers were present. This happened as Russia and America increased tensions over Syria. Russia's actions followed the decision of the State Department to discontinue talks with this country on Syria.

Gertz wrote that the nuclear buildup is raising new fears that Putin is planning to break away from the limits of the New START treaty rather than comply with the accord. Russian has deployed 249 warheads above the warhead limit set by the treaty to be reached by February 2018. Since the treaty went into effect in 2011, Russia increased its total warhead stockpile from 1,537 warheads to 1,796 warheads, an increase of 259. At the same time, the Obama administration cut U.S. nuclear forces by 433 warheads during the same period.

It is obvious that former President Obama willfully and deliberately downgraded America's military superiority making America a lesser superpower. This was treason and dereliction of duty!

Republicans in Congress should have denounced this unilateral disarmament while the enemies of America are getting stronger militarily. The biased mainstream media did not criticize Obama's endangering our national security. After all, if Russia and China were to attack America and defeat it in a World War III, all Democrats, Republicans, and independents would suffer alike. This is not a matter of politics but of survival.

Gertz wrote that Air Force General John E. Hyten, nominee for the position of commander of the U.S. Strategic Command, warned the Senate during a hearing in September 2016 that Russia was modernizing both its strategic and tactical nuclear weapons. General Hyten stated the following to the Senate Armed Services Committee: "It seems clear that Russia has been making large investments in its nuclear weapon programs as well as modernizing both its strategic and non-strategic nuclear weapons. In addition to advancing nuclear capabilities, Russia is emphasizing new regional and strategic approaches, and declaring and demonstrating its ability to escalate if required. Collectively, Russian development of advancing weapons capabilities and its evolving war fighting doctrine is concerning."

Air Force General John E. Hyten

Gertz explained the following: "Under New START, the United States and Russia agreed to reduce deployed nuclear warheads to 1,550 warheads. Deployed land-based and submarine-launched missiles and bombers will be cut to 700. Missile launchers and non-deployed heavy bombers will be reduced to 800."

Gertz also said, "While U.S. nuclear forces are very old and in need of modernization, Russian nuclear forces are being modernized. By 2020, nuclear missile submarines, land-based missiles, and bombers will be modernized, with 70 percent of the nuclear forces replaced with advanced systems, according to U.S. officials."

Russia abandoned the 2000 agreement on plutonium reduction

Russia announced on October 4, 2016 that it had abandoned a 2000 agreement to reduce stockpiles of plutonium originally intended for nuclear weapons. Gertz said that Pentagon spokesman Peter Cook reported that, with respect to the Russian rejection of the plutonium agreement, "We're disappointed with their decision."

Gertz wrote that other alarming signs of Russian nuclear weapons advances include intelligence reports that indicate that Moscow is expanding underground nuclear command. This is a violation of the New START treaty. Putin is also planning to double its nuclear warhead stockpiles for new multiple-warhead missiles.

Obama, who was the architect of the destruction of the United States, ignored Russia's rapid reaming and modernization of its nuclear arsenal and moved forward with a unilateral disarmament scheme. This was dereliction of duty and treason!

President Trump needs to upgrade the nuclear triad to defend America from China and Russia.

The aggressive behavior by China and Russia requires a strong response. This is why it is of utmost importance that Donald J. Trump upgrades the nuclear triad to defend America from China and Russia. Fortunately, the President Trump supports a revamping of U.S. nuclear forces at an estimated cost of $500 billion. It would take several years to improve the nuclear arsenal. In the meantime, the Pentagon is developing new weapons, which are classified. The 2017 Pentagon budget consists an estimated $62.2 billion and represents 11% of the total budget. Pentagon's efforts to replace the nuclear triad of submarines, land-based missiles, and the B-21 bomber over the next decade will remain classified.

The B-21 bomber is being developed to eventually replace the B-52 of the 1950s.

Conclusion

Russia and China are committing acts of unimpeded aggression around the world. Former President Obama, with the help of Hillary Clinton when she served as Secretary of State, willfully and deliberately downgraded America's military superiority and made America a lesser superpower. Both of them have weakened American power abroad.

The disastrous Obama administration legacy fostered danger and insecurity in the world. Former Obama seriously endangered our national security. Donald J. Trump needs to reverse the immense damage done by Obama and Clinton. The policy of Obama and Clinton of unilateral nuclear disarmament must stop.

Donald J. Trump has promised to rebuild our military. He has appointed competent retired generals to the Cabinet and the White House. Only when America has the capability to wield overwhelming nuclear and military power can America deter its enemies from threatening Americans and its allies. As President Ronald Reagan said, "Freedom is no more than one generation away from extinction." Our survival is at stake! We need America to be resurgent and not to be America in decline!

CHAPTER 13

Fidel Castro, the bloody dictator, died at the age of 90

Fidel Castro died at the age of 90.

Mass murderer tyrant Fidel Castro and his assassin-in-series brother Raúl Castro almost brought nuclear war between America and the Soviet Union in 1962. Cuba was and still is an enemy of America Cuba has resulted in enormous problems to 11 American presidents. The mass-murdering regime has exerted oppressive and total control over the suffering Cuban people.

In 2016, the bloody dictator Raúl Castro, who succeeded his older brother as president of Cuba, announced on Cuban television the death of dictator Fidel Castro "with profound pain". The cause of death was not immediately disclosed. Dictator Raúl Castro confirmed the news in a brief speech stating that "The commander-in-chief of the Cuban revolution died at 10:29 pm."

The Cuban tyrannical regime observed nine days of mourning for the death of the oppressive dictator Fidel Castro. After two days of observances in Revolution Plaza in Havana, Fidel Castro's ashes were taken across the country to the city of Santiago de Cuba. The communist regime offered a final Mass for the atheist murderer. The ceremony took place on December 4, 2016 and the ashes were interred in the cemetery of Santa Efigenia.

During 47 long years, the tyrant Fidel Castro maintained an iron grip over Cuba and kept close ties with the Soviet Union, China, North Korea, Venezuela, Nicaragua, Bolivia, Iran, and other Islamic radical regimes in the Middle East. Fidel Castro inspired communist anti-American leaders throughout Latin America and other parts of the world. It provided funds and logistical support for communist insurgencies throughout the world. Cuba was, and continues to be, a terror nation and one that practices human trafficking.

From the very beginning of Fidel Castro's coming to power, revolutionary violence and intimidation became daily event. First, the summary executions without due process of law of those who were accused of supporting the government of Fulgencio Batista were implemented. These executions astounded not only the Cubans but the entire world. Since the beginning of the revolution anyone who opposed the dictatorship was shot on the wall or sent to in prison for many years to achieve complete obedience through fear.

Donald Trump's reaction to the death of the Cuban dictator

Donald Trump posted on Twitter on November 26, 2016 "Fidel Castro is dead!" at the news of the death of the bloody tyrant of Cuba at the age of ninety. Later, he issued a longer statement condemning the "brutal dictator" and wishing for a free Cuba.

President Trump stated the following: "Today, the world marks the passing of a brutal dictator who oppressed his own people for nearly six decades. Fidel Castro's legacy is one of firing squads, theft, unimaginable suffering, poverty and the denial of fundamental human rights. While Cuba remains a totalitarian island, it is my hope that today marks a move away from the horrors endured for too long, and toward a future in which the wonderful Cuban people finally live in the freedom they so richly deserve."

"Though the tragedies, deaths and pain caused by Fidel Castro cannot be erased, our administration will do all it can to ensure the Cuban people can finally begin their journey toward prosperity and liberty. I join the many Cuban Americans who supported me so greatly in the presidential campaign, including the Brigade 2506 Veterans Association that endorsed me, with the hope of one day soon seeing a free Cuba."

Barack Obama's reaction to the death of Fidel Castro

A completely different reaction came from then President Barack Obama who offered condolences to the Castro's family. Obama said the following: "At this time of Fidel Castro's passing, we extend a hand of friendship to the Cuban people. History will record and judge the enormous impact of this singular figure on the people and the world around him." Obama's comments were outrageous! Cuban-Americans, who voted in great numbers for Donald Trump rejecting Obama's and Hillary Clinton's policy on Cuba, know that history has already judged the terrible and diabolical legacy of the Cuban tyrant.

The comments of Marxist Obama were immediately denounced by Florida Republican Senator Marco Rubio, who called these remarks "pathetic." Senator Rubio stated the following: "Sadly, Fidel Castro's death does not mean freedom for the Cuban people or justice for the democratic activists, religious leaders, and political opponents who Fidel Castro and his brother have jailed and persecuted. The dictator has died, but the dictatorship has not."

Republican Congresswoman Ileana Ros-Lehtinen stated the following: "President-elect Trump has correctly stated that Obama's overtures to the Castro regime were one-sided and only benefited the Cuban regime. I hope that the new administration, under the leadership of President Trump, seizes this moment as an opportunity to reaffirm its commitment to the Cuban people that it will pressure the Castro regime by rolling back these executive actions of the Obama administration."

Statement by Bear Witness Central

On November 26, 2016, Bear Witness Central, the patriotic organization, with this writer as its South Florida Director, issued the following statement on the death of the communist dictator and murderer Fidel Castro: "The Cuban people were betrayed by Fidel Castro when 57 years ago, he came to power in a bloody revolution that installed a Communist totalitarian dictatorship. The people of Cuba have suffered an inhuman repression, hundreds of thousands unjustly imprisoned, millions of broken and destroyed families, oppression of free speech and the murder of tens of thousands of people during his reign in power. The Cuban people deserve the freedoms and democracy that we Americans have. There needs to be a change in Cuba and it needs to come soon!"

Although it is not correct to celebrate the death of another human being, Bear Witness Central reported that the death of Fidel Castro was an enormous and infinitely justifiable exception. Alberto de la Cruz wrote in *Babalu Blog* the following: "His passing is not simply the death of an old man; it is the death of an intrinsically evil, despotic, and demonic plague that not only caused so much misery, pain, and bloodshed in Cuba, but in other parts of the world as well. This makes the death of Fidel, a malevolent and vile beast, a death worth celebrating."

This writer and his wife Haydée celebrated the death of the Cuban tyrant,
the serial assassin Fidel Castro, in the streets of Miami.

Miami-Dade County, home to over one million Cuban Americans, exploded in jubilation over the death of Fidel Castro

After the news of the death of the Cuban tyrant became known on the night of November 15, 2016 or very early in the morning on November 16, thousands of Cuban Americans began an all-night and all-day celebration in Greater Miami. The celebrations went on for several days.

Cuban Americans took to the streets of Miami to celebrate the death of the communist dictator Fidel Castro the following day, November 26.

This writer was interviewed by journalist Ana Cuervo from *Telemundo Channel* on the meaning of the death of Fidel Castro.

Pictures of Fidel Castro in 1961, 2000, and 2016

Conclusion

For nearly 50 years, the bloody tyrant Fidel Castro and his murderer brother Raúl Castro almost brought nuclear war between American and the Soviet Union during the October Missile Crisis in 1962. Fidel Castro may have been involved in the assassination of President John F. Kennedy in 1963.

Cuba was and continuous to be an enemy of America. Cuba has brought to the United States tons of drugs, spies to damage our national security, and intelligence agents to steal from Medicare and Medicaid. Fidel Castro has sent tens of thousands of refugees to America to create chaos and disruption at different times, the worst having been the Mariel influx.

These actions have created enormous problems to 11 United States presidents. The brutal communist regime has exerted oppressive and total control over the suffering people of Cuba. Fidel Castro maintained an iron grip over the Cuban people and kept close ties with the Soviet Union, China, North Korea, Venezuela, Nicaragua, Bolivia, Iran, and other Islamic radical regimes in the Middle East.

The Cuban regime also inspired and assisted communist anti-American leaders to take power throughout Latin America. It gave financial and logistical support to numerous communist guerrillas in the Western Hemisphere, Africa, Asia, and other parts of the world. Fidel Castro presided over the longest and most brutal regime in the Western Hemisphere.

During his many years in power, 17,000 to 18,000 children, women, and men were executed; over 300,000 were incarcerated; 100,000 died at sea or were devoured by sharks when trying to escape; and over two million became refugees as they left the island prison. In the process, Fidel Castro became one of the richest individuals in the world while the standard of living in Cuba became one of the worst in the Americas.

Fidel Castro's regime destroyed the social cohesion of the Cuban people by creating neighborhood committees for the defense of the revolution that spied on those who criticized the regime. The dictator ruined the economy of the prosperous island that was the third largest in Latin America when he assumed power.

Fidel Castro destroyed the freedom of the press by confiscating all newspapers and radio and television stations. Freedom of worship ended yet many years later was partially restored. The excellent public and private schools and universities were taken over and replaced by entities of communist indoctrination. Private property was abolished.

Fidel Castro's legacy is one of separation of families, firing squads and extrajudicial assassinations, abject poverty, unimaginable horror and suffering, terror and brutality, and the denial of fundamental human and civil rights. While Cuba still is an oppressive totalitarian island, it is this writer's hope that President Trump would reverse the series of illegal and shameful unilateral concessions with no Quid Pro Quo or nothing in return granted to Cuba over the last years. There is more repression and arbitrary arrests in Cuba today after former President Obama recognized Cuba diplomatically and gave endless concessions to this brutal regime.

President Trump has promised that his administration will do everything possible to ensure that the Cuban people could finally begin their journey towards prosperity and liberty. One can only hope that with God's help one day soon Cuba will be a free, democratic, and sovereign nation.

The ashes of Fidel Castro were taken from Havana to Santiago de Cuba to be buried in Santa Efgenia cemetery.

CHAPTER 14

Members of the United Nations General Assembly praised the brutal dictator Fidel Castro and the United States will withdraw from UNESCO

It is shameful that members of the Club of Dictators, which is what the United Nations General Assembly is, praised Fidel Castro, one of the worst bloody tyrants of the world. For nearly 50 years, the tyrant Fidel Castro and his brother Raúl Castro almost brought nuclear war between America and the Soviet Union during the October Missile Crisis. Cuba was, and continuous to be, an enemy of America. The communist regime of Cuba has brought tons of drugs, many spies to damage America's national security, and intelligence agents to steal from ObamaCare, Medicare, and Medicaid.

The mass-murdering communist regime has exerted oppressive and total control over the suffering people of Cuba for almost 57 years. Fidel Castro maintained an iron grip over the people of Cuba and kept close ties with the Soviet Union and eventually with Russia, China, North Korea, Venezuela, Nicaragua, Bolivia, Syria, Iran, Iraq, and other Islamic radical regimes in the Middle East. Cuba became the center of terrorism in the world.

The regime also inspired communist anti-American leaders throughout Latin America and other parts of the world. Fidel Castro assisted the communist and radical guerrillas in Latin America, Africa, Middle East, and other parts of the world. Fidel Castro presided over the longest and most brutal regime in the Western Hemisphere.

Tens of thousands have been killed or wounded in revolutions all over the world led by communist leaders who were trained in Cuba and given logistical and economic support by the Cuban oppressive regime.

The United States will withdraw from UNESCO

UNESCO building

On October 12, 2017, the Department of State announced that the United States will withdraw from United Nations Educational, Scientific, and Cultural Organization (UNESCO) on December 31, 2018 citing bias on Israel as one of the reasons. The decision could be revisited. Why?

Farnaz Fassihi wrote an article titled "U.S. to Exit UNESCO, Citing Bias on Israel" which was published in the *Wall Street Journal* on October 13, 2017. The reporter wrote that the State Department said that the United States will withdraw from UNESCO, a move that could further strain relations between the Trump administration and the United Nations. The State Department said the decision to leave UNESCO "was not taken lightly" and reflects American concerns over the need for overhauls in the United Nations, as well as its "continuing anti-Israel bias." The withdrawal will take effect at the end of the year.

President Ronald Reagan withdrew from UNESCO in 1980 because it said the organization had become politicized. The United States rejoined in 2003. However, since 2011, it has withheld funds to UNESCO amounting to $542.67 million because of its decision to confer membership to the Palestinian territories. Israeli Prime Minister Benjamin Netanyahu said his country was also preparing to exit UNESCO "in parallel with the United States."

Nimrata "Nikki" Haley born on January 20, 1972 is the United States Ambassador to the United Nations.

Fassihi explained that after arriving at the United Nations, U.S. Ambassador Nikki Haley has criticized what she has called a bias against Israel both in the Security Council and at various U.N. agencies. She has said that the United States is reviewing its commitment to the U.N.'s Human Rights Council, citing concerns coming from issues related to Israel, Iran, and Venezuela and warning that the U.S. would withdraw from the Human Rights Council without changes. In July 2017, UNESCO designated the Old City of Hebron and Tomb of the Patriarchs as Palestinian heritage sites despite diplomatic efforts by Israel and political pressure from the U.S. to stop the designation. Ambassador Nikki Haley said that "The United States will continue to evaluate all agencies within the United Nations system through the same lens."

Conclusion

President Trump needs to take a serious look at the United Nations and consider the withdrawal of the United States, not just from UNESCO. The Trump administration was successful in demanding a reduction of the budget of the UN which was reduced by over $250 million. The president should also consider a significant reduction of the funds given to this institution that would like to take away America's sovereignty, wealth, Constitution, Armed Forces, internet, and so forth.

CHAPTER 15

Trump makes excellent appointments to protect our National Security

Retired four-star General James N. "Mad Dog" Mattis became Secretary of Defense.

President-elect Donald J. Trump has made two outstanding selections to protect America from its enemies. One is retired General James N. "Mad Dog" Mattis as Secretary of Defense and the second is retired Marine Corps General John Francis Kelly as Secretary of Homeland Security, who later became White House Chief of Staff.

This writer has a chapter in his book *The Gathering Threat of Russia, China, and Their Allies Against America* (2016) with the title "Russia, the Center of Global Terrorism, Uses Radical Islam as a Weapon Against the West" where he discussed how former President Barack Obama made the United States a superpower in complete retreat. The enemies of America, including Russia, China, Iran, North Korea, Venezuela, Cuba, and radical Islam, did not fear President Obama. The allies of America did not trust or respect Obama to defend them from their enemies.

The CIA director during Obama administration, John Brennan, voted for the Communist Party ticket in 1976 yet was hired by the agency four years later. It is clear that standards for hiring intelligence officers have been dramatically lowered.

Then President-elect Donald J. Trump met with General Mattis for a little over one hour on November 20, 2016. He later stated on Twitter the following: "General James "Mad Dog" Mattis, who is being considered for Secretary of Defense, was very impressive yesterday. A true General's General!" On December 1, 2016, then President-elect Trump announced at a rally in Cincinnati that he was going to nominate General Mattis for Secretary of Defense. As General Mattis retired from the military in 2013, his nomination required a waiver of the National Security Act of 1947, which requires a seven-year waiting period before retired military personnel can assume the role of Secretary of Defense.

Retired General John Francis Kelly became Secretary of Homeland Security and was later appointed as White House Chief of Staff.

President Donald J. Trump with retired General James N. "Mad Dog" Mattis

President-elect Donald J. Trump with Retired General John Francis Kelly

General Kelly is the former commander of the U.S. Southern Command located in Miami-Dade County, Florida. General Kelly previously served as the commanding general of the Multi-National Force—West in Iraq from February 2008 to February 2009. On December 7,

2016, then President-elect Donald J. Trump announced his selection of General Kelly as Secretary of Homeland Security.

Conclusion

President Donald J. Trump has made excellent appointments to protect our national security and U.S. boundaries. The liberal and socialist media has criticized these appointments by alleging that there are too many generals in the Trump admiration. However, previous Democratic and Republican presidents have nominated many retired generals to important posts in their administrations. The liberal mainstream media will attack and criticize Donald J. Trump every day. But who cares? This media is completed discredited. The media has clearly shown how biased it was during the 2016 presidential election and previous elections.

CHAPTER 16

Obama Ends the Wet Foot, Dry Foot Policy and the Cuban Medical Professional Parole

Cubans fleeing the island prison in a tiny raft will not be allowed to enter the United States and will be deported to Cuba even if the bloody regime will put them in jail.

On January 12, 2017, President Barack Obama abruptly ended the Wet Foot, Dry Foot policy established by President Bill Clinton in 1995. Obama also ended the Cuban Medical Professional Parole Program established by President George W. Bush in 2006 that allowed Cuban medical doctors, nurses and dentists who had been sent by the Cuban regime by force to countries in Latin America, Africa, and Asia to receive visas that allowed them to enter the United States. Both of these changes were requested by the Cuban bloody dictator Raúl Castro. President Obama was happy to comply with these outrageous requests by the Cuban regime.

The Cuban Medical Professional Parole Program

The termination of the Cuban Medical Professional Parole Program was shameful since these Cuban health professionals were treated by the Cuban government as slaves. They were forced to leave their families behind in Cuba for two years and were sent to Third World countries against their will. This program was started by President George W. Bush and was known as

"Barrio Afuera" (neighborhood outside) in 2006. "Barrio Adentro (neighborhood inside) was the name of the program initiated by the former dictator Hugo Chávez in Venezuela.

For years, the communist regime of Venezuela sent 100,000 barrels of free oil in exchange for the enslaved medical doctors, dentists, nurses, and others who were sent against their will to work in that nation. Now, of course, Venezuela is bankrupt and has had to drastically reduce the shipment of free oil to Cuba.

This writer had a cousin in the city of Camagüey, Cuba who was happily married with two kids. Thugs from the Cuban secret police came to his office one day and told him that he needed to go home and prepare his bags since he would be sent to Venezuela in a few hours. This writer's cousin said that he did not want to go to Venezuela as he was happily married and had two young children. His request to stay in Cuba was denied. He was forced to leave his wife, small children, brothers and sisters, and parents behind and that very day he was sent to a remote city in Venezuela. He was placed in a house that belonged to a communist family who supported the brutal regime of Venezuela. Secret police from Cuba closely supervised several doctors who had been sent with him to that remote city.

This writer's cousin was not allowed to watch Venezuelan television, only Cuban television. He had to remain in Venezuela for two years before he could return home. Cuba is a nation that participates in human trafficking worldwide and, yet Barack Obama removed Cuba from the list of nations that participate in human trafficking.

Other nations in Latin America, Africa, and Asia would pay the Cuban regime $5,000 a month for these Cuban professionals yet the Cuban doctors were given a salary of $200 a month. The Mafia that runs the Cuban regime enriched themselves with the millions of dollars that came as a result of human trafficking.

From 2006 to 2015 more than 8,000 Cuban doctors, nurses, and dentists were given visas to enter the United States. In 2015, 1,663 Cuban health professionals came to the United States.

The Wet Foot, Dry Foot Policy

As a result of another shameful concession given by former President Obama to the Cuban regime, Cubans were no longer allowed to stay and become legal residents if they enter the United States illegally. Cubans were promptly deported back to the island prison where they could face incarceration and harassment. It is true that other immigrants were not given this privilege, and this has been resented by other Latin Americans.

The repeal by former President Obama of this longstanding immigration policy that allowed Cubans who made it to the United States soil to stay and become legal residents became effective immediately. Sadly, the Cuban regime gave no assurances about the treatment of those sent back to their country of birth.

The Wet Foot, Dry Foot policy was prepared in 1995 by President Bill Clinton as a revision of a more liberal immigration policy. Until then, Cubans captured at sea who were trying to make their way to the United States were permitted to remain in this country and were able to become legal residents after a year. The United States was reluctant to send people back to the communist island, and then run by the brutal dictator Fidel Castro. The Cuban regime generally refused to accept repatriated citizens.

Former president Obama, with less than a week left as president, used an administrative rule change to end this policy. President Trump could undo that rule immediately if he so desires. He has criticized Obama's policy aimed at improving relations with Cuba.

Many Cubans were fearful that the current immigration policy would change, and they would not be allowed to enter the United States. As a result of this concern, tens of thousands of Cubans left the island prison and entered Ecuador since the normalization of relations between the United States and Cuba. Cuban families, often with small children, crossed from that nation to Colombia, Central America, and Mexico in an effort to cross the border into the United States. There are still thousands who are left in several countries of Latin America and would not be allowed to come to America. Since October 2012, more than 118,000 Cubans have presented themselves at ports of entry along the border, according to statistics published by the Homeland Security Department.

Many Cuban Americans wondered why Obama would want to make it more difficult for Cubans to stay in America and pursue citizenship. Several thousands of Syrian refugees have entered this country even though FBI and other intelligence agencies officials have testified in Congress that there may be terrorists posing as refugees. Tens of thousands unaccompanied minors and thousands of adults have also entered America from its southern border. Many Cuban Americans believe that the reason for these changes in policies was Obama-s desire to give more gifts to his new friend, the brutal dictator Raúl Castro. Perhaps it was payback because the majority of Cuban Americans in the United States voted for Donald Trump.

The Cuban communist officials praised Obama's action, calling the new agreement "an important step in advancing relations" between the United States and Cuba that "aims to guarantee normal, safe and ordered migration." Leaving Cuba is a crime. Whether the Cubans sent back to Cuba under Obama's new policy were tortured, jailed, or executed is an open question but not one that Barack Obama cares about. Open borders are now allowed for unaccompanied children and adults from Central America and Mexico and Islamic terrorists, everyone except Cubans.

Former president Obama's Statement on ending the Wet Foot, Dry Foot Policy and the Cuban Medical Professional Parole Program was as follows: "Today, the United States is taking important steps forward to normalize relations with Cuba and to bring greater consistency thought immigration policy. The Department of Homeland Security is ending the so-called Wet Foot, Dry Foot policy, which was put in place more than 20 years ago and was the signed for a different era.

Effective immediately, Cuban nationals who attempt to enter the United States illegally and do not qualify for humanitarian relief will be subject to removal, consistent with U.S. law and enforcement priorities. By taking this step, we are treating Cuban migrants the same way we treat migrants from other countries. The Cuban government has agreed to accept the return of Cuban nationals who have been ordered removed, just as it has been accepting the return of migrants interdicted at sea.

Today, the Department of Homeland Security is also ending the Cuban Medical Professional Parole Program. The United States and Cuba are working together to combat the diseases that endanger the health and lives of our people. By providing preferential treatment to Cuba medical personnel, the medical bodily program contradicts those efforts, and risks harming the Cuban people. Cuba medical personnel will now be eligible to apply for asylum at United States embassies and consulates around the world, consistent with the procedures for all foreign nationals.

The United States is the land of immigrants, has been enriched by the contributions of Cuban Americans for more than a century. Since I took office, we have put the Cuban-American community at the center of our policies. With this change we will continue to welcome Cubans as we welcome immigrants for other nations, consistent with our laws. During my administration, we work to improve the lives of the Cuban people-inside of Cuba-by providing them with greater access to resources, information and connectivity to the wider world. To staining that approach is the best way to ensure that Cubans can enjoy prosperity, pursue reforms, and determine their own destiny. As I have said in Havana, the future of Cuba should be in the hands of the Cuban people."

Cuban Americans in Congress from both political parties denounced Barack Obama.

Almost immediately, Cuban Americans from both political parties wrote statements denouncing the changes made by outgoing President Barack Obama. The *Babalú Blog* published an article describing the comments made by three Cuban Americans in Congress. Below are the comments made by Ileana Ros- Lehtinen, Mario Díaz-Balart, and Bob Menendez.

Congresswoman Ileana Ros-Lehtinen (Republican from southern Florida) stated the following:

"Castro uses refugees as pawns to get more concessions from Washington so there is no reason to do away with the Cuban medical doctor program, which is a foolhardy concession to a regime that sends its doctors to foreign nations in a modern-day indentured servitude. The repeal of the Cuban Medical Professional Parole Program was done because that's what the Cuban dictatorship wanted, and the White House caved to what Castro wants, instead of standing up for U.S. democratic values and seeking the return of fugitives from U.S. justice like Joanne Chesimard or seeking compensation for U.S. citizens for their confiscated properties.

In another bad deal by the Obama administration, it has traded wet foot/dry foot for the elimination of an important program which was undermining the Castro regime by providing an outlet for Cuban doctors to seek freedom from forced labor which only benefits an oppressive regime."

Republican Congressman Mario Díaz-Balart from South Florida stated the following:

"With just eight days left in his administration, President Obama has found one more way to frustrate the democratic aspirations of the Cuban people and provide yet another shameful concession to the Castro regime. Under President Obama's misguided view, after having removed the Castro regime from the state sponsor of terror list and granting diplomatic recognition, the next logical step is denying oppressed Cubans the presumption of political asylum.

Since 1966, the Cuban Refugee Adjustment Act has provided a lifeline to generations of Cubans fleeing oppression. Many made the treacherous journey to begin their lives anew in freedom, and others perished trying to escape. In addition, the Cuban Medical Professional Parole Program provided a way for doctors forced to work under inhumane conditions for paltry salaries in foreign lands to escape their servitude.

President Obama's policy toward the Castro regime has not improved human rights or increased liberty on the island. To the contrary, documented political arrests reached close to 10,000 in 2016 as renowned activists such as Berta Soler, Danilo Maldonado Machado "El Sexto," and labor activists including Ivan Carrillo Hernandez suffered brutal arrests just in the past few weeks. El Sexto remains in prison today and his American lawyer, Kim Motley, was harassed and interrogated while in Cuba simply for representing him. Cubans are leaving the island in record numbers, and many of the 53 who were released as part of the Obama-Castro deal were subsequently rearrested.

President Obama's numerous concessions and extension of diplomatic recognition to the murderous Castro regime does not constitute an achievement. To the contrary, his policy has been a succession of betrayals of America's longstanding commitment to human rights and freedom, and a betrayal of the Cuban people who have suffered under oppression for far too long. This last act of diminishing lifelines to Cubans languishing in totalitarianism is one final despicable betrayal of a people who deserve better from an American president.

With just eight days left in his administration, President Obama has found one more way to frustrate the democratic aspirations of the Cuban people and provide yet another shameful concession to the Castro regime. Under President Obama's misguided view, after having removed the Castro regime from the state sponsor of terror list and granting diplomatic recognition, the next logical step is denying oppressed Cubans the presumption of political asylum.

Since 1966, the Cuban Refugee Adjustment Act has provided a lifeline to generations of Cubans fleeing oppression. Many made the treacherous journey to begin their lives anew in freedom, and others perished trying to escape. In addition, the Cuban Medical Professional Parole Program provided a way for doctors forced to work under inhumane conditions for paltry salaries in foreign lands to escape their servitude.

President Obama's policy toward the Castro regime has not improved human rights or increased liberty on the island. To the contrary, documented political arrests reached close to 10,000 in 2016 as renowned activists such as Berta Soler, Danilo Maldonado Machado "El Sexto," and labor activists including Ivan Carrillo Hernandez suffered brutal arrests just in the past few weeks. El Sexto remains in prison today and his American lawyer, Kim Motley, was harassed and interrogated while in Cuba simply for representing him. Cubans are leaving the island in record numbers, and many of the 53 who were released as part of the Obama-Castro deal were subsequently rearrested.

President Obama's numerous concessions and extension of diplomatic recognition to the murderous Castro regime does not constitute an achievement. To the contrary, his policy has been a succession of betrayals of America's longstanding commitment to human rights and freedom, and a betrayal of the Cuban people who have suffered under oppression for far too long. This last act of diminishing lifelines to Cubans languishing in in totalitarianism is one final despicable betrayal of a people who deserve better from an American president."

Senator Bob Menendez Democrat from New Jersey stated the following: "As a beacon of light for those fleeing persecution and oppression, the United States has a rich history of creating programs specifically designed to provide a safe haven and refuge for those who truly need it. Throughout their murderous reign, hundreds of thousands of Cubans have fled from the Castros' regime seeking safe haven in the United States. Those who further risked their lives by sea and reached our shores have been afforded the opportunity to expedite their claims to U.S. citizenship.

The fact is the recent ill-conceived changes in American policy towards Cuba have rewarded the regime with an economic lifeline while leaving every day Cubans less hopeful about their futures under a brutal totalitarian dictatorship. And while more needs to be done to prevent the small universe arriving from Cuba who may seek to exploit the privileges and freedoms that come with the Wet-Foot Dry-Foot policy, those few actors should not destroy our efforts to protect the many who are forced to flee persecution.

To be sure, today's announcement will only serve to tighten the noose the Castro regime continues to have around the neck of its own people. Congress was not consulted prior to this abrupt policy announcement with just nine days left in this administration. The Obama administration seeks to pursue engagement with the Castro regime at the cost of ignoring the present state of torture and oppression, and its systematic curtailment of freedom."

Senator Marco Rubio denounced Obama's reversal of the Wet Foot, Dry-Foot.

Alberto de la Cruz said that Senator Rubio stated that the sudden increase of Cubans migrating from the island over the past two years was a direct result of Obama's new Cuba policy of embracing the Castro regime. Nevertheless, after Obama created a migration crisis from Cuba, he suddenly decided to slam shut the door. The Florida senator sharply criticized the Obama Administration's decision to end the Wet Foot, Dry Foot Policy. The new policy eliminated the preferential treatment of Cuban migrants. Senator Rubio slammed President Obama's Cuba policy saying that it contributed to the rise in Cuban migration since 2014.

The senator from Florida admitted that changes to the Cuban Adjustment Act were needed, but argued that "we must work to ensure that Cubans who arrive here to escape political persecution are not summarily returned to the regime." The senator has been a strong opponent of Obama's efforts to normalize relations with the Cuban regime.

Senator Rubio also agreed with the comments made by Representatives Ileana Ros- Lehtinen and Mario Díaz-Balart and Senator Bob Menendez, who opposed the elimination of the Cuban Medical Professional Parole Program. The program allowed Cuban doctors to seek asylum in the United States. "For decades, the Castro regime has forced thousands of doctors to go abroad as a tool of its foreign policy," said Senator Rubio. The Florida Republican stated that he had discussed the issue with Vice President Mike Pence and welcomed Trump's commitment to repeal the Obama Cuba policy.

Conclusion

Obama's policy toward the brutal Castro regime was a complete failure. The policy did not improve human rights or increased liberty on the island. On the contrary, the regime increased its repression. Obama's Cuban policy, as stated by Congressman Mario Díaz-Balart, "has been a succession of betrayals of America's longstanding commitment to human rights and freedom, and a betrayal of the Cuban people who have suffered under oppression for far too long."

CHAPTER 17

Obama retaliated against Russia over hacking

Russian dictator Vladimir Putin met with President Barack Obama on the sidelines of the G-20 Summit in Hangzhou, China in September 2016.

On December 30, 2016, Carol E. Lee and Paul Sonne wrote an article titled "Obama Sanctions Russia, Expels 35" which was published in the *Wall Street Journal*. The reporters explained that then President Obama retaliated against Russia's alleged use of cyber-attacks to interfere with the 2016 presidential election. Obama imposed sanctions on Russian agencies and companies and expelled 35 suspected intelligence operatives from the United States in one of the greatest diplomatic confrontations between Washington and Moscow since the end of the Cold War. Russia threatened to retaliate but then changed course when members of Congress asked for even stiffer sanctions and an investigation into Moscow's cyber-attacks.

Obama said the cyber-attacks "could only have been directed by the highest levels of the Russian government." He said, "We will continue to take a variety of actions at a time and place of our choosing, some of which will not be publicized."

Russia has continued to deny its involvement in the election-related hacks. The spokesman of the Russian government spokesman, Dmitry Peskov, said that "the principle of reciprocity applies here." Peskov stated that Russian President Vladimir Putin would formulate a response that would create "considerable discomfort in the same areas" for the United States. As it has been indicated, Russia decided not to respond to America's sanctions. The President-elect Donald Trump said then that he was going to review the situation in a meeting with U.S. intelligence officials.

Russian Foreign Minister Sergei Lavrov, left, meets with President Vladimir Putin, center, and Defense Minister Sergei Shoigu at the Kremlin in Moscow on December 29, 2016.

Lee and Sonne explained the following: "The sanctions target Russia's military intelligence agency, the Main Intelligence Directorate, or GRU, for tampering, altering or causing the misappropriation of information with the purpose or effect of interfering with the election. The measures also cite Russia's main security agency, the Federal Security Service, for assisting the GRU in the activities. Also sanctioned were three Russian companies the administration accused of providing material support for the GRU's cyber operations and four top Russian officials who run the military intelligence agency." The sanctions impose asset freezes and travel bans on individuals and prohibit U.S. citizens and companies from doing business with them.

The State Department expelled 35 intelligence agents allegedly serving as diplomats from the Russian embassy in Washington, D.C. and the Russian consulate in San Francisco. The Russian officials and their families were given 72 hours to leave America after the State Department said they "were acting in a manner inconsistent with their diplomatic status."

The State Department informed Russia that, as of December 30, 2016, it would deny access to two Russian government-owned compounds in the United States. One is a summer retreat for Russian embassy officials on the eastern shore of Maryland and the other is a compound for Russian diplomats on Long Island, New York. The White House accused Moscow of using the recreational compounds for intelligence-related purposes.

Lee and Sonne said that the Department of Homeland Security and the FBI issued a joint report, titled "Grizzly Steppe," giving additional technical details about the hacking of the election, including implicated IP addresses, virus signatures, and file hashes. The report indicated that the hacking group, known as Cozy Bear or APT 29, penetrated the network of an American political party in the summer 2016 while a second group, known as Fancy Bear or APT 28, penetrated the network in the spring 2016. It said Russian intelligence actors gained access and stole content from senior party members. The report warned that individuals associated with Russian intelligence were launching spear phishing campaigns even after the election. Many Republicans in Congress said President Obama had taken too long to punish Russia after years of Russian aggression. Senate Majority Leader Mitch McConnell (Republican from Kentucky) said the next Congress should take tougher actions. Senate Democrats praised the decision of the Obama administration to target new Russian officials and entities with sanctions.

On December 29, 2016, then President-elect Donald J. Trump, who had said a day earlier that "we ought to get on with our lives" when asked about retaliatory moves against Russia—appeared open to accepting the U.S. intelligence assessment. Trump stated the following: "It's time for our country to move on to bigger and better things. Nevertheless, in the interest of our country and its great people, I will meet with leaders of the intelligence community next week in order to be updated on the facts of this situation."

Is there conclusive evidence that Russia used cyber-attacks to interfere with the 2016 presidential election?

Cliff Kincaid wrote an article titled "Obama's Evidence Against Russia Falls Flat" which was published on the *Accuracy in Media* website on December 30, 2016. Kincaid explained that Obama and Democrats have been stating that there is proof that Russia hacked into Democratic Party computers for the purpose of obtaining and planting information that would help elect Donald J. Trump as president. However, the reporter said that proof was not provided when former President Obama issued an executive order and announced the expulsions of 35 Russians from America and sanctions against Russian officials. Then President-elect Donald J. Trump seemed in no hurry to come to any rash conclusions, saying he would meet with "leaders of the intelligence community" in order to be "updated on the facts of this situation."

Kincaid pointed out that the Obama administration's Joint Analysis Report on alleged "Russian malicious cyber activity" is very weak and vague in key aspects. The reporter stated the following: "It would have been nice if reporters had read the pathetically thin report before concluding that there was substance to it, and that Trump was somehow derelict in not accepting what Obama had to offer. Only four-and-a-half pages of the 13-page report purport to examine alleged Russian hacking activities. The rest of the report gives advice on how to provide security for computer networks. It looked like the report was padded in order to make it seem more authoritative than it really was."

A separate White House press release went into some more detail, alleging that "the disclosures of alleged hacked e-mails on sites like DCLeaks.com and *WikiLeaks* are consistent with the Russian-directed efforts. But being consistent with is not proof."

Kincaid said that the Joint Analysis Report, described as "the result of analytic efforts between the Department of Homeland Security (DHS) and the Federal Bureau of Investigation (FBI)," includes a "DISCLAIMER" stating that it is "for informational purposes only" and that the DHS "does not provide any warranties of any kind regarding any information contained within." The reporter said that "It sounded like the kind of warning that comes with a possibly defective product."

The report stated that this alleged Russian campaign, designated as "GRIZZLY STEPPE," was an activity by Russian civilians and military intelligence services and was "part of an ongoing campaign of cyber-enabled operations directed at the U.S. government and private sector entities." Kincaid asked that if it was ongoing, why did it take so long for Obama to act? The reporter concluded his article by saying that Obama's "evidence" raises questions about the worth and value of the intelligence agencies that apparently provided it. No wonder Trump wants to wait and see.

In a surprise decision Vladimir Putin said Russia will not retaliate against America

It is believed that Putin's unexpected decision was designed to repair relations with America under President-elect Donald J. Trump. Putin stated, "We will formulate further steps in restoring Russian-American relations according to the policy that the administration of President Donald Trump conducts."

President-elect Donald J. Trump said on Twitter that Putin's decision not to respond to Obama's sanctions was a "Great move. I always knew he was very smart!"

Vladimir Putin said Russia will not expel any American diplomats in response to the executive order of the Obama administration that sanctions Moscow over alleged interference with the 2016 presidential election.

Conclusion

The Obama administration failed to protect America from cyber-attacks from Russia, China, North Korea, and other enemy nations. Many Republicans in Congress said former President Obama took too long to punish Russia after years of Russian aggression. It was late then for Obama to act tough as he was a weak leader and made America a superpower in complete retreat. Thanks to Obama's foreign policy America's enemies were emboldened and did not fear America and its allies did not trust America to defend them. Just look at the shameful position that Obama took toward America's ally, Israel, at the United Nations.

The editorial from the *Wall Street Journal* of December 30, 2016 pointed out the following: "Obama's timid responses so far to Moscow—and to attacks from China and North Korea— have emboldened its hackers to meddle in the U.S. political process. The Russian regime is nothing if not a respecter of power, and only a U.S. President willing to exercise it will get the Kremlin to stop…On December 29, the transition released a more considered statement from Mr. Trump repeating that it's time to move on but that in the interest of our country he'd meet with U.S. intelligence officials next week in order to be updated on the facts of this situation. He's wise to do so lest Mr. Putin treat him as a cyber-patsy the way he has Mr. Obama."

President Trump and his advisers need to study carefully the Joint Analysis Report titled "Grizzly Steppe" issued by the Department of Homeland Security (DHS) and the Federal Bureau of

Investigation (FBI) to determine its accuracy. If Russia was involved, then some type of action will be required. If the evidence is weak and inconclusive, then it is time to move on.

This writer believes that Russia is America's number one geopolitical enemy. President Trump should try to develop a better relationship with Moscow, but he needs to be very firm with that nation's dictator Vladimir Putin. Russia wants to recreate the old Soviet Union and has threatened America and its NATO allies with nuclear war.

CHAPTER 18

CIA Director John Brennan and Donald J. Trump

President Donald J. Trump

On January 15, 2017, then President-elect Donald J. Trump asked if CIA Director John Brennan himself was responsible for leaking a dossier of unverified information to the press about his alleged sexual activities in Russia. This question was raised by Trump after CIA Director John Brennan appeared on the "Fox News Sunday" program on January 15, 2017. Brennan criticized Donald Trump's comparison of the intelligence community to Nazi Germany. Brennan said that Trump's remarks were "outrageous." Trump had said that the person working in the intelligence community who had leaked the 35-page dossier of totally unverified information on him was acting in a similar fashion to a Nazi. Leaking by intelligence officials is, of course, illegal and a crime.

CIA Director John Brennan

John Brennan stated the following: "What I do find outrageous is equating intelligence community with Nazi Germany. I do take great umbrage with that and there is no basis for Mr. Trump to point fingers at the intelligence community for leaking information that was already available publicly."

Trump issued a series of tweets in which he questioned whether CIA Director Brennan was personally behind *BuzzFeed*'s recent publication of a 35-page dossier of totally unverified information on him. Then President-elect Trump did not appear to be convinced, in spite of the statements from John Brennan and from the Director of National Intelligence James Clapper earlier that the intelligence community had no involvement with the leaked dossier. Brennan stated in his interview with *Fox News* that "there is no interest in undermining the president-elect."

Is the intelligence community out to get Trump?

Cliff Kincaid wrote an article titled "The CIA's War on Trump, Continued" which was published in the website *Accuracy in Media* on January 13, 2017. The reporter pointed out that New York Democratic Senator Chuck Schumer warned that the intelligence community is out to "get" President Trump. Kincaid wrote that "Daniel Benjamin, a Brookings Institution expert who served in the Clinton administration, says that Trump's treatment of his spies will come back to bite him in the form of devastating leaks to the media that will make him look foolish or incompetent."

Kincaid mentioned that Daniel Benjamin stated the following: "The intelligence community doesn't leak as much as the Pentagon or Congress, but when its reputation is at stake, it can do so to devastating effect. Trump's attacks on the intelligence community will come back to haunt him." Benjamin did not deny that many believe that President Obama's CIA and its director John Brennan were behind the recent leaks to the *Washington Post* and *New York Times* showing Donald J. Trump as a Russian puppet. The implication is that the CIA and the rest of the intelligence community will seek further revenge on President Trump if he continues to criticize them.

At a news conference, Donald Trump said regarding the leaks about his meetings with intelligence officials, "I think it's pretty sad when intelligence reports get leaked out to the press. I think it's pretty sad. First of all, it's illegal. You know, these are classified and certified meetings and reports."

Kincaid noted that "it appears that some intelligence officials believe they are above the law and can use illegal leaks to damage an elected President who has been critical of their work product." *BuzzFeed* published a dossier of a leaked document offering unsubstantiated claims of Trump being sexually compromised by Russian officials. CNN summarized the document and *BuzzFeed* published it in its entirety.

President Trump denounced these leaks with Director of the Office of National Intelligence James Clapper. Clapper said that he had called Trump about them and expressed his "profound dismay at the leaks that have been appearing in the press…" Clapper said that he and Donald J. Trump "both agreed that they are extremely corrosive and damaging to our national security." Clapper added that he did not believe the leaks came from within the Intelligence Community.

Cliff Kincaid concluded his article by raising the following two questions: "Is the CIA really the invisible government that the so-called conspiracy theorists have warned about? Is there a deep state that tries to run the government behind-the-scenes"? In a previous article, Kincaid said John Brennan voted for the Communist Party USA two years before he joined the CIA.

Is CIA Director John Brennan a Wahhabi Muslim?

Barack Obama nominated John Brennan as director of the CIA in January 2013, following the resignation of General David Petraeus.

Who is John Brennan?

New sparks fly between CIA, Senate Intelligence Committee Tensions between the CIA and its congressional overseers erupted anew this week when CIA Director John Brennan refused to tell lawmakers who authorized intrusions into computers used by the Senate Intelligence Committee to compile a damning report on the spy agency's interrogation program. According to *Wikipedia*, John Owen Brennan was born on September 22, 1955. Brennan, the son of Irish immigrants, was born and raised in North Bergen, New Jersey. He attended the Immaculate Heart of Mary Elementary School and graduated from St. Joseph of the Palisades High School in West New York, New Jersey. He graduated from Fordham University in New York City with a Bachelor of Arts in political science in 1977. During his junior year abroad, he learned Arabic while he was taking Middle Eastern studies subjects at the American University in Cairo, Egypt.

Brennan graduated with a Master of Arts in government with a concentration in Middle Eastern studies from the University of Texas at Austin in 1980. He speaks Arabic fluently. Brennan is married to Kathy Pokluda Brennan. They have one son and twin daughters.

Wikipedia explained that Brennan's 25 years with the CIA included work as a Near East and South Asia analyst, station chief in Saudi Arabia, and director of the National Counterterrorism Center. Brennan began his CIA career as an analyst at the CIA headquarters in Langley, Virginia. In 1996, he was the CIA station chief in Riyadh, Saudi Arabia when the bombing of the Khobar Towers killed 19 U.S. servicemen.

In 1999, Brennan was appointed chief of staff to George Tenet, who was then Director of the CIA. Brennan became deputy executive director of the CIA in March 2001.

John Brennan served as an advisor to Barack Obama on foreign-policy and intelligence issues during the 2008 presidential campaign and transition. In 2009, Obama wanted to nominate Brennan for director of the Central Intelligence Agency. However, Obama was forced to withdraw his nomination over concerns regarding the support of Brennan of the CIA's rendition and forceful interrogations, such as water boarding under President George W. Bush. Instead, Brennan was appointed Deputy National Security Advisor for Homeland Security and counterterrorism and assistant to the president, a position which did not require Senate confirmation. His responsibilities included overseeing plans to protect the country from terrorism and respond to natural disasters. He met with the President daily.

Obama nominated Brennan as director of the CIA on January 7, 2013, following the resignation of General David Petraeus. The ACLU called for the Senate not to proceed with the appointment until it could be confirmed that "all of his conduct was within the law" at the

CIA and White House. John Brennan was confirmed by the Senate Intelligence Committee on March 5, 2013 by a vote of 12 to 3.

Wikipedia pointed out that in August 2009, Brennan criticized some of the anti-terror policies of the George W. Bush administration, saying that water boarding had threatened national security by increasing the recruitment of terrorists and decreasing the willingness of other nations to cooperate with the United States. He also described the focus of the Obama administration of calling terrorists as being "extremists" and not "jihadists." Brennan said that using the second term, which means one who is struggling for a holy goal, gives "these murderers the religious legitimacy they desperately seek" and suggests the United States is at war with the religion of Islam.

This appeasement of terrorists by the Obama administration and Brennan by changing their name was completely ignored by everyone all terrorists are known as jihadists. In February 2010, he said on *Meet the Press* that he was tired of Republican members of Congress using national security issues as political footballs and making allegations when they did not know the facts. As president, Obama had already stated that he had full confidence in John Brennan in spite of the CIA scandal of the hacking of Senate's computers. Obama was not interested in finding out whether John Brennan had committed perjury by stating that the CIA had done nothing wrong. Why did Obama protect his CIA director?

Jack Cashill wrote an article regarding Jerome Corsi book, *Where is the Birth Certificate?* Cashill wrote the following regarding this book: "In March 2008, contract employees for the State Department were caught breaching the passport files of the three still viable presidential candidates, Obama, McCain, and Hillary Clinton. While the media allowed Obama to pontificate about the sanctity of confidential records, they spared the public the knowledge that Obama's file was uniquely visited on three occasions and that that visitor just happened to work for Obama adviser John Brennan, now Deputy National Security Adviser. Two weeks later, Obama disclosed for the first time that he had visited Pakistan in 1981, a fact curiously missing from both of his books. The media predictably averted their gaze."

Did Brennan's employee, who had access to the passport records, destroy Obama's mother passport? This passport has mysteriously disappeared. At the time, Brennan's company had a contract with the State Department to assist with the processing of passports. If so, Obama owes a large debt to Brennan. What if the passport of Obama's mother indicated that she was in Kenya when he was born? Of course, since the passport disappeared, we will never know, but it makes one wonder. Obama may have something else in common with Brennan. Both of them may be hidden radical Muslims and extreme leftists.

Brennan was being sworn in as CIA Director on March 8, 2013 after being confirmed by the Senate.

Is John Brennan a Muslim with a dangerous worldview who is unfit to serve as Director of the CIA?

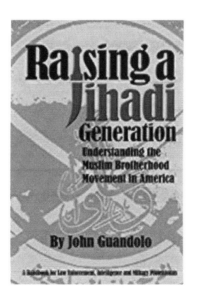

John Guandolo is the author of *Raising a Jihadi Generation: Understanding the Muslim Brotherhood Movement in America* (2013).

Drew Zahn wrote an article entitled "Shock Claim: Obama Picks Muslim for CIA Chief" which was published on *WND* on February 10, 2013. Zahn explained that John Guandolo, a former Marine and combat veteran and an expert on Islam who worked for the FBI's Counterterrorism Division for eight years, stated that John Brennan is a converted Muslim.

The reporter explained that Guandolo was being interviewed by Tom Trento on the radio when he stated the following: "Mr. Brennan did convert to Islam when he served in an official capacity on behalf of the United States in Saudi Arabia. That fact alone is not what is most disturbing. His conversion to Islam was the culmination of a counterintelligence operation against him to recruit him. The fact that foreign intelligence service operatives recruited Brennan when he was in a very sensitive and senior U.S. Government position in a foreign country means that he's either a traitor... Or he has the inability to discern and understand how to walk in those kinds of environments, which makes him completely unfit to be the director of Central Intelligence."

"Are you kidding me?" Trento asked John Guandolo. "The head of the CIA is a Muslim? For real? Are you sure?" Guandolo replied, "Yes, I am." Guandolo then stated the following: "The facts of the matter are confirmed by United States government officials who were also in Saudi Arabia at the time that John Brennan was serving there and has direct knowledge. These are men who work in very trusted positions. They were direct witnesses to this growing relationship with individuals who work for the Saudi government and others and they witnessed his conversion to Islam."

He told Tom Trento on a radio interview the following: "My contention is that Brennan is wholly unfit for government service in any national security capacity, and that would specifically make him unfit to be director of Central Intelligence. First, he has interwoven his life professionally and personally with individuals that we know are terrorists. He has overseen and approved and encouraged others to bring known leaders of Hamas and the Muslim Brotherhood into the government in positions to advise the United States government on counterterrorism strategy as well as the overall War on Terror."

"Second, Brennan has proven through his own comments publicly that he is clueless and grossly ignorant of al-Qaeda's strategy. Third and finally, what some would say is the most disturbing, is that Brennan did convert to Islam. I think the larger news is that that conversion is the culmination of the work of people in Saudi Arabia who worked for the Saudi government, and that makes John Brennan just naïve, foolish, dangerously ignorant and totally unfit for this position. That in and of itself, again, shouldn't be shocking to people. Mr. Brennan. They have the clip where he specifically says during a public address... He said during that speech that he has learned and gets his understanding of his worldview in large part from Islam. It shouldn't be a large lead to imagine he has converted to Islam."

As president, Obama pardoned the traitor Bradley/Chelsea Manning

Then President Obama and the Democrats criticized the leaks published by Julian Assange in *WikiLeaks* that were damaging to the corrupt Hillary Clinton. Those criticisms regarding leaks did not matter to Obama when they came from traitor Army soldier, Bradley/Chelsea Manning.

On January 17, 2017, Obama, while still president, commuted Chelsea Manning's sentence to a total of seven years of confinement dating from the date of arrest. Manning was released on May 17, 2017. Obama's own Secretary of Defense Ash Carter and the military were opposed to the commutation of Manning, who severely damaged America's national security. It set a terrible precedent for future traitors who may leak or share national secrets.

House of Representative Speaker Paul Ryan called it "just outrageous," tweeting that "Chelsea Manning's treachery put American lives at risk and exposed some of our nation's most sensitive secrets." He accused Obama of setting a "dangerous precedent." Alabama Senator Tom Cotton said Manning should be treated like a traitor and not as a martyr.

Vice President Mike Pence said this pardon was a mistake since Private Manning compromised the national security of the United States. Senator Marco Rubio and other Republicans in Congress denounced this shameful pardon. Democrats in Congress maintained their silence.

Chelsea Elizabeth Manning was born as Bradley Edward Manning in 1987. Manning is a transgender woman who said she had felt female since childhood and wanted to be known as Chelsea.

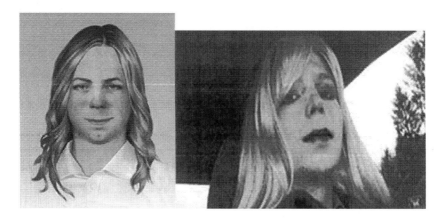

Bradley/ Chelsea Manning

Chelsea Manning was formerly Bradley Manning, an Army soldier who was convicted by court-martial in July 2013 of violations of the Espionage Act and other offenses. Manning gave over more than 700,000 classified U.S. military documents to *WikiLeaks*. These documents included battlefield reports from Afghanistan and Iraq and State Department's cables. Manning was sentenced in August 2013 to 35 years of imprisonment.

Conclusion

Former President Obama and many Democratic politicians criticized for weeks the leaks published by Julian Assange in *WikiLeaks* given to him by Russia that were damaging the corrupt Hillary Clinton. However, the criticisms regarding leaks did not matter to Obama when they came from a traitor Army soldier since the outgoing president shamefully commuted his 35-year sentence by a court martial.

It is quite obvious that John Brennan shared with Obama his love for Islam, which is much more that a religion, as it is a way of life with Shariah law. Similar to the former president, Brennan wanted to bring more members of the Muslim Brotherhood into the government of the United States. This dangerous and outrageous treason was denounced by many high-ranking retired admirals and generals as well as by this author.

It does not surprise this author that CIA Director Brennan may be behind these leaks with false information, as Donald J. Trump suspects. Trump has said many times that he does not want to accept Muslims from nations that have many Islamic terrorists. Brennan resents Trump's victory as much as his boss Obama.

Part 2

DONALD J. TRUMP IN THE WHITE HOUSE

CHAPTER 19

A new era began with the swearing-in of Donald J. Trump

Donald J. Trump took the Oath of Office on two bibles being held by his wife Melania as his ten-year-old son watched. Supreme Court Chief Justice John Roberts administered the Oath of Office.

On January 20, 2016 at noon, President Donald J. Trump took the Oath of Office presenting a completely different agenda than that of Barack Obama. He promised to take rapid action in implementing his bold new agenda to make America great and safe again. On his first day, President Trump signed an executive order directing agencies to reduce the burdens of the Affordable Care Act or ObamaCare.

White House Chief of Staff Reince Priebus directed federal agencies to impose an "immediate regulatory freeze." Earlier President Trump had stated in his inaugural address on the West Front of the Capitol, "The time for empty talk is over. Now arrives the hour of action." It was clear that the era of business as usual was over in the nation's capital.

President Trump presented his America First nationalist vision in his speech to the nation. The official White House website switched immediately as President Trump delivered his inaugural address, reflecting a new agenda for the new administration.

President Donald J. Trump delivered his inaugural address as tens of thousands braved the rain and the cold weather to see the swearing-in ceremony and listen to the speech of the 45th president.

President Trump delivered a short Inaugural Address and stated the following:

"Chief Justice Roberts, President Carter, President Clinton, President Bush, President Obama, fellow Americans, and people of the world: Thank you.

We, the citizens of America, are now joined in a great national effort to rebuild our country and to restore its promise for all of our people. Together, we will determine the course of America and the world for years to come. We will face challenges. We will confront hardships. But we will get the job done. Every four years, we gather on these steps to carry out the orderly and peaceful transfer of power, and we are grateful to President Obama and First Lady Michelle Obama for their gracious aid throughout this transition. They have been magnificent.

Today's ceremony, however, has very special meaning. Because today we are not merely transferring power from one administration to another, or from one party to another -- but we are transferring power from Washington, D.C. and giving it back to you, the American People.

For too long, a small group in our nation's Capital has reaped the rewards of government while the people have borne the cost. Washington flourished -- but the people did not share in its wealth. Politicians prospered, but the jobs left, and the factories closed. The establishment protected itself, but not the citizens of our country. Their victories have not been your victories; their triumphs have not been your triumphs; and while they celebrated in our nation's capital, there was little to celebrate for struggling families all across our land.

That all changes -- starting right here, and right now, because this moment is your moment: it belongs to you. It belongs to everyone gathered here today and everyone watching all across America. This is your day. This is your celebration. And this, the United States of America, is your country.

What truly matters is not which party controls our government, but whether our government is controlled by the people. January 20th 2017, will be remembered as the day the people became the rulers of this nation again. The forgotten men and women of our country will be forgotten no longer.

Everyone is listening to you now. You came by the tens of millions to become part of a historic movement the likes of which the world has never seen before. At the center of this movement is a crucial conviction: that a nation exists to serve its citizens. Americans want great schools for their children, safe neighborhoods for their families, and good jobs for themselves. These are the just and reasonable demands of a righteous public.

But for too many of our citizens, a different reality exists: Mothers and children trapped in poverty in our inner cities; rusted-out factories scattered like tombstones across the landscape of our nation; an education system flush with cash, but which leaves our young and beautiful students deprived of knowledge; and the crime and gangs and drugs that have stolen too many lives and robbed our country of so much unrealized potential.

This American carnage stops right here and stops right now. We are one nation -- and their pain is our pain. Their dreams are our dreams; and their success will be our success. We share one heart, one home, and one glorious destiny.

The oath of office I take today is an oath of allegiance to all Americans. For many decades, we've enriched foreign industry at the expense of American industry; subsidized the armies of other countries while allowing for the very sad depletion of our military; we've defended other nation's borders while refusing to defend our own; and spent trillions of dollars overseas while America's infrastructure has fallen into disrepair and decay.

We've made other countries rich while the wealth, strength, and confidence of our country has disappeared over the horizon. One by one, the factories shuttered and left our shores, with not even a thought about the millions upon millions of American workers left behind.

The wealth of our middle class has been ripped from their homes and then redistributed across the entire world. But that is the past. And now we are looking only to the future. We assembled here today are issuing a new decree to be heard in every city, in every foreign capital, and in every hall of power.

From this day forward, a new vision will govern our land. From this moment on, it's going to be America First. Every decision on trade, on taxes, on immigration, on foreign affairs, will be made to benefit American workers and American families. We must protect our borders from the ravages of other countries making our products, stealing our companies, and destroying our jobs. Protection will lead to great prosperity and strength.

I will fight for you with every breath in my body -- and I will never, ever let you down. America will start winning again, winning like never before. We will bring back our jobs. We will bring back our borders. We will bring back our wealth. And we will bring back our dreams.

We will build new roads, and highways, and bridges, and airports, and tunnels, and railways all across our wonderful nation. We will get our people off of welfare and back to work -- rebuilding our country with American hands and American labor. We will follow two simple rules: Buy American and hire American.

We will seek friendship and goodwill with the nations of the world -- but we do so with the understanding that it is the right of all nations to put their own interests first. We do not seek to impose our way of life on anyone, but rather to let it shine as an example for everyone to follow.

We will reinforce old alliances and form new ones -- and unite the civilized world against radical Islamic terrorism, which we will eradicate completely from the face of the Earth. At the bedrock of our politics will be a total allegiance to the United States of America, and through our loyalty to our country, we will rediscover our loyalty to each other.

When you open your heart to patriotism, there is no room for prejudice. The Bible tells us, "How good and pleasant it is when God's people live together in unity." We must speak our minds openly, debate our disagreements honestly, but always pursue solidarity. When America is united, America is totally unstoppable. There should be no fear -- we are protected, and we will always be protected.

We will be protected by the great men and women of our military and law enforcement and, most importantly, we are protected by God. Finally, we must think big and dream even bigger. In America, we understand that a nation is only living as long as it is striving. We will no longer accept politicians who are all talk and no action -- constantly complaining but never doing anything about it.

The time for empty talk is over. Now arrives the hour of action. Do not let anyone tell you it cannot be done. No challenge can match the heart and fight and spirit of America. We will not fail. Our country will thrive and prosper again. We stand at the birth of a new millennium, ready to unlock the mysteries of space, to free the Earth from the miseries of disease, and to harness the energies, industries and technologies of tomorrow.

A new national pride will stir our souls, lift our sights, and heal our divisions. It is time to remember that old wisdom our soldiers will never forget: that whether we are black or brown or white, we all bleed the same red blood of patriots, we all enjoy the same glorious freedoms, and we all salute the same great American Flag.

And whether a child is born in the urban sprawl of Detroit or the windswept plains of Nebraska, they look up at the same night sky, they fill their heart with the same dreams, and they are infused with the breath of life by the same almighty Creator. So, to all Americans, in every city near and far, small and large, from mountain to mountain, and from ocean to ocean, hear these words:

You will never be ignored again. Your voice, your hopes, and your dreams will define our American destiny. And your courage and goodness and love will forever guide us along the way.

Together, we will make America strong again. We will make wealthy again. We will make America proud again. We will make America safe again. And yes, together, we will make America great again. Thank you. God bless you. And God bless America."

A new vision for America

On January 20, 2016, Judson Berger wrote on *FoxNews.org* an article titled "Trump pursues new vision on first day as president." He explained that a top issue was President Trump's "America First Energy Plan," which included a commitment to eliminate Obama's policies to curb global warming and regulate U.S. waterways. The Trump administration considered these regulations "harmful and unnecessary policies" that hurt the economy. "Lifting these restrictions will greatly help American workers, increasing wages by more than $30 billion over the next seven years," the White House website stated. The White House website also posted plans for the military, foreign policy, the economy, and more. The jobs plan committed to "pro-growth tax reform" including a reduction in the corporate tax rate.

Berger pointed out that President Trump signed nomination papers for his Cabinet choices and also signed his first legislation allowing retired General James Mattis to serve as Defense Secretary. The Senate later confirmed retired General Mattis to lead the Pentagon, as well as retired General John Kelly to lead the Department of Homeland Security. Senate Democrats refused to consider more Cabinet nominees on the first day.

Berger explained that anti-Trump protesters in Washington, D.C. smashed the windows of businesses, burned a car, and clashed with police– who used pepper spray and tear gas to try to control the crowds. However, tens of thousands of President Trump supporters also came out, watching the 45th president's inaugural address from the National Mall and later the parade.

The West Dade Trump Victory Office volunteers celebrated President Donald J. Trump inaugural events

Martie raised her arms in excitement as Donald J. Trump took the Oath of Office. Roberto Godoy, a Miami-Dade Republican Executive Committee member, stood behind this writer who is also an elected member of the Miami-Dade Republican Executive Committee.

Another volunteer, Rene Espinosa, held an American flag as he watched with over 100 volunteers and friends of the West Dade Trump Victory Office in Miami. This writer was Office Manager of that office, one of three in Miami-Dade County and one of 29 in Florida.

This writer and one of the volunteers of the West Dade Trump Victory Office, Martie Mees, watched as Donald J. Trump became the 45th president of the United States at Las Vegas restaurant in Miami.

One volunteer does a victory sign and Magaly Alfonso, a member of the Junta Patriótica Cubana, held a sign "Cubanas for Trump." This writer showed a Trump Pence sign, one that he kept for himself out of the hundreds he distributed when he served as Manager of the West Dade Trump Victory Office in Miami.

Miguel Alvarez, former President of the Brigade 2506 Veterans Association, Eli César, a Brigade member who held the insignia of the Brigade 2506, and this writer, also a brigade member, displayed a Trump Pence sign.

Antonio D. Esquivel, President of the Junta Patriótica Cubana, and his wife Gloria shared a victory sign with this writer during the Watching Victory Party at Las Vegas restaurant in Miami.

This writer appeared in this picture with two hard-working volunteers, Maria Magdalena Estupiñan and Marcelino Totorica, a member of the Junta Patriótica Cubana. Marcelino came to the West Dade Trump Victory Office every day.

Conclusion

President Trump presented his America First nationalist anti-globalist vision in his speech to the nation. The president criticized how in the past America subsidized the armies of other countries while allowing for the very sad depletion of our military; enriched foreign industry at the expense of American industry; defended other nation's borders while refusing to defend our own; and spent trillions of dollars overseas while America's infrastructure fell into disrepair and decay.

President Trump criticized severely the Washington establishment saying that for too long, a small group in our nation's Capital had reaped the rewards of government while the people had borne the cost. Washington flourished, but the people did not share in its wealth. Politicians prospered, but the jobs left, and the factories closed. The establishment protected itself, but not the citizens of our country. Their victories have not been your victories; their triumphs have not been your triumphs; and while they celebrated in our nation's capital, there was little to celebrate for struggling families all across our land. He promised to improve the economy so that he forgotten men and women of our country will be forgotten no longer.

President Trump promised to work on his agenda rapidly and said the time for empty talk was over. Now arrived the hour of action. It was clear that the era of business as usual was over in the nation's capital. The president said that he was going to reinforce old alliances and form new ones and unite the civilized world against radical Islamic terrorism, which we would eradicate completely from the face of the Earth. It is very important to note that unlike his weak predecessor, President Trump used the term "radical Islamic terrorism."

President Trump said that every domestic and foreign policy would place America First. He said that every decision on trade, on taxes, on immigration, on foreign affairs, would be made to benefit American workers and American families. The president promised to bring back jobs and wealth to America. He vowed to improve America's neglected infrastructure by building new roads, and highways, bridges, airports, tunnels and railways across America. President Trump said that he wanted to get Americans off of welfare and back to work, rebuilding our country with American hands and American labor.

It is clear to this writer that Donald J. Trump will be one of our finest president and commander-in-chief. He is bringing back prosperity and jobs and making Make America Great Again and America Safe Again. A new era in our beloved country started with President Trump who is leaving behind the failed domestic and foreign policies of Barack Obama.

CHAPTER 20

General John Kelly is the White House Chief of Staff and former Secretary of Homeland Security

President Donald Trump and retired U.S. Marine Corps General John Kelly

President Donald J. Trump appointed retired U.S. Marine Corps General John Kelly as Secretary of the Department of Homeland Security and later White House Chief of Staff. John Kelly is a highly respected Marine Corps general, who served three tours in Iraq and lost a son in combat in Afghanistan. Among his many assignments, General John Kelly served as the top Marine commander in Iraq in 2008 when he commanded the Marine force based in Anbar province.

Retired U.S. Marine Corps General John Kelly and his wife are a Gold Star family

General Kelly's son, Marine First Lieutenant Robert Kelly, age 29, was killed on November 9, 2010 while conducting combat operations in Helmand province, Afghanistan. The military calls a Gold Star family those unfortunate parents who lose a son or a daughter in combat. Lieutenant Robert Kelly was assigned to the 3rd Battalion, 5th Marine Regiment, 1st Marine Division, I Marine Expeditionary Force, at Camp Pendleton, California. First Lieutenant Robert Kelly was a graduate of Florida State University in Tallahassee, Florida.

General John Kelly's two sons, Marine Lieutenant Robert Kelly and Captain John Kelly Junior, are standing next to their father.

General John Kelly wrote this letter to family and friends after the death of his brave son:

"As I think you all know by now our Robert was killed in action protecting our country, its people, and its values from a terrible and relentless enemy, on 9 November, in Sangin, Afghanistan. He was leading his Grunts on a dismounted patrol when he was taken. They are shaken, but will recover quickly and already back at it. He went quickly and thank God he did not suffer. In combat that is as good as it gets, and we are thankful. We are a broken hearted - but proud family. He was a wonderful and precious boy living a meaningful life. He was in exactly the place he wanted to be, doing exactly what he wanted to do, surrounded by the best men on this earth - his Marines and Navy Doc.

The nation he served has honored us with promoting him posthumously to First Lieutenant of Marines. We will bury our son, now First Lieutenant Robert Michael Kelly USMC, in Arlington National Cemetery on 22 November. Services will commence at 1245 at Fort Myer. We will likely have a memorial receiving at a yet to be designated funeral home on 21 November.

The coffin will be closed. Our son Captain John Kelly USMC, himself a multi-tour combat veteran and the best big brother on this earth, will escort the body from Dover Air Force Base to Arlington. From the moment he was killed he has never been alone and will remain under the protection of a Marine to his final resting place.

Many have offered prayers for us and we thank you, but his wonderful wife Heather and the rest of the clan ask that you direct the majority of your prayers to his platoon of Marines, still in contact and in "harm's way," and at greater risk without his steady leadership. Thank you all for the many kindnesses we could not get through this without you all. Thank you all for being there for us. The pain in unimaginable, and we could not do this without you.

In his final Pentagon news conference, he spoke about the loss of his son — a topic he does not often discuss publicly. General Kelly stated the following: "To lose a child is — I can't imagine anything worse than that. I used to think, when I'd go to all of my trips up to Bethesda, Walter Reed, I'll go to the funerals with the secretaries of defense that I could somehow imagine what it would be like. When you lose one in combat, there's a — in my opinion — there's a pride that goes with it, that he didn't have to be there doing what he was doing. He wanted to be there. He volunteered."

General Kelly receives occasional letters from Gold Star families who are asking, 'Was it worth it?' He responds as follows: "And I always go back with this: It doesn't matter. That's not our question to ask as parents. That young person thought it was worth it, and that's the only opinion that counts."

General John Kelly military career

The Department of Defense published General Kelly biography stated: "General Kelly enlisted in the Marine Corps in 1970, and was discharged as a sergeant in 1972, after serving in an infantry company with the 2nd Marine Division, Camp Lejeune, North Carolina. Following his graduation from the University of Massachusetts in 1976, he was commissioned and returned to the 2nd Marine Division, where he served as a rifle and weapons platoon commander, company executive officer, assistant operations officer, and infantry company commander.

General John Kelly was born and raised in Boston, Massachusetts.

Sea duty in Mayport, Florida followed, at which time he served aboard aircraft carriers *USS Forrestal* and *USS Independence*. In 1980, then Captain Kelly transferred to the U.S. Army's Infantry Officer Advanced Course in Fort Benning, Georgia. After graduation, he was assigned to Headquarters Marine Corps, Washington, DC, serving there from 1981 through 1984, as an assignment monitor. Captain Kelly returned to the 2nd Marine Division in 1984 to command a rifle and weapons company. Promoted to the rank of Major in 1987, he served as the battalion's operations officer.

In 1987, Major Kelly transferred to the Basic School, Quantico, Virginia, serving first as the head of the Offensive Tactics Section, Tactics Group, and later Director of the Infantry Officer Course. After three years of instructing young officers, he attended the Marine Corps Command and Staff College, and the School for Advanced Warfare both located at Quantico.

After, completing duty under instruction and being selected as Lieutenant Colonel, he was assigned as Commanding Officer, 1st Light Armored Reconnaissance Battalion, 1st Marine Division, at Camp Pendleton, California. Holding this command position for two years, Lieutenant Colonel Kelly returned to the East Coast in 1994 to attend the National War College in Washington, D.C. He graduated in 1995 and was selected to serve as the Commandant's Liaison Officer to the U.S. House of Representatives, Capitol Hill, where he was promoted to the rank of Colonel.

In 1999, Colonel Kelly transferred to joint duty and served as the Special Assistant to the Supreme Allied Commander, Europe, in Mons, Belgium. He returned to the United States in 2001, and was assigned to a third tour of duty at Camp Lejeune, now as the Assistant Chief of Staff G-3 with the 2nd Marine Division.

In 2002, he was selected to the rank of Brigadier General, Colonel Kelly again served with the 1st Marine Division, this time as the Assistant Division Commander. Much of Brigadier General Kelly's two-year assignment was spent deployed in Iraq. He then returned to the Headquarters Marine Corps as the Legislative Assistant to the Commandant from 2004 to 2007.

Promoted to major general, he returned to Camp Pendleton as the Commanding General, I Marine Expeditionary Force (Forward). He was deployed to Iraq in early 2008 for a year-long mission, replacing II Marine Expeditionary Force (Forward) as Multinational Force-West in Al Anbar and western Ninewa provinces. Lt Gen Kelly commanded Marine Forces Reserve and Marine Forces North from October 2009 to March 2011. General Kelly comes to United States Southern Command from his previous position as the Senior Military Assistant to the Secretary of Defense from March 2011 to October 2012."

At Southern Command, General Kelly spoke bluntly about his need for more resources to fight the drug trade. During a 2014 hearing, he told the Senate Armed Services Committee that he did not have the ships or surveillance assets to get more than 20% of the drugs leaving Colombia for the United States.

General Kelly served as Combatant Commander of the United States Southern Command from November 19, 2012 to January 16, 2016 and soon after that assignment he retired. The United States Southern Command (USSOUTHCOM) is located in the city of Doral in Miami-Dade County. It is one of nine United Combatant Commands in the United States Department of

Defense. According to *Wikipedia*, the Southern Command is responsible for providing contingency planning, operations, and security cooperation for Central and South America, the Caribbean, their territorial waters, and for the force protection of U.S. military resources at these locations. USSOUTHCOM is also responsible for ensuring the defense of the Panama Canal and the canal area.

Immigration enforcement is a familiar issue for General John Kelly. As a former head of the Southern Command, General Kelly worked with the Department of Homeland Security (DHS) to dismantle migrant smuggling networks. General Kelly also worked closely with Immigration and Customs Enforcement.

General John Kelly's opening statement during his confirmation hearing in the Senate

"Mr. Chairman, Ranking Member McCaskill, and distinguished Senators of the Committee, please accept my thanks and appreciation for considering my nomination to lead the men and women of the U.S. Department of Homeland Security. Senator McCain and Secretary Gates – I am grateful that each of you took the time to be here on my behalf, and for your kind words.

Please allow me to introduce my family. My wife, Karen, is here, as are my daughter and son-in-law. Anyone who has answered the call to serve our country knows that the personal sacrifices of public service are often felt most acutely by their families. As the wife and mother to three strong-willed Marines and one determined FBI agent, Karen has been my anchor and I'm grateful for her love and partnership.

Over the past 45 years, I have been privileged to serve my nation as both an enlisted Marine and an officer. I have led platoons and divisions. I have held senior command positions in Iraq and served as the Combatant Commander of the U.S. Southern Command and as the Senior Military Assistant to two Secretaries of Defense—Secretaries Gates and Panetta. I have worked with our allies, across agencies, the private sector, and with independent experts to identify innovative, comprehensive solutions to current and emerging threats.

These assignments—while varied—shared the common characteristics of working within and leading large, complex, and diverse mission-focused organizations, while under great pressure to produce results. I am humbled to once again be called to serve, this time with the men and women of the Department of Homeland Security. As I solemnly swore before God when I entered the Marine Corps, if confirmed, I will faithfully support and defend the Constitution of the United States against all enemies foreign and domestic—every second of every day.

I believe in America and the principles upon which our country and way of life are guaranteed. I believe in respect, tolerance, and diversity of opinion. I have a profound respect for the rule of law and will always strive to uphold it.

I have never had a problem speaking truth to power, and I firmly believe that those in power deserve full candor and my honest assessment and recommendations. I love my country, and I will do everything within my power to preserve our liberty, enforce our laws, and protect our citizens. I recognize the many challenges facing the Department of Homeland Security—and should I be confirmed—I look forward to partnering with you all to protect the homeland.

I look forward to discussing the future of this Department and answering the Committee's questions. Thank you for this opportunity.

Conclusion

Donald J. Trump has made a superb selection with General John Kelly as Secretary of Homeland Security and later as White House Chief of Staff. General Kelly said, "I will faithfully support and defend the Constitution of the United States against all enemies foreign and domestic—every second of every day." The fact is that General Kelly is a great patriot who has defended America everywhere every second of every day for 45 years.

CHAPTER 21

Mile Pompeo, the CIA Director

On January 23, 2017, Republican Congressman Mike Pompeo from Kansas was confirmed as CIA Director by a 66 to 32 vote in the Senate. On November 18, 2016, he was nominated by then President-elect Donald J. Trump as Director of the Central Intelligence Agency. Pompeo was the third Cabinet nominee to be approved by the Senate.

Who is Michael Richard "Mike" Pompeo?

Michael Richard "Mike" Pompeo was born on December 30, 1963. On November 18, 2016, he was nominated by then President-elect Donald J. Trump as Director of the Central Intelligence Agency.

According to *Wikipedia*, Mike Pompeo served as a Congressman for Kansas's 4th Congressional District since 2011. He was born in Orange, California. Pompeo graduated first in his class in 1986 at the U.S. Military Academy at West Point. He majored in Mechanical Engineering.

Upon graduation, Pompeo served in the Army as an Armor Branch cavalry officer from 1986 to 1991. During this time, he patrolled the Iron Curtain before the fall of the Berlin Wall. He was assigned to the 2nd Squadron, 7th Cavalry in the Fourth Infantry Division. He served his last tour during the Gulf War.

Subsequently, Pompeo received a J.D. from Harvard Law School, where he was an editor of the Harvard Law Review. He worked as a lawyer and founded several businesses. Upon his election to Congress, Pompeo was appointed to the Permanent Select Committee on Intelligence and the Energy and Commerce Committee. He also served on the House Select Committee on Benghazi.

Pompeo criticized former President Obama for being indecisive and not supporting the military. He has supported the surveillance programs of the National Security Agency. In a 2013 speech on the House floor, Pompeo said Muslim leaders who fail to denounce acts of terrorism done in the name of Islam are "potentially complicit" in the attacks.

On November 18, 2016, John Hayward wrote an article titled "Ten Things You Did Not Know about Representative Mike Pompeo" which was published in the website *Breitbart*. Hayward stated the following:

"1. Pompeo, 52, graduated first in his class at West Point in 1986, with a major in mechanical engineering. His Army service included patrolling the Berlin Wall before it came down. "My generation was the tail end of the Cold War," Pompeo said during a 2014 visit to Kansas State, where he discussed the battle against the Islamic State. He added: Before that, you had Nazism. This will ultimately be this generation's fight, this battle where radical Islam continues to want to take on the West in fundamental ways, in the same way these other ideologies wanted to do before. I think we're going to be at this for a while. We ought to be vigorous and thoughtful and effective in the way we respond. In a 2011 profile of soldiers in Congress published by the Association of the United States Army, Pompeo is quoted as saying, I still remember the first acronym I learned, BLUF: Bottom Line Up Front. I still try to communicate that way. No reason to dance around getting to the point."

"2. He continued his education at Harvard Law School after completing his active-duty Army service in 1991, and was an editor at the *Harvard Law Review*. He worked as a lawyer in Washington for several years, at the powerful law firm Williams & Connolly. When he arrived here after graduating first in his class at West Point and serving with distinction as an Army officer, he was bent on going into politics, law professor Mary Ann Glendon recalled in a 2011 interview continuing: When he went into business instead, I felt real regret to see yet another young person of great integrity and ability swerve from his original path. But in fact, he didn't. Mike waited until he and his wife, Susan, had raised their son and assured a sound financial footing for the family. This past November, he was elected to the U.S. Congress from the 4th District of Kansas."

"3. As Professor Glendon said in her interview, Pompeo did not go into politics immediately after his time as a D.C. lawyer. Instead, he returned to his hometown in Orange County, California, and founded a company called Thayer Aerospace with some friends from his West Point days. After serving as Thayer CEO for more than a decade, he sold Thayer and became president of Sentry International, a Wichita-based company that sells oil field equipment…"

"4. Pompeo serves on both the House Intelligence and House Energy and Commerce committees. He was also appointed to the House Select Benghazi Committee."

"5. Perhaps surprisingly, given his business background, Pompeo's net worth is rated below average by various public interest sites – 69 percent below the average member of Congress, according to InsideGov, which pegs his net worth at $345,011."

"6. Pompeo was elected to Congress in 2010 on the Tea Party wave and is now serving his third term. He was, at one point, seen as a dark-horse challenger to Rep. Paul Ryan (R-WI) for Speaker of the House. There were also rumors he was considering a Senate run. While we have had our share of strong differences – principally on the politicization of the tragedy in Benghazi – I know that he is someone who is willing to listen and engage, both key qualities in a C.I.A. director," Rep. Adam Schiff (D-CA), ranking Democrat on House Intelligence Committee, said in praise of Pompeo on Friday morning."

"7. Pompeo was originally a supporter of Senator Marco Rubio's (R-FL) presidential bid, moving his support to Trump after it became clear he would be the GOP nominee. He is close to Vice President-elect Mike Pence, having served with him when Pence was in Congress. During a breakfast for Kansas delegates to the Republican National Convention in July 2016, he called Pence a "friend and mentor" whose "values … are very much like those of us in Kansas. You have seen him make good decisions in his business life, his family life – with his children, so I am excited for a commander-in-chief who fearlessly puts America out in front, Pompeo said of Trump at the same event."

"8. He is a strong critic of the Iran nuclear deal, remarking on Twitter that he is looking forward to rolling back this disastrous deal with the world's largest state sponsor of terrorism. Among other actions, he has sponsored bills to increase sanctions on Iran and to require the Obama administration to investigate Iran for violating the Geneva Convention in its treatment of ten captured American sailors last year. He also unsuccessfully attempted to obtain a visa to visit Iran and observe its most recent round of elections."

"9. Pompeo has supported online surveillance programs. He has said former NSA contractor Edward Snowden should be "brought back from Russia and given due process." He stated, "I think the proper outcome would be that he would be given a death sentence" because he "put friends of mine, friends of yours who serve in the military today at enormous risk because of the information he stole and then released to foreign powers.""

"10. Pompeo has been accused of Islamophobia by the Council on American-Islamic Relations (CAIR is a Muslim Brotherhood Front), for statements such as this one, made after the Boston Marathon bombing in 2013: "When the most devastating terrorist attacks on America in the last 20 years come overwhelmingly from people of a single faith, and are performed in the name of that faith, a special obligation falls on those that are the leaders of that faith." He continued, "Instead of responding, silence has made these Islamic leaders across America potentially complicit in these acts and more importantly still, in those that may well follow.""

Testimony of Congressman Mike Pompeo before the Senate Select Committee on Intelligence during his confirmation hearing on January 12, 2017

Congressman Mike Pompeo stated the following:

"Should I be fortunate enough to be confirmed by the Senate, I hope to visit you more often from Langley than I have from across the Capitol. I mean this not as a criticism of relations between the two Houses of Congress, but a recognition of how much value I would place on relations between the CIA and its Congressional overseers. Since I first joined the House Permanent Select Committee on Intelligence (HPSCI) in the 112th Congress, I have felt a special appreciation for the hard work that goes into Congressional oversight. The tremendous honor we have in overseeing the intelligence community is only tempered by the sobering burden of grappling in secret with the many national security challenges facing our country.

I would like to thank President-elect Trump for nominating me to serve in this role and for the faith he has shown in me. It is an honor to be selected as the next steward of the premier intelligence agency that is the CIA. I look forward to working with Senator Dan Coats, nominee for the Director of National Intelligence, and supporting him in his critical role, if we are both confirmed...

My job will be to stay clearly on the side of intelligence collection and objective analysis of our national security challenges—presenting factual intelligence and sound judgments to policymakers, including this Committee. I have spent the majority of my life outside the realm of politics – as a cavalry officer in the United States Army, then as a litigator, and then running two manufacturing businesses. Returning to duty requiring hard work and unerring candor is something that is in my bones.

Today, I would like to first briefly sketch some of the specific challenges facing the U.S.; second, address trends in intelligence I have seen from my post on HPSCI; and finally, describe what I see as the CIA's role in addressing these challenges.

Threat Environment

First, as many have noted, this is the most complicated threat environment the U.S. has faced in recent memory. The litany is now familiar:

- As Director Clapper acknowledged at the beginning of 2016: "there are now more Sunni violent extremist groups, members, and safe havens than at any time in history."

- ISIS remains a resilient movement, has metastasized, and shockingly has controlled major urban centers in the Middle East for well over two years. Whereas a few years ago, we focused on stemming the flow of foreign fighters going to Syria and Iraq, today, the concern is making sure they, and those they inspire, are prevented from expanding their reach, returning home, or slaughtering more innocent people.

- Syria is a failed state and has become one of the worst humanitarian catastrophes of the 21st century. This conflict has led to the rise of extremism, sectarianism, instability in the region and Europe, and the worst refugee crisis the world has faced in recent memory.

- Iran – the leading state sponsor of terror – has become an emboldened, disruptive player in the Middle East, fueling tension with our Sunni allies.

- Russia has reasserted itself aggressively, invading and occupying Ukraine, threatening Europe, and doing nearly nothing to aid in the destruction of ISIS.

- As China flexes its muscles and expands its military and economic reach, its activities in the South and East China Seas and in cyberspace are pushing new boundaries and creating real tension.

- North Korea has dangerously accelerated its nuclear and ballistic missile capabilities, with little regard for international pressure.

- In an increasingly inter-connected world, the cyber domain presents new and growing challenges. Using evolving cyber tools, state and non-state actors continue to probe U.S. systems, exploit vulnerabilities, and challenge our interests.

Intelligence Trends

Intelligence is vital to every national security issue facing the United States. As some have said, it is the "lifeblood" of national security and is more in demand than ever.

- Intelligence enables better-informed decisions by reducing uncertainty; it is critical in seeking to avoid strategic or tactical surprise, and to giving our armed forces superior domain awareness.

- We rely on intelligence from around the globe to keep danger from our shores. High quality precision intelligence enables our military efforts. More and more, intelligence is critical to making effective other elements of national power including sanctions against weapons proliferators, cyber criminals, perpetrators of war crimes, and terrorist financiers.

- We share capabilities and intelligence to improve relationships in furtherance of our national security objectives. Foreign governments and liaison services are vital partners in preventing attacks and providing crucial intelligence. It is important that we thank our foreign partners for standing with us.

- There are at least five long term trends making the urgency of recognizing and supporting intelligence critically important.

- First, the Intelligence Community finds itself a potential victim of a longer term negative budgetary trend. Given the vital role of intelligence in national security, and given the increasing threats we face, this makes little sense.

- Second, technological advancement across the globe, even by non-hostile countries, is challenging the U.S. advantage, as commercial technologies spread into the hands of those who wish us harm. The world is gaining on the U.S.

- We have long seen this dynamic with the proliferation of chemical and biological weapons and ballistic missile technology, but increasingly in the cyber domain, countries thought to be unsophisticated, such as North Korea, have overcome what appear to be low technological barriers of entry to engage in offensive cyber operations. The U.S. must continue to invest wisely to maintain a decisive advantage.

- The effects of dislocation, lack of governance, and the rise of non-state actors threaten our national security and present critical challenges to the Intelligence Community. This is creating new targets for CIA's intelligence collection and analysis that compete for attention with the usual state suspects and bad actors.

- Finally, the insider threat problem has grown exponentially in the digital age. Counterintelligence is a perennial issue and we must be increasingly aware that those within our agencies have access to millions of files. By the same token, the use of digital assets by foreign actors creates intelligence opportunities.

CIA's Role

I want to talk in more detail about today's challenges. The greatest threats to our national security have always been the CIA's top priorities. And the CIA has always been at the forefront of America's comprehensive efforts to meet these threats. Since September 11, 2001, the CIA's activities have been extraordinary. As the tip of the spear in the war on terrorism, the CIA has put tremendous pressure on our enemies, reducing their freedom to plan, communicate and travel.

The CIA has always played integral roles in America's fight against radical Islamic terror. It sounded warning bells before 9/11 of al Qaeda's growing global reach. CIA officers were the first into Afghanistan to lay the groundwork for the military effort that struck a major blow to al Qaeda and drove the Taliban from power. From understanding and tearing apart al Qaeda in Iraq networks, to the hunt for bin Laden, the CIA has been at the forefront of the fight every step of the way.

My outline above of hard targets and challenges merely skims the surface of the potential threats facing the United States. If confirmed, it will be the CIA's mission to bring other pressing problems, risks, and challenges from regions and countries that don't always make the front page to the attention of senior policymakers. Indeed, if we are doing our job, we will help U.S. policy makers act early to prevent such problems from becoming front page news.

- It will also be the CIA's mission, and my own, to ensure the Agency remains the best in the world at its core mission: discovering the truth and searching out information.

- In this complex threat environment, we must gather intelligence from the most elusive targets and in the most difficult environments. We will need to rely on liaison services and new relationships, which are critical to gathering information around the world. Even so, U.S. intelligence must continue to expand its global coverage to keep up with these threats. While intelligence sharing relationships with our friends and allies are important, they cannot replace our own unilateral recruiting and operations. To protect America, the CIA must continue to be the world's premier espionage service.

- One obvious emerging area for increased focus – both unilaterally and in conjunction with our partners – is the cyber domain. The internet – and the connectivity of our world, systems, and devices – is a borderless, global environment, easily and frequently exploited by sophisticated adversaries like China and Russia, as well as by less sophisticated adversaries like Iran and North Korea, non-state actors, terrorist groups, criminal organizations, and hackers. While NSA and Cyber Command play leading roles, cyber has become critical to virtually every intelligence operation and CIA must continue to operate at the forefront on this issue.

- As the President-elect has made clear, one of my top priorities, if confirmed, is to assist in defeating ISIS. Radical Islamic terrorism is both a symptom and a catalyst of the terrible conflicts raging in the Middle East that have created both a humanitarian and strategic catastrophe. The enduring capability of al Qaeda and its affiliates, the rise and resilience of ISIS and Islamic extremists in Libya and across the Middle East, and the brutality of al Shabaab and Boko Haram, should remind us of the need to maintain an aggressive counterterrorism posture. It is also critical to address what manifestations of this threat and ideology emerge – beyond ISIS and al Qaeda.

- We must also be rigorously fair and objective in assessing the Joint Comprehensive Plan of Action. As the deal permits domestic enrichment and other nuclear research and development, U.S. policymakers will need increased intelligence collection and insightful analysis. While as a Member of Congress I opposed the Iran deal, if confirmed, my role will change. It will be to drive the Agency to aggressively pursue collection operations and ensure analysts have the time, political space, and resources to make objective and methodologically sound judgments. If confirmed, I will present their judgments to policymakers.

- The same goes for Russia. It is a policy decision as to what to do with Russia, but I understand it will be essential that the Agency provide policymakers with accurate intelligence and clear-eyed analysis of Russian activities.

- The Agency must also serve as the nation's sentinel for new and emerging threats and trends, monitoring the convergence of rogue actors and capabilities, and sources of instability that can spread across the globe and undermine U.S. national security. This means that the Agency needs the means, capabilities, reach, and awareness to understand and convey where threats are emerging and how U.S. interests may be vulnerable. This requires constant innovation, analytic rigor, and operational flexibility – hallmarks of the CIA.

As a Member of the House Intelligence Committee, I fully appreciate the need for transparency with the Congressional oversight committees. If the Intelligence Community does not secure the support of the appropriate Congressional authorities for its activities, the legislative backlash from controversial intelligence failures and controversies can be severe and counterproductive.

We owe it to our constituents to get to the bottom of intelligence failures – as this Committee did with the pre-war Iraq intelligence. But we owe it to the brave Americans of the intelligence community not to shirk our responsibility when unauthorized disclosures to the media expose controversial intelligence activities, or when Edward Snowden, from the comfort of his Moscow safe house, misleads the American people about the NSA's surveillance activities.

I cannot stress strongly enough how proud of the CIA's workforce Americans would be if they could peek behind the curtains, as the Committee gets to do, to see them in action. The incredible talent, bravery, and ingenuity these patriots put on the line every day in defense of our country are constant inspirations to me.

On my first visit out to the CIA headquarters a few years ago, I was walking through an analytical targeting cell. I saw a woman who appeared as though she had not slept for weeks, poring over a data set on her screen. I stopped, introduced myself and asked her what she was working on. She said she thought she was just hours away from solving a riddle about the location of a particularly bad character that she had been pursuing for months. She was not about to abandon her post. She had her mission and its completion would make America safer. A true patriot. In the past years, I have come to know that there are countless men and women just like her working to crush our adversaries with world class intelligence operations.

As these quiet professionals' grapple with an overwhelming series of challenges in this increasingly uncertain world, they deserve our support and our respect. When we ask them to do difficult things, they should not have to wonder whether we will stand beside them if things go sideways. We should have their backs. Full stop.

When there are intelligence failures, operations that go off the rails, or controversial disclosures, if I am fortunate enough to be confirmed, I pledge to come to the Committee in a timely fashion – and be as forthcoming as possible. But I believe that leaders of the Intelligence Community and Congress owe it to the young men and women who risk their lives for us to do our utmost to keep mistakes from being politicized.

This past weekend, I visited Arlington National Cemetery. I've done this many times, but on this visit, I paid special attention to the markers that commemorate CIA officers who have perished ensuring our freedom and working to meet America's intelligence demands.

From Afghanistan to Korea and from Lebanon to Africa, and in so many places most Americans will never know, Agency officers put their lives at risk. Too often, because of the nature of their work, we know little about these men and women and what they do. What we do know, is that they were prepared to give so much for each of us. We know the sacrifices of the families of each CIA officer as well. As I walked among these heroes, I was reminded of the sacred trust that will be granted to me if I am confirmed. I will never fail it.

I am honored to have been nominated to lead the finest intelligence agency the world has ever known—working to keep safe the people of the greatest nation in the history of civilization. If confirmed, I will be sworn to defend the United States Constitution for the third time in my life – first as a soldier, then as a member of the House of Representatives, and, now, to work for the President and with each of you. I look forward to your questions today."

President Donald J. Trump spoke at the CIA headquarters

President Donald J. Trump spoke at the CIA headquarters on January 21, 2017.

The president said the following: "But I want to say that there is nobody that feels stronger about the intelligence community and the CIA than Donald Trump. There's nobody...Very, very few people could do the job you people do. And I want to just let you know, I am so behind you. And I know maybe sometimes you haven't gotten the backing that you've wanted, and you're going to get so much backing. But we're going to do great things. We're going to do great things. We've been fighting these wars for longer than any wars we've ever fought. We have not used the real abilities that we have. We've been restrained. We have to get rid of ISIS. Have to get rid of ISIS. We have no choice. Radical Islamic terrorism. And I said it yesterday -- it has to be eradicated just off the face of the Earth. This is evil. This is evil. And you know, I can understand the other side. We can all understand the other side. There can be wars between countries, there can be wars."

"But I met Mike Pompeo, and it was the only guy I met. I didn't want to meet anybody else. I said, cancel everybody else. Cancel. Now, he was approved, essentially, but they're doing little political games with me. But I met Mike Pompeo, and it was the only guy I met. I didn't want to meet anybody else. I said, cancel everybody else. Cancel. Now, he was approved, essentially, but they're doing little political games with me. He was one of the three. Now, last night, as you know, General Mattis, fantastic guy, and General Kelly got approved. And Mike Pompeo was supposed to be in that group. It was going to be the three of them. Can you imagine all of these guys? People respect -- you know, they respect that military sense. All my political people, they're not doing so well. The political people aren't doing so well but you. We're going to get them all through, but some will take a little bit longer than others."

"But Mike was literally -- I had a group of -- what, we had nine different people? Now, I must say, I didn't mind cancelling eight appointments. That wasn't the worst thing in the world. But I met him, and I said, he is so good. Number one in his class at West Point... I believe that this group is going to be one of the most important groups in this country toward making us safe, toward making us winners again, toward ending all of the problems. We have so many problems that are interrelated that we don't even think of, but interrelated to the kind of havoc and fear that this sick group of people has caused. So, I can only say that I am with you 1,000 percent."

"I just wanted to really say that I love you, I respect you. There's nobody I respect more. You're going to do a fantastic job. And we're going to start winning again, and you're going to be leading the charge. So, thank you all very much. Thank you -- you're beautiful. Thank you all very much. Have a good time. I'll be back. I'll be back. Thank you."

Conclusion

Congressman Mike Pompeo was an excellent choice for the position of Director of the CIA. The agency has had problems in the past but having an intelligent patriot at the head of this important intelligence agency, such as Mike Pompeo, who will provide excellent leadership is a major step in the right direction.

CHAPTER 22

WikiLeaks released thousands of documents from the CIA

On March 7, 2017 Julian Assange's *WikiLeaks* released 8,761 documents and files from the CIA's Center for Cyber Intelligence dated between 2013 and 2016 that allegedly exposed CIA software tools used to break into technology such as smartphones, internet-connected televisions, and computer operating systems, and message applications. The *WikiLeaks* massive release of documents and files could be the worst breech in the CIA's history.

WikiLeaks indicated that the stolen documents are only 1% of what it has and that later other documents will be dumped. It also pointed out that the classified information is bigger in size and significance than the collection of National Security Agency documents revealed by former U.S. intelligence contractor Edward Snowden. This really hurts America's national security and the theft occurred when Obama was president and the Marxist Wahhabi Muslim John Brennan was his CIA Director.

Senator John McCain (Republican from Arizona) was very concerned about *WikiLeaks'* threat to release the CIA code. "It's of the utmost seriousness. If they can hack the CIA they can hack anybody," he told the *Daily News* on March 7. "They've shown a capability that they can hack into our most important secrets, our most important classified material. That's what bothers me," he said. Senator McCain further indicated he wanted to see a "greater emphasis" from the Trump administration in dealing with the issue, and speculated that Russia may have been involved, given its previous ties to *WikiLeaks*. Senator John McCain and others need to be equally concerned with the shameful spying on Americans by the CIA!

Julian Assange is the founder of the anti- secrecy organization *WikiLeaks*.

Julian Assange alleged to have received the files — nicknamed "Vault 7" — from a former CIA contractor, saying that the "archive appears to have been circulated by former U.S. government hackers and contractors in an unauthorized manner." Assange is a traitor but, at least, he informed Americans of the extent of the CIA spying on Americans.

On March 8, 2017, Paul Sonne wrote an article titled "CIA Tapped Holes in Devices, *WikiLeaks* Dump Allegedly Reveals" which was published in the *Wall Street Journal*. Sonne explained that the stolen CIA documents and files indicate that the agency was able to hack into many popular consumer products, including Apple's iOS, the mobile operating system used on iPhones. Hacking tools for the iPhone are considered especially valuable because the technology is so widely used. One particular hacking tool appears to remain on an iPhone even after it has been rebooted, which would make it particularly valuable to a hacker.

Sonne pointed out that many of the documents posted by *WikiLeaks* include entries for tools such as Shoulder Surfer, which can extract data from a Microsoft Exchange database without the need for credentials, and Weeping Angel, a joint program with British intelligence to hack Samsung's internet-connected television and transform it into a covert listening device. The documents also showed how the CIA developed the ability to activate the camera and microphone of a person's smartphone and covertly and surreptitiously retrieve an individual's geolocation and audio and text communications. This writer owns an Apple smartphone and the most modern Samsung television, and it is an outrage that CIA could spy on him!

Shane Harris and Paul Sonne wrote an article titled "WikiLeaks Dumps Trove of Purported CIA Hacking Tools" which was published in the *Wall Street Journal* on March 8, 2017. The reporters said that one intelligence source indicated that some of the information *WikiLeaks* released involves the tools that the CIA uses to hack computers and other devices. This person said that disclosing the information would jeopardize ongoing intelligence-gathering operations.

The Central Intelligence Agency headquarter is located in McLean, Virginia.

WikiLeaks said the CIA "lost control of the majority of its hacking arsenal" and characterized the archive as "an extraordinary collection" of more than several hundred million lines of code. The ripped off documents and files is likely to disrupt or halt many ongoing intelligence operations, said a former intelligence officer who has worked on cyber espionage, and could implicate the CIA in past operations, including some that might be under investigation in foreign countries where the agency was spying.

Congressman Devin Nunes (Republican from California and chairman of the House Intelligence Committee) said the United States was "early on" in an investigation into the matter and described the leaks as "very, very serious." "We are extremely concerned," Mr. Nunes said. Again, he should also be concerned by the massive spying by the CIA on Americans.

Harris and Sonne explained the following: "One CIA group revealed in the documents, known as Umbrage, maintains a library of malicious software components taken from commercial and foreign sources found in-the-wild. So far, security experts have found evidence in this trove that the CIA collected malware components believed to have been used by foreign countries. This library appears to give the CIA the ability to deploy hacking tools and techniques that have been known to work in operations by other countries overseas, said one former Western intelligence official. The Umbrage library would also provide a useful reference for identifying foreign hackers trying to penetrate U.S. systems, said a former U.S. intelligence officer. And it could also be used to mask a U.S. operation and make it appear that it was carried out by another country, the former officer said. That could be accomplished by inserting malware components from, say, a known Chinese, Russian or Iranian hacking operation into a U.S. one."

Congressman Devin Nunes

The Wall Street editorial

On March 8, 2017 the *Wall Street Journal* wrote the following editorial:

"Tuesday's (March 7) *WikiLeaks* dump of a major chunk of what it claims is the CIA's "hacking arsenal" ought to be an eye-opener for anyone still laboring under the delusion that *WikiLeaks*'s Julian Assange or former National Security Agency contractor Edward Snowden are not out to weaken the United States. This leak of CIA documents appears to disclose for America's enemies a key advantage against the asymmetric threats of this new century: better technology that provides better intelligence. *WikiLeaks* says the 8,761 documents and files were ripped off from an isolated, high-security network situated inside the CIA's Center for Cyber Intelligence in Virginia. It further says these documents were circulated among former U.S. government hackers and contractors—and that one of them shared the info with *WikiLeaks*. So far former government officials quoted in news reports say the leaked information looks genuine, and the *WikiLeaks* press release promised more to come."

"Much of this *WikiLeaks* dump deals with ways the CIA has found to get into electronic devices such as iPhones and Android phones. These methods include—as Edward Snowden clarified in a tweet—end runs around the encryption of such popular apps as *Signal* or *WhatsApp* without having to crack the apps themselves. The leaks also expose other areas of CIA interest such as an agency effort to hack into the control panels of cars and trucks. Another tool exposed by the leaks turned Samsung Smart TVs into microphones that could then relay conversations back to the CIA even when the owner believed the set was off."

"The losses from this exposure are incalculable. These tools represent millions of dollars of investment and man-hours. Many will now be rendered moot as terrorists or foreign agents abandon traceable habits. Merely because America's enemies are barbaric—think al Qaeda or Islamic State—does not mean they are stupid. One reason it took so long to hunt down Osama bin Laden is because he took pains to establish a sophisticated communications system to evade U.S. intelligence tracking. The costs will also include the time and effort U.S. intelligence agencies will now have to expend investigating how the information was lost. This includes retracing any missed computer hacks and trying to find out who stole and released the secrets."

"Some on the political left and right want to treat Messrs. Snowden and Assange as heroes of transparency and privacy. But there is no evidence that U.S. spooks are engaging in illegal spying on Americans. The CIA's spying tools are for targeting suspected terrorists and foreign agents. As for *WikiLeaks*, note how it never seems to disclose Chinese or Russian secrets. The country they loathe and want to bring low is America."

The National Security Agency (NSA) was spying on Americans

The nation has been aware since 2013 that the National Security Agency (NSA) collected tens of thousands e-mails from Americans over the years. The NSA collected Internet communications from fiber optic cables and, in the process, gathered thousands of e-mails and other Internet activities by Americans. NSA said that such collections were inadvertent.

The Americans who were spied upon did not have any ties to terrorism, according to the documents that were declassified by the Obama administration on August 21, 2013. James Clapper, Director of National Intelligence, declassified these documents after a directive by former President Barack Obama to try to reduce the growing public consternation over the government's enormous surveillance programs. This information, instead of reducing the increasing concerns, would only add more fuel to the fire as more and more people are now aware that our nation was becoming surveillance or a police state.

The Foreign Intelligence Surveillance Court (FISA) that supervises NSA surveillance programs had ruled the program unconstitutional, forcing the NSA to change its practices. The chief judge of the court, John Bates, stated in his ruling that it was the third instance in less than three years in which the NSA had disclosed a substantial misrepresentation regarding the scope of the program.

In 2013, Democratic and Republican legislators reacted with great concern at this news. Senator Tom Udall, Democrat from New Mexico, stated the following: "Mass collection of Americans e-mails without a warrant is unacceptable, and I believe it is unconstitutional. We need to ensure the government is focused on foreign threats and terrorism, not mass collection of communication by innocent American citizens."

Senator Bob Corker, Republican from Tennessee and the top Republican on the Foreign Relations Committee, wrote a letter on August 22, 2013 to Obama asking for a briefing for senators by September 13, 2013 of all surveillance programs. Senator Corker stated the following: "Given the scope and scale of the disclosures to date, and a significant likelihood of more to come, it is now all the more important that the administration come to Congress and provides a full accounting of the totality of these efforts."

On August 21, 2013, the *Wall Street Journal* reported that former officials of intelligence agencies have revealed that our government has built a surveillance system with the capacity to reach as much as 75% of the U.S. Internet traffic and that, in some cases, it retains the content. Obama refused the request by many in Congress to overhaul Section 702 of the 2008 Foreign Intelligence Surveillance Act Amendments. This law permits the NSA to search vast databases of individual Americans e-mails without court warrants. This is, of course, another violation of the Constitution by former President Obama.

The Obama White House tried to contain the damage from these alarming revelations. Deputy White House Press Secretary Josh Earnest insisted that the federal government did not spy on Americans. The Obama administration for many months decided not to make this information public, insisting that each branch of government was properly informed about American phone and Internet surveillance programs.

Conclusion

The spying by the NSA was going on at the same time that the CIA's was also spying on Americans from 2013 to 2016 relying on tools used to break into technology such as smartphones, internet-connected televisions and computer operating systems, and message applications. This writer was a victim of the constant spying by the Obama administration. He has written many articles and six books on Obama and his corrupt administration and that is why he was harassed and intimidated. On December 20, 2015 at 12:30 a.m., this writer sent the information for the back cover of his book, *Obama, Hillary, and Radical Islam*, through his two private and one free e-mail to the publishing house. It was rejected repeatedly. When the publisher sent him an e-mail, it was also rejected in an effort to obstruct communications.

As the United States continued on the road to a totalitarian society during the Obama years, critics like this writer and others were tried to be silenced. This writer wrote six books on Barack Obama, three of them in Spanish—*¿Obama o McCain?* (2008), *El Verdadero Obama: Sus conexiones marxistas, socialistas y radicales* (2010), and *¿Obama o Romney?* (2012). *America in Decline* (2014), *Obama, Hilary, and Radical Islam* (2016), and *The Gathering Threat of Russia, China, and Their Allies Against America* (2016) were written in English.

In a nation of over 55 million Hispanics, this writer is the only American of Cuban origin who has strongly criticized the president in books and articles in both English and Spanish published in various websites, newspapers, and magazines since 2008. He has exposed the past of America's most radical president in history and denounced the many scandals, crimes, and acts of treason committed by the Obama administration.

This writer is frequently interviewed by local and national radio and television stations, including NTN 24 from Bogotá, Colombia, which is seen in Latin America and the United States. On December 18, 2014, this writer was being interviewed in Spanish by a radio station in Orlando (which interviews him once and sometimes twice a week) that has 25,000 watts. The station has a large audience in central Florida and along part of the I-4 corridor. On that day, when this writer began to criticize the Obama administration for illegally lifting most of the Cuban embargo in violation of the Helms Burton Law, the station was put off the air for an hour and 45 minutes.

In another situation, this writer was explaining in an interview by a reporter from the same station the terrorist links of the president's brother, Malik Obama, when the lights went off. The strange situation is that those things only happened when this writer has been interviewed. He suspects that the intent was to force the station to stop interviewing him.

This writer also speaks in many cities in Florida and at national conferences. Why was he such a threat to the Obama administration? Don't we as citizens have the right to criticize and denounce those who we elect into office? If the government intimidates, harasses, and spies Americans for covering the many scandals of the Obama administration, can Americans truly say that they live in a law-abiding Constitutional Republic?

Many strange things have happened to this writer which leads him to believe that during the Obama years Americans were living in, at best, a surveillance nation and, most likely, in a police state. This writer felt that during the years of the Obama administration he was living back in Cuba, his native country, and was being spied upon by the secret police of that tyrannical regime. This writer has been the victim of the many illegal actions most probably perpetrated by the Obama administration or hackers or spies who are his supporters. The Fourth Amendment of the Constitution gives Americans the right to be free in their own homes free from unreasonable governmental intrusion. More than likely the Obama administration or his followers have taken that right away from this writer.

One day this writer was writing in Microsoft Word in his personal computer at home an article called "Is China a Gathering Threat to our National Security?" which was later published in the website *bwcentral.org* on March 18, 2014 and in a book. This writer was explaining in his article that in March 2009 the U.S. Navy ship, the *Impeccable*, a surveillance ship, was sailing about 70 nautical miles from the submarine base in Hainan Island, China when it was confronted by 10 Chinese Navy ships.

The Chinese dropped planks into the water and forced the U.S. ship to stop. Chinese sailors used long poles to smash the surveillance instruments that were being towed behind the ship. The *Impeccable* was harassed for some time until it retreated from the area. To add insult to injury, the Chinese crew of one of the ships dropped their pants and showed their bare bottoms in the direction of the Americans. This, of course, was an act of war.

Much to his surprise, an article on the very same topic that he was writing about appeared, unexpectedly and without explanation, in the middle of his own article. It was an article written by Bill Gertz three months earlier entitled "Chinese Naval Vessel Tries to Force U.S. Warship to Stop in International Waters." This article had been published on the *Washington Free Beacon* website on December 13, 2013.

Bill Gertz explained that on December 5, 2013 the guided missile cruiser *USS Cowpens* was sailing in international waters in the South China Sea, which China has illegally claimed as its territory. The U.S. warship was following the Chinese aircraft carrier the *Liaoning* at the time. According to American officials, a Chinese Navy vessel ordered the cruiser *USS Cowpens* to stop. The cruiser refused to obey the order because it was operating in international waters and, so it continued on its course. Suddenly, a Chinese tank landing ship sailed in front of the cruiser and the stopped suddenly, forcing the U.S. Naval vessel to abruptly change its course in what resulted in a dangerous maneuver. This was another act of war which former President Obama ignored.

This writer was stunned that someone, who was reading every word of his article, sent him another article into his computer regarding a Navy ship which had also been harassed by the Chinese navy. Obviously, the spy wanted to help him write a better article and also let him know that he was being spied upon. This writer will forever be thankful to that spy. However, it was too bad that the spy did not become a whistleblower and let the nation know how journalists and authors of books are being spied in violation of the First of the Fourth Amendments of the Constitution.

For months before this incident, occasionally, when this writer would try to send through his Yahoo e-mail an article that he had written about a subject that criticized the Obama administration, the blue beach ball would go on turning forever and his article would not be sent. However, if he later tried later to send it with a different subject, such as "Hola," the same article would be sent without difficulty. This writer has spoken to other journalists and writers who have told him that the same thing had happened to them

It is also happening to people who are simply sharing articles written by others. Obviously, someone reads what Americans write or share and, if not in agreement with the Obama administration, the information would not be allowed to be sent. This is absolutely illegal and outrageous!

Much more serious things have happened to this writer. Oftentimes, someone rewrites the e-mails that this writer has sent from his private computer to someone else's private computer. This is being done in an effort to impede his communication with others. Additionally, e-mails that are sent to him are often intercepted, so he does not receive them.

This writer wrote seven e-mails to an individual who invited him to present his book, *America in Decline* (2014), to a Republican club in Central Florida. His e-mails were sent from Yahoo and they were changed electronically by adding the following: "Please reply to frankdevarona@holmail.com." His last name was misspelled, and the Hotmail e-mail does not exist. Later, he was able to speak to the person who had invited him and was able to schedule the presentation. This is quite dangerous as someone could write an e-mail from his private computer to a criminal and then he could be blamed for something he did not write. This is actually very scary. This writer felt that he was living in the nation described by George Orwell's novel *1984*.

About four or five ago, this writer received the visit of an FBI agent at his house who asked him questions about a neighbor who lived in the back. He had the feeling that the agent was interested on him and not on his neighbor, although he could have been wrong. This writer showed the FBI agent the books that he had written on Barack Obama to let him know that he was not afraid. Months later, someone entered his house and left the back door unlocked. Since nothing was stolen, this led him to suspect that illegal microphones may have been placed inside his house. It will not surprise this writer if his phone lines have been hacked and bugged.

This writer is the South Florida director of a patriot organization called Bear Witness Central. His organization has two websites, one in English, www.bwcentral.org, and one in Spanish, www.libertadusa.com. Both of the websites are under constant cyber-attack and are frequently disabled in spite of the many firewalls that have been installed. Bear Witness Central has received over 100,000 cyber-attacks in a three-day period in the English website. On one occasion, all of the videos were erased and, frequently, over 400 articles written by his writer have been erased. Sadly, all of his articles have recently disappeared again!

Another director of Bear Witness Central and this writer received a threating message from an Islamic radical from Europe soon after they spoke in a C-Span televised national conference.

They both had to notify their police departments, which in turn notified the FBI and the Department of Homeland Security.

This writer's computer and printer have been destroyed and on one occasion his list of e-mail contacts was erased. He often needs to request the services of a computer technician to repair his computer and printer.

Why is this writer being treated as a criminal when he is a patriot who is concerned about what is happening in America and the increasing threats by enemy nations and Islamic radicals to America's national security? As a United States citizen, his First and Fourth Amendments were violated with impunity during the Obama years. Why was someone trying to silence this writer and interfere with his communications with others? America changed radically after Barack Obama came to power in January 2009.

It seems that our nation is using the same tactics used by the KGB in the Soviet Union or Russia as well as the former Stasi secret police of East Germany and Seguridad del Estado, the Cuban secret police. During the Obama years America looked more like the Big Brother society described in George Orwell novel *1984*.

Thank God America elected Donald J. Trump as president on November 8, 2016. This writer feels very relieved that the federal government will not harass him anymore. However, when this writer sees how the Trump administration is being attacked by the "Deep State" officials in intelligence agencies, who are leaking illegally classified information in an effort to undermine the Trump administration, he wonders if his nightmare might not be over.

CHAPTER 23

The surveillance on Donald J. Trump and others

All the mainstream media newspapers, magazines, and television channels as well as the Democratic Party have called repeatedly President Donald J. Trump a liar for accusing Barack Obama of "wiretapping," which means surveillance or espionage on him and his team. Sadly, even the Republican newspaper the *Wall Street Journal* wrote an editorial denouncing President Donald Trump as a liar and "fake president."

Larry Klayman is a prominent activist, journalist, and international lawyer.

Klayman has written of two books, *Fatal Neglect: the United States Government's Continuing Failure to Protect American Citizens from Terrorism* (2007) and *Whores: Why and How I Came to Fight the Establishment* (2009). He is working on a third book dealing with the breakdown of our political and legal systems.

During the administration of President Ronald Reagan, Larry Klayman was a Justice Department prosecutor. He founded Judicial Watch and Freedom Watch, both outstanding organizations that are government watchdog groups. These organizations also promote ethics in government and individual freedoms and liberties. Larry Klayman often appears as commentator on television and radio and is a weekly columnist for *WND.com*. He also writes a regular blog for *Newsmax* called "Klayman's Court."

Currently, whistleblower Dennis Montgomery, who worked as a contractor for the Central Intelligence Agency (CIA) and the National Security Agency (NSA), is being represented by lawyer Larry Klayman. During his work Montgomery discovered that these two intelligence agencies were spying, not only on businessman Donald Trump before he ran for president, but also on the Chief Justice of the Supreme Court John Roberts, 156 judges, and many others. Montgomery, along with his lawyer Larry Klayman, went to the FBI and obtained immunity for what he did, as opposed to Edward Snowden who fled the country and gave NSA classified information to Russia.

In the wake of the Trump Tower "wiretapping" (meaning surveillance), Larry Klayman, on Dennis Montgomery's behalf, said that Montgomery had evidence that security agencies have been involved in "systematic illegal surveillance on prominent Americans," including Donald Trump. According to Klayman, Montgomery also said these agencies had manipulated voting in Florida during the 2008 presidential election. Klayman has written that his client, former NSA and CIA contractor Dennis Montgomery, holds the key to disproving the false claims of those representatives and senators on the House and Senate intelligence committees who have said, as well as FBI Director James Comey and NSA Director Mike Rodgers, that there is no evidence that the president and his men were wiretapped.

California Republican Congressman Devin Nunes is the Chairman of the House of Representatives Select Committee on Intelligence.

Larry Klayman wrote an article on *WND.com* titled "The Whistleblower Devin Nunes Must Hear From" which was published on March 24, 2017. He explained that on March 20, 2017, he delivered a letter to California Republican Congressman and Chairman of the House of Representatives Select Committee on Intelligence Devin Nunes and all the members of the House Select Committee on Intelligence. Klayman urged the committee to investigate the "widespread illegal surveillance, not just of President Donald J. Trump and his team both before and after his inauguration but also of hundreds of millions of other innocent Americans by the intelligence agencies." Klayman gave the name to the House of Representatives Intel Committee of a whistleblower, Dennis Montgomery, who as a former National Security Agency (NSA) and Central Intelligence Agency (CIA) contractor left the spy agencies with 47 hard drives and over 600 million pages of information. Klayman obtained a grant of immunity for Montgomery from FBI Director James Comey.

James Clapper was Obama's Director of National Intelligence from August 9, 2010 to January 20, 2017. He committed perjury when he told Congress that the NSA did not spy on Americans. Clapper later admitted that he lied to Congress, yet he has not received punishment.

Klayman pointed out that this information, according to Dennis Montgomery, indicated that the intelligence agencies, particularly under former Obama Director of National Intelligence James Clapper and former Obama CIA Director John Brennan and their minions, had "spied illegally and unconstitutionally on prominent Americans, including the chief justice of the Supreme Court, other SCOTUS justices, 156 judges, prominent businessmen like Donald Trump as well as him."

During Brennan's time as CIA Director, it was revealed that the United States government conducted massive global surveillance, including heads of nations, who are allies of America. While Brennan was director of the CIA, his agency hacked into the computers of Senate employees who were working on a report on the CIA torture abroad. Brennan severely criticized Donald Trump on national television, an action never done by any other CIA director in history. Brennan converted to Islam and, before he worked for the CIA, he voted for the Communist Party USA.

Larry Klayman wrote that in addition to the mass surveillance revealed by Edward Snowden, the CIA and the NSA, during the Obama administration, spied on "anyone who was anyone" in terms of their perceived status in society. He believes that the reason for the mass surveillance of prominent people and judges was the potential for extortion and blackmail by the Obama administration.

John Brennan was Director of the Central Intelligence Agency (CIA)
from March 8, 2013 to January 20, 2017.

Klayman is outraged that in spite of Dennis Montgomery coming forward about two years ago, FBI Director James Comey, his General Counsel and Special Agents James Baker, Walter Giardina, and William Barnett have refused to act on this scandalous information. He said that it was for this reason that he contacted Chairman Devon Nunes and the other members of the House Intelligence Committee about this apparent cover-up. He would like for the Intel committee to allow Montgomery to testify and produce proof of this "Orwellian Big Brother" violation of the constitutional rights of not just President Donald J. Trump, but of all Americans.

Klayman pointed out that Chairman Nunes has even asked whistleblowers like Montgomery to come forward. He said that "all of Montgomery's classified information is currently in the possession of the FBI, as well as a video of his three-hour interview before Special Agents Giardina and Barnett, at FBI Field Headquarters in Washington, D.C."

Klayman regrets that FBI Director Comey failed to disclose this information to the House Intelligence Committee when he himself testified in open session on March 20, 2017, which was the same day that he delivered his letter to Chairman Nunes. Klayman thinks that due to his letter perhaps other whistleblowers have come forward.

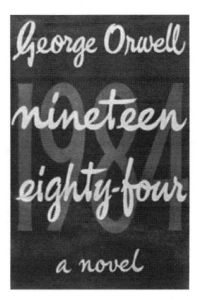

George Orwell's famous novel *1984* was written in 1949. This writer believes that Americans are currently living in the Big Brother society described in this novel

Klayman, as well as this writer who have said many times that America is a police state, raised the following question: "How can this nation function and the citizenry live in freedom if they are subjected to what is in effect and in practice a police state, forecast by George Orwell in his famous book *1984*? How can I talk with my clients as a lawyer, and preserve our attorney-client and work product privileges, when our communications are subject to surveillance, and how can the president and his team carry out the affairs of state if they are under the gun of corrupt and dishonest intelligence agency czars like Clapper and Brennan, who wield the power to destroy them, as they did with Gen. Michael Flynn most recently? Of course, we cannot!"

Klayman explained in his letter to Chairman Nunes and the Committee that the future of the United States hangs in the balance. He said it is time for good men in the Trump administration and the few in Congress, like Chairman Nunes, to "clean house of the cockroaches that infest our body politic and threaten to bring the nation down."

Klayman pointed out that whistleblower Dennis Montgomery, who is risking his life and liberty to reveal this continuing threat to America, may not live much longer as he suffers from a potentially fatal brain aneurism. He concluded his article by stating the following: "And, that is why Chairman Nunes and the House Intelligence Committee must move quickly, unlike the apparently compromised FBI Director James Comey, to get to the truth. And, when all of this truth comes out, from Montgomery and other sources, the criminally minded, like former Obama Director of National Intelligence Clapper and former Obama CIA Director John Brennan and their pro-Obama minions still embedded in the intelligence agencies, and perhaps even former President Obama himself, must be indicted, prosecuted and ultimately convicted of high crimes against not just President Trump and his team, but also against all Americans."

James Comey became FBI Director on September 4, 2013, after being nominated by President Barack Obama and confirmed by the Senate.

"In short, the time has finally come for the corrupt political and government elite to be held to account before the non-discriminatory blind bar of Lady Justice, to prevent this tyranny from ever occurring again! If we do not succeed in this quest, all of our freedoms will be forever lost," said Klayman

Conclusion

It is very important for Congressman Devin Nunes as the Chairman of the House of Representatives Select Committee on Intelligence and his committee to allow whistleblower Dennis Montgomery to testify and present the 600 million pages of documents taken from the CIA and the NSA. This writer has written in books and articles and stated at conferences that America has become a police state. He himself has been spied upon as well as millions of Americans.

President Donald Trump was telling the truth when he said he was spied upon as well as members of his team. It is up to him as president to put an end to the illegal mass surveillance of Americans by intelligence agencies, especially since he was one of the victims of the police state created by former President Barack Obama. President Trump needs to prosecute former President Barack Obama and his officials for violating the Constitution as they spied on millions of Americans. Trump should also fire Comey and Rodgers for lying to Congress and making him look as if he was the liar.

By now, President Trump is aware that Obama is the leader of the "Deep State" and has created a "Shadow Government" in his Kalorama mansion, which is located two miles from the White House. Obama is not only working to undermine Trump's presidency but also to force him to resign or be impeached. Either the president the drains the swamp quickly or he will be eaten alive by the creatures of the swamp!

CHAPTER 24

Obama is leading a Civil War against Trump with the help of the Deep State and he must be stopped

Former President Obama is the leader of the Deep State/Anonymous Network and has created a "Shadow Government." He is waging a civil war or a silent coup against President Donald J. Trump. Obama wants to oust President Trump from the presidency either by forcing his resignation or through his impeachment.

To the immense surprise of the very liberal and corrupt mainstream media, the Hillary Clinton campaign, and those who made the fake polls, Donald J. Trump was elected president on November 8, 2016. The members of the globalist elite who control most of the mainstream media, Islamic radicals, communists, socialists, and anarchists began an organized campaign to undermine and possibly destroy the presidency of Donald J. Trump. These unprecedented efforts to undermine and possibly bring an impeachment on President Donald J. Trump have intensified.

George Soros, his foundation, and the many socialist organizations that he has funded as well as those in charge of the Rockefeller Foundation, the Rockefeller Family Foundation, the Carnegie Foundation, the Ford Foundation, the Ties Foundation, and other groups have hired and paid thugs to conduct violent massive demonstrations in cities across the United States.

George Soros and his multimillionaire's allies have funded over 170 radical organizations, including Black Lives Matter, which is a domestic terrorist group.

Communists and radicals protested in many cities across the nation. These paid criminals burned cars, broke windows, vandalized businesses, and fought police officers in the United States. Many of them openly displayed communist flags and posters accusing President Trump of being a fascist. Communists always accuse people who disagree with Marxism of being fascists.

Hundreds and even thousands radicals thugs closed roads and rioted damaging businesses and police cars in many cities. These radicals, many of whom were paid to commit acts of violence by Soros and others, were screaming that they did not want Donald J. Trump as their president. During these rent-a-mobs rioting, President Obama and Hillary Clinton remained silent.

On November 9, 2016, the Party for Socialism and Liberation, a Marxist revolutionary group, burned an image of Donald Trump in front of the Los Angeles City Hall.

Communists held signs that proclaimed that capitalism must go!

Change.org collected several million signatures to persuade the individuals who were elected to the Electoral College to change their votes to deny the White House to Donald J. Trump. The Democratic Party refused to accept its defeat. The increasingly socialist Democratic Party should not have selected the very corrupt Hillary Clinton as its standard bearer. But the party did, and Hillary Clinton was rejected by the American voters.

The Soros funded Change.org collected signatures requesting that the electors of the Electoral College, prior to meeting on December 19, 2016 in Washington, D.C., reject Donald Trump and select Hillary Clinton as president.

The effort to deny the presidency to Donald Trump failed. However, two electors who had pledged to vote for Trump were persuaded to vote for someone else. Hillary Clinton was actually the one who lost the most electoral votes when the Electoral College met in Washington, D.C. Several of her pledged electors voted for someone else. This conspiracy to deny the White House to Donald J. Trump is unprecedented in the history of this nation. However, it clearly showed the immense hatred of the Left, the globalist elite, and the complicit mainstream media for the Republican president.

On January 20, 2017, the day that Donald J Trump was inaugurated as president, hundreds of thugs burned U.S. flags, beat up people, and vandalized stores, banks, and all types of businesses in Washington, D.C. These paid criminals also blocked many streets so that Trump supporters could not reach the Mall to hear Donald Trump's inaugural speech. In the nation's capital, police officers arrested 211 of these criminals and charged them with felony riot, which carries a penalty of up to 10 years in prison and a fine up to $250,000. However, the millionaires who paid and hired these criminals to commit acts of violence were not indicted.

When President Donald J. Trump issued an executive order banning the entry to America of people from seven countries of the Middle East, Obama's appointed federal judges blocked the president's executive order. When President Trump revised the original order, and eliminated Iraq from the list of countries, it was rejected for the second time by Obama's appointed federal judges. All of these rulings by these judges were unconstitutional since the president, according to the law, has the right to forbid the entry of foreigners from any nation, as it was done previously by President Barack Obama and President Jimmy Carter. These judges as well as the Democratic Party that supported them will have blood on their hands should an immigrant from these countries were to enter the United States and commit acts of terrorism.

Obama's Anonymous Network, also known as the Deep State

On March 7, 2017, Daniel Greenfield, a journalist at the Freedom Center, wrote an article titled "Obamagate: Exposing the Obama Deep State" which was published in the website *FrontPage-Mag.com*. The reporter explained that soon after Donald J. Trump obtained the GOP nomination for president, President Obama's officials filed a wiretapping request. Obama targeted Trump for destruction from the very beginning as soon as it was clear he would be the nominee.

When Trump was on the verge of winning as a candidate, Obama's officials did it again. They filed another wiretapping request. Since he won the presidential election in November 2016, Barack Obama and officials, who are still serving in the federal government, have been doing everything they can to bring him down. Greenfield said that Obama's third term has begun, and our Republic is in danger.

The Foreign Intelligence Surveillance Court

All wiretapping and electronic surveillance requests must be approved by the Foreign Intelligence Surveillance Court (FISA), which was established in 1978. The Court sits in Washington, D.C. and is composed of eleven federal district court judges who are designated by the Chief Justice of the Supreme Court. Each judge serves for a maximum of seven years and their terms are staggered to ensure continuity on the Court. By statute, the judges must be drawn from at least seven of the United States judicial circuits and three of the judges must reside within 20 miles of the District of Columbia. Judges typically sit for one week at a time on a rotating basis.

Pursuant to FISA, the Court entertains applications submitted by the United States Government for approval of electronic surveillance, physical search, and other investigative actions for foreign intelligence purposes. Most of the Court's work is conducted ex parte as required by statute and due to the need to protect classified national security information.

Greenfield said that by May 2016, it was clear that Donald J. Trump had locked down the Republican Party nomination. On the following month, the Obama administration asked permission to wiretap the Trump campaign to the Foreign Intelligence Surveillance Court (FISA). The Foreign Intelligence Surveillance Court denied the request. It is still unknown whether the FISA request targeted Donald J. Trump or only members of his campaign. As Greenfield said, it was "silly to pretend that the submission of such a request a month after he became the presumptive GOP nominee was apolitical."

Greenfield explained the following: "The second, narrower, FISA request came through in October 2016. This one was approved. The reason for getting a FISA request in October was even more obvious than June. October is the crucial month in presidential elections. It's the month of the October Surprise when the worst hit pieces based on the keenest opposition research is unleashed. Obama's opposition research on Trump involved eavesdropping on a server in Trump Tower. Nixon would have been very jealous."

FBI Director Comey stated that the agency is investigating whether members of the Trump's 2016 campaign collaborated with the Russian government and said that there was no evidence of wiretapping of Donald Trump

According to the testimony of Federal Bureau of Investigation Director James Comey before the House of Representative Permanent Select Committee on Intelligence on March 20, 2017, the agency is investigating whether members of Donald J. Trump's 2016 campaign collaborated with the Russian government to influence the presidential election. This investigation started in late July 2016 and is still going on. Comey's announcement of an active FBI investigation was a rare step by the head of the FBI, especially given the fact that that it directly affects President Donald J. Trump, the current president. Comey's statements contradicted the testimony of the former Director of Intelligence, James Clapper, who said that that there was no collusion between the members of the Trump campaign and Russia.

Federal Bureau of Investigation Director Comey as well as National Security Agency Director Admiral Mike Rogers said that they had "no information" that supports President Trump's claims that Barack Obama wiretapped him during the campaign. They basically called the president a liar since he had sent a Twitter massage on March 4, 2017 stating the following: "How low President Obama gone to tap my phones during the very sacred election process. This is Nixon/Watergate Bad (or sick) guy."

Democrats and some Republicans in Congress as well the media criticized the president, who kept insisting that he was under surveillance by President Obama. Many demanded Obama to offer a retraction and an apology. How can the FBI investigate members of the Trump campaign without surveillance? Others have evidence that there was indeed surveillance by the British intelligence services at the request of the Obama administration.

Congressman Nunes announced that communications by the Trump campaign were "incidentally" monitored by the intelligence community

Speaking to reporters on Capitol Hill, Republican Congressman Devin Nunes, Chairman of the House Intelligence Committee, said that there has been "significant developments" in the investigation of his committee into Obama administration´s surveillance of the Trump team.

Congressman Nunes announced that communications by the Trump campaign were "incidentally" monitored by the intelligence community. Representative Nunes stated the following: "First, I recently confirmed that on numerous occasions, the intelligence community incidentally collected information about U.S. citizens involved in the Trump transition. Details about U.S. persons associated with the incoming administration, details with little or no apparent foreign intelligence value, were widely disseminated in intelligence community reporting. Third, I have confirmed that additional names of Trump transition team members were unmasked. Fourth and finally, I want to be clear. None of this surveillance was related to Russia, or the investigation of Russian activities or of the Trump team."

Congressman Nunes stated that the information was collected in November and December 2016 and January 2017—the transition period after the election. He said he had seen "dozens" of reports involving Donald J. Trump and his team, which were brought to his attention by a concerned but unidentified party. According to Congressman Nunes, the information was collected as part of "normal foreign surveillance" and not related to any criminal investigation. He said repeatedly that the surveillance had nothing to do with the investigation of ties between the Trump campaign and Russia.

Representative Nunes suggested that a source had provided new information showing that the Obama administration incidentally collected information on then President-Elect Donald Trump and the Trump campaign. He also said that some of the Trump team members whose communications were picked up may have been illegally unmasked by the intelligence community. The California Republican added that he had confirmed that "additional names of Trump transition team members" were unmasked. None of the surveillance was related to Russia or the investigation into Russia's activities prior to the election.

House of Representative Select Intelligence Committee Chairman Devin Nunes spoke to reporters during a press conference at the U.S. Capitol on March 22, 2017.

Representative Nunes was asked, "Do you think right now that the NSA or a member of the intelligence community was spying on Trump during the transition period?" He answered, "Well, I guess it all depends on one's definitions of spying." He said, "I'm really alarmed by the unmasking." The California Republican said he is demanding more information from intelligence agencies. Later, Congressman Nunes headed to the White House to brief President Trump and others in his administration. After the briefing, Representative Nunes stated regarding the surveillance that "perhaps it was legal but is not right."

White House Press secretary Sean Spicer read from Congressman Nunes' statement during his press briefing on March 22, 2017. President Trump told reporters that he felt "somewhat" vindicated by Nunes' comments. The director of the FBI and the NSA virtually called Trump a liar since he had sent a Twitter message accusing Obama of spying on him and both of them said it had not happened. Well, it did happen!

Did Obama and/or his White House violate any law?

Peter Hoekstra is a former member of the United States House of Representatives, representing Michigan's 2nd congressional district from 1993 to 2011. Hoekstra is a member of the Republican Party who served as Chairman of the House Intelligence Committee from 2004 to 2007.

Peter Hoekstra wrote an article titled "Did Obama Abuse Raw Intelligence?" which was published in the *Wall Street Journal* on March 24, 2017. He said that it was positively astonishing and remarkable that Congressman Devin Nunes revealed on March 22 that Donald Trump campaign officials were caught up in the inadvertent collection of intelligence. He said that not all details are known. It could include conversations between Trump transition staff and foreign officials whose conversations were subject to intelligence monitoring.

Peter Hoekstra stated the following: "Things begin to get a little frightening when we learn that this inadvertent collection of Trump staff conversations was followed up with transcriptions of those conversations and the disclosure (or unmasking) of the persons involved in the conversation. These transcripts would be considered raw intelligence reports… The raw transcripts of masked persons—or unmasked persons, or U.S. persons who can be easily identified—making their way to the White House is very likely unprecedented. One can only imagine who, at that point, might be reading these reports. Valerie Jarrett? Susan Rice? Ben Rhodes? The president himself? We don't know, and the people who do aren't talking at the moment."

Hoekstra said that when he was chairman of the House Intelligence Committee he could not recall how many times he asked to see raw intelligence reporting. His request was denied because raw intelligence is just not made available to policy makers. In the testimony given by

FBI Director James Comey, he said there was no basis to support the tweet from President Trump that his "wires" had been tapped by Barack Obama.

Hoekstra wrote the following: "What he didn't say—and wasn't asked—was whether information was collected on Trump staff by other means. Then there's Mr. Comey's testimony that the FBI had been investigating Trump staff for eight months. It almost certainly included surveillance; an investigation without surveillance would approach farcical. Admiral Rogers told the House Intelligence Committee that there are strict controls in place for masking and unmasking the identities of people caught up in the inadvertent collection of information and the distribution of this kind of material. It now appears he either misled the committee or doesn't know what's happening inside his own agency. If Mr. Nunes is right, the rules either weren't followed or were much less stringent than Adm. Rogers let on. Last, and rather damningly, I believe that Mr. Comey and Admiral Rogers would have to have known that raw transcripts of captured conversations that included members of the Trump team were at the White House. It is inconceivable that people in those positions of power would not know. While this may not be criminal, it is at least a cause for them to be fired."

The former Chairman of the House of Representatives Intelligence Committee said that his greatest concern was that the awesome powers of our intelligence community might have been corrupted for political purposes. Hoekstra explained that it was clear there have been serious errors of judgment and action among our otherwise professional intelligence community and that was truly scary. He ended his article by saying, "We have to learn the entire truth before anyone, in or out of Congress, can again have confidence in our intelligence community."

Valerie Jarrett, who was born in Shiraz, Iran, is a red diaper baby whose relatives were Marxists. She married the son of the Chicago communist journalist Vernon Jarrett, who worked closely with Obama's mentor Frank Marshall Davis.

Valerie Jarrett moved into Barack Obama's Kalorama mansion in Washington, D.C., which has become the "Shadow White House Government" to plot operations against President Donald J. Trump. Jarrett served as the Senior Advisor to President Barack Obama and Assistant to the President for Public Engagement and Intergovernmental Affairs in the Obama administration from January 20, 2009 to January 20, 2017.

Daniel Greenfield stated the following: "One is the elected President of the United States. The other is the Anti-President who commands a vast network that encompasses the organizers of Organizing for Action (OFA), the official infrastructure of the Democratic National Committee (DNC) and Obama Anonymous Network, a Shadow Government of loyalists embedded in key positions across the government…And that the Obama Anonymous Network of staffers embedded in the government was the real threat. Since then Obama's Kalorama mansion has become a Shadow White House?"

Valerie Jarrett was the most influential adviser to both Barack and Michelle Obama. In 1991, Jarrett served as deputy chief of staff for Chicago Mayor Richard Daley and she hired Michelle Robinson, then engaged to Barack Obama.

Greenfield wrote that the Obama Anonymous Network is doing everything it can to bring down an elected government. Valerie Jarret has moved into the Shadow White House to help Obama in planning operations against Trump.

Tom Perez is the Chair of the Democratic National Committee.

Thomas Edward "Tom" Perez was elected Chair of the Democratic National Committee on February 25, 2017. After being elected, Perez named Congressman Keith Ellison, an Islamic radical, as deputy chair. Ellison had run against him with the support of the communist Senator Bernie Sanders. Tom Perez was the Secretary of Labor from 2013 to 2017. Prior to that position, Perez served as Assistant Attorney General for the Civil Rights Division of the Department of Justice under the corrupt Attorney General Eric Holder. He supported Holder in all his violations of the Constitution, which eventually led Congress to declare Holder in Contempt of Congress for refusing to turn in documents.

Keith Ellison is the Deputy Chair of the Democratic National Committee.

Keith Ellison was elected to the House of Representatives in 2007 in Minnesota and then re-elected. Ellison was the first Muslim to be elected to Congress, and along with André Carson of Indiana, is one of two Muslims now serving in Congress. Tom Perez appointed him as Deputy Chair of the Democratic National Committee. Ellison is a co-chair of the Marxist Congressional Progressive Caucus and Chief Deputy Whip.,

In November 2016, progressive groups and United States senators, including the Marxist Bernie Sanders of Vermont, supported Ellison for chair of the Democratic National Committee. On February 25, 2017, minutes after defeating him on the second ballot, newly-elected Chairman Tom Perez motioned for Ellison to be elected his Deputy Chair, which was approved by a unanimous voice vote of DNC members. Ellison has an anti-Semitism past which he has not genuinely repudiated. More troubling is the close association Congressman Ellison with the Muslim Brotherhood front organization Council on American-Islamic Relations (CAIR) and the co-founder, Nihad Awad, who has publicly supported Islamic terrorism.

Greenfield pointed out that Obama controls the opposition and that he will have a great deal of power to choose future members of Congress and the 2020 presidential candidate. The reason Obama did not move from Washington, D.C. is that the nation's capital has "the infrastructure of the national government." Obama does not just want to be in charge of the Democratic Party. He wants to run the United States. Obama runs the Deep State, also known as Anonymous, which is a network of political appointees, bureaucrats, and personnel scattered across numerous government agencies who are loyal to him.

After the election, Greenfield pointed out that Obama's people went to work with his network of political organizations. Others remained embedded in the government. While the former group would organize the opposition, the latter group would sabotage, undermine, and try to bring down Trump. The reporter said that this was "an unprecedented campaign for full spectrum dominance was being waged in domestic politics" and "weaponizing unelected government officials to wage war on an elected government which is a coup."

Greenfield has referred to Obama's actions to undermine President Trump as a "coup." The reporter described the ongoing coup as follows: "The first layer partnered congressional Democrats with Obama administration personnel to retain control of as much of the government as possible by the Obama Deep State. They did it by blocking President Trump's nominees with endless hearings and protests. The second layer partnered congressional Democrats with the deeper layer of Obama operatives embedded in law enforcement and intelligence agencies who were continuing the Obama investigations of Trump. This second layer sought to use the investigation to force out Trump people who threatened their control over national security, law enforcement and intelligence. It is no coincidence that their targets, Flynn and Sessions, were in that arena. Or that their views on Islamic terror and immigration are outside the consensus making them easy targets for Obama Anonymous and its darker allies."

Greenfield explained that Obama used the same tactics when he went after the Iran Deal opponents. Once again, members of Congress were spied on and the information was leaked to friendly media outlets of the pro-Obama mainstream media. Before the wiretapping of the group of Donald J. Trump, the NSA was passing conversations of opponents of the Iran Deal to the White House, which were used to coordinate strategies to support Obama's ill-advised Iranian deal.

When Obama was president, he hacked reporters like *FoxNews'* James Rosen and *CBS News'* Sharyl Attkisson. His very corrupt Attorney General Eric Holder spied on over 100 reporters from the Associated Press for several months. Obama eavesdropped on members of Congress who opposed to the Iran Deal.

This writer was also subjected to illegal surveillance. Why? He wrote six books and hundreds of articles denouncing the many violations of the Constitution and the crimes committed by President Obama, Secretary of State Hillary Clinton, and others in his administration. In addition, this writer spoke at national, state, and local conferences and was and continuous to be interviewed by national and international radio and television stations.

However, what former President Obama is doing now is even more disturbing. He is trying to overthrow President Trump.

Greenfield said that in the last days of the Obama administration, the president "passed along unfiltered personal information to the other agencies where Obama loyalists were working on their investigation targeting Trump." He accused the NSA of making it possible for the "Shadow White House" to still gain intelligence on its domestic enemies. And who is the target of the "Shadow White House?" None other than the President of the United States.

Greenfield believes that currently the nation has a President and an Anti-President and a government and a shadow government. Greenfield believes that the anti-President controls more of the government through his shadow government than the real President.

Daniel Greenfield concluded his illuminating article by explaining the following: "The Obama network is an illegal shadow government…Its shadow side is not only illegal, but a criminal attack on our democracy. Obama no longer legally holds power. His Deep State network is attempting to overturn the results of a presidential election using government employees whose allegiance is to a shadow White House."

"Tactics that were illegal when he was in office are no longer just unconstitutional, they are treasonous. Obama Inc. has become a state within a state. It is a compartmentalized network of organizations, inside and outside the government, that claim that they are doing nothing illegal as individual groups because they are technically following the rules within each compartment, but the sheer scope of the illegality lies in the covert coordination between these revolutionary cells infecting our country."

"It is a criminal conspiracy of unprecedented scope. Above all else, it is the most direct attack yet on a country in which governments are elected by the people, not by powerful forces within the government. Obama's Shadow Government is not just a war on President Trump. It is a war on that government of the people, by the people and for the people. If he succeeds, then at his touch, it will perish from the earth. Obama's third term has begun. Our Republic is in danger."

Did President Obama illegally order the surveillance of Trump and members of his campaign?

It is possible that President Obama illegally spied on the Trump transition team in an attempt to undermine and, if possible, destroy the Republican president. A serious investigation needs to be conducted by the Justice Department.

President Trump told Tucker Carlson on *Fox News* on March 15, 2017 why he tweeted what he did: "Well, I've been reading…I think it was January 20…*New York Times* article where they were talking about wiretapping…. I think they used that exact term." It is well known that Obama's appointees to intelligence agencies have leaked classified information to the *New York Times*. So, President Trump is correct in believing that he was under surveillance by the Obama administration. Below one can see the headlines of the *New York Times* on January 20, 2017, the very day that Donald J Trump was inaugurated as president.

On March 21, 2017, Cliff Kincaid wrote an article titled "Trump vs. FoxNews on Wiretapping" which was published in the website *Accuracy in Media*. He explained that *FoxNews* has been caught misrepresenting its own interview with Congressman Devin Nunes (Republican from California and Chairman of the House of Representative Permanent Select Committee on Intelligence) on the subject of the alleged wiretapping of President Trump. *FoxNews* fired, either temporarily or permanently, one of its respected commentators, Judge Andrew Napolitano, for raising the possibility of the British NSA, known as GCHQ or Government Communications Headquarters, role in gathering intelligence on Trump and his associates.

Congressman Nunes stated the following in *Fox News*: "…The President doesn't go and physically wiretap something. So, if you take the President literally, it didn't happen." But Trump has referred to "wiretap" in quotes, to refer to surveillance. Nunes went on, "I think the concern that we have is that are—*were there any other surveillance activities* that were used unmasking the names."

Kincaid pointed out that unmasking refers to obtaining the name of an American citizen in a surveillance report. However, the personal privacy of citizens is supposed to be protected under U.S. law because he/she was not the target of the surveillance that captured the conversation. The reporter explained that on March 20, 2017, President Trump Press Secretary Sean Spicer stated the following: "Before President Obama left office, Michael Flynn was unmasked and then illegally his identity was leaked out to media outlets, despite the fact that, as NSA Director Mike Rogers said, that unmasking and revealing individuals endangers 'national security.' Not only was General Flynn's identity made available, Director James Comey refused to answer the question of whether or not he'd actually briefed President Obama on his phone calls and activities."

The New York Times

Late Edition

Today, some sunshine giving way to clouds, rain late, high 46. Tonight, rain and drizzle, low 40. Tomorrow, clouds giving way to some sunshine, high 54. Weather map, Page B14.

© 2017 The New York Times Company   NEW YORK, FRIDAY, JANUARY 20, 2017 $2.50

TRUMP ARRIVES, SET TO ASSUME POWER

WIRETAPPED DATA USED IN INQUIRY OF TRUMP AIDES

EXAMINING RUSSIAN TIES

Continued on Page A16

The F.B.I. is leading the investigations, aided by the National Security Agency, the C.I.A. and the Treasury Department's financial crimes unit. The investigators have accelerated their efforts in recent weeks but have found no conclusive evidence of wrongdoing, the officials said. One official said intelligence reports based on some of the wiretapped communications had been provided to the White House.

Obama White House

Kincaid wrote that after having Congressman Nunes on the network's "*FoxNews* Sunday" show, *FoxNews* claimed that he said that "phones at President Donald Trump's campaign headquarters in midtown Manhattan were never tapped during last year's election campaign, contrary to President Trump's earlier, unsubstantiated assertion." However, that is not what Congressman Nunes said.

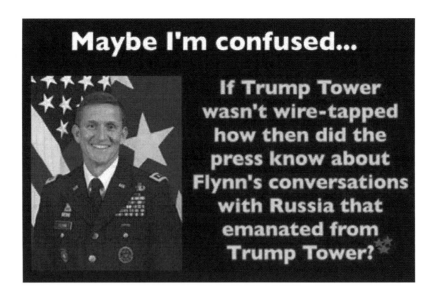

Maybe I'm confused...

If Trump Tower wasn't wire-tapped how then did the press know about Flynn's conversations with Russia that emanated from Trump Tower?

General Michael Flynn

Congressman Nunes explained, "...The one crime we know that's been committed is that one, the leaking of someone's name through the FISA system. That is—that is a crime that's been committed." At the March 20, 2017 hearing Congressman Nunes repeated in his prepared opening statement that "...It's still possible that other surveillance activities were used against President Trump and his associates." On *FoxNews Sunday*, Nunes said that "still remaining out there is the unmasking of names and the leaking of names...we have a lot of surveillance activities in this country and I think the concern that the Trump administration has is, you know, were they actually using surveillance activities to know what they were up to, because we know that that happened with General Flynn. We know that his name was unmasked, and we know that it was leaked out to the press."

As stated earlier, the mainstream media reported FBI Director James B. Comey's testimony at the hearing saying that the FBI and the Justice Department had "no information that supports" President Trump's tweets about wiretapping. Kincaid wrote that there could have been "other surveillance activities." It is known that a former British intelligence agent was involved in gathering "intelligence" against Donald J. Trump in the form of the fake "Trump Dossier," and was paid by donors associated with the Hillary Clinton campaign. Parts of that "dossier" were passed on to Trump by the U.S. intelligence community.

Even though just a few high officials of the intelligence services met with Donald Trump at Trump Towers, one of them leaked this report to the media in order to damage and undermine the president. Kincaid had earlier written a special report explaining that it is well-known that the British National Security Agency, known as Government Communications Headquarters (GCHQ), collaborates with the United States NSA. He further explained that a declassified document on the NSA's own website confirms the collaboration with NSA/GCHQ dating back decades. *FoxNews* senior judicial analyst and commentator Judge Andrew Napolitano said his sources confirmed that there was such an arrangement in the matter of the "wiretapping" of Trump and/or his associates.

The building in Great Britain, known as the doughnut, is the headquarters of Government Communications Headquarters (GCHQ) and collaborates with the United States NSA.

FoxNews immediately suspended Judge Napolitano. The anti-Trump *FoxNews* anchor Shepard Smith said on-air the following: "*FoxNews* cannot confirm Judge Napolitano's commentary. *FoxNews* knows of no evidence of any kind that the now-President of the United States was surveilled at any time, anyway." As Cliff Kincaid points out, the phrase "knows of no evidence" does not suggest any independent investigation of this information.

Kincaid wrote that one of Judge Napolitano's sources was former CIA operative Larry Johnson. The former CIA operative came forward and said the following: "I reached out to friends in the Intel community and asked them about the possibility that a back channel was used to get the Brits to collect on Trump associates. My sources said, 'absolutely.' I later confirmed this via a cutout with a person who is a Senior Intelligence Service executive in the CIA."

Kincaid raised the following question in the face of this evidence of collaboration. Why NSA Director Mike Rogers tried to insist at the hearing on March 20 that the NSA never asked the British to conduct surveillance of Trump? So why did the intelligence community accept and circulate the Trump dossier?

Senator Charles Grassley (R-IA) wrote a letter to FBI director James Comey noting that it was the former British intelligence agent Christopher Steele was "creating these memos as part of work for an opposition research firm connected to Hillary Clinton." He also noted that the *Washington Post* had reported that the FBI had reached an agreement a few weeks before the 2016 presidential election "to *pay the author* of the unsubstantiated dossier alleging a conspiracy between President Trump and the Russians, Christopher Steele, to continue investigating Mr. Trump." Grassley added the following: "The idea that the FBI and associates of the Clinton campaign would pay Mr. Steele to investigate the Republican nominee for President in the run-up to the election raises further questions about the FBI's independence from politics, as well as the Obama administration's use of law enforcement and intelligence agencies for political ends." It is important to note that this unsubstantiated dossier has been completely disregarded as being false.

Cliff Kincaid explained that even though FBI director Comey confirmed to the House Intelligence Committee that the investigation into the Trump campaign's alleged relationship with Russian officials continues, there was no firm commitment to get to the bottom of the source (or sources) of the leaks to the media that are designed to damage the Trump administration. Congressman Nunes said his House of Representatives Intelligence Committee wanted to pursue the matter, saying the following: "Numerous current and former officials have leaked purportedly classified information in connection to these questions. We aim to determine who has leaked or facilitated leaks of classified information so that these individuals can be brought to justice."

As Cliff Kincaid explained in a previous article, if the FBI Director wanted to find out the source or sources of these illegal and felonious leaks of classified information, there is a way to do it. The FBI can subpoena *Washington Post* columnist David Ignatius, the recipient of the illegal leak of the classified information naming or "unmasking" Michael T. Flynn.

Kincaid explained that reporter David Ignatius is a well-known mouthpiece of the CIA. Later, the *Washington Post* said that in regard to the General Flynn matter, "Nine current and former officials, who were in senior positions at multiple agencies at the time of the calls, spoke on the condition of anonymity to discuss intelligence matters." Leaking classified information is illegal and a violation of the Espionage Act. It is a felony punishable by up to 10 years in prison. To make matters worse, Jeff Bezos, the owner of the *Washington Post*, does business with the CIA and the NSA through the provision of computer cloud capabilities.

Congressman Trey Gowdy (Republican from South Carolina) was not able to obtain exact figures from the FBI Director Comey or NSA Director Rogers on the number of individuals at these agencies able to "unmask"—and therefore leak—a name. Such a number is absolutely vital in any identification of the leakers. Director Comey admitted that the heads of the intelligence agencies and various Obama White House officials could have acquired access to unmasked names. But as White House spokesman Spicer noted at the White House press briefing, FBI Director Comey would not talk about any discussions he may have had with President Obama on the matter. Cliff Kincaid concluded his articles by saying that any serious investigation of the illegal surveillance and leaking will have to be led and conducted by the committee headed by Republican Congressman Nunes.

Chart showing some of the members of the Deep State in the Justice Department, and the FBI.

What is the Deep State?

On March 14, 2017, *Newsmax* published an article titled "Gingrich: 'Deep State' Exists." It explained that the "Deep State," is a shadowy network of powerful entrenched federal and military interests who are trying to undermine the president Donald J. Trump. White House high officials and President Donald Trump believe America's intelligence agencies have conspired to leak harmful information to embarrass him. The article pointed out that President Trump's chief strategist had promised to dismantle the permanent Washington "administrative state." White House spokesman Sean Spicer says, "people that burrowed into government" are trying to sabotage the president.

Former Speaker of the House of Representatives Newt Gingrich stated the following: "Of course, the Deep State exists. There's a permanent state of massive bureaucracies that do whatever they want and set up deliberate leaks to attack the president. This is what the deep state does: They create a lie, spread a lie, fail to check the lie and then deny that they were behind the lie... They are fighting to keep hold of their power. "

The article explained that the growing federal bureaucracy, including its intelligence agencies, has thousands of employees who predate President Donald J. Trump, a mix of career staffers, and those appointed by President Barack Obama, whose replacements have yet to be named. Some of these individuals have offered illegal leaks, including sensitive documents, to reporters in order to undermine the president. President Trump has said that these leakers are utilizing the tactics used by Nazi Germany.

Asked if the White House believes there is "a Deep State that's actively working to undermine the president," White House spokesman Spicer said recently, "I don't think it should come as any surprise that there are people that burrowed into government during eight years of the last administration and, you know, may have believed in that agenda and want to continue to seek it."

Sean Hannity, a *Fox News* commentator who has close ties to President Trump, stated in one of his shows that there are "Deep State Obama holdover government bureaucrats who are hellbent on destroying this president." "It's time for the Trump administration to begin to purge these saboteurs before it's too late," Hannity said.

Some observers think that Obama's decision to remain in Washington, D.C. after leaving office is evidence that he is leading the resistance. "He's only there for one purpose and one purpose only and that is to run a shadow government that is totally going to upset the new agenda," said Congressman Mark Kelly, a Pennsylvania Republican, at a recent meeting in his home district last week. His office later walked back the remarks. However, Congressman Kelly was right in his statement and should not have retracted it.

Obama has returned to his role as a radical socialist community organizer

Saul D. Alinsky's goal for the *Rules for Radicals* was to create a guide for future community organizers to use in uniting low-income communities, or "Have-Nots", in order for them to gain social, political, legal, and to take power away from the Haves. Alinsky wanted to train a new generation of radicals to destroy capitalism. On March 14, 2017, Aaron Klein wrote an article for *Breitbart* titled "Obama vs. Trump: Ex-President Returns to Radical Community Organizing to Save his Tattered Legacy." Klein explained that President Donald Trump is dismantling key parts of Barack Obama's legacy.

Saul D. Alinsky wrote *Rules for Radicals* in 1971 and he dedicated his book to Lucifer.

It is for this reason that the former president has returned to his roots as a Saul Alinsky-style radical community organizer. According to several sources, the former president and his associates' main objective is to stop President Trump's domestic and foreign policy agendas. Obama is fighting to stop President Trump's agenda on all fronts from immigration reform, border security, to replacing ObamaCare. Obama and his associates may be seeking no less than Trump's impeachment. Obama is encouraging the filing of legal motions against the president as well as supporting the protest movements targeting President Trump and top administration officials.

Klein pointed out that as "President Trump works to fix America's porous borders, repair the faltering economy, replace Obama's failed healthcare law, combat radical Islamic terrorism, contend with the threat of Obama's nuclear deal with Iran, and address the issue of illegal immigration, the former president is trying to undermine the current president." The *Daily Mail* reported that "Obama's goal, according to a close family friend, is to oust Trump from the presidency either by forcing his resignation or through his impeachment."

Klein said that a group of former top lawyers for the Obama administration created their own organization to utilize legal advocacy methods to target Trump's policies. The group is called United to Protect Democracy. These radical lawyers are in partnership with an organization that is heavily financed by billionaire George Soros. They are led by a lawyer of former President Obama who previously worked at a Soros-financed global activist outfit.

There is also evidence of Obama-connected support for protests that have targeted Trump. Obama established a group called Organizing for Action (OFA). This group has partnered with the newly-formed Indivisible Project for "online trainings" on how to protest Trump's agenda. *Breitbart News* reported that indivisible leaders are openly associated with groups financed by billionaire George Soros.

Obama's OFA has established more than 250 offices throughout the United States. OFA has trained almost 60,000 radicals in a six-week course designed to undermine the presidency of Donald Trump. They have planned 400 protests in 42 states.

Klein wrote that Organizing for Action is a so-called community organizing project that evolved from Obama's 2012 campaign organization, Organizing for America. No president in U.S. history has ever created a nonprofit group such as this one, which was described by the *Washington Post* as "advocating for the president's policies." OFA has hired 14 field organizers in states home to key senators as part of its campaign to defend Obama's signature healthcare law.

Writing for the *New York Post*, researcher and reporter Paul Sperry reported that Obama "is intimately involved in OFA operations and even tweets from the group's account. In fact, he gave marching orders to OFA foot soldiers following Trump's upset victory."

Perry further reported the following on OFA: "In what's shaping up to be a highly unusual post-presidency, Obama isn't just staying behind in Washington. He's working behind the scenes to set up what will effectively be a Shadow Government to not only protect his threatened legacy, but to sabotage the incoming administration and its popular America First agenda. He's doing it through a network of leftist nonprofits led by Organizing for Action. Normally you'd expect an organization set up to support a politician and his agenda to close up shop after that candidate leaves office, but not Obama's OFA. Rather, it's gearing up for battle, with a growing war chest and more than 250 offices across the country."

Klein said that *Politico* recently reported the OFA-affiliated Indivisible, a group that has been aided by MoveOn.org and the American Civil Liberty Union (ACLU). The associations between the OFA-affiliated Indivisible, the Soros-financed MoveOn.org, and ACLU are important since the latter two groups have been central in efforts to stop Trump. MoveOn.org and Indivisible planned a massive anti-Trump Tax March in Washington and in at least 60 other locations on April 15, 2017.

The ACLU held training sessions for several hundreds of radicals, also via the Internet in Miami, Florida. The head of the ACLU said that he has hundreds of lawyers who will attack President Trump in every way possible.

Aaron Klein, a reporter at WND.com, extensively documented Obama's ties to Alinsky ideology. David Horowitz, founder of the David Horowitz Freedom Center and a former 1960's radical, considers Alinsky to be the "communist/Marxist fellow-traveler who helped establish the dual political tactics of confrontation and infiltration that characterized the 1960s and have remained central to all subsequent revolutionary movements in the United States."

Conclusion

Former President Barack Obama, with the help of George Soros and other billionaire socialist friends, has created an illegal "Shadow Government" to try to overturn the results of the presidential election. He is using federal employees who support an ideology similar to his radical Marxist ideology. Obama's "Shadow Government" is not only illegal, but also a criminal attack on our constitutional Republic. Never before in the history of America has this country witnessed a former president trying to overthrow the current president.

Obama's actions and tactics, which were illegal when he was in office, are no longer just unconstitutional but also treasonous. Obama has created a state within a state. It is a criminal conspiracy of unprecedented scope. Obama is attacking directly a duly elected president and is trying to destroy the presidency of Donald Trump. It is looking more and more like a coup d'état.

If President Donald J. Trump is able to prove that President Barack Obama violated his rights by conducting an illegal wiretapping or surveillance on him, there would be grounds to indict

Barack Obama. All the leakers in the intelligence agencies who unmasked Trump associates and leaked classified information must be identified, fired, and indicted. President Trump must order quickly an investigation with loyal and patriotic intelligence service officers. Obama must be stopped!

As Sean Hannity said, "it's time for the Trump administration to begin to purge these saboteurs before it's too late." President Donald J. Trump needs to order the Justice Department and other agencies of his government to investigate the criminal and illegal "Shadow Government" of Barack Obama and his allies. Indictments need to be issue against those who are paying criminals to commit acts of violence across America. If President Trump does not hurry to drain the swamp, he will be swallowed by the swamp in Washington, D.C.

CHAPTER 25

An Iman with ties to the Muslim Brotherhood is the main plaintiff opposing Trump's travel ban in Hawaii

Ismail Elshikh, who was born in Egypt and is the Imam of a Muslim Brotherhood-connected mosque in Honolulu, Hawaii, said he is suffering "irreparable harm" by President Donald J. Trump's temporary travel ban.

Hassan al-Banna founded the terrorist organization Ikhwan or the Muslim Brotherhood in Egypt in 1928.

This radical terror organization has been banned in Egypt, Bahrain, Syria, Saudi Arabia, Russia, and the United Arab Emirates but operates freely in America. The Muslim Brotherhood is a transnational Sunni Islamic organization.

The Muslim Brotherhood's well-known slogan is "God is our objective. The Prophet is our leader. The Qur'an is our law. Jihad is our way. Dying in the way of God is our highest hope. God is greater!" How can America allow this terror organization and its many fronts to operate in America?

Imam Ismail Elshikh, who leads a mosque with ties to the Muslim Brotherhood, is the main plaintiff in the Hawaii case blocking President Trump's revised temporary travel ban. During the presidential campaign, Donald J. Trump talked about declaring the Muslim Brotherhood a terrorist organization. Now it is a Muslim Brotherhood-backed imam who is playing a key role in blocking his executive order on immigration.

Imam Ismail Elshikh, age 39, is the leader of the largest mosque in Hawaii and claims to be suffering "irreparable harm" from the president's executive order. This order places a 90-day ban on travel to the United Sates from six countries. One of those six countries is war-torn Syria. Elshikh's mother-in-law is Syrian and would not be able to visit her family in Hawaii for 90 days if Trump's ban were allowed to go into effect.

State Attorney of Hawaii Doug Chin, right, is standing in this picture with Imam Ismail Elshikh and other members of the Muslim Association of Hawaii.

The majority of the 5,000 Muslims in Hawaii attend Imam Ismail Elshikh's mosque, the Muslim Association of Hawaii, which is located in a residential area in Manoa, Honolulu. The mosque, despite its ties to the terror and subversive radical organization, the Muslim Brotherhood, is fighting President Trump's temporary travel ban with the help of State Attorney of Hawaii, Doug Chin, and Derrick K. Watson, an Obama-appointed federal judge who was Obama's classmate in Harvard Law School.

Thousands of Muslims attend services at Muslim Association of Hawaii mosque in Honolulu with ties to the Muslim Brotherhood.

Imam Elshikh was born and raised in Cairo, Egypt, the home base of the Muslim Brotherhood. The stated goal of this terrorist organization is to spread Shariah law throughout the world and its slogan is "the Qur'an is our law and Jihad is our way." Imam Elshikh is living in the United States with a green card, which gives him permanent legal status.

The North American Islamic Trust (NAIT)

Evidence supporting that the Muslim Association of Hawaii mosque has ties to the Muslim Brotherhood is found in the court records of Honolulu County. These records list the North American Islamic Trust (NAIT) as the deed holder. The North American Islamic Trust is based in Plainfield, Indiana and owns many Islamic properties in North America.

Wikipedia reported that many Muslim organizations founded by Islamic immigrants who came to America during the 1960s have roots in the Muslim Students Association (MSA). It is well known that MSA is a Muslim Brotherhood front.

Beginning in the 1970s, NAIT helped provide Islamic college and university students with mosques so they could continue to worship Islam. NAIT serves as the trustee of approximately 200 Islamic centers, mosques, and schools. The properties of those mosques are estimated to be worth in the hundreds of millions of dollars. NAIT holds the titles of over 325 properties in 42 states. The organization also holds the deeds of about one-fourth of the mosques in America. NAIT says it "does not administer these institutions nor interfere with their daily management, but is available to support and advise them regarding their operation in conformity with the Shariah."

Wikipedia reported that many NAIT-supported mosques have been involved in terrorist activities. One of these mosques was the Islamic Academy of Florida in Hillsborough County, Florida. Sami Al-Arian founded this mosque in 1992. The Islamic Academy of Florida was described in a 2003 federal indictment as the headquarters of a terrorist cell working on behalf of the Palestinian Islamic Jihad. This terror group was responsible for the murders of more than 100 people. The federal indictment stated that the offices of the Academy of Florida were used to communicate with Islamic Jihad operatives. On March 2, 2006, Al-Arian entered a guilty plea to a charge of conspiracy to help the Palestinian Islamic Jihad terror organization. Al-Arian was sentenced to 57 months in prison. An order was issued for his deportation following his prison term.

Wikipedia reported that in August 2004 Mohammed M. Hossain and Yassin M. Aref, two leaders of a mosque in Albany, were arrested on charges that they took part in, what they thought was, a plot to import a shoulder-fired missile and assassinate a Pakistani diplomat in New York City. They were convicted and sentenced to 15 years in prison in 2007. In 2007, federal prosecutors brought charges against Holy Land Foundation for allegedly funding the terrorist activities of Hamas and other Islamic terrorist organizations. NAIT was named as an unindicted co-conspirator in the case, along with the Council on American-Islamic Relations (CAIR) and the Islamic Society of North America (ISNA).

On July 1, 2009, U.S. District Court Judge Jorge Solis upheld NAIT's designation as an unindicted co-conspirator. He did, however, rule that it should not be made public. He determined there is "ample" evidence tying NAIT to Hamas. The Holy Land Foundation, for example, transferred money to Hamas through a joint NAIT/ISNA bank account.

Wikipedia stated the following: "Other terrorism-connected mosques controlled by NAIT include: the Islamic Society of Boston, where a dozen terrorists have worshipped, including the 2013 Boston Marathon bombers Dzhokhar Tsarnaev and Tamerlan Tsarnaev; Islamic Community Center of Phoenix, where worshippers included two ISIS-inspired terrorists who attacked a Dallas-area event in 2015; and Dar al-Hijrah Islamic Center, where some of the 9/11 hijackers worshipped and got help obtaining IDs and housing, followed by the 2009 Fort Hood shooter and several other terrorists who have attended the mosque just outside Washington."

The website *WND* reported that NAIT is closely linked to other Muslim Brotherhood-linked entities. It was founded in Indiana in 1973 by the Muslim Students Association and is today a "constituent organization" of the Islamic Society of North America (ISNA). Both have Muslim Brotherhood origins. Declassified FBI memos dated 1987-1988 showed that agency investigators identified NAIT as a foreign-financed Muslim Brotherhood front.

WND reported that an FBI memo states the following: "As reported above by [name redacted] the IIIT [International Institute of Islamic Thought], NAIT, ISNA and various other Muslim organizations under the direction and control of the IKHWAN [Muslim Brotherhood] in the United States has as its ultimate goal political control of all non-Islamic governments in the world."

WND reported the following: "The same FBI memo cites a source that has traveled worldwide on orders of NAIT, ISNA and the International Institute of Islamic Thought. He is convinced that this organization has a secret agenda which includes the spread of the Islamic Revolution to all non-Islamic governments in the world which does include the United States. He said that the entire organization is structured, controlled and funded by followers and supporters of the Islamic Revolution as advocated by the founders of Muslim Brotherhood in Egypt. Another 1987 FBI memo states that many leaders of NAIT support the Iranian Islamic Revolution and the group receives money from Saudi Arabia, Iran, Libya, Kuwait and other Middle Eastern countries. It says NAIT is financing those seeking a separate black nation in the U.S. and have also indicated their support of terrorism in the U.S. to further the revolution. NAIT is supporting Jihad in the U.S."

NAIT's Islamic Book Service has advertised "Milestones" by Sayyid Qutb, the Muslim Brotherhood preacher who inspired Osama Bin Laden, as a "top seller." John Guandolo, a former FBI counter-terrorism specialist and now private consultant to law enforcement, said all mosques under the "Muslim Association of" moniker are typically affiliated with the Muslim Brotherhood. However, instead of banning the Muslim Brotherhood, the United States is letting a Brotherhood-backed imam dictate U.S. refugee and visa policy, Guandolo said.

The website *Discover the Networks* stated the following: "Because NAIT controls the purse strings of these many properties, it can exercise ultimate authority over what they teach and what activities they conduct. Specifically, the Trust seeks to ensure that the institutions under its financial influence promote the principles of Sharia law and Wahhabism."

The Trump administration has said it is considering banning the Muslim Brotherhood in America by including it on the State Department's list of foreign terrorist organizations. President Trump's secretary of state, Rex Tillerson, described the Muslim Brotherhood as "an agent of radical Islam."

Former U.N. Ambassador John Bolton stated to *Breitbart News* in February 2017 that the United States should declare the Muslim Brotherhood a terrorist organization. Bolton sated the following: "The fact is, the Brotherhood is a front for terrorism. A number of Arab majority-Muslim countries, like Egypt and Saudi Arabia and the United Arab Emirates, have already designated it as a terrorist organization. I've had Muslim leaders from the Middle East say to me, 'Are you people blind to what's going on right in front of you and the role that the Brotherhood performs, really on an international basis?'"

The unconstitutional ruling made by U.S. federal judge Derrick K. Watson

Derrick K. Watson

On March 15, 2017, Derrick K. Watson, age 50, an Obama-appointed federal judge, stroke President Trump's temporary travel ban Executive Order. Judge Watson graduated from Harvard Law School along with former President Barack Obama. The six nations in Trump's list for a 90-day moratorium on visas and a 120-day pause on refugee resettlement are Iran, Libya, Syria, Yemen, Sudan, and Somalia.

In an unconstitutional ruling, federal judge Derrick Watson ruled that President Trump's temporary 90-day ban on travel to the United States from six countries amounted to a "Muslim ban." Doug Chin, Hawaii's Attorney General, along with co-plaintiff Imam Elshikh, claimed the ban would irreparably harm the state's tourism industry and the Muslim families.

This successful lawsuit alleged the following: "That the Executive Order subjects portions of the State's population, including Imam Elshikh and his family, to discrimination in violation of both the Constitution denying them their right, among other things, to associate with family members overseas on the basis of their religion and national origin. The State purports that the Executive Order has injured its institutions, economy, and sovereign interest in maintaining the separation between church and state."

Judge Derrick K. Watson's language was very harsh. He severely criticized the government for being "illogic" and for presenting arguments he said were "not true." In addition to stopping the Trump administration from enforcing the travel ban, Judge Watson described Donald J. Trump's past comments about Muslims as "remarkable" evidence that his order was motivated by animosity toward a religious faith. Judge Watson believes Iranians, Sudanese, Libyans, Syrians, Somalis, and Yemenis have the same constitutional rights as American citizens

The unconstitutional decision, issued just hours before President Trump's travel ban was to go into effect, resulted in an angry response from the president. At a rally in Tennessee, Florida on that same day, President Donald J. Trump accused Judge Watson of acting "for political reasons" and stated that the ruling "makes us look weak."

Did Obama visit Judge Derrick K. Watson prior to his ruling?

A source close to the former president stated to the *Daily Mail* that Obama's ultimate goal was to force Trump to step down, either through resignation or impeachment. The source also stated that the former president is "dismayed at the way Trump is tearing down his legacy—ObamaCare, the social safety net and the welcome mat for refugees he put in place." Obama has created a nerve center in his mansion just two miles from the White House, which is serving as a war room for his bid to lead an "insurgency" against Trump to sabotage his presidency.

How long is President Donald J. Trump going to tolerate Obama's shadow government that undermines his presidency?

The *RedStateWatcher* website reported that Obama met with Judge Derrick K. Watson a day before his unconstitutional decision. *InfoWars, Geteway Pundit*, and *bwcentral.org* websites reported that former President Barack Obama visited Hawaii two days before the ruling by this federal judge.

On March 16, 2017, Jim Hoft wrote an article titled "Obama Paid Surprise Visit to Hawaii 48 Hours before Hawaii Judge Rules against Trump Temporary Refugee Ban (Updated)" which was published by the website *Gateway Pundit*. The reporter explained that former President Barack Obama made a surprise visit to Honolulu, Hawaii on March 13, 2017. This visit took place just two days before U.S. District Court Judge Derrick Watson, who presides in Honolulu, ruled against President Trump's temporary refugee ban from six Middle East nations.

Hoft stated the following: "Coming off a string of high-profile meetings, former President Barack Obama made an unannounced return to Hawaii. Just three months removed from his last official holiday visit as president, Obama was spotted dining at Buzz's Lanikai Monday night. Local Democrats tried their best to keep it under wraps the whole day."

Paul Joseph Watson wrote an article on March 16, 2017 entitled "Coincidence? Obama Makes Surprise Visit to Hawaii 48 hours Before Judge Blocks Trump Travel Ban" which was published by the *InfoWars* website. Watson explained that the decision by U.S. District Court Judge Derrick Watson in Hawaii to block President Donald Trump's travel ban was announced less than 48 hours after Barack Obama made a surprise visit to Honolulu. This surprise visit by the former president has led some to speculate that Obama may have plotted with the judge, who he originally appointed. Derrick Watson was nominated by Obama as federal judge in November 2012. He graduated from Harvard law school in the same year as Obama.

Watson reported that the newspaper *Honolulu Star* wrote that Obama "made an unannounced return to Hawaii Monday, March 13, 2017 just three months after his last official holiday visit as president, arriving with a small entourage that included a Secret Service detail. Obama had dinner at the Noi Thai restaurant, which is just minutes away from the courthouse and that Obama was "likely within five minutes of the judge's house at one point on the drive over." Watson concluded his article by stating that "Given that Obama appointed the judge, graduated in the same year as him and visited Honolulu and was within minutes of the judge less than

48 hours before Judge Watson made a major ruling that blocked Trump's travel ban, it doesn't take a wild-eyed conspiracy theorist to insinuate that the two could have met."

The Supreme Court Allowed the Trump Administration to Enforce the Travel Ban

The Supreme Court allowed the Trump administration to fully enforce a ban on immigrants from eight countries.

The Supreme Court in a 7 to 2 decision handed the Trump administration a major victory on December 4, 2017 by permitting the White House to fully impose the president's travel ban for residents of six Muslim-majority countries. These nations are Chad, Iran, Libya, Somalia, Syria, and Yemen. The travel ban also includes North Korea as well as Maduro's regime officials and their families in Venezuela. The two dissenting members of the Supreme Court were Justices Ruth Bader Ginsburg and Sonia Sotomayor. The other seven voted to strike down the lower-court orders that blocked the policy.

The Supreme Court lifted stays imposed by lower courts and allowed the President Trump's executive order to take effect while legal challenges proceed. The Supreme Court said in two one-page orders that lower court rulings that partly blocked the latest ban should be put on hold while courts of appeals consider the cases.

The extreme liberal San Francisco-based 9th U.S. Circuit Court of Appeals and the 4th U.S. Circuit Court of Appeals in Richmond, Virginia will be holding arguments on the legality of the ban. Both courts of appeals are dealing with the issue promptly. After their rulings, the Supreme Court is to hear and decide the issue by the end of June 2018.

The December 4, 2017 decision by the Supreme Court showed that the high court looks favorably on the latest version of President Trump's travel ban. This is the third version of the travel ban or extreme vetting order that until now has repeatedly been blocked by federal judges. Attorney General Jeff Sessions called the ruling "a substantial victory for the safety and security of the American people."

Conclusion

It is clear that the Supreme Court will issue a final ruling in mid-2018 in support of the Trump administration permanent travel ban on immigrants from eight nations. The very liberal courts of appeals more than likely will rule against the executive order issued by President Trump. However, when these cases come before the highest court in the nation, these rulings will be reversed. The Constitution allows presidents to have broad authority on which individuals from foreign countries are allowed to come to America.

The rulings by the federal judge in Hawaii and by a Maryland federal judge blocking President Trump's executive order temporarily banning travel to the United States from six countries are clearly unconstitutional. Under the law the president may ban foreigners from entering America.

The hypocrisy of these judges as well as of the Democrats in Congress is immense as both presidents Obama and Carter blocked entrance to the United States of citizens from Iraq and Iran for several months and no one complained. These federal judges and the Democrats will have blood on their hands if someone from these six countries, which are full of Islamic terrorists, kills or injures Americans.

The Trump administration reported to be considering banning the Muslim Brotherhood in America by including it on the State Department's list of foreign terrorist organizations. President Trump's secretary of state, Rex Tillerson, described the Muslim Brotherhood as "an agent of radical Islam." President Trump needs to work with Congress to expedite the bill to ban the Muslim Brotherhood and its many front organizations in the nation.

CHAPTER 26

President Donald J. Trump's Address to Congress

President Donald J. Trump addressed a joint session of Congress as Vice President Mike Pence and House Speaker Paul Ryan, Republican from Wisconsin, looked on.

On February 28, 2017, President Donald J. Trump spoke brilliantly for the first time to a joint session of Congress. He presented a vision looking ahead to a better future for all Americans and stated his agenda and priorities.

The president focused on civil rights and the fight against discrimination, renewal of the American spirit, greatness and a new national pride, unity and strength, the creation jobs, the improvement of inner cities, the need for bipartisanship, the improvement of education, adherence for the rule of law, a merit-based immigration system, liberty and justice, the improvement of infrastructure, and the construction of the Keystone and Dakota Access Pipelines. He also spoke on the wall and border security, support of NATO, economy and prosperity, fighting crime and drug cartels, tax and regulatory reform, safety, opportunities, and fighting the drug epidemic. The President also talked about the need to repeal and replace ObamaCare, defend our allies, rebuild the military, improve vetting procedures, fight Islamic terrorists and protect America, have free trade and fair trade, and improve national security. It was one of the best presidential addresses to Congress in the history of this country.

On February 28, 2017, S.A. Miller and Dave Boyer wrote in the *Washington Times* that President Trump wanted to jump-start his legislative agenda. The reporters explained that the president asked Republicans and Democrats in Congress to work with him "to crack down on illegal immigration, increase economic growth and rebuild the U.S. military — sticking to the campaign promises that resonated with blue-collar Americans and put him in the White House." President Trump tried to explain his vision to a deeply divided nation, a bitterly split Congress, and a mainstream news media that he considers among of his enemies. He repeatedly made appeals for unity and for Democrats to put aside long-standing disputes to work toward a common goal of bettering the lives of Americans. He insisted that both sides of the aisle needed to support his "America First" agenda.

On March 1, 2017, Erick Erickson wrote an article on his blog entitled "Last Night, the Man Became the President". He pointed out that presidential addresses to joint sessions of Congress are quickly forgotten.

Erickson stated the following: "While the speeches are forgotten, the impressions they leave will live on. Last night, Mr. Trump finally became President Trump. That should scare the crap out of Democrats. President Trump's speech was, frankly, a conventional speech to a crowd that favors convention. He sounded the part. He hit the right notes. His remarks on Ryan Owens and having Mrs. Owens there were electric and unifying. It was a moment of non-partisanship in a hyper-partisan age. That moment allowed all but the most cynical partisans to be American, not partisan. The President put the nation ahead of the tribe. It matters because things have felt out of sorts for some time and the last month has been discombobulating and confusing for so many people. Last night, President Trump restored normalcy. It has a different rhythm and a different cadence, but it is familiar. That familiarity is reassuring."

Erickson added the following: "The President's performance should scare Democrats because they had placed their bets that President Trump is incapable of rising to the occasion. But he did. They cannot now rely on letting President Trump self-immolate. They are now going to have to relate to real people in the heartland again, but how can they? President Trump connected with the middle class across demographic lines and Americans witnessed a Democratic Party sitting on their hands. When the Congress gave Mrs. Owens a standing ovation, Keith Ellison — the would be chair of the DNC — and Debbie Wasserman Schultz refused to stand. Last night, the President showed he really has found his footing. He showed he really can be up to the task of being everyone's President. He showed he is invested in the job…And Americans had every reason to feel reassured that things will be okay in the Age of Trump." Keith Ellison, a radical Muslim who supports Muslim Brotherhood groups, later became the vice chair of the DNC

Conclusion

This writer believes President Trump spoke brilliantly for the first time to a joint session of Congress. He presented a vision looking ahead to a better future for all Americans and stated his agenda and priorities.

President Trump connected with the middle and working classes across demographic lines. Americans witnessed many members of the Democratic Party being disrespectful and sitting on their hands.

President Trump's speech was one on the best given by a president to both houses of congress in history. President Trump sounded very presidential. His remarks on the late Navy Seal Ryan Owens in the presence of his widow, who was in the audience, were electrifying and unifying.

CHAPTER 27

Judge Neil Gorsuch was an excellent appointment to the Supreme Court

President Donald J. Trump nominated a conservative judge, Neil Gorsuch, to be an Associate Justice of the Supreme Court. The president appeared with Judge Gorsuch and his wife Louise.

On January 31, 2017, President Donald J. Trump fulfilled an important campaign promise and nominated a conservative judge, Neil Gorsuch, to be an Associate Justice of the Supreme Court to fill the seat left vacant after the death of Justice Antonin Scalia. Later the Senate confirmed his appointment. As he introduced his nominee in the East Room of the White House, President Trump said that Judge Gorsuch was "the very best judge in the country." President Trump added the following: "I took the task of this nomination very seriously. Millions of voters said this was the single most important issue to them when they voted for me. I am a man of my word. I will do what I say, something that people has been asking for in Washington for a very long time…Judge Gorsuch has outstanding legal skills, a brilliant mind, tremendous discipline, and has earned bipartisan support."

After the president introduced him, Judge Gorsuch stated the following: "The president had trusted me with a most solemn assignment. Justice Scalia was a lion of the law. Agree or disagree with him, all of his colleagues on the bench shared his wisdom and his humor. And like them, I miss him. In our legal order it is for Congress and not the courts to write new laws. It is the role of judges to apply, not alter, the work of the people's representatives. A judge who likes every outcome he reaches is very likely a bad judge."

Judge Neil McGill Gorsuch was born in 1967.

Judge Gorsuch promised that, if confirmed, he would labor to live up to the standard set by Justice Antonin Scalia, whose death in February 2016 created the vacancy. He cast himself firmly in the Scalia mold of a judge who would not place his own views over his duty to follow the law.

In September 2016, during the presidential campaign, Donald J. Trump promised that he would choose a conservative judge similar to Justice Antonin Scalia. He presented the nation a list of 21 conservative judges who were submitted by him by several conservative organizations which included the name of Judge Neil Gorsuch.

As the president said, millions of individuals in the nation voted for him on his promise to nominate conservatives to the Supreme Court. Millions were worried that if Hillary Clinton won the presidential election, she would appoint extreme leftist liberal judges to the Supreme Court of the nation.

On May 10, 2006, Neil Gorsuch was nominated by President George W. Bush to the United States Court of Appeals for the Tenth Circuit. Two months later, on July 20, 2006, Neil Gorsuch was confirmed unanimously by the Senate. He had previously been recommended by the American Bar Association, which is mostly a liberal group.

Judge Gorsuch is a proponent of all originalism and textualism in interpreting the Constitution. This means that, as he stated in the White House, he will be "a faithful servant of the Constitution and the laws of the nation." He will not be an activist judge who would legislate from the Supreme Court as many liberal judges have done over the years. He will interpret the laws passed by Congress and the president in terms of the Constitution.

Wikipedia has an excellent biography of Judge Neil Gorsuch. The information below was obtained from *Wikipedia* and other sources.

Early life and education

Neil Gorsuch was born in Denver, Colorado and grew up in Washington, D.C. His father is David Gorsuch and his mother, Anne Gorsuch Burford. She was appointed by President Ronald Reagan as the first woman to head the Environmental Protection Agency. Neil Gorsuch is Episcopalian.

Judge Gorsuch's academic credentials are beyond reproach. He graduated from the best universities in the world. In 1988, he received a Bachelor's of Art degree with honors from Columbia University. While a student at that university, he wrote articles for the *Columbia Daily Spectator*, the student newspaper. He co-founded an alternative conservative student newspaper, *The Fed*.

Neil Gorsuch graduated from Harvard Law School with honors in 1991. One of his classmates at Harvard Law School was former President Barack Obama. Judge Gorsuch received a Marshall Scholarship to attend the University College at Oxford University. He received a Doctor of Philosophy in Law degree in 2004.

Career

Neil Gorsuch had outstanding judges as mentors. He clerked for Judge David B. Sentelle in the United States Court of Appeals for Washington, D.C. from 1991 to1992 and then for the United States Supreme Court with justices Byron White and Anthony Kennedy from 1993 to 1994. Justice Kennedy, age 80, still serves on the highest court of the land.

During the following 10 years, Neil Gorsuch was a lawyer at the Washington, D.C. law firm of Kellogg, Huber, Hansen, Todd, Evans and Figel. From 2005 to 2006, he served as Principal Deputy to the Associate Attorney General Robert McCallum at the Department of Justice. He served as a Visiting Professor at the University of Colorado Law School.

United States Court of Appeals for the Tenth Circuit

As stated earlier, on May 10, 2006, Gorsuch was nominated by President George W. Bush to the United States Court of Appeals for the Tenth Circuit. He was unanimously confirmed by the Senate. Below are some of his most important rulings:

Money in politics

Judge Gorsuch issued a ruling that states that giving money to politicians while running campaigns is a "fundamental right" that should be afforded the highest standard of constitutional protection, known as strict scrutiny.

Freedom of religion

Judge Gorsuch is a defender of the freedom of religion. In two rulings, Judge Gorsuch sided with Christian employers and religious organizations. These were the cases of Hobby Lobby Stores versus Sebelius and the case of Little Sisters of the Poor. In the Hobby Lobby case, Judge Gorsuch held that the requirement in ObamaCare or the Affordable Care Act that employers provide insurance coverage for contraceptives without a co-payment violated the rights of those employers that object to use of contraceptives on religious grounds.

Judge Gorsuch wrote the following: "The Affordable Care Act's mandate requires them to violate their religious faith by forcing them to lend an impermissible degree of assistance to conduct their religion teaches to be gravely wrong. And as we have seen, it is not for secular courts to rewrite the religious complaint of a faithful adherent, or to decide whether a religious teaching about complicity imposes 'too much' moral disapproval on those only 'indirectly' assisting wrongful conduct. Whether an act of complicity is or isn't 'too attenuated' from the underlying wrong is sometimes itself a matter of faith we must respect."

The Hobby Lobby case was a high-profile religious liberty case that later was reviewed by the Supreme Court. Judge Gorsuch wrote a concurring opinion which asked the court to decide if the 1993 Religious Freedom Restoration Act allows a closely held for-profit company to deny its employees contraceptive coverage based on religious objections. His opinion was largely vindicated when the Supreme Court ruled in a 5 to 4 decision in favor of Hobby Lobby.

Death penalty

Judge Gorsuch favors a strict reading of the Antiterrorism and Effective Death Penalty Act of 1996. In a 2003 case, Judge Gorsuch denied requests of death-row inmates seeking to escape executions.

Legal philosophy

Judge Gorsuch believes in what has been described as originalism, which means that the Constitution should be interpreted as the Founding Fathers would have interpreted it. He also believes in textualism, which is the idea that statutes should be interpreted literally, without considering the legislative history and the underlying purpose of the law.

He is opposed to judicial activism. He has stated that judges should strive "to apply the law as it is, focusing backward, not forward, and looking to text, structure, and history to decide what a reasonable reader at the time of the events in question would have understood the law to be—not to decide cases based on their own moral convictions or the policy consequences they believe might serve society best."

Abortion

Judge Gorsuch has never written an opinion on Roe versus Wade. However, many believe that based on the opinions expressed in his book opposing euthanasia and assisted suicide, he may tend to rule in favor of pro-life in the future of abortion and related cases.

Euthanasia

Judge Gorsuch covered the most thorough overview of the ethical and legal issues raised by assisted suicide and euthanasia--as well as the most comprehensive argument against their legalization—ever published. He evaluated the strengths and weaknesses of leading contemporary ethical arguments for assisted suicide and euthanasia. He reviewed the evidence and case histories from the Netherlands and Oregon, where the practices have been legalized. Judge Gorsuch analyzed the arguments for legalization as well as the impact of key Supreme Court decisions on the debate. He looked at the history and evolution of laws and attitudes regarding assisted suicide and euthanasia in U.S. society.

Judge Gorsuch wrote the book *The Future of Assisted Suicide and Euthanasia* 2009.

After assessing the strengths and weaknesses of arguments for assisted suicide and euthanasia, Neil Gorsuch provided a powerful moral and legal argument against their legalization. This argument is based on a principle that, surprisingly, has largely been overlooked in the debate--the idea that human life is intrinsically valuable, and that intentional killing is always wrong. At the same time, Judge Gorsuch left wide latitude for individual patient autonomy and the refusal of unwanted medical treatment and life-sustaining care, permitting intervention only in cases where an intention to kill is present.

Those on both sides of the assisted suicide issue will find Gorsuch's analysis to be a thoughtful and stimulating contribution to the debate about one of the most controversial public policy issues of today. Judge Gorsuch stated that "retaining the laws banning assisted suicide or euthanasia … based on the idea that all human beings are intrinsically valuable and the intentional taking of human life by private persons is always wrong". He said he was a strong opponent of euthanasia.

States' rights

Judge Gorsuch was described by a professor at the University of Denver Law School as "a predictably socially conservative judge who tends to favor state power over federal power".

Personal life

Judge Gorsuch and his wife, Louise, have two teenage daughters, Emma and Belinda, and live in Boulder, Colorado. In addition to his book *The Future of Assisted Suicide and Euthanasia*, Gorsuch was one of 12 co-authors of *The Law of Judicial Precedent* (2016).

Democratic senators unsuccessfully tried to block the nomination of Judge Gorsuch

Senate Schumer failed to stop the confirmation by the Senate of Judge Gorsuch.

Only minutes after the announcement, Democrat Senate Minority Leader Charles E. Schumer from New York announced plans for a filibuster to block the judge. Democrat Senator Jeff Merkley from Oregon led fellow Democrats on a mission to filibuster any nominee by President Trump as a payback for the treatment of Judge Garland whose nomination was not acted upon by the Republicans in the Senate in the last year of the presidency of Obama. Democratic senators refused to remember that Senator Schumer said the Democrats would not confirm any justice to the Supreme Court who President George W. Bush would nominate in his last two years in office.

It was difficult for Senate Democrats to explain their new dislike for Judge Gorsuch. As stated earlier, the Senate confirmed him for the federal bench in 2006 by a unanimous voice vote, including support from Chuck Schumer, Barack Obama, Joe Biden, and Hillary Clinton. President Trump asked Republicans in the Senate to exercise the so-called nuclear option, which is a change in the rules of the Senate to eliminate the 60-vote threshold for filibusters. If the nuclear option is implemented, justices of the Supreme Court could be confirmed with 51 votes in the Senate.

Conclusion

President Donald J. Trump has nominated one of the most conservative, extremely intelligent judges in America. Judge Gorsuch was later confirmed by the Senate. He is the youngest justice. This means that he could stay in the bench for many years.

Mat Staver, Founder and Chairman of Liberty Counsel, stated the following: "It's time to return this country back to the rule of law where judges interpret the original meaning of the Constitution and the laws before them. Judicial activism is destroying the judiciary and will ultimately weaken the role of the judicial in the eyes of the people. The only power that courts have is the trust of the people that judges will act fairly and put aside personal bias. From the Supreme Court to the state courts, the role of judges is to judge fairly. If they want to be legislators, then let them run for office. Judicial activism has no place on the bench."

Americans need to be very grateful to President Donald J. Trump for delivering on his promise to nominate excellent, competent, and very intelligent conservative judges to the highest court of the land. Hopefully, during his tenure, the president will have the opportunity to nominate other conservative justices to the Supreme Court.

CHAPTER 28

America Strikes Syria

Destroyer launches a Tomahawk cruise towards Shayrat Syrian airfield.

Trump's strike of Syria sent a signal to its dictator to not use banned chemical weapons against its people. It also was a signal for Russia as this country signed an agreement to remove all chemical weapons but has not enforced it. This was the first direct U.S. strike on Assad regime and has altered the dynamics between America and Russia.

President Trump issued the following statement:

"On Tuesday, the Syrian dictator Bashar al-Assad launched a horrible chemical weapons attack on innocent civilians. Using a deadly nerve agent, Assad choked out the lives of helpless men, women, and children. It was a slow and brutal death for so many. Even beautiful babies were cruelly murdered in this very barbaric attack. No child of God should ever suffer such horror."

"Tonight, I ordered a targeted military strike on the airfield in Syria from where the chemical attack was launched. It is in this vital security interest of the United States, to prevent and deter the spread and use of deadly chemical weapons. There can be no dispute that Syria used banned chemical weapons violated its obligations under the Chemicals Weapon Convention, and ignored the urging of the U.N. Security Council. Years of previous attempts at changing Assad's behavior have all failed, and failed very dramatically."

President Donald J. Trump joined, from left to right, Defense Secretary Jim Mattis, Secretary of State Rex Tillerson, and Commerce Secretary Wilbur Ross on Friday at Mar-a-Lago in Palm Beach, Florida.

"As a result, the refugee crisis continues to deepen, and the region continues to destabilize threatening the United States and its allies. Tonight, I call on all civilized nations to join us in seeking to end the slaughter and bloodshed in Syria, and also to end terrorism of all kinds and all types. We ask for God's wisdom as we face the challenge of our very troubled world. We pray for the lives of the wounded and for the souls of those who have passed. And we hope that as long as America stands for justice, then peace and harmony will in the end, prevail. Good night and God bless America and the entire world."

Pentagon officials said the 59 Tomahawk missiles strike launched from two destroyers destroyed 20 Syrian planes, the base air defense system, airplane hangars, ammunition bunkers, and fuel depots. The Pentagon did not target the runway. Russia denounced strongly the U.S. attack and ended its military working relationship with the United States in Syria, increasing the danger of a military confrontation with the two nations.

Paul Sonne, Felicia Schwartz, and Carol E. Lee wrote an article on the *Wall Street Journal* explaining that President Donald Trump's decision to strike the Syrian airfield was a signal to Russia that his administration was willing to use force, contrary to his predecessor, even if it meant upsetting the Kremlin and its allies. Officials in the Trump administration have been saying that America must approach Russia from a position of strength before relations with Moscow can improve. President Trump wanted to send the rest of the world a signal in one of his earliest foreign-policy test.Click For Sound

"This is bigger than Syria," a senior administration official said. "It's representative of how he wants to be seen by other world leaders. It is important that people understand this is a different administration," the official added.

Sonne, Schwartz, and Lee explained this was the first direct U.S. strike on the Assad bloody regime since the beginning of the Syrian conflict. It altered the dynamics between America and Russia over Syria. An immediate result was Russia's declaration that it had cancelled the agreement with America to coordinate aircraft flights over Syria to prevent conflicts. This action by Putin could increase the risk of an incident over Syria, where U.S. aircrafts fly regularly in the campaign against Islamic State. The U.S. strike against Syria could lead to unpredictable reactions by dictator Assad and his allies, in particular Iran and its Lebanese ally, Hezbollah.

Republican Senate Foreign Relations Committee Chairman Bob Corker from Tennessee

Sonne, Schwartz, and Lee pointed out that Senate Foreign Relations Committee Chairman Bob Coker said, "Hopefully, this is something that very much changes the type of conversation that will take place between Putin and Tillerson when they meet." Senator Corker said the operation showed "the kind of pushback" Mr. Putin understands.

Later Senator Corker began a series of attacks against President Trump. Since his popularity in his state had diminished significantly, Senator Corker announced that he was not going to seek reelection. Senator Corker was the only Republican senator to vote against the Senate tax cut bill in December 2017. His hatred for the president is immense!

"I think that there can be a shared commitment to defeat ISIS and also agree that you can't gas your own people," White House press secretary Sean Spicer said. "There is a mutual level of human decency that I think we can expect out of everybody," he added.

For years, Obama administration officials at the State Department and the Pentagon expressed frustration with the unwillingness of the White House to use greater force in Syria, leaving former Secretary of State John Kerry with little leverage in his negotiations with Russia. Many of them approved the decision to strike Mr. Assad.

Russia's avowed cancellation of the military channel between Moscow and Washington is one way the Russians can make future U.S. unilateral strikes more difficult, said Michael Kofman, a Russian defense expert and research analyst at the Virginia-based Center for Naval Analyses. "They want to make sure that we don't have a channel where we can call them and announce we are bombing somewhere in Syria," Kofman said.

Mr. Putin has been able to undertake risky military gambits in places such as Syria and Ukraine in part because he has a lock on domestic politics in Russia, with little criticism or opposition. This is a luxury the White House does not enjoy.

"I think they calculate that if this is a game of chicken, that we'll probably be the first ones to swerve to the side of the road," said Michael Carpenter, the former U.S. deputy assistant secretary of defense for Russia under Mr. Obama. "They calculate that. It remains to be seen if that's the case," Carpenter added.

Syrian dictator Bashar al-Assad shakes hands with his friend and ally, Russian dictator Vladimir Putin.

Conclusion

President Donald Trump's decision to strike the Syrian airfield sent a strong message to Russia that his administration was willing to use force, contrary to his predecessor, even if it meant upsetting the Kremlin and its allies. The Trump administration has been saying that America must approach Russia from a position of strength before improving relations with Moscow. President Trump wanted to send to the rest of the world a signal in one of his earliest foreign-policy test.Click For Sound

The impact of this strike goes beyond Syria. It represents how President Trump wants to be seen by other world leaders. It is important that people understand that this is a different administration. The era of weakness with the enemies of America is finally over!

CHAPTER 29

President Donald Trump Nominated Jerome Powell as Chairman of the Federal Reserve

Jerome Hayden Powell was born on February 4, 1953 in Washington, D.C.

On November 2, 2017, President Donald J. Trump nominated Jerome (Jay) Powell to serve as the 16th chairman of the Federal Reserve. He served as a member of the Federal Reserve Board of Governors since 2012. Previously, Powell worked in several globalists Wall Street firms. Jay Powell was confirm by the Senate 85-13 on January 23, 2018. Four Republican Senators voted NO: Marco Rubio, Ted Cruz, Rand Paul, and Mike Lee. Why? Perhaps because he is a globalist banker from Wall Street.

According to *Wikipedia*, Jerome H. Powell graduated in 1971 from the Jesuit Georgetown Preparatory School. Four years later he received a Bachelor of Arts degree in political science from Princeton University. From 1975 to 1976 Powell worked as legislative assistant to Senator Richard Schweiker from Pennsylvania. He returned to study and earned a Juris Doctor degree from the Law Center at Georgetown University in 1979, where he was editor-in-chief of the *Georgetown Law Journal.*

In 1979, Powell moved to New York City and worked as a clerk to a judge and as a lawyer. From 1984 to 1990 Powell worked at the investment bank Dillon, Read and Co. He became vice president of the bank and concentrated on financing, merchant banking, and mergers and acquisitions.

Between 1990 and 1993, Powell served in the Treasury Department with Nicholas F. Brady, the former chairman of Dillon, Read & Co. In 1992, Powell was appointed Under Secretary of the Treasury for Domestic Finance. He then went back to work for Dillon, Read & Co.

From 1997 to 2005 Powell was a partner at the very powerful Carlyle Group where former President George H.W. Bush was a member. After leaving the Carlyle Group, Powell founded Severn Capital Partners, a private investment firm focused on specialty finance and opportunistic investments in the industrial sector. In 2008, Powell became a managing partner of the Global Environment Fund, a private equity and venture capital firm.

In December 2011, Powell was nominated to the Federal Reserve Board of Governors by President Barack Obama. He took office on May 25, 2012 to fill the unexpired term of Frederic Mishkin, who had resigned. In January 2014, Powell was nominated for another term and, in June 2014, he was confirmed by the Senate in a 67-24 vote.

In 2017, Powell reported that he had a net worth between $19.7 million and $55 million, making him the richest member of the Federal Reserve Board of Governors. Powell is a registered Republican. In 2008, he contributed $30,800 to the John McCain 2008 presidential campaign.

What is the Federal Reserve (the Fed)?

The Federal Reserve Bank (the Fed) is not a federal agency. The Fed is a banking cartel made up of national and international banks that issues money out of thin air. This very powerful private central bank was created on December 23, 1913 by Insiders bankers and their allies in the government. The Federal Reserve Act, when it was signed by President Woodrow Wilson, was unconstitutional. Article 1, Section 8 of the Constitution clearly states that only Congress has the power to issue or print the currency and determine its value.

There are many books that explain the role of the banking cartel that created the Federal Reserve Bank and assumed control over finances of the United States and practically over its entire government. The best book on this topic is *The Creature of Jekyll Island: A Second Look at the Federal Reserve,* 5th Edition (2010) written by G. Edward Griffin.

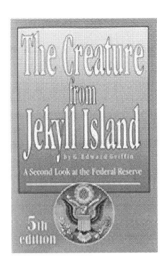

The Creature from Jekyll Island became the Number One best seller in Amazon's category of money and monetary policy.

It also ranked 32nd in the non-fiction category. This book is a classic exposé of the Federal Reserve Bank. It explains the most blatant scam in history. The book has 608 pages and describes how the Federal Reserve Bank is the cause of inflation, depression, prosperity, boom-bust cycles, and wars. Former Congressman Ron Paul has called *The Creature from Jekyll Island* a "superb analysis" and has indicated "to be prepared for one heck of a journey through time and mind." Ron Paul agreed with the conclusions of G. Edward Griffin.

Jekyll Island, an island off the coast of Georgia, is where the conspirators secretly met in November 1910. The secret meeting was called by Senator Nelson Aldrich, Republican from Rhode Island and chairman of the Senate Banking Committee. Aldrich's daughter, Abby, married John D. Rockefeller, Jr. Sixty years after this secret meeting, Aldrich's grandson, Nelson Aldrich Rockefeller became the vice president of the United States under President Gerald Ford. Previously, Nelson Rockefeller had served as governor of New York and had run unsuccessfully for the presidential nomination of the Republican Party.

Another grandson of Senator Nelson Aldrich was the late David Rockefeller. He had served as chairman of the Council of Foreign Relations (founded in 1921) and was one of the founders of the Bilderberg Group in 1954 and the Trilateral Commission in 1973.

The purpose of the secret meeting at Jekyll Island that Senator Nelson Aldrich called upon was to create the Federal Reserve Bank. In addition to Senator Aldrich, five other individuals met at the Jekyll Island Club House in 1910. (This writer has been several times to this place in Jekyll Island.)

The five individuals were the following:

- Abraham Piatt Andrew, Assistant Secretary of the U.S. Treasury.

- Frank A. Vanderlip, president of the National City Bank of New York, the most powerful bank at that time, who represented William Rockefeller and the international investment banking house of Kuhn, Loeb & Company.

- Henry P. Davison, senior partner of the J.P. Morgan Company.

- Benjamin Strong, head of J.P. Morgan's Banker Trust Company, who later became the head of the Federal Reserve Bank.

- Paul M. Warburg, a partner in Kuhn, Loeb & Company, a representative of the Rothschild banking dynasty in England and France, and brother to Max Warburg, who was head of the Warburg banking consortium in Germany and the Netherlands. These six individuals, along with the bankers who they represented, made up approximately 25% of the total wealth of the entire world.

Ron Paul wrote the book *End of the Fed* in 2010.

Criticisms of the Federal Reserve Bank

Former Republican Congressman Ron Paul, who served in the House of Representatives Banking Committee and ran for president several times, wrote the book *End of the Fed* (2010). He severely criticized the Federal Reserve. Amazon described Congressman Paul's book as follows: "Most people think of the Fed as an indispensable institution without which the country's economy could not properly function. But in, *End of the Fed*, Ron Paul draws on American history, economics, and fascinating stories from his own long political life to argue that the Fed is both corrupt and unconstitutional. It is inflating currency today at nearly a Weimar or Zimbabwe level, a practice that threatens to put us into an inflationary depression where $100 bills are worthless. What most people don't realize is that the Fed -- created by the Morgans and Rockefellers at a private club off the coast of Georgia -- is actually working against their own personal interests."

Both Ron Paul and his son, Republican Senator Rand Paul, from Kentucky have repeatedly requested that an independent audit of the Federal Reserve Bank be conducted by the Controller General of the Congress. Bills have been filed over the years but none of them were approved by Congress.

Conclusion

If the Senate approves the nomination of Jerome (Jay) Powell to serve as the 16th chairman of the Federal Reserve, he will replace Janet Yellen when her term expires. Powell's career in the very powerful Wall Street globalist financial institutions and in the Council of Foreign Relations-controlled Treasury Department will be of immense help to him. Currently, the Fed is in the process of gradually selling a portfolio of $4.2 trillion in mortgages and Treasury bonds purchased after the financial crisis of 2007 and 2008. Since the Fed is a banking cartel, can anyone explain how it is possible for a group of private banks to have so much money to buy trillions of mortgages and Treasury bonds?

There is a definite need for an independent audit of the Federal Reserve Bank to be conducted by the Controller General of the Congress. Americans need to know who are the owners of this private banking cartel that has so much power over the United States.

CHAPTER 30

Treasury and Commerce Departments issued new sanctions against Cuba

On June 16, 2017, President Donald Trump signed his Cuba policy directive on new sanctions against the communist regime at the Manuel Artime Theater in Miami.

It took several months for the Departments of the Treasury, Commerce, and State and the White House National Security Council to implement the Cuban sanctions based upon the policy directive of the president. During this delay, the shameful Cuban policy of the Obama administration of unilateral concessions without a Quid Pro Quo or nothing in return continued to be in effect.

The new sanctions on the mass-murdering Cuban regime took effect on November 9, 2017. However, the sanctions were weakened by bureaucrats in the federal government. Cuban Americans in Congress from Florida as well as this writer and many supporters of President Trump were disappointed.

On November 9, 2017, the Department of Treasury's Office of Foreign Assets Control (OFAC) and the Department of Commerce's Bureau of Industry and Security implemented the Cuban sanctions announced by President Donald Trump on June 16, 2017. The Treasury, Commerce, and State Departments stated that the rules are aimed at prohibiting American tourists and U.S. businesses to engage with the Cuban military, intelligence, and security services. The intent of the regulations is to promote business to the Cuban private sector. The United States will prohibit Americans from doing business with dozens of Cuban government-run hotels, shops, tour groups, and other entities identified by the State Department.

On November 9, 2017, Patricia Mazzei, Nora Gámez Torres, and Mimi Whitefield wrote an article titled "Policy on Cuba Restricts Travel, Partners" which was published in the *Miami Herald*. The reporters explained that under the new regulations Americans will be prohibited from doing business with 180 businesses connected to the Cuban military and intelligence and security services. These corporations include "83 hotels, stores, marinas, tourist agencies, industries and even two rum makers owned by the government. U.S. companies will be barred from investing in a sprawling economic development zone in Mariel that Cuba envisions as crucial to its commercial future."

Treasury Secretary Steve Mnuchin

Treasury Secretary Steve Mnuchin said in a statement, "We have strengthened our Cuba policies to channel economic activity away from the Cuban military and to encourage the government to move toward greater political and economic freedom for the Cuban people."

The new regulations are designed to cut off funds to Raúl Castro's oppressive regime and tighten U.S. travel to the communist island. However, Florida Republicans in Congress were very critical of the new regulations, stating that they did not go far enough in punishing the Cuban government.

Mazzei, Gámez Torres, and Whitefield wrote the following: "The Treasury, Commerce and State departments, together with the National Security Council, worked for months on the regulations, which took longer than some members of Congress and U.S.-Cuba policy experts expected. Sanctions against other countries, most notably North Korea, took priority for the administration, which continues to be understaffed in State and other agencies. The White House also had to deal with the ongoing mystery over an alleged sonic attack against U.S. diplomats in Havana. While Washington has not accused the Cuban government of causing the attacks, it holds Havana responsible for not protecting American diplomats while on Cuban soil and has reduced the U.S. Embassy staff by 60 percent. But an administration official said at a morning briefing that the regulations had nothing to do with the acoustic incidents."

Congressman Mario Diaz-Balart

Republican Congressman Mario Diaz-Balart from South Florida said in a statement the following: "Today's announced regulations include some positive first steps. I am disappointed, however, that the regulations do not fully implement what the President ordered. It is clear that individuals within the bureaucracy who support the former administration's Cuba policy continue to undermine President Trump."

Similar to Congressman Diaz-Balart, Republican Senator Marco Rubio from Florida blamed federal bureaucrats for writing softer regulations than the ones President Trump called for. Representative Diaz-Balart and Senator Rubio "have fretted for months that career civil servants — particularly in State — favor former President Barack Obama's Cuba opening and have pushed back against the more hardline policy endorsed by Trump," wrote the *Miami Herald* reporters.

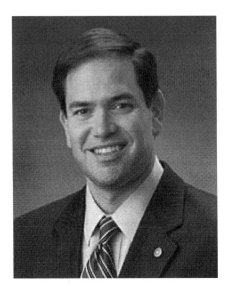

Republican Senator Marco Rubio

Republican Senator Marco Rubio from Florida pointed out that the new regulations restricting U.S. business and travel to Cuba do not go as far as President Donald Trump intended. Regarding the regulations, Senator Rubio stated the following: "The regulatory changes announced today by Treasury and Commerce begin to implement President Trump's June 2017 policy for enforcing U.S. sanctions laws against the Castro regime. Unfortunately, however, bureaucrats in the State Department who oppose the President's Cuba policy refused to fully implement it when they omitted from the Cuba Restricted List several entities and sub-entities that are controlled by or act on behalf of the Cuban military, intelligence or security services. I remain confident that this effort by some in the State Department to undermine the President's directive will be addressed."

Patricia Mazzei pointed out that Senator Rubio asked for the addition of Gran Caribe and Cubanacan, which are owned by the Cuban tourism ministry and not the military. The reporter explained that "Tourism Minister Manuel Marrero Cruz is an army colonel — a link Rubio signaled should be enough to land the two holding companies on the U.S. restricted list."

The delay in issuing the regulations allowed U.S. companies to finalize business deals with the Cuban regime and travel agencies to book rooms in military-owned hotels in 2017 and beyond

Mazzei, Gámez Torres, and Whitefield said that the delay in issuing the sanctions permitted American companies such as Caterpillar to finalize business deals with Cuba that will be unaffected by the new restrictions. The Caterpillar agreement allows the multinational to build up a warehouse and distribution operation at the Mariel Special Economic Development Zone. Another business, Deere & Co., also completed a deal to sell John Deere tractors to the Cuban government for use by agricultural cooperatives. This writer does not understand how the Trump administration approved these two business deals with Cuba. It seems to this writer that these two deals with the Cuban regime violate the United States economic embargo under the Helms Burton law.

The Port of Mariel was built by the Brazilian multinational Odebrecht Company in 2014.

The modern Port of Mariel was built by the very corrupt Brazilian Odebrecht Company with funding from the government of radical President Dilma Rousseff. Rousseff was impeached and fired as president of Brazil for corruption and former Marxist President Luiz Inácio Lula da Silva is being investigated for corruption. Odebrecht owners are in jail in Brazil for bribing officials in Brazil and many nations in Latin America.

On January 27, 2014, the port of Mariel was completed. Present at the inauguration were the assassin-in-series dictator Raúl Castro, Venezuelan bloody dictator Nicolás Maduro, and radical Brazilian President Dilma Rousseff. The port of Mariel has more than a dozen big cranes, a 700-meter-long pier which can handle the world's biggest container ships, a highway, and a rail line to Havana. The port of Mariel was financed by Brazil's state development bank in a deal negotiated directly between dictator Raúl Castro and Luiz Inácio Lula da Silva, the former radical Brazilian president. The port of Mariel includes a 180-square-mile foreign trade zone.

The reporters explained that the Mariel Special Economic Development Zone will be among the 180 entities restricted by the United States, as will Almacenes Universales and Terminal de Contenedores de Mariel, S.A., two companies that run the seaport's container terminal. The new regulations will exempt business with Cuban airports and seaports, allowing permissible trade to continue and airlines and cruise lines to operate as they do now. Most travel arranged prior to the publication of the regulations will also be allowed.

Augusto Maxwell, an Akerman attorney whose clients include companies that are doing business with Cuba and was probably in favor of Obama Cuban policy, stated the following: "The Trump administration has edited, not undone, the Obama opening. The regulations are nowhere as severe as some people had feared." Maxwell added that "Companies can still apply for specific licenses to do business with Cuban entities on the prohibited list, but they would have to demonstrate how a deal would clearly benefit the Cuban people vs. benefiting the Cuban military." Another Miami lawyer whose clients include cruise lines, Pedro Freyre, said, "This is a step back, a step sideways but the core of the relationship is still there."

The new sanctions will end some of the Obama administration provisions and take specific action to prohibit doing business with the enterprises run by Grupo de Administración Empresarial, S.A. or GAESA. This military-run business conglomerate is owned by the Revolutionary Armed Forces and controls more than 50 enterprises.

Reporter Gámez Torres stated the following: "If you're a U.S. traveler in Cuba and you buy a bottle of water in the supermarket or a souvenir in a store, or you rent a car or a hotel room, it's very likely that you're putting money into the pockets of the military-run GAESA, which experts say controls nearly 60% (others estimate 80%) of the Cuban economy. GAESA operates in virtually every profitable area of the Cuban economy, controlling hotel chains, car rental agencies and sales companies, banks, credit card and remittance services, supermarkets, clothing shops, real estate development companies, gasoline stations, import and export companies, shipping and construction companies, warehouses and even an airline."

The reporter pointed out that GAESA is the owner of Gaviota hotel chain, which owns nearly 29,000 rooms in Cuba and serves an estimated 40% of the entire nation's foreign tourism. Gaviota has signed management contracts for 83% of its rooms with international hotel chains, including Spain's Meliá and the Swiss-based Kempinski.

The immense power of General Luis Alberto Rodríguez López Calleja

General Luis Alberto Rodríguez López Calleja is or was the son-in-law of Cuban bloody dictator Raúl Castro. Half or more than half of Cuba's business activity is run through General Rodríguez López Calleja.

Michael Smith wrote an article titled "Want to Do Business in Cuba? Prepare to Partner with the General" which was published in the website *SmithMarkets* on September 30, 2015. The article originally appeared in the November 2015 issue of *Bloomberg Markets* under the named "Cuba: The Price of Doing Business in a New Economy." Smith explained that in order to conduct most businesses in Cuba, investors must meet with General Luis Alberto Rodríguez López Calleja, who is or was Raúl Castro's son-in-law. Smith visited Cuba and said that he saw Havana's redevelopment in progress. Near El Floridita, where Ernest Hemingway once drank daiquiris, the hulking Manzana de Gómez building is being transformed into a five-star hotel.

The hotel is now completed. It is owned by Gaviota, the tourist corporation that belongs to the military and is run by the Swiss luxury hotel chain Kempinski. This is how foreign corporations must do business in communist Cuba. Under the new sanctions, Americans are prohibited from staying in this hotel since it is owned by the military.

This luxury hotel has on the first-floor stylish boutiques that sell perfumes, stereos, and Montblanc, Versace, and Armani goods. These stores are owned by CIMEX, a Cuban business conglomerate taken over by GAESA in 2010. CIMEX, founded by the Ministry of the Interior, includes financial services, a chain of shops, and import and export agencies. Americans will not be able to stay at hotel Gran Manzana de Gómez, Havana's new five-star hotel managed by Kempinski under contract with Gaviota. Americans will not be able to shop at its ground-floor luxury arcade. However, Americans will still be able to stay at private accommodations as well as at the many hotels throughout the island operated by other Cuban tourism companies, such as Cubanacan and Gran Caribe.

The five-star hotel Gran Manzana de Gómez is owned by Gaviota.

Brisas Trinidad del Mar in Trinidad is one of 28 hotels run by Cubanacan.

Senator Rubio is correct when he said all the hotels run by Cubanacan and Gran Caribe should have been included in the ban since all of them belong to the oppressive regime. Gran Caribe is Cuba's foremost hotel group that operates many four- and five-star hotels across Cuba. The hotels owned by Gran Caribe are located in Cuba's most important destinations and range from landmark properties, such as the Hotel Nacional de Cuba and the historic Hotel Inglaterra in Havana, to hotels on beautifully stretched beaches in Varadero and on the keys overlooking crystal clear waters.

Today Cuba is a state capitalist run by the military mafia element which is deeply embedded within communist Cuba. Obama's shameful unilateral concessions to the oppressive communist regime and in violation of the Helms-Burton Law allowed American hotel chains to run hotels owned by the military. All these hotels are grandfathered by the new sanctions.

Smith stated the following: "General Rodriguez has worked directly for Raúl Castro. He's the gatekeeper for most foreign investors, requiring them to do business with his organization if they wish to set up shop on the island... General Rodriguez doesn't just count Castro as a longtime boss. He is family. More than 20 years ago, Rodriguez, a stocky, square-jawed son of a general, married Deborah Castro, Raúl's daughter. In the past five years, Castro has vastly increased the size of Rodriguez's business empire, making him one of the most powerful men in Cuba. General Rodriguez's life is veiled in secrecy. He's rarely been photographed or quoted in the media, and his age isn't publicly known."

Smith pointed out that the Cuban dictator Raúl Castro has been slowly and cautiously opening the island to private enterprise since he assumed control of the country in 2006. There are now 201 types of private businesses permitted in the island (restaurants and bed-and-breakfasts are the largest categories). These private businesses employ a million people or a fifth of the Cuban workforce.

The military dictatorship that runs Cuba imposes high taxes on all small private businesses. These businesses can be closed at any time by the communist regime. Often, police officers and military officials show up at the private restaurants called "paladares" and eat for free. Dictator Raúl Castro has legalized the sale of homes and cars, allowed more travel to certain individuals and denied travel to others, and allowed private farming and cooperative businesses. It is estimated that Cubans own 2.6 million cell phones, although service is poor and expensive.

Smith pointed out that the Castro regime has kept the big-money industries in the hands of the state. Much of these industries are managed by his son-in-law. General Rodríguez's Grupo de Administración Empresarial, S.A. or GAESA runs companies that account for more than half the business revenue produced in Cuba. Other economists say it may be closer to 80%, according to Smith.

Smith said that GAESA owns almost all of the retail chains in Cuba and 57 of the mainly foreign-run hotels from Havana to the country's finest Caribbean beaches. GAESA has restaurant and gasoline station chains, rental car fleets, and companies that import all products, from cooking oil to telephone equipment. General Rodríguez is also in charge of Cuba's most important base for global trade and foreign investment, which is the new container ship terminal and 180-square-mile foreign trade zone in Mariel.

Smith pointed out that for the majority of people in Cuba, the reforms of dictator Raúl Castro have not addressed the most basic need, which is a living wage. Salaries average just 584 pesos or about $24 a month. That is, the average salary represents the cost of 4.4 pounds of chicken breasts, a couple bags of rice and beans, and four rolls of toilet paper in a GAESA's Panamericana supermarket.

During his visit to Cuba, Smith learned that most of the people have "to scrape and hustle to put together a decent living." Nearly everyone Smith met in Havana has a story of moonlighting in odd jobs and even stealing to make up for the dismal pay. He pointed out that a friend of his father sells Cohiba cigars stolen from the factory where he works. A young engineer drives tourists around in his mother's Lada, a Russian car, to supplement his $19.59 monthly salary as a university professor.

Smith said that Cuba's most profitable state companies under GAESA are run by General Luis Alberto Rodríguez. The most significant addition to GAESA was Cimex, which had been run for three decades by military commanders chosen by Fidel Castro. Adding the Cimex companies more than doubled the size of GAESA. More recently, General Rodríguez took over Habaguanex, the state company that owns the best commercial real estate in Old Havana, including 37 restaurants and 21 hotels.

Sadly, many multinational corporations from the United States and other nations want to make Cuba the China of the Caribbean. These corporations would like to use Cuban workers, who make between $20 and $25 a month and have no rights whatsoever. These multinational corporations do not care about the suffering of the Cuban people under the worst and longest dictatorship of the Western Hemisphere.

The State Department, which is full of globalist anti-Trump officials, will be charged with keeping the "list of restricted entities and sub entities associated with Cuba" updated. Companies not listed among the 180 entities will not be restricted, even if they have military ties. Enforcing these sanctions will be very difficult. Assigning the monitoring to the Department of State officials, many of whom belong to the Council of Foreign Relations, is absurd since most of are in favor of Obama Cuban policy.

The Four Points by Sheraton Hotel in Havana is owned by the military-run Gaviota and managed by the U.S. Corporation Starwood hotel chain.

Mazzei, Gámez Torres and Whitefield stated the following: "How closely the government will enforce the new rules remains unclear. No additional enforcement resources are being added to Treasury's Office of Foreign Assets Control, which under Obama relied on an honor system when it came to be policing U.S.-Cuba travel. Senior administration officials said Wednesday travelers would be required to retain records of their itineraries and expenses, which will be subject to review." The reporters summarized the new sanctions against the Cuban regime as follows:

1. Prohibits most U.S. business dealings with Cuban military enterprises.

2. Makes exceptions for business with Cuban airports and seaports. Airlines and cruise lines will continue to operate as they do now.

3. Lists 180 companies with ties to the Cuban military and intelligence and security services that are off limits for Americans.

4. Imposes new restrictions on Americans who fall into three categories of admissible travel to the island.

5. Emphasizes that travelers must retain records of all transactions they make in Cuba for five years.

6. Retains current policies on family travel.

7. Prohibits U.S. travelers from staying at hotels run by the Cuban military.

8. Greatly expands a list of prohibited officials who are not eligible to receive remittances and gift parcels sent from the United States.

The list of 180 entities may expand and sanctions may be strengthened

White House Deputy to the President and Director of Policy and Interagency Coordination, Dr. Carlos Díaz-Rosillo, this writer, and Antonio Esquivel, President of the Cuban Patriotic Council at the Cuban Diaspora Museum in Miami

On November 10, 2017, White House Deputy to the President and Director of Policy and Interagency Coordination, Carlos Díaz-Rosillo, spoke on the United States and Cuba relations at the invitation of the Cuban Studies Program. The event was held at the Cuban Diaspora

Museum in Miami, Florida. This writer and others at the meeting told Dr. Díaz-Rosillo, who has an important position in the White House, that we thought the new sanctions needed to be strengthened. He said the list of the 180 entities was a living document and could be expanded. This writer pointed out that the many hotels throughout the island run by the Ministry of Tourism, under the names of Cubanacan and Gran Caribe, should have been included in the ban since all of them bring millions to the oppressive regime.

This writer said that Cuba should be added to the list of terrorist countries and the list of countries that are engaged in human trafficking. Additionally, he told Dr. Díaz-Rosillo that allowing cruise ships and airlines to bring tens of thousands of American tourists to Cuba who would be transported by regime buses, taken to regime restaurants, stores, night clubs, monuments, and museums contradict the objectives of the new regulations. It also contradicts warning of the Department of State that stipulates that Americans should not travel to Cuba.

This writer thanked Dr. Díaz-Rosillo for coming to Miami to talk to us and hear our concerns. This writer is very pleased that such a brilliant individual as Dr. Díaz-Rosillo, who is very familiar with Venezuela and who grew up in Miami with a Cuban-born mother, is advising the president on U.S. policy with Venezuela and Cuba. As indicated earlier, the new regulations were prepared by the Departments of the Treasury, Commerce, and State and the White House National Security Council. This writer is optimistic that President Donald Trump, who is committed to a free and democratic Cuba, may want to increase the sanctions against Cuba when he hears the input by Cuban Americans in Congress and in the United States.

The United States is still investigating the sonic and ultrasonic attacks against American diplomats and their families in Havana. If the conclusion of this lengthy investigation reveals that the Cuban regime was involved or tolerated such attacks, this writer is certain that President Trump will break diplomatic relations with Cuba and hopefully initiate a regime change strategy to end the longest and mass-murdering tyrannical regime in the Western Hemisphere.

Conclusion

Cuban American patriots who worked very hard to elect Donald J. Trump as president hope that he will strengthen the announced sanctions since they are weak. American tourists will be able to stay in many hotels which will bring income to the brutal regime. Approximately 60% of Cuban Americans voted for Donald Trump on November 8, 2016. This author has sent all the recommendations explained in this article to the White House several times. And he will continue to do it!

The sanctions should have been much stronger, especially after the president said that Cuba was responsible for injuring American diplomats and members of their families with sonic attacks. The State Department also warned Americans not to travel to Cuba. However, during 2017 over one million American tourists visited the island prison. It does not make any sense to allow Americans to stay in hotels run by the regime tourist department and allow cruise lines and airlines to bring thousands of American tourists to the island to enrich the military mafia in Cuba.

Cuban Americans approved Republican presidential candidate Donald Trump's promises that he would reverse Obama's Cuban policy. They hoped that the president would reverse, if not all, almost all of the shameful unilateral concessions given by Obama to the Cuban regime in exchange for nothing, except increase repression, beatings, and arbitrary arrests of peaceful opponents.

Upholding the Helms- Burton Law is crucial. Restating the important sections of the Helms-Burton Law was necessary and President Trump did it in his speech in Miami. The president stated the following: "We will not lift sanctions on the Cuban regime until all political prisoners are free, freedoms of assembly and expression are respected, all political parties are legalized, and free and internationally supervised elections are scheduled."

President Trump spoke how Cuba sent illegal weapons to North Korea and helps the regime in Venezuela to oppress its people. Yet, the president did not state that he wants to place Cuba back in the list of terrorist-supporting nations. Nor did the president say that he wants to put Cuba back in the list of nations that participate in human trafficking. It is very important that President Trump takes these two actions very soon.

The new Cuban policy of President Trump allows the United States airlines and cruise lines to continue providing service to the island. With the restrictions on travel, it is likely that the numbers of Americans visiting Cuba will diminish, thus reducing the cash flow to the Cuban military. However, the Treasury and State Departments must strictly enforce the new travel restrictions to the full extent of the law. Otherwise, American tourists will continue to stay in military-owned hotels, use military-owned taxis, buy in military owned stores, and eat and drink in military-owned restaurants and nightclubs.

Cuba has never paid back any ill-advised nation or corporation that sold products on credit to the military in the island. Perhaps, the majority of Americans do not understand that the Export and Import Bank pays in cash when American corporations sell products on credit to nations that have no credit and never pay back what they receive. American taxpayers are swindled in each of these transactions.

This practice must be stopped. The Export and Import Bank needs to be abolished as it represents welfare for rich corporations. The Cuban corporations controlled by the military never pay back what they purchase. If American farmers want to sell their products in Cuba, let the military pay in cash for what they buy.

The new Cuban policy has the goal of weakening the military dictatorship by denying it easy access to dollars through the military-owned tourist industry and by restricting travel. However, none of these announced measures will overthrow the Cuban communist regime, which is the longest and harshest military dictatorship in the Western Hemisphere.

Cuba can still buy what it needs from other nations and receive their tourists in military-controlled businesses. It is important that all Western nations condemn the rogue and illegitimate Cuban regime as they did with South Africa during apartheid. Sadly, instead of implementing economic sanctions in Cuba, Western nations have continued to do business as usual with the military dictatorship for many years.

Venezuela and Cuba are strong allies. Both nations assist Islamic terror groups. There is a Hamas office in Havana. Cuba has always been a center of terrorism. Similar to Venezuela, the Cuban military participates in drug trafficking. Cuba has an occupation Army in Venezuela assisted by its intelligence services. Venezuela sends financial help to Iran's militia Hezbollah.

Venezuela sends uranium to Iran, a close ally. The fates of their communist regimes are interrelated. Venezuela and Cuba are national security threats to the United States and both are close allies of Russia and China. President Trump needs to sanction economically high officials in the regime and high ranking military officers of both nations. It was very positive that the Trump administration sanctioned 10 more Venezuelan regime leaders on November 9, 2017. The number of chavistas sanctioned is now 40. Cuban regime officials also need to be added to the black list of oppressors and punished.

Frequently, these oppressors come to the United States to invest in property with the stolen funds from their nations. Freezing the assets of the high-ranking oppressors in the United States is an effective way to punish those who abuse their fellow citizens. If President Trump wants to implement regime change in communist Venezuela and Cuba, he needs to implement an economic embargo in Venezuela and stop purchasing petroleum from that terror narco nation. The communist regime in Venezuela cannot survive a total economic embargo from the United States. If democracy were to be restored in Venezuela, that nation would cease supplying free oil to communist Cuba. The Cuban regime would also collapse in a short time.

This writer realizes that those drastic steps are very difficult to implement by the Trump administration. International bankers, other nations, and the globalist elite of the New World Order would oppose such a policy labeling it as inhumane. It is inhumane for Western nations to remain silent to all the killings, beatings, and arrests and to conduct business as usual with these two unrepented bloody regimes.

If such a courageous regime change policy were implemented successfully by President Donald Trump, he would go down in history as the liberator of two savage and bloody communist regimes that have brought extreme suffering to their people and other nations throughout the world. Mr. President, Make the America Great and Save Again!

CHAPTER 31

The U.S. economy continuous
to improve under President Trump

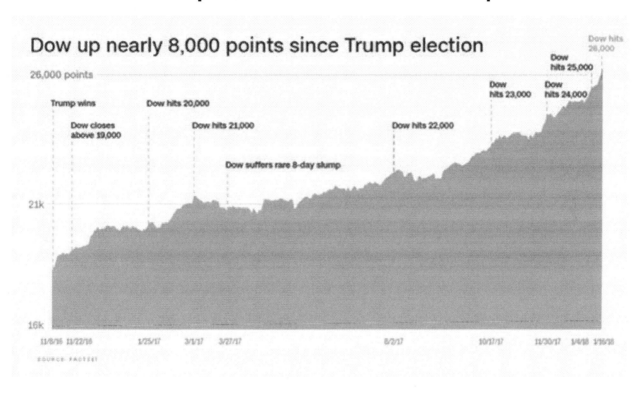

On January 17, 2018, The Dow Jones industrial average closed above 26,000 mark for the first time in its 121-year history. It increased 322.79 points to an astounding record of 26,115.65. The stock market has grown by 40% since the election as president of Donald J. Trump in spite of the daily attacks of the corrupt mainstream media, the Democrats, and the Deep State.

On January 17, the *USA Today* said the following: "It was the Dow's best one-day point gain in 14 months, or since the day before Donald Trump was elected president. The fresh milestone comes just 13 calendar days after the 30-stock index topped 25,000, marking the fastest 1,000-point climb in its history, according to S&P Dow Jones Indices.

President Donald Trump deserves a lot of credit for the improvement of the economy and the soaring stock market. By eliminating costly regulations to businesses and passing the Tax Cuts and Jobs Act in December 2017, the president has improved the economy which is now growing at more than 3% of the Gross National Product (GNP) with a 4.1% unemployment rate the lowest in 17 years, and a 6.8 % African American unemployment rate, the lowest in 45 years. Latino unemployment has decreased. Two million less people are receiving food stamps. Two millions jobs were created. Consumer confidence is an all-time high.

The Tax Cuts and Jobs Act slashed the corporate tax rate to 21% from 35%. USA Today reported that "Wall Street analysts have been boosting their 2018 earnings forecasts for U.S. companies at the quickest pace in a decade." Of course, since the stock market has risen so quickly, it is possible that a correction may come in the future.

The optimism on Wall Street regarding corporate profits is what ultimately drives stock market prices. Earnings have been strong all year and analysts are predicting for next year higher market prices.

Jerome (Jay) Hayden Powell was born on February 4, 1953.

Jerome Powell is a member of the Federal Reserve Board of Governors and has served in this board since 2012. On November 2, 2017, President Donald Trump nominated Powell to serve as the next Chairman of the Federal Reserve to replace Janet Yellen when her term ended..

Jay Powell, President Trump's choice to replace Janet Yellen at the Federal Reserve, has said he will continue the Fed policies. He supported these raising rates at a gradual pace. Powell also said he believes existing bank regulations are tough enough. Instead, he expressed a desire for "appropriate ways" to ease some rules.

Reuters said that Federal Reserve Chair Janet Yellen told Congress on November 29, 2017 that "the economic expansion is increasingly broad based across sectors" and that she expected that "the economy will continue to expand." President Trump wants lower taxes to lift annual GDP growth to 3% or higher on a sustained basis.

The unemployment rate is 4.4%, the lowest in 17 years. After the president's election, and before he assumed office, he persuaded several multinational corporations not to move their factories to Mexico and other countries. The president issued many executive orders eliminating burdensome regulations on businesses. One executive order issued by the president stated that for every new regulation, two had to be eliminated. Tens of thousands of jobs were created by the business-friendly President Trump.

Consumer confidence has increased dramatically, and the commercial deficit has been reduced as more U.S businesses are exporting more goods. The president has stated that the trade agreements will no longer damage America.

Fake news by *ABC News* brought the stock market down

ABC News Brian Ross delivered an inaccurate report on former National Security Director Michael Flynn which brought the stock market down.

On December 1, 2017, *ABC News* journalist Brian Ross reported incorrectly that former White House National Security Director Michael Flynn, who pleaded guilty to lying to the FBI, would testify that President Donald J. Trump directed him during the campaign to make contact with Russian officials. As a result, the Dow Jones plunged by 330 points.

On December 3, 2017, President Donald Trump criticized *ABC News* and suggested those who lost money in the stock market after the Michael Flynn's report should consider suing the network. The network soon issued a "clarification," stating that President Trump had asked Michael Flynn during the transition "to find ways to repair relations with Russia and other hot spots." Conservatives and members of the media criticized the network for not calling it a "correction."

On December 2, announced that Brian Ross was suspended without pay for four weeks, Later, ABC News said that it will not allow reporter Ross to cover stories related to President Trump. After the stock market investors discovered that the report from Brian Ross was fake news, the Dow Jones recovered quickly. On December 4 it increased to 24, 290 points.

Conclusion

Fake news has a negative impact on the stock market. The destroy Trump mainstream media needs to be careful when reporting lies and misinformation on the president and his administration for it will hurt the economy and the national security.

President Donald J. Trump deserves a great deal of credit for improving the economy and creating new jobs. The GDP is increasing over 3% in the last two quarters. Corporate profits have increased along with consumer confidence. The stock market has grown an unprecedented almost 6,000 points. Oppressive business regulations have been eliminated. Oil and gas production have increased considerably. The president approved the Keystone XL oil pipe as well as the Dakota oil pipe, which will bring Canadian oil to the American refineries in Texas.

In spite of all the economic progress, President Trump is subjected to daily attacks by the corrupt mainstream media, by members of the Deep State embedded in the federal government including intelligence agencies, by Democrats in Congress, and by hundreds of radical organizations funded by Soros and Obama.

Now that Congress passed the Tax Cut legislation and the president signed it into law, the economy will continue to soar, and tens of thousands of new jobs will be created.

CHAPTER 32

President Trump wants to end lottery visas and chain migration

Akayed Ullah, a Bangladesh national, injured five individuals when he tried to detonate a suicide bomb in New York City.

Akayed Ullah arrived in the United States in 2011 as a "chain migrant" of his uncle, who had previously come to the country through the visa lottery. Ullah, a legal permanent resident of the United States, reportedly told police he was inspired by ISIS to carry out the attack. Chain migration allows new immigrants to the United States to bring an unlimited number of foreign relatives with them. President Donald J. Trump has been asking for an end of lottery visas and chain migration and for a merit-based immigration system during his campaign and in the White House.

On December 12, 2017, Brian Freeman wrote an article titled "Trump Calls on Congress to End Chain Migration, Visa Lottery Program" which was published by *Newsmax*. Freeman said that President Donald Trump demanded Congress to end both chain migration and the diversity visa lottery program, saying they present a danger to national security. The president said the legal immigration programs were to blame for two recent terror attacks in New York City since that is how the terrorists in each of these incidents legally entered the United States.

President Trump stated the following: "We're gonna end both of them. We're going to end 'em. Fast. Congress must get involved immediately, and they are involved immediately, and I can tell you we have tremendous support."

"The terrible harm that this flawed system [of extended-family chain migration] inflicts on America's security and economy has long been clear. America must fix its lax immigration system, which allows far too many dangerous, inadequately vetted people to access our country," said the president.

Freeman explained that President Trump made those comments after Akayed Ullah, who tried to detonate a bomb in the city's subway system on December 11, 2017. Ullah came to America from Bangladesh in 2011 on a visa for children of siblings of American citizens, according to the Department of Homeland Security. In October 2017, another terrorist in another attack in New York City was found to have legally arrived in the United States using the visa lottery program.

Sarah Sanders was appointed White House press secretary by President Trump in July 2017.

White House press secretary Sarah Huckabee Sanders had also sent a similar message. She said, "We must protect our borders, we must ensure that individuals entering our country are not coming to do harm to people, and we must move to a merit-based immigration system."

Akayed Ullah attended a terror-linked mosque

On December 13, 2017, Edwin Mora wrote an article titled "Radicalized in New York': NYC Subway Jihadist Attended Terror-Linked Mosque" which was published by *Breitbart*. Mora said that Akayed Ullah, the failed New York City subway bomber, attended a terrorist-linked mosque in Brooklyn that was once funded by the Saudi government.

Mora explained the following: "Ullah attended the Masjid Nur Al-Islam mosque, known to have many terrorist links and used to be funded by the Saudi Arabian government. Among the members, the son of a former imam at the mosque, Adnan Gulshair el-Shukrijumah, became a senior member of al-Qaeda and another member, Abdul Rasheed, was convicted for plotting to blow up the United Nations (U.N.) building and the Holland Tunnel…The Bangladeshi terrorist was close to the mosque's Imam and was often seen with him at afternoon prayers," the *New York Times* learned from a regular attendee identified only as Mohammad… Ullah's brother also reportedly attends a mosque with a history of terrorist associations. Ahsan Ullah was reportedly an attendee of Masjid al-Salam, the same mosque where the infamous blind sheikh Omar Abdel-Rahman used to preach. Rahman is considered the mastermind behind the 1993 bombing of the World Trade Center. Abdel Rahman died in February 2017."

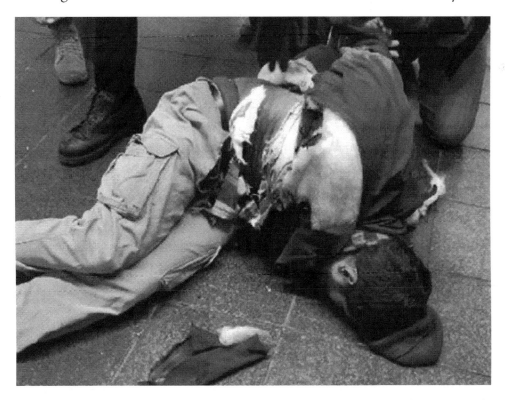

Akayed Ullah's bomb exploded prematurely and he injured himself and five others.

New York Governor Andrew Cuomo told CNN that "Fortunately for us, the bomb partially detonated. He did detonate it, but it did not fully have the effect that he was hoping for."

Conservative commentator Michelle Malkin criticized Republicans and Democrats in Congress for failing to end the so-called diversity visa lottery program

On December 13, 2017, John Binder wrote in *Breitbart* that conservative commentator Michelle Malkin appeared on *Fox News Channel*'s "Fox & Friends." She criticized both Republicans and Democrats in Congress for failing to end the so-called diversity visa lottery program.

This failed immigration policy has been exploited by foreign terrorists. Binder said that Malkin attacked the Republican-led Congress "for not having already ended the visa lottery, where 50,000 visas are randomly given out to foreign nationals from a multitude of countries." Those countries include Afghanistan, Algeria, Bangladesh, Egypt, Iraq, Lebanon, Libya, Nigeria, Saudi Arabia, Somalia, Syria, Trinidad and Tobago, Venezuela, Yemen, and Uzbekistan.

Malkin stated the following: "There are millions of people around the world who are clamoring to get in here the right way and the fact that we still do it randomly tells you how much insanity — politically incorrect sanity — has set in. I mean, it was just seven weeks ago with the truck jihadist, who also got in here through the Diversity Visa Lottery and also benefitted from the chain migration insanity that we had people saying 'Oh yeah, we've got to get rid of it! We've got to get rid of it! 'And I'm so exasperated my friends because I've been calling for the end of this program for the last 15 years."

"We should value citizenship and entry into this country much more than we have been and both parties have shrugged their shoulders. There have been legislative bills, stand-alone bills, to eliminate the Diversity Visa program for the last 15 years."

"They've gathered dust. The SAFE Act, before the House Judiciary Committee in 2011, just sat there doing nothing. We've got the RAISE Act, which is co-sponsored by Tom Cotton and David Perdue, which would have eliminated the Visa Lottery program. It's been gathering dust. How many more people have to die or be threatened before we get rid of this stupidity?"

Breitbart News reported that under the visa lottery system, 14,869 Bangladeshi nationals entered the U.S. between 2007 and 2012. "This man that came in –or whatever you want to call him –brought in, with him, other people," President Trump said during his Cabinet meeting on December 13, 2017. "And he was a point, he was the point of contact—the primary point of contact for, and this is preliminary—23 people that came in, or potentially came in with him," he added.

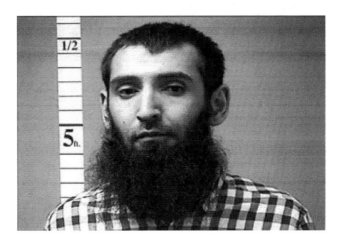

Sayfullo Saipov came to America in 2010 from Uzbekistan under a Diversity Visa Program.

On October 31, 2017, Sayfullo Saipov drove a rented truck into cyclists and runners for about one mile alongside a bike path in Lower Manhattan in New York City. He killed eight people and injured eleven others. After crashing the truck into a school bus, Saipov left the truck and was shot in the abdomen by a policeman and arrested. A flag and a document indicating allegiance to the Islamic State or ISIS were found.

John Binder explained that chain migration occurs when immigrants come to America simply to be united with a relative already living in this nation. The type of visa Saipov had could have allowed dozens of his family members into America. The Department of Homeland Security told *FoxNews* that Saipov was admitted to the U.S. "upon presentation of a passport with a valid diversity immigrant visa to U.S. Customs and Border Protection in 2010."

Many Republicans in Congress support the president in reforming the immigration system to one based on merit

John Binder said that Congressional Republicans supported the president's call for "extreme vetting" and the repeal or reform of the Diversity Visa Lottery Program. "The lottery system, I've always been against it because it's random—completely random," Chairman of the House Homeland Security Committee Michael McCaul (Republican from Texas) stated on *FoxNews*' "Fox & Friends" on December 13, 2017. "I thought it should be merit-based...I have been working with Chairman Bob Goodlatte to abolish this system, and I think this case just further demonstrates why that is absolutely necessary," he added.

Binder pointed out that Congressman Bob Goodlatte (Republican from Virginia) said he has called for ending the diversity visa lottery "for years" and has sponsored legislation to do that. Congressman Goodlatte said the following: "This flawed policy is just foolish in the age in which we live. Those in the world who wish us harm can easily engage in this statistical gamble with nothing to lose. Our immigration policy should be based primarily on our national needs, security, and economics and not in part on any arbitrary system." Senator John McCain (Republican from Arizona) said the Diversity Visa Program should be scrapped and replaced with a merit-based immigration system.

Binder explained that Republican senators David Perdue from Georgia and Tom Cotton from Arkansas proposed eliminating the Diversity Visa Lottery Program as part of the RAISE Act. Senator Perdue said that "While Senate Democrats originally created the Diversity Visa Lottery in 1990 many have supported legislation that would have eliminated it in the years since." Senator Perdue added, "I hope we can include this area of common ground as we work to fix our broken immigration system and strengthen our national security."

Conclusion

Congress needs to end chain migration and lottery visas and create a merit-based system as it is done in most countries in the world. America's immigration policy should be based primarily on national needs, security, and economics.

There have been legislative bills, stand-alone bills, to eliminate the Diversity Visa program for the last 15 years. But none have become law. It is time to act before more Americans are killed by terrorists coming by lottery visas or chain migration.

The FBI and police departments need to investigate what imams are saying in mosques in America in order to stop the radicalization of Muslims who may become domestic terrorists.

CHAPTER 33

Trump needs to declassify Obama's Secret Directive 11

Roger Aronoff and this writer spoke at the America at
Crossroads Benghazi Conference in Jacksonville, Florida.

On December 3, 2017, this writer attended the America at Crossroads Conference dealing with Libya and Benghazi in Jacksonville, Florida. It was also a tribute to Ambassador Christopher Stevens, his aide Sean Smith, and two diplomatic security officers, former Navy SEALs Glen Doherty and Tyrone Woods, who were killed in Benghazi due to the criminal negligence and dereliction of duty of the Obama administration. Among the speakers at the conference were my friend and one of my heroes, Roger Aronoff, who created the Citizens' Commission on Benghazi (CCB) that published the *Interim Report How America Switched Sides in the War on Terror* in April 2014 and the final *Report Dereliction of Duty* in July 2016. (It can be read at the aim.org website.)

Roger Aronoff set up the Citizens' Commission on Benghazi (CCB) in September 2013 to investigate the causes and circumstances involving the attacks of September 11, 2012 on the U.S. diplomatic compound and the nearby CIA Annex in Benghazi, Libya. Among the members selected by Roger Aronoff were Brigadier General Charles Jones (Ret.), Admiral James Lyons (Ret.), General Thomas McInerney (Ret.), former CIA officer Clare Lopez, former CIA officer Wayne Simmons, former CIA officer Kevin Shipp, General Paul Vallely (Ret.), former Congressman and Lieutenant Colonel (Ret.) Allen West, and Captain Larry Bailey (SEAL Ret.).

Retired CIA official Clare Lopez and this writer spoke at the America at
Crossroads Benghazi Conference in Jacksonville, Florida.

Two retired CIA officers, Clare Lopez and Kevin Shipp, who served in the Citizens' Commission on Benghazi, spoke at the conference about a secret and classified Presidential Study

Directive 11 executed by President Barack Obama. This treasonous document is still classified but part of the information of Presidential Study Directive 11 has leaked out.

Clare Lopez and Kevin Shipp said that the Presidential Study Directive 11 was Obama's secret plan to turn the Middle East to Iran and North Africa to al-Qaida and the Muslim Brotherhood. President Donald J. Trump needs to declassify this document to show Americans how Barack Obama is a traitor who should be indicted as well as other members of his administration.

Roger Aronoff appeared on *The Blaze* with Dana Loesch before Hillary Clinton came to testify at the hearing of the House of Representative Select Committee on Benghazi on October 22, 2015 on her role in Libya. He explained the following: "While the failures to either provide sufficient security for Ambassador Chris Stevens, or to remove him before the attacks occurred on September 11, 2012, is an important issue, it is certainly not the only one that Mrs. Clinton must answer for. Two new articles out in the last day present powerful arguments and lines of questioning that should be pursued. One is from *The Washington Times*, which lays out new evidence showing how the U.S. facilitated the flow of arms to militia groups in Libya, many of which went to al-Qaeda-linked groups. This violated both American law and a U.N. resolution."

"The other article is by Nancy Youssef in *The Daily Beast*, where she questions the wisdom, motives and strategy that led the U.S. and NATO into the war in Libya in the first place. She points out that while President Obama may have been reluctant at first, with no stated plans to remove Libyan leader Muammar Qaddafi that is exactly what happened, with no plans in place for what would come after Qaddafi. And what has followed is a failed state."

Aronoff wrote that both of these points were made in the Interim Report by the Citizens' Commission on Benghazi (CCB) of April 2014 and received little attention at the time. Many in the media kept asking what more was there to learn. Aronoff pointed out that the CCB had prepared a list of questions that he hoped would be asked during the House of Representative Select Committee on the Benghazi hearing on October 22, 2015.

Sadly, none of the great questions prepared by Roger Aronoff were used. Congressional Republican leaders were aware of the crimes committed by Secretary of State Hillary Clinton and President Obama in Libya but feared that if this information was revealed to Americans, they would have to impeach Obama and indict Hillary Clinton and others. This writer believes that the Congressional Republicans feared a civil war or the declaration of martial law by Obama and the suspension of the Constitution and the presidential elections.

The Republicans, either due to fear or perhaps directed by the members of the globalist elite who belong to the very powerful Council of Foreign Relations, Bilderberg Group, and Trilateral Commission and selected Barack Obama as president, decided to let the traitor finish his term in office. Now Republicans are watching how Obama is the leader of the Deep State, which is trying to destroy the presidency of Donald J. Trump.

Ambassador Christopher Stevens, his aide Sean Smith, and two diplomatic security officers, former Navy SEALs Glen Doherty and Tyrone Woods, were killed in Benghazi.

These four Americans were killed in Benghazi due to the criminal negligence and dereliction of duty of the State and Defense Departments and the White House. The crimes committed by Barack Obama and Hillary Clinton, which resulted in the deaths of these four Americans, have been covered up by the corrupt mainstream media. But justice must prevail.

Frank de Varona wrote the book *Obama, Hillary Clinton, and Radical Islam* in 2016.

Obama, Hillary Clinton, and Radical Islam discusses the reasons why the House of Representatives need to impeach Obama and why the Department of Justice need to indict Hillary Clinton for their Middle Eastern gunrunning operation in Libya and Syria, the Benghazi cover-up, and other crimes. The book has several chapters dealing with Libya and Benghazi. It also explains the history and the infiltration of the Muslim Brotherhood in the government.

Stephanie Jason and this writer spoke at the America at Crossroads Benghazi Conference in Jacksonville, Florida.

Stephanie Jason, similar to this writer, is a director of *Bear Witness Central*. She has visited Libya over 40 times and knew Ambassador Christopher Stevens very well. Stephanie Jason, who is an expert on national security and the Middle East, spoke at the conference.

Dinesh D'Souza was the keynote speaker at the conference. He dedicated one of his books to this writer.

Obama's Presidential Study Directive 11

On June 7, 2015, Daniel Greenfield wrote an article titled "Directive 11: Obama's Secret Islamist plan" which was published in *Frontpage Magazine*. Greenfield explained that behind the Libyan Civil War; the unrest in Egypt, Yemen, Syria, and across the region; the rise of the Islamic State or ISIS; and the Middle East's civil wars is Obama's Presidential Study Directive 11. Greenfield said that Directive 11 was used to guide American policy in the Middle East without being officially submitted. The Directive 11 group was "just finishing its work" when the Arab Spring began.

Greenfield stated the following: "Directive 11 brought together activists and operatives at multiple agencies to come up with a tailored approach for regime change in each country. The goal was to manage the political transitions. It tossed aside American national security interests by insisting that Islamist regimes would be equally committed to fighting terrorism and cooperating with Israel. Its greatest gymnastic feat may have been arguing that the best way to achieve political stability in the region was through regime change. What little we know about the resulting classified 18-page report is that it used euphemisms to call for aiding Islamist takeovers in parts of the Middle East. Four countries were targeted. Of those four, we only know for certain that Egypt and Yemen were on the list. But we do know for certain the outcome."

It is now known that the Obama administration overthrew President Hosni Mubarak of Egypt, a faithful ally for decades, to place in power the Muslim Brotherhood, which collaborated with al-Qaeda, Hamas, and Iran, before being undone by a counterrevolution. Yemen is currently controlled by Iran's Houthi terrorists and al-Qaeda.

Greenfield pointed out that the coup d'état against President Mubarak with the coordination of liberals, Islamists, and the military strongly resembled what happened in Indonesia in 1998 when a coup ousted its longtime leader General Muhammad Suharto. The largest most pronounced similarity may be that the Muslim mobs in Indonesia targeted the Chinese, many of whom are Christians, while the Muslim mobs in Egypt targeted Coptic Christians.

Greenfield explained the following: "It was obvious why Obama would have considered the Islamization of Indonesia and the purge of Christians under the guise of democratic political change to be a fine example for Egypt. While we don't know the full contents of Directive 11 and unless a new administration decides to open the vaults of the old regime, we may never know. But we do know a good deal about the results. Obama's insistence that human rights be made a core national security interest paved the way for political and military interventions on behalf of Islamists. Obama had never been interested in human rights; his record of pandering to the world's worst genocide plotters and perpetrators from Iran to Turkey to Sudan made that clear. When he said human rights, Obama really meant Islamist power. That was why Obama refused to intervene when the Muslim Brotherhood conducted real genocide in Sudan, but did interfere in Libya on behalf of the Brotherhood using a phony claim of genocide."

"Positioning Samantha Power (later she became the American ambassador at the United Nations) in the Office of Multilateral Affairs and Human Rights at the National Security Council (NSC) was part of the process that made over the NSC from national security to servicing a progressive wish list of Islamist terrorist groups that were to be transformed into national governments. Power, along with Gayle Smith and Dennis Ross, led the Directive 11 project."

"Secret proceedings were used to spawn regime change infrastructure. Some of these tools had official names, such as The Office of The Special Coordinator for Middle East Transitions which currently reports directly to former Ambassador Anne Patterson (in Egypt) who told Coptic Christians not to protest against Morsi. After being driven out of the country by angry mobs over her support for the Muslim Brotherhood tyranny, she was promoted to Assistant Secretary of State for Near Eastern Affairs. The Office is still focused on outreach to emergent political, economic and social forces in Egypt, Tunisia, and Libya even though counterrevolutions have pushed out Islamists in Egypt and Tunisia, while Libya is in the middle of a bloody civil war in which an alliance of the Muslim Brotherhood and al-Qaeda controls the nation's capital."

Greenfield said that Gayle Smith, one of the three leaders of Directive 11, contacted the International Union of Muslim Scholars, a Muslim Brotherhood group that supported terrorism against American soldiers in Iraq, to assist the Muslim Brotherhood President of Egypt Morsi to stay in power. Presidential Study Directive 11 said Greenfield ended up giving us the Islamic State through its Arab Spring. The document claimed that regional stability could only be achieved through Islamist radical regime change, which brought chaos in the Middle East. The Islamic State was born in an environment of violent civil wars created by Obama's Directive 11.

Mohamed Morsi was elected president of Egypt in 2012.

Mohamed Morsi served as president of Egypt from June 30, 2012 to July 3, 2013. General Abdel Fattah el-Sisi removed Morsi from office in the 2013 Egyptian coup d'état after the June 2013 Egyptian protests.

Greenfield explained that during the Arab Spring protests, Egyptian Foreign Minister Ahmed Aboul Gheit told Secretary of State Hillary Clinton that his government could not hand over power to the Muslim Brotherhood. "My daughter gets to go out at night. And, God damn it, I'm not going to turn this country over to people who will turn back the clock on her rights, said Foreign Minister Gheit." Sadly, that was exactly what Hillary Clinton and Barack Obama wanted to do. Countless women were raped in Egypt. Beyond Egypt, Hillary and Obama's policy saw Yazidi and Christian women actually being sold into slavery. Many were crucified in Syria and Iraq. Obama and Clinton have a lot of blood on their hands.

On June 3, 2015, Bill Gertz Obama wrote an article titled "Secretly Backing Muslim Brotherhood" which was published in the *Washington Times*. Gertz said that President Obama and members of his administration supported the Muslim Brotherhood. The policy of backing the terror organization of the Muslim Brotherhood was outlined in a secret directive called Presidential Study Directive 11.

The directive, Gertz pointed out, was produced in 2011 and explained the support of the Obama administration to the political reform in the Middle East and North Africa, according to officials familiar with the classified study. Efforts to force the administration to release the directive or portions of it under the Freedom of Information Act have been unsuccessful.

Gertz said that White House National Security Council spokeswoman Bernadette Meehan declined to comment on the Presidential Study Directive 11. "We have nothing for you on this," she said.

The directive, which was executed by Obama, explains why his administration chose the Muslim Brotherhood as "a key vehicle of U.S. backing for so-called political reform in the Middle East." The Muslim Brotherhood was labeled a terrorist organization by the governments of Saudi Arabia, Egypt, and the United Arab Emirates (UAE). The UAE government also has labeled two U.S. affiliates of the Muslim Brotherhood, the Council on American-Islamic Relations and the Muslim American Society, as terrorist support groups. Hillary Clinton Praised the Muslim Brotherhood.

On October 14, 2016, Joseph Schmitz wrote an article titled "Hillary Clinton Praised the Muslim Brotherhood" which was published by *Newsmax*. Schmitz said that Hillary Clinton's support for the Muslim Brotherhood led President el-Sisi of Egypt to endorse Donald Trump over Hillary Clinton after meeting separately with them in September 2016 in New York. "For years, Hillary Clinton has been in bed with the Muslim Brotherhood, which Egypt and other predominantly Muslim countries recently declared an international terrorist organization," explained Schmitz.

The Muslim Brotherhood's motto since its founding in 1928 has been, "Allah is our objective; the Prophet is our Leader; the Quran is our law; Jihad is our way; dying in the path of Allah is our highest hope." Schmitz wrote than in September 2010, the Muslim Brotherhood's Supreme Guide declared jihad against the United States and Israel six months before the so-called "Arab Spring."

Schmitz pointed out that veteran national security reporter Bill Gertz broke a news story about Hillary Clinton's collusion with the Muslim Brotherhood. He described "newly released talking points for Hillary Clinton's meeting in July 2012, two months before the deadly Islamic terrorist attack in Benghazi, Libya, with the newly-elected Muslim Brotherhood president of Egypt, Mohammed Morsi."

According to another released State Department document, even after the September 11, 2012, the Benghazi terrorist attack that killed U.S. Ambassador to Libya Chris Stephens, Sean Smith, Tyrone Woods, and Glen Doherty, Hillary Clinton's deputy secretary of state wrote a letter to the Muslim Brotherhood president of Egypt. The letter concluded saying "As I said when we met, the United States also remains committed to helping Egypt address regional issues, including Syria and Iran."

Joseph Schmitz stated the following: "Perhaps the biggest bombshell in Bill Gertz' new Hillary Clinton-Muslim Brotherhood exposé is this: The CIA also covertly backed the Muslim Brotherhood in Egypt, according to Egyptian news outlets. In December 2013, the news website *Al Bashayer* published audio recordings of a CIA delegation that met with Muslim Brotherhood Deputy Khairat al-Shatir and Brotherhood official Isam al Haddad at the U.S. Embassy in Cairo on Jan. 8, 2013... The CIA asked the Muslim Brotherhood leaders to open a back channel to al-Qaida 'to secure the safe exit of U.S. troops' from Afghanistan."

On June 14, 2012, Secretary of State Hillary Clinton met with then Egyptian President Mohammed Morsi in Cairo, Egypt.

This same Arab Spring led to Secretary of State Hillary Clinton's diplomatic disasters in Egypt, Libya, and Syria — while she carried out President Obama's Presidential Study Directive 11.

The Muslim Brotherhood logo

The Justice Department needs to bring an indictment against Barack Obama

Conclusion

Presidential Study Directive 11 codified the Obama administration alliance with the Muslim Brotherhood into American foreign policy. Its support for radical Islamist takeovers in many Middle East nations and in Libya paved the way for civil wars that culminated in the violence that gave birth to ISIS and covered the region in blood.

Presidential Study Directive 11, which was executed by President Barack Obama, remains classified to this day. President Trump needs to declassify this vile document to let Americans and others in the world know that Obama, Hillary Clinton, and many others in the Obama administration engaged in high treason and dereliction of duty. The Justice Department needs to bring indictments to the former president and all the members of his administration who were responsible for the deaths, injuries, and tortures of tens of thousands in the Middle East and North Africa as well as the millions who had to flee their nations. Justice must be done.

CHAPTER 34

President Trump announced his National Security Strategy

On December 18, 2017, President Trump released his National Security Strategy.

The *DipNote*, the Department of State official blog, wrote that President Donald J. Trump announced his National Security Strategy (NSS) on December 18, 2017. The *DipNote* stated the following: "The strategy sets a positive strategic direction for the United States that will restore America's advantages in the world and build upon our country's great strengths. The NSS is a reflection of President Trump's belief that putting America first is the duty of our government and the foundation for effective U.S. leadership in the world. The NSS identifies four vital national interests, or four pillars: protect the homeland, the American people, and American way of life; promote American prosperity; preserve peace through strength; and advance American influence."

"In his remarks, President Trump outlined the new strategy as one based on a principled realism, guided by our vital national interests, and rooted in our timeless values. This strategy recognizes that, whether we like it or not, we are engaged in a new era of competition."

President Donald Trump said that "To succeed, we must integrate every dimension of our national strength, and we must compete with every instrument of our national power." He added, "Our government's first duty is to its people, to our citizens — to serve their needs, to ensure their safety, to preserve their rights, and to defend their values."

Secretary of State Rex Tillerson released a statement on December 18, 2017 in support of the new NSS. Secretary Tillerson said "The United States faces a 21st century global environment that presents unconventional threats from non-state actors, as well as challenges to our economic and national security from traditional state actors."

Additionally, Secretary Tillerson stated the following: "President Trump's new National Security Strategy brings to bear all elements of American power to protect our people, generate new economic opportunities, and advance our interests and democratic principles. The State Department will work closely with other federal agencies and our allies and partners around the world to implement this strategy."

Nikki Haley is the U.S. Ambassador to the United Nations.

U.S. Ambassador to the United Nations Nikki Haley said the following: "President Trump's National Security Strategy is a comprehensive, strong, and principled roadmap to keep America safe and protect our interests throughout the world. Above all else, this strategy puts the American people at the center of every decision and action we take on behalf of the national security of the United States."

President Donald J. Trump Announced a National Security Strategy to Advance America's Interests

Logo of the White House National Security Council

The White House explained that President Donald J. Trump's National Security Strategy sets a positive strategic direction for the United States that will restore America's advantages in the world and build upon our country's great strengths. The 2017 National Security Strategy builds on the 11 months of Presidential action to restore respect for the United States abroad and renew American confidence at home.

The National Security Strategy stated the following:

- Revisionist powers, such as China and Russia, that use technology, propaganda, and coercion to shape a world antithetical to our interests and values;

- Regional dictators that spread terror, threaten their neighbors, and pursue weapons of mass destruction;

- Jihadist terrorists that foment hatred to incite violence against innocents in the name of a wicked ideology, and transnational criminal organizations that spill drugs and violence into our communities.

The Strategy articulates and advances the President's concept of principled realism. It is realist because it acknowledges the central role of power in international politics, affirms that strong and sovereign states are the best hope for a peaceful world, and clearly defines our national interests. It is principled because it is grounded in advancing American principles, which spread peace and prosperity around the globe.

I. PROTECT THE HOMELAND: President Trump's fundamental responsibility is to protect the American people, the homeland, and the American way of life.

- We will strengthen control of our borders and reform our immigration system to protect the homeland and restore our sovereignty.

- The greatest transnational threats to the homeland are: Jihadist terrorists, using barbaric cruelty to commit murder, repression, and slavery, and virtual networks to exploit vulnerable populations and inspire and direct plots. Transnational criminal organizations, tearing apart our communities with drugs and violence and weakening our allies and partners by corrupting democratic institutions.

- America will target threats at their source: we will confront threats before they ever reach our borders or cause harm to our people.

- We will redouble our efforts to protect our critical infrastructure and digital networks, because new technology and new adversaries create new vulnerabilities.

- We are deploying a layered missile defense system to defend America against missile attacks.

II. PROMOTE AMERICAN PROSPERITY: A strong economy protects the American people, supports our way of life, and sustains American power.

- We will rejuvenate the American economy for the benefit of American workers and companies, which is necessary to restore our national power.

- America will no longer tolerate chronic trade abuses and will pursue free, fair, and reciprocal economic relationships.

- To succeed in this 21st century geopolitical competition, America must lead in research, technology, and innovation. We will protect our national security innovation base from those who steal our intellectual property and unfairly exploit the innovation of free societies.

- America will use its energy dominance to ensure international markets remain open, and that the benefits of diversification and energy access promote economic and national security.

III. PRESERVE PEACE THROUGH STRENGTH: An America strengthened, renewed, and rejuvenated will ensure peace and deter hostility.

- We will rebuild America's military strength to ensure it remains second to none.

- America will use all of the tools of statecraft in a new era of strategic competition—diplomatic, information, military, and economic—to protect our interests.

- America will strengthen its capabilities across numerous domains — including space and cyber — and revitalize capabilities that have been neglected.

- America's allies and partners magnify our power and protect our shared interests. We expect them to take greater responsibility for addressing common threats.

- We will ensure the balance of power remains in America's favor in key regions of the world: the Indo-Pacific, Europe, and the Middle East.

IV. ADVANCE AMERICAN INFLUENCE: As a force for good throughout its history, America will use its influence to advance our interests and benefit humanity.

- We must continue to enhance our influence overseas to protect the American people and promote our prosperity.

- America's diplomatic and development efforts will compete to achieve better outcomes in all arenas—bilateral, multilateral, and in the information realm—to protect our interests, find new economic opportunities for Americans, and challenge our competitors.

- America will seek partnerships with like-minded states to promote free market economies, private sector growth, political stability, and peace.

- We champion our values – including the rule of law and individual rights – that promote strong, stable, prosperous, and sovereign states.

- Our America First foreign policy celebrates America's influence in the world as a positive force that can help set the conditions for peace, prosperity, and the development of successful societies."

Conclusion

After many years of irresponsible cuts in the Department of Defense's budget by the Obama administration, President Donald Trump is rebuilding America's military strength to ensure it remains second to none. The President is strengthening the military including space and cyber capabilities that have been neglected. He is improving and deploying a missile defense system to defend America against missile attacks.

President Trump is protecting the critical infrastructure and digital networks of the United States, because new technology and new adversaries create new vulnerabilities. He is improving the economy. Lastly, the National Security Strategy sets a positive strategic direction for the United States that will restore America's military and diplomatic strength in the world.

CHAPTER 35

Tax Cuts and Jobs Act is approved

President Donald J. Trump, Vice President Mike Pence, Senate Majority Leader Mitch McConnell, House Speaker Paul Ryan, and other Congressional Republicans celebrate in the White House the passing of the Tax Cuts and Jobs Act.

On December 20, 2017, President Donald J. Trump, Vice President Mike Pence, Republican congressional leaders, and Republican members of the Senate and the House celebrated the passing of the Tax Cuts and Jobs Act at the White House. This was a major accomplishment as overhauling the tax system in a significant way had not been done since President Ronald Reagan.

During a speech on the South Lawn of the White House, President Trump said the following: "We broke every record ... It's the largest tax cut in the history of our country. This is going to mean companies are going to be coming back. You know, I campaigned on the fact that, you know, we're not going to lose our companies anymore. They have tremendous enthusiasm right now in this country and we have companies pouring back into our country."

When President Trump and Republican lawmakers were celebrating their legislative success, many large corporations made announcements of pay raises for their employees and new investments on plants and equipments. AT&T announced it would pay a $1,000 bonus to 200,000 of its employees and invest $1 billion in America as a result of the coming corporate tax cuts.

Other large corporations followed. Comcast said it would give its over 100,000 employees $1,000 bonuses and spend $50 billion to improve and extend broadband plant capacity. Boeing said it would spend $300 million on its workers and in charity.

Wells Fargo and Fifth Third Bancorp announced raises for all employees. These corporate announcements are evidence that the Republican tax plan would soon start delivering for workers. By January 2018, over 40 major companies had given bonuses and/or raised the salary of tens of thousands their employees. Hopefully, many others would follow.

The president said that the individual mandate repeal included in the Republicans' tax legislation "essentially repealed ObamaCare because taxpayers will no longer face a penalty if they decline to purchase health insurance." He added, "We are making America great again." "You haven't heard that, have you?" the president asked.

House Speaker Paul Ryan congratulated President Trump's "exquisite presidential leadership" for helping guide the tax reform bill through Congress over the past several months. "Mr. President, thank you for getting us over the finish line," Speaker Ryan said.

On December 22, 2017, President Donald Trump signed the Tax Cuts and Jobs Act at the White House before leaving for his Christmas vacation in Florida.

Senate Majority Leader Mitch McConnell went through a large list of President Trump's accomplishments before praising the president for his efforts to pass tax cuts and reform. Senator McConnell stated the following: "We've cemented the Supreme Court right of center for a generation. Mr. President, thanks to your nominees, we've put 12 circuit court judges in place. You've ended the overregulation of the American economy and that, coupled with what we did last night and what the House did this morning means America is going to start growing again. "

Vice President Mike Pence, who worked arduously with his former colleagues in Congress, stated the following: "President Donald Trump is a man of his word. He's a man of action and with the strong support of these members of Congress. President Donald Trump delivered a great victory for the American people. We made history today, but as the president said when we gathered this morning ... we're just getting started."

House of Representatives approves biggest tax overhaul in 30 years

"Today, we give the people of this country their money back. This is their money, after all," House Speaker Paul Ryan said shortly before the historic vote. With Treasury Secretary Steven Mnuchin and others watching from the gallery, the House passed the bill by a vote of 227-203, overcoming united opposition from Democrats and 12 Republicans who voted against it.

However, the House of Representatives had to vote on the bill a second time when the Senate parliamentarian pointed out that three of the minor provisions of the Bird Rule were violated. The Senate fixed the glitch and voted on December 20 on a party-line 51-48 vote after midnight and sent the bill to the House. The House of Representatives voted shortly after noon and passed the historic bill 224-201. The 12 GOP votes against the bill came from Republican representatives from the high-tax states of New York, New Jersey, and California. They did not like that the bill reduced the deductions from state and local taxes.

On December 20, 2017, Marisa Schultz and Bob Fredericks wrote an article titled "Congress sends GOP tax bill to Trump to sign" which was published in the *New York Post*. The reporters said a jubilant President Trump stated the following: "People are starting to see how great this historic victory was, the passage of the massive tax cuts and reform that's — a lot of reform in there, but the tax cuts supersede, and I said very specifically 'use the word tax cuts'. It will be an incredible Christmas gift for hard-working Americans. I said I wanted to have it done before Christmas. We got it done."

Earlier, President Trump took to twitter to once again criticize the Destroy Trump mainstream media for saying the reforms are a giveaway to the rich and big business. "The Tax Cuts are so large and so meaningful, and yet the Fake News is working overtime to follow the lead of their friends, the defeated Dems, and only demean. This is truly a case where the results will speak for themselves, starting very soon. Jobs, Jobs, Jobs!" tweeted the president.

On December 19, 2017, Speaker of the House Paul Ryan, R-Wis, Kevin Brady, R-Tex, and other Republican representatives celebrate the passing of the bill Tax Cuts and Jobs Act.

The bill also allows oil drilling in Alaska's Arctic National Wildlife Refuge, which other presidents tried to do without success for over 40 years. Thanks to President Trump America will soon become an energy independent nation.

David Morgan and Amanda Becker wrote an article on *Reuters* on December 18, 2017, explaining that the House of Representatives approved the biggest overhaul of the American tax system in more than 30 years. The bill, called the Tax Cuts and Jobs Act, was sent to the Senate, where it was approved later in the evening.

Morgan and Becker wrote the following: "The plan includes steep tax cuts for corporations and wealthy taxpayers, as well as temporary tax cuts for some individuals and families. It repeals a section of the ObamaCare health system and allows oil drilling in Alaska's Arctic National Wildlife Refuge, just two of many narrow changes added to the bill to secure sufficient to win its passage. Middle-income households would see an average tax cut of $900 next year, while the wealthiest 1% of Americans would see an average cut of $51,000, according to the nonpartisan Tax Policy Center, a think tank in Washington."

President Donald Trump and Republicans in Congress believe that Tax Cuts and Jobs Act will improve the economy and job growth. They also see the legislation as key to retaining their majorities in the House and Senate in the November 2018 elections.

Democrats in the House of Representatives criticized the bill and their House Democratic Leader Nancy Pelosi said the following regarding the bill: "A Frankenstein monster riddled with carve-outs and loopholes that falls far short of the Republican promise of simplifying the tax code. This monster will come back to haunt them."

Tax Cuts and Jobs Act

The *Congress.gov* website explained that the Tax Cuts and Jobs Act bill amends the Internal Revenue Code to reduce tax rates and modify policies, credits, and deductions for individuals and businesses. With respect to individuals, the bill does the following:

- Replaces the seven existing tax brackets (10%, 15%, 25%, 28%, 33%, 35%, and 39.6%) with four brackets (12%, 25%, 35%, and 39.6%).

- Increases the standard deduction.

- Repeals the deduction for personal exemptions.

- Establishes a 25% maximum rate on the business income of individuals.

- Increases the child tax credit and establishes a new family tax credit.

- Repeals the overall limitation on certain itemized deductions.

- Limits the mortgage interest deduction for debt incurred after November 2, 2017, to mortgages of up to $500,000 (currently $1 million).

- Repeals the deduction for state and local income or sales taxes not paid or accrued in a trade or business.

- Repeals the deduction for medical expenses.

- Consolidates and repeals several education-related deductions and credits.

- Repeals the alternative minimum tax, and the estate and generation-skipping transfer taxes in six years.

- With respect to businesses, the bill reduces the corporate tax rate from a maximum of 35% to a flat 21% rate (25% for personal services corporations). And also does the following:

- Allows increased expensing of the costs of certain property.

- Limits the deductibility of net interest expenses to 30% of the business's adjusted taxable income.

- Repeals the work opportunity tax credit.

- Terminates the exclusion for interest on private activity bonds.

- Modifies or repeals various energy-related deductions and credits the taxation of foreign income, and imposes an excise tax on certain payments from domestic corporations to related foreign corporations.

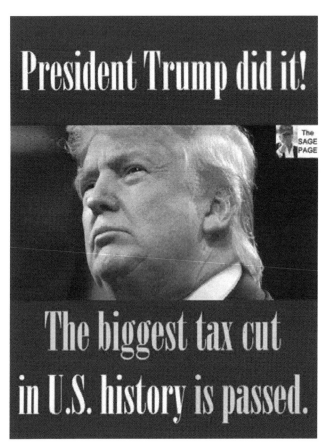

President Donald Trump and Republicans in Congress have achieved an enormous victory for the American people. For more than 30 years, the tax code had not been reformed. President Trump fulfilled one of his major promises during his campaign by lowering taxes for individuals, small businesses, and large corporations.

The Tax Cuts and Jobs Act will improve the economy and job growth. Multinational corporations will be able to better compete in the world and their trillions abroad will now be able to return to America

Conclusion

Not a single Democrat in the House and the Senate voted for the bill. Senate and House Democratic leaders and others slammed the bill. This writer hopes that when Americans see the improvement of the economy, the creation of tens of thousands new and better paid jobs, corporations giving raises and bonuses to their employees, and more money in their pockets, they will remember that not one Democrat supported the Tax Cuts and Jobs Act. The Democrats need to be held accountable in future elections.

CHAPTER 36

Major accomplishments of the Trump administration in 2017 and the Schumer government shutdown and his surrender

There is no question that the Trump administration had a long list of major accomplishment in 2017. Thus far Donald Trump has already had an extraordinary presidency—more bold and courageous, than any recent American president.

On December 30, 2017, Joan Swirsky wrote an article titled "A Year of Spectacular Accomplishments for President Trump" that was published in the *Free Canadian Press* website. Joan Swirsky summarized the president's list of achievements as follows:

"**ECONOMY**

- Enactment of the massive tax cuts and jobs-creation law which eliminates the ObamaCare mandate and provides incentives for corporations to repatriate trillions stashed overseas to avoid America's unnecessarily high tax rates and consumers to have greater choice in healthcare options.

- A Latino unemployment rate that is has hit a record low in the 45-year history of government tracking,

- A black unemployment rate hitting a 17-year low—after nearly two decades of double-digit unemployment,

- An unexpectedly high growth rate of 3.3% in the third quarter of 2017…with projections for the fourth quarter edging into the magic number of 4%,

- The unemployment rate hitting a 17-year low, the lowest since 2000,

- Mortgage applications for new homes rise to a seven year high,

- Lowest gas prices in more than 12 years,

- A boom in manufacturing jobs, with 171,000 having been created under President Trump, in stark contrast to the 16,000 manufacturing jobs lost in the poseur president's final year, and the manufacturing unemployment rate just 2.6%, the lowest in history.

- In addition, a booming stock market, with a gain of more than $4 trillion in wealth, the DOW over 24,000, and for the first time ever, rising 5,000 points in one year, and the S&P and NASDAQ setting all-time highs,

- A decrease in the U.S. debt by $101-billion dollars! (In his first five months, the poseur president Barack Obama increased the U.S. debt by $771-billion dollars).

- The president convinced companies such as Ford, Chrysler and Carrier Air Conditioners to manufacture and build plants in the United States and Corning announced it was investing $500 million in new U.S. production, creating 1,000 new jobs. Foxconn, the world's largest contract electronics manufacturer, which makes the iPhone, announced in July it was investing $10 billion in Wisconsin to build a factory that will employ 3,000 workers directly and up to 22,000 workers indirectly.

- *According to Ambrose Evans-Pritchard, international business editor of the London Telegraph, "American companies have stashed* trillions of dollars overseas in what amounts to the greatest cash reserve in the world," and President Trump, as part of his tax reform, is bringing that money back to the U.S.

- POTUS reversed the Dodd-Frank Act, financial-regulation legislation in which regulators were given too much power and big banks were given special treatment.

- Refused his $400,000 a year salary as president, took just one dollar, and donated to the Park Service, Veterans Affairs.

- Signed Executive Order for an Apprentice program to train skilled works to fill six-million open positions.

- Reduced White House payroll by $22 million.

DOMESTIC POLICY

- President Trump is destroying MS 13, and other illegal immigrant gangs.

- He has reset an agenda for space exploration by NASA.

- Exposed the national media for the leftist activism base it is.

- Exposed the Democratic Party as corrupt, issueless, and powerless.

- Exposed the fecklessness, and fraud of the GOP.

- Exposed the deep state to public view.

- Exposed the corruption of our bureaucracies by the Obama administration.

- In addition, the president has:

- Rolled back the roadblocks to coal mining, which cost the industry $81 million a year,

- Ended the ban on oil drilling in Alaska's Arctic National Wildlife Refuge (ANWR), opening up more than a million acres to oil exploration, which will create unprecedented job boom and total energy independence for the U.S.

- Approved the Dakota Access Pipeline project and the construction of the Keystone XL oil pipeline from Canada, which are expected to create more than 42,000 jobs and $2 billion in earnings.

- Rejected the Paris Climate Accords, which perpetuated the hoax of global warming, saving the U.S. billions in money-extorting regulations,

- On immigration, submitted to Congress a 70-point proposal that calls for increased border security, enforcement of immigration laws, funding of "the wall" on our southern border, removing illegal aliens in "sanctuary cities," and ending extended-family chain migration, et al.

- Deported thousands of illegal aliens,

- Appointed Constitution-abiding Neil Gorsuch to the Supreme Court,

- Appointed like-minded judges to 12 Appellate Courts and had 73 conservative judges confirmed,

- Added some 100 new immigration judges.

- Canceled or delayed over 1,500 planned oppressive regulatory actions, eliminating 22 old regulations for every one new regulation—22-1!

- **Withdrawn** from participation in the United Nations Global Compact on Migration, another significant departure from the global governance policies of the poseur president's administration.

- **Withdrawn** from the United Nation's Educational, Scientific and Cultural Organization (UNESCO) because of the agency's "anti-Israel bias

- Created commission on child trafficking and voter fraud.

- Declared a nationwide Public Health Emergency on opioids and laid out a new five-point strategy to fight the crisis.

- Negotiated the release of six U.S. humanitarian workers held captive in Egypt.

- Traveled to Poland for the annual. G-20 meeting where he pushed again for funding of women entrepreneurs.

- Launched the United States-Canada Council for Advancement of Women Entrepreneurs and Business Leaders with Canadian Prime Minister Justin Trudeau in February.

- Prioritized women-owned businesses for some $500 million in SBA loans.

- Reinstated and expanded the Mexico City Policy that blocks some $9 billion in foreign aid being used for abortions.

- Worked with Congress on a bill overturning an Obama regulation that blocked states from defunding abortion providers.

- Food stamps under Pres. Trump have been reduced to their lowest levels in seven years, down in 46 of 50 states, with 1.5 million fewer subscribers.

- The Trump administration reached a very substantial settlement in a class action lawsuit brought by more than 400 conservative groups illegally targeted by the poseur president's Internal Revenue Service.

FOREIGN POLICY

- Increased the sanctions on Iran and refused to recertify Obama's disastrous agreement with the nuke-hungry mullahs,

- Bombed a Syrian airfield and destroyed a fifth of Assad's jet fighters,

- Took the gloves off our military and ended ISIS's "caliphate,"

- Rolled back Obama's cringing concessions to Cuba,

- Put Russia on notice by recommitting to the Magnitsky Act and increasing sanctions on regime oligarchs,

- Unleashed U.N. Ambassador Nikki Haley on "the anti-American pygmy states infesting that 'cockpit in the Tower of Babel' (the United Nations),

- The president's 11-day Asian trip—to Pearl Harbor, Hawaii; Tokyo, Japan; Seoul, South Korea; Beijing, the People's Republic of China; Danang, the Socialist Republic of Vietnam; and in Manila, the Philippines—succeeded in bolstering "resolve to combat North Korean nuclear adventurism and Islamic terrorism, and to promote his signature 'America First' trade policies… after eight years of pathetic servility, weakness, and apology tours" by the poseur president.

- During the trip, President Trump scuttled the Trans-Pacific Partnership, saying: *"We will no longer enter into large agreements that tie our hands, surrender our sovereignty, make meaningful enforcement practically impossible,"* and produce "unfair trade practices and enormous trade deficits for the United States."

- Vice President Mike Pence announced that the U.S. will quit funding refugee programs carried out by the United Nations, given its failure to protect Christian [and other] minorities "in the wake of genocide and the atrocities of terrorist groups."

MILITARY

- President Trump removed the poseur president's crushing Rules of Engagement in combat, which tied the hands of our military and resulted in both greater combat and civilian casualties. And he empowered military leaders to "seize the initiative and win," reducing the need for a White House sign off on every mission.

- ISIS has lost 98% of its territory and that now, fewer than 1,000 ISIS fighters remain in Iraq and Syria. And *Fox News* reports that number is down "from a peak of nearly 45,000 just two years ago. U.S. officials credit nearly 30,000 U.S.-led coalition airstrikes and regional partners on the ground for killing more than 70,000 jihadists.

- In addition, President Trump signed the National Defense Authorization Act for fiscal year 2018, which approves one of the largest defense spending increases in the past 30 years. The NDAA does the following:

- Increases the size of our forces for the first time in 7 years,

- Authorizes funds for the continued defeat of ISIS and to cover critical missile defense capabilities to confront the threat posed by North Korea,

- Takes concrete steps to rebuild U.S. military readiness

- Approves a 2.4% pay raise for our troops—the largest in 8 years!

VETERANS

- Signed the Veterans Accountability and Whistleblower Protection Act to allow senior officials in the Department of Veterans Affairs to fire failing employees and establish safeguards to protect whistleblowers,

- Authorized $2.1 billion in additional funds for the Veterans Choice Program in healthcare; allowed private healthcare choices for veterans,

- Launched an online "Access and Quality Tool" providing veterans with a way to access wait time and quality of care data."

Joan Swirsky ended her article by stating the following: "After the big-hearted people of America gave a community organizer with not one microsecond of executive or foreign affairs experience a chance to lead the greatest, strongest, most generous country on earth, those same big-hearted people regained their sanity and voted for an American patriot with vast executive experience to seize the reins of power and—literally—to save both America and Western civilization! For those of us who value safety, a strong military, a booming economy, high employment, a belief in the sanctity of life, and a reverence for the U.S. Constitution, the election of Donald J. Trump was a Godsend. And we fervently believe that under his leadership, the best, indeed, is yet to come!"

Donald Trump has had a spectacular success as president since he was inaugurated on January 20, 2017.

On December 28, 2017, Sarah Westwood and Gabby Morrongiello wrote an article titled "Trump's Top 9 Accomplishments of 2017 that was published by the *Washington Examiner*. The reporters stated the following:

1. Judicial appointments

President Trump shattered an all-time record earlier this month when the Senate confirmed his 12th federal appeals court nominee, marking the only time in history a U.S. president has made more than 11 appellate appointments during his first year in office.

With those appellate appointments, a new Supreme Court justice, and his investiture of several other low-court judges, Trump has rapidly and radically changed the federal judiciary this year. The president's close relationship with conservative groups like the Heritage Foundation and Federalist Society has ensured that nearly all of his judicial nominees fit the mold of Justice Neil Gorsuch, a strict originalist who succeeded the iconic conservative Justice Antonin Scalia after being confirmed by the Senate last April…

Many conservatives see the president's judicial appointments as his biggest accomplishment yet, noting that Trump's progress in this area will likely be the most enduring element of his post-presidential legacy. With 59 nominations (including U.S. Attorneys) and 19 confirmations in the Senate so far, even legal conservatives who begrudgingly voted for Trump are likely to be pleased."

2. Tax reform

"Very few political strategists thought Trump could pass a tax bill earlier this fall after congressional Republicans failed to fulfill their promise of repealing and replacing ObamaCare.

Months of intraparty squabbling, disagreements between Republican leaders and White House officials, and provocative tweets from the president ultimately doomed GOP efforts to undo healthcare law. But when it came to overhaul the tax code – a top priority for Trump and House Speaker Paul Ryan – things changed on Capitol Hill."

3. Individual mandate repeal

"Through tax reform, Trump fulfilled another key campaign promise: repealing Obamacare's individual mandate. Senate Republicans included a measure to kill the mandate in their initial tax bill, paving the way for its subsequent inclusion in the final tax reform package that cleared the president's desk. The mandate, which required Americans to carry health insurance or pay an annual penalty as part of ObamaCare, was long seen by GOP voters as the worst element of the 2010 healthcare law."

4. Deregulation

"During its month's long legislative dry spell, the Trump administration touted deregulation as an area in which the president continued to make progress despite congressional gridlock. Trump came into office promising to slash two existing regulations for each new one his administration enacts. The president has since said the White House beat its goal by a lot this year, as officials canceled or delayed more than 1,500 regulations in the first 11 months of Trump's presidency."

"The administration has said Trump ultimately cut 22 regulations for each new one enacted this year, saving taxpayers billions of dollars over the coming years. Trump has repeatedly credited his deregulation push with the economic growth that has flourished during his first year in office."

5. Cutting government waste

"Less than three months into his presidency, Trump issued an executive order directing every federal agency to determine "where money is being wasted [and] how services can be improved. Though the order never set a desired number for the cuts, several Cabinet-level departments have since found ways to shrink their payroll and consolidate internal programs."

"The most attention-grabbing reforms have occurred at the State Department, where Secretary of State Rex Tillerson has eliminated several coordinators for sanctions policy, offered early retirement incentives to hundreds of career employees, and promised to redesign the agency.

Office of Management and Budget Director Mick Mulvaney has also been busy overseeing the reduction of duplicative programs and wasteful spending. His agency killed 59 guidance and policy documents in June that officials had deemed "obsolete" or inefficient…"

6. Travel ban

"Despite initially attracting criticism from across the political spectrum for its botched rollout, Trump's so-called travel ban scored a major victory later this year when the Supreme Court ruled to allow the entire policy to take effect."

"The administration was forced to revise the policy in September following several lawsuits in federal court and a partial ruling by the Supreme Court. Administration officials added North Korea, Venezuela, and Chad to its list of countries from which immigrants would temporarily be blocked from entering the U.S., and removed Sudan. The original ban had drawn scrutiny from liberal critics of the administration for imposing a religious test, as it exclusively targeted seven Muslim-majority countries: Iran, Iraq, Libya, Sudan, Somalia, Syria, and Yemen."

"Such legal complaints — brought by the state of Hawaii and the American Civil Liberties Union — failed to hold up when the revised version of the ban came before the nine-member Supreme Court in early December. Despite previous moves by lower-court judges to limit its scope, the high court permitted the updated ban to be implemented pending appeal. The Constitution and acts of Congress confer on the President broad authority to prevent aliens abroad from entering this country when he deems it in the nation's interest," U.S. Solicitor General Noel Francisco had argued in court papers ahead of the decision."

President Donald Trump is looking forward to implementing his agenda in 2018.

7. Defeating the Islamic State

"Trump repeatedly credited his decision to ease restrictions on the rules of engagement with the military's victory over the Islamic State in key strongholds this year. When U.S.-backed coalition forces drove Islamic State fighters from their headquarters in Raqqa, Syria in October, the White House highlighted Trump's efforts to give commanders on the ground more decision-making authority than his predecessor gave them. The liberation of Raqqa marked a pivotal moment in the war against the Islamic State…"

"The terror organization saw its numbers and territorial holdings decimated this year. A U.S-led coalition helped to free Mosul from the Islamic State in July 2017, a victory that denied the extremist group the largest city under their control. In early October, coalition forces notched another victory when 1,000 Islamic State fighters surrendered as Iraqi Security Forces closed in on Hawija, the last of the terror group's strongholds in Iraq."

8. Recognition of Jerusalem

"Despite pressure to preserve a status quo that his predecessors had left untouched for decades in Israel, Trump made waves on the international stage this month when he formally recognized Jerusalem as the capital of Israel and announced plans to move the U.S. embassy there from its present location in Tel Aviv. Trump had vowed as a presidential candidate to move the U.S. embassy to Jerusalem, and the White House framed his decision in early December as the fulfillment of a campaign promise."

"Former presidents from Bill Clinton to Barack Obama had granted waivers that allowed the U.S. embassy in Israel to remain in Tel Aviv despite legislation Congress passed in 1995 that required the embassy to move to Jerusalem. Previous administrations cited concerns about the effects such a move would have on the Israeli-Palestinian peace process when delaying the embassy relocation effort for more than 20 years. Trump, however, decided he could not sign the second waiver to arrive at his desk since taking office without signaling a policy change toward Jerusalem."

9. Withdrawal from Paris climate agreement

"Trump's decision in June 2017 to pull the U.S. out of a sweeping international climate pact drew some of the loudest and most pointed criticisms from his liberal detractors to date. Proponents of the climate deal claimed the U.S. would forever lose prestige in the global community if it walked away from the agreement, which former President Obama had negotiated without congressional input."

"But Trump ultimately followed through on a campaign promise to withdraw from the agreement despite objections from several of his closest advisers. The internal negotiations pitted his daughter and son-in-law, Jared Kushner, against some of his more populist advisers, such as then-chief strategist Steve Bannon and then-EPA chief Scott Pruitt. The outcome of the battle behind closed doors in the West Wing was viewed at the time as a major victory for the nationalist wing of the White House staff, which had counseled Trump not to cave under pressure to soften his hardline."

The Schumer government shutdown and his surrender

On January 22, 2018, President Donald Trump signed a bill ending the three-day government shutdown.

The closing of the government was initiated by Democratic Senator Minority Leader Chuck Schumer from New York and the vast majority of the Democrats in the Senate. Pandering to the extreme radicals in the Democratic Party and the senators who are planning to run for president in 2020, Senator Schumer demanded a DACA (Deferred Action for Childhood Arrivals) solution with the approval of a Continuing Resolution (CR) of the budget. This was done by Senate Democrats without considering the immigration bill of building a wall in the southern border, an end to chain migration, and lottery visas of the Republican Party and President Donald Trump. The Democrats initiated a filibuster and the 60 votes to end it were not there. Thus began an unnecessary and reckless government shutdown damaging the national security and sending a wrong message to America's enemies. It was legislative arson of the worst kind!

The Democrats miscalculated badly. If they thought the American people were going to support a shutdown of the federal government over children brought illegally to America by their parents while the men and women of the Armed Forces and first responders went without pay, as well as all federal employees except those who were extremely necessary, they were badly mistaken. Republicans had added to the CR the funding children's insurance for six years which was something the Democrats wanted.

Holding the government hostage over DACA was a terrible idea by Senator Schumer.

Pitting undocumented youngsters against soldiers, sailors, and marines was a no win proposition. It was utter madness! Democrats in the Senate and the House of Representatives showed the nation that did not care about the Armed Forces and national security. Democrats in Congress better hope that Americans would forget in the midterm elections what they did disrupting the government over DACA. Democrats are also hoping that Americans would not realize how their once center left party has become a Marxist and pro Muslim Brotherhood party advocating open borders.

President Trump and Senate Republicans held firm and refused to consider any DACA reforms until the government shutdown ended. Polls went against the Democrats. A Harvard-Harris poll indicated 56% disapproval over the closing the federal government over DACA and a 34%

approval. Polling also showed a majority of Americans backed the immigration plan of President Trump on ending lottery visas, chain migration, and building a border wall.

The House and the Senate voted on January 22, 2018 to end the government shutdown, extending funding for three weeks, following a deal being reached between Senate Minority Leader Chuck Schumer and Senate Majority Leader Mitch McConnell regarding assurances related to consider a DACA and immigration bill. The House passed the continuing resolution 266-159, with 36 more yes votes than the four-week resolution they passed last week. The Senate passed the CR 81 to 18.

Schumer was severely criticized for caving in and surrendering to Republicans by radicals and some Senate Democrats who wanted to continue the government shutdown until the Dreamers were legalized. Those voting NO were the radical Democratic senators considering running for president in 2020: Corey Booker from New Jersey, Kamela Harris from California, Elizabeth Warren from Massachusetts, Kirsten Gillibrand from New York, and Bernie Sanders from Vermont.

All of these radical Democratic senators were appealing to the Marxists and hard core Left of the Democratic Party who want to legalize all the illegals knowing that the vast majority would vote Democratic in future elections. If they succeed in giving citizenship to all the millions of undocumented immigrants, the Democratic Party would be in power forever and it will be the end of the Constitutional Republic of the United States and the end of freedom and liberty!

Senator McConnell stated the following: "But we should not let the political feuds or policy disagreements obscure the simple fact that every member of this body cares deeply about the challenges facing our country. It's evident that this government shutdown is doing nothing, absolutely nothing to generate bipartisan progress on the issues the American public care about."

President Donald Trump called for Senate Republicans to change the Senate's rules to resolve the funding impasse as the government shutdown continued. The president wanted Senator McConnell to invoke the so-called "nuclear option" that would allow bill to be approve in the Senate by a simple majority as the Democrats did when Obama was president. This would stop the obstructionism and thereby remove leverage for Senate Democrats.

As CNN explained the "Senate rules impose a threshold of 60 votes to break a filibuster, and Senate Republicans currently hold a slim majority of 51 votes, meaning even if they can unite their members, they need nine more votes to end debate." The White House is calling for the Senate to change its rules and move the threshold to a simple majority of 51 votes. A spokesman for McConnell said in response to the tweet by the president that the Senate Republican Conference does not support changing the 60-vote rule.

President Donald Trump in a Tweet stated "Big win for Republicans as Democrats cave on Shutdown. Now I want a big win for everyone, including Republicans, Democrats and DACA, but especially for our Great Military and Border Security. Should be able to get there. See you at the negotiating table"!

It will be a very difficult negotiating an immigration agreement with the Democrats. Already Senator Schumer went back on his previous agreement of partially funding the border wall. This writer believes that the president is right and the nuclear option should be adopted by Senate Republicans, after all it was done by Democrats in the Senate before.

Continuing resolutions are hurting the military. Half of the combat aircraft are unable to operate due to lack of parts and proper maintenance. The Air Force needs an additional 1,500 pilots and due to the lack of funds pilots fly 15 hours a month instead of the required 30 hours. Only five of 58 combat brigades are ready to fight today. This situation is extremely dangerous as America is facing many international threats. Former President Obama seriously cut the Pentagon budget as he tried to destroy America as a superpower and now the increasingly extreme radical Democrats in Congress are doing the same.

Conclusion

In spite of all the enormous domestic and international problems faced by America and all the efforts of the Deep State and the complicit corrupt mainstream media, President Trump has had major accomplishments in his first year in office. The mid-term elections in 2018 are crucial for the Trump administration to keep control of the House of Representatives and expand the numbers of Republicans in the Senate. The president should try to be diplomatic in his tweets and remarks to prevent his many enemies and the Destroy Trump mainstream media to viciously attack and distract him from his agenda to Make America Great and Safe Again.

May God bless the president, his family, and all those in his administration! May God bless America and protect it from all its enemies!

Made in the USA
Columbia, SC
30 May 2018